D0931440

WHAT'S THE PLAY AND WHERE'S THE STAGE?

What's the Play and Where's the Stage?

A Theatrical Family of the Regency Era

Alan Stockwell

25.95

VESPER HAWK

WHAT'S THE PLAY AND WHERE'S THE STAGE?

Copyright © Alan Stockwell 2015

All Rights Reserved

Hardback: ISBN 978-0-9565013-6-3

Paperback: ISBN 978-0-9565013-7-0

Published by VESPER HAWK PUBLISHING

www.vesperhawk.com

MONEY
HISTORICAL NOTE

The currency in use during the period was based on pounds, shillings and pence (*£ s d*).

$£1 = 20$ shillings $\qquad$ 1 shilling $= 12$ pence

These denominations were rendered variously as, for example,

£209 or 209*l*	(Two hundred and nine pounds)
£37.10s	(Thirty seven pounds and ten shillings)
£203.14.6 or	(Two hundred and three pounds, fourteen shillings and sixpence)
7/- or 7s	(7 shillings)
4/6 or 4/6d	(four shillings and sixpence – colloquially called "four and six")

A guinea was originally a gold coin whose value was fixed in 1717 as £1.1s.0d. Although the coin itself was abolished in 1813 the term guinea survives to the present day and the value in modern UK currency is £1.05.

The forms 209*l* and 7s were chiefly used in the Georgian period but in the text money is shown in the more familiar £209 and 7/- manner of the twentieth century.

CONTENTS

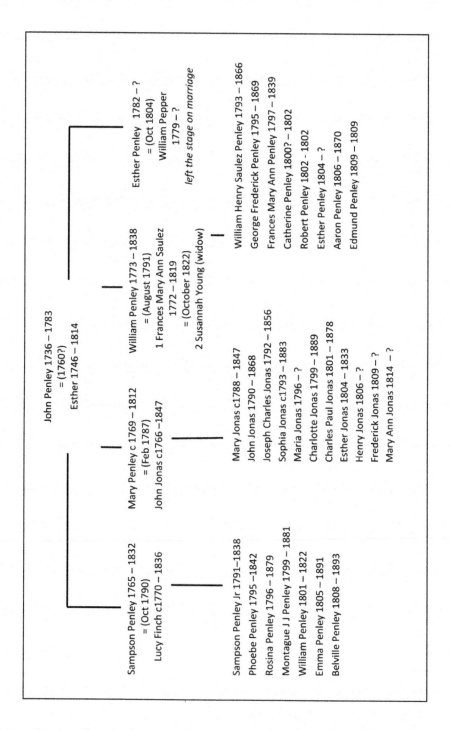

John Penley 1736 – 1783
= (1760?)
Esther 1746 – 1814

Sampson Penley 1765 – 1832
= (Oct 1790)
Lucy Finch c1770 – 1836

Sampson Penley Jr 1791–1838
Phoebe Penley 1795 –1842
Rosina Penley 1796 – 1879
Montague J J Penley 1799 – 1881
William Penley 1801 – 1822
Emma Penley 1805 – 1891
Belville Penley 1808 – 1893

Mary Penley c 1769 – 1812
= (Feb 1787)
John Jonas c1766 –1847

Mary Jonas c1788 – 1847
John Jonas 1790 – 1868
Joseph Charles Jonas 1792 – 1856
Sophia Jonas c1793 – 1883
Maria Jonas 1796 – ?
Charlotte Jonas 1799 – 1889
Charles Paul Jonas 1801 – 1878
Esther Jonas 1804 – 1833
Henry Jonas 1806 – ?
Frederick Jonas 1809 – ?
Mary Ann Jonas 1814 – ?

William Penley 1773 – 1838
= (August 1791)
1 Frances Mary Ann Saulez
1772 – 1819
= (October 1822)
2 Susannah Young (widow)

William Henry Saulez Penley 1793 – 1866
George Frederick Penley 1795 – 1869
Frances Mary Ann Penley 1797 – 1839
Catherine Penley 1800? – 1802
Robert Penley 1802 - 1802
Esther Penley 1804 – ?
Aaron Penley 1806 – 1870
Edmund Penley 1809 – 1809

Esther Penley 1782 – ?
= (Oct 1804)
William Pepper
1779 – ?
left the stage on marriage

Penley Family Tree of the two generations featured in the text

OVERTURE

STRICTLY SPEAKING, the Georgian period began with the accession of George I in 1714 and lasted until the death of George IV in 1830. The point has usually been stretched to include George's brother William who succeeded him, reigning until 1837 which was the start of the Victorian Era. The nine years from 1811 to 1820 when poor old George III was unable to rule on account of his mental instability was occupied by the Prince of Wales acting as Regent for his father, that sub-period becoming known as the Regency.

A period in excess of 100 years should not be regarded as a whole, there are too many changes taking place during four generations. Contrarily, the Regency era is considered to be longer than the basic decade when it was formally in place, as it gave rise to distinctive trends in architecture, literature, fashions, politics and culture which started before and ended after.

The period between 1795 and 1837 is the transition from Georgian to Victorian and is loosely referred to as the Regency era. It was a period of great contrasts: glamour and filth, elegance and warfare, fine architecture and squalid rookeries, extreme wealth and dire poverty. The upper classes lived a rarefied life style that never impinged on the lower orders who could only gape in wonder at these creatures that seemed to them as exotic as birds of paradise.

But there was one place where the aristocracy, middle and working classes could, and did, mingle – the theatre. George III in his box laughed along with his poorest subjects in the gallery, and thrilled to the same dramas. The entertainment business was one place where democracy flourished, London stars toured the provinces with their 'hits', and lowly-born actresses married nobility.

Much has been written about David Garrick and the theatre of his time. Many words have been spilt recording the life and deeds of those later Georgian and Regency eminences the Kembles, Kean, Macready and Grimaldi. However, very little has appeared in print revealing the work and lives of the thousands of unknown toilers in the theatrical profession during this latter period. This has caused an imbalanced dichotomy in theatre history as reviewers, critics and historians invariably lavish their attention on the great and good of the London theatre, whereas a far larger audience witnessed the entertainment of the provincial common people. The history of the Georgian theatre does not entirely repose on outstanding performances of Shakespeare by brilliant actors of note on the London stage, there was also a world outside.

Two acts of Parliament, one in 1788 and one of 1843, bracket a period of great upsurge in the nation's theatrical activity followed by a rapid cooling. In half a century an entire entertainment industry boomed and bust.

Throughout the country, family troupes toured their own restricted circuits of country theatres. Few have been recorded, knowledge is scant. Sampson Penley and his brother-in-law John Jonas headed a typical company of family players but – as their separate stories will reveal – in many respects they and their two dozen children were also unique individuals.

The Jonas & Penley Company of Comedians is a paradigm of the troupes of this era. By focussing on the particular we illuminate the general.

PROLOGUE

WHEN SERIAL STORIES were popular in magazines, each instalment used to commence with *New Readers Start Here* followed by a summary of what had already gone before in the story.

This prologue provides a five-minute crash-course in the history of the English Theatre to set the scene for what follows. Theatre historians may skip this and plunge straight into Act One but other readers may find it useful for understanding some of the subsequent references to apparent oddities and regulations.

Discounting the Roman occupation, the first theatre in this country arose in 1576. It was built in London, closely modelled on existing bull- and bear-baiting pits. Roughly circular like a large cylinder open to the sky but with sheltered galleries lining the walls, it was simply called The Theatre. Several other theatres built on similar lines followed.

These theatres were all in London, and going to see a play became both fashionable and popular. A constant supply of new plays was required. They were churned out by Marlowe, Shakespeare, Jonson, Webster and all the other Elizabethan playwrights that we know to this day. It is quite astonishing that novice authors writing for a new medium should so rapidly become accomplished playwrights that their works remain as our classics 400 years later.

After such an auspicious start we might expect a steady development and expansion of the theatre industry, but such was halted by the Civil War and the execution of Charles I. The country came under the heavy hand of that major killjoy Oliver Cromwell. He banned everything – pubs, football, dancing, women's make-up, coloured clothing, even Christmas. He turned what had been feast days into fasting days and was a right old misery. So, of course, he tore down all the theatres. Theatre and the performance of plays completely disappeared.

Fortunately Cromwell did not last for ever, and when Charles II was restored to the throne theatre also returned. While exiled in France, Charles had enjoyed not only the theatre in Paris but the spectacle of actresses. Yes, actual real live women on the stage! The English theatre had never had females on the stage, women's parts being played by boys and young men.

Charles II was known as the Merry Monarch and he gave permission by Royal Patent for two theatres to be built in London. Unlike the old open-air public venues these were smaller indoor theatres. After a hesitant start the two patents resolved into the Theatre Royal, Covent Garden and the Theatre Royal, Drury Lane. These two theatres are still there to this day, the present versions being the fourth incarnation in each case. One is the Royal Opera House and the other the home of spectacular musicals. But when created they were the only theatres in the land that were permitted to present plays. As time passed, the two were variously known as the major, royal, legitimate theatres or simply CG and DL in shorthand. In 1767 a further patent was granted by George III turning the 'Little Theatre in the Hay' into the Theatre Royal, Haymarket with a licence limited to the summer months.

Throughout the country the larger more important towns clamoured to have legitimate theatres for themselves as in the capital, so little by little other patents were granted directly by the king. Theatres that were granted patents, which we would call licences today, were: Edinburgh 1767; Bath 1768; Norwich 1768; York & Hull jointly 1769; Liverpool 1771; Manchester 1775; Chester 1777; Bristol 1778; Margate 1786; and Newcastle 1787. These theatres were designated 'theatres royal' and whilst today we regard Theatre Royal, similar to the Empire or the Palace as just a name, in those days it had a definite legal significance of great importance. It would take a bold mayor or JP to interfere with a building that had acquired rights from the king himself. These provincial theatres were full of actors who aspired to tread the boards of Drury Lane and Covent Garden, for it was only in those theatres that actors could make their fame and fortune emulating the great names of the past. Theatrical entertainment in the rest of the land was provided by troupes of travelling players living a hand-to-mouth existence setting up wherever they could, either with the permission of local officers or by flouting the law. An act of 1737 grouped travelling players with rogues, vagabonds, vagrants and sturdy beggars and dictated 'effectual punishments for sending them whither they ought to be sent.'

Fortunately for the actors these laws were widely disregarded because there was no central method of local government; towns and villages were mainly self-regulated. The control of a community still rested with aldermen and councillors, the mayor and magistrate being the men who mattered. Thus, to be allowed to perform, travelling players were obliged to curry favour with these important officials.

In most towns there were not many suitable places in which to present plays. Inns, which often had rooms that occupied an entire floor, were popular venues. Other suitable large rooms included assembly halls which were usually used for dances, card parties and other social events. Barns were also widely used, with many a barn becoming 'The Theatre' for several weeks before returning to barn status at harvest time.

But touring players with enterprising managers wanted better conditions than fit-ups in pubs and barns so started building theatres for themselves. Their patrons, also demanding better accommodation, found prominent citizens willing to instigate the creation of a theatre in their community without the benefit of a royal patent. These improvements did not, of course, happen overnight and there were many strolling players of dubious talent in companies of obvious poverty still roaming for years to come. Companies such as the one where Romeo and Mercutio had only one coat between them – when Romeo entered he wore it properly whilst Mercutio made his entrances wearing it inside out!

So that is the position as our story properly begins . . .

ACT ONE

MESSRS. JONAS AND PENLEY

'Those spirited and deserving managers'

SCENE ONE
1782 - 1803
THE TURN OF THE CENTURY

GOING TO SEE A PLAY at the end of the 18th Century was not an unalloyed pleasure. If you were a Londoner you could make your way most evenings in the winter season to one or other of the two patent theatres. Having walked through unpaved streets full of mud and ordure and avoided being mugged by footpads, there you could purchase a seat in the boxes for 7/- (a week's wage for a common labourer) or 3/- in the pit or 1/- in the gallery. Whichever part of the house you sat in, you would perch on a backless bench and, as both patent houses had capacities in excess of 3000, those in the furthest cheapest seats would be peering through the smoky, smelly gloom of candles and oil lamps, straining to hear the unamplified voices of the nation's finest actors who, at the turn of the century, were headed by John Philip Kemble and his sister Mrs Siddons, Dora Jordan, George Frederick Cooke and Joseph Grimaldi.

The two patent houses provided the best theatrical experience on offer – great music played by the most talented musicians, the finest scenic devices that could be painted by man, classic and new plays, all melded into a programme of delights starting at seven o'clock and carrying on until 11, and often past midnight.

On the other hand, if you did not live in London or one of the few provincial cities with a patent theatre that would provide a more modest but recognisable version of all that, you could wait until a travelling troupe called at your town or village and set up in the local pub or some farmer's barn. If you lived in Wapping in 1782 you could visit the Paviour's Arms in New Gravel Lane at Shadwell where Mrs Penley's Company of Comedians was dedicated to bringing the finest works from the great London theatres to its own humble audience. Perhaps 'company' is an exaggeration as Mrs Penley's troupe comprised a rag-tag bunch of four actors.

The play *Chrononhotonthologos* by Henry Carey, written some 50 years previously, was a nonsense affair that made fun of the bombastic tragedies that were popular at the time and contained hidden satire striking at the then Prime Minister Sir Robert Walpole, King George II and his queen.

It is a moot point whether the inhabitants of Wapping were amused by cod-heroic dialogue on the lines of:

> Go, call a Coach, and let a Coach be call'd,
> And let the Man that calls it be the Caller;
> And, in his calling, let him nothing call,
> But Coach! Coach! Coach! O for a Coach ye Gods!

They were probably more amused by characters with silly names such as King Chrononhotonthologos and Queen Fadladinida of Queerummania, but the version they would see was not the splendid original from Drury Lane with its cast of 18, spectacular scenery and full orchestra. Mrs Penley did the play with two men and two women in the club room of the pub with a lone fiddler providing the score.

The receipts hovered between 4/6 and 5/- a night divided between the company, meagrely providing for a group of starving actors who regarded a bowl of Irish stew once a week as a treat.

Mrs Penley's was typical of many such groups that relied on staying for a few days in a place before moving on. These troupes also played in the big London fairs such as Bartholomew and Smithfield and were not necessarily poverty stricken. Flockton was a famous puppet showman who died a wealthy man, while a sixteen-year-old youth called John Richardson, who had briefly been part of Mrs Penley's gallant little troupe, went on to become the owner of a magnificent travelling theatre that outlived him by a further 100 years. But there was a lot of competition – Bartholomew Fair often had as many as ten puppet shows at any one time. Puppet shows were widely used to evade the regulations appertaining to the censorship of the live theatre. One such regular puppet showman was John Jonas.

But if pickings are slim the answer is to pack up and move on, which is what Mrs Penley did. She obtained work for her players from Timothy Moore who had a company playing in the club room of a pub at Brompton, a village near Chatham, so the troupe packed up and, with bundles of costumes on their backs and bits of scenery tucked under their arms, made their way on foot to the Gravesend boat. At Brompton they met with better luck, and business was good in spite of playing in opposition to Mrs Sarah Baker whose company was acting in a stable at nearby Rochester.

Older than Mrs Penley, Sarah Baker, from a family of fairground acrobats, had married a man in her parent's company and when she was early widowed became a puppeteer, travelling with her young family around the fairs of the south-east. Gradually she extended her activities from acrobatics and puppets, becoming a proper theatre company. Although at this time she was, like Mrs Penley, working at fairs and in barns, she soon built up a circuit of permanent theatres at major towns throughout Kent. All Mrs Baker's theatres had a single entrance and she was always the only person to sit taking the money. She was uneducated, unable to read or write, and known for her earthy language. The word most often used to describe Mrs Baker is 'formidable'. On one occasion she was obliged to act as the prompter, and when an actor faltered and no prompt was forthcoming, he asked for the word whereupon his employer said 'I don't know what word you want!' and threw the prompt book on to the stage. Mrs Baker will keep cropping up from time to time as our story unfolds.

The origins of Mrs Esther Penley are more obscure. There was a husband, one John Penley, born in 1736. Esther was ten years younger and it is believed they married about 1760. They produced several children including Sampson (born 1765), Mary (about 1769), William (1773) and Esther (about 1782). It is not known when John Penley died, whether he was a showman, whether showbusiness descended from Esther's family, or whether Esther took to it in desperation.

However, the real subjects within these pages are Mrs Penley's children and grandchildren who, dragging themselves up from obscurity, became established as one of the most reputable theatrical families in the provincial Georgian and Regency theatre. Probably you have never even heard of them for, after many vicissitudes not only in this country but abroad, the entire family reverted to time's oblivion leaving only one grandchild eminent enough to make the pages of the *Dictionary of National Biography*. The story uncovered here is no less fascinating because the participants have been hitherto unknown.

On 18 February 1787 at Rotherhithe, Mary Penley married John Jonas, a well-established puppeteer and actor who performed at Bartholomew Fair annually from 1790 to 1798. Jonas signed the parish register, Mary made her mark which indicates she could not write. That does not necessarily mean she was unable to read and, as she was to take small roles in plays, she must have had some ability, or relied on learning from the spoken word. Jonas's background is unknown. He was born in 1766 and there is a record of a clown and acrobat of that name in Astley's circus troupe from Sadler's Wells playing at Birmingham in 1776. This may have been his father, or the very young Jonas himself. There is evidence in John Jonas's later life of some expertise in acrobatics.

Three years later, Mary's brother Sampson married Lucy Finch at Marylebone on 21 October 1790, and the following year on 3 August younger brother William married Frances Mary Ann Saulez at Lambeth.

As a result of these marriages, the three young couples banded together to form the Jonas & Penley Company. In those days, touring companies of actors were usually named on the lines of 'Mr Blank and his Company of Comedians' even though they would present tragedies, melodramas, musical pieces (even opera), as well as farces and comedies. The term 'comedian' was used as a synonym for player, embracing both actors and actresses. Sampson himself, soon becoming the dominant partner, eschewed convention, preferring the style 'Messrs Jonas and Penley' in his advertisements.

The Jonas & Penley company was formed at an opportune time in theatre history as all the irregularity and doubts for country theatrical companies were swept away by the Licensing Act of 1788 allowing local magistrates to license theatres to open for a maximum of 60 days per annum. This act cleared the way for a boom in theatre construction. The travelling companies now had better security, the aim being to build up a circuit of theatres in one manageable geographical area. These theatres were modest little playhouses closely similar in design and dimensions, enabling stock scenery to be transported from theatre to theatre thus cutting rehearsal times on near identical stages to a minimum.

They were rarely buildings of architectural merit and often were not even part of the street scene, being constructed down alleys and tucked-away corners just as their predecessors, the fit-up barns, had been. All these playhouses were constructed on similar lines – usually plain and rectangular – inside, a raised stage at one end, often occupying as much as half the area. The remaining space had boxes ranged round the walls at the same level as the stage, thus the space in front of them, betwixt boxes and stage, became a sunken pit filled with rows of backless benches. Above the boxes at the rear would be a small balcony of three or four rows of benches, and one or two rows of benches stretching along the long sides above the side boxes known as 'slips'. Some theatres might have an extra tier of boxes, giving a larger capacity while utilising the same footprint.

When not in use as a theatre, a portable floor could be placed over the pit, joining up with the stage so making a flat area for dances, auctions, dinners etc. Using a theatre for such events did not come under the licensing rules.

The admission prices in Georgian country theatres were remarkably consistent over a long period. As a norm, box seats were 3/-, Pit 2/-, Gallery 1/-. The atmosphere was extraordinarily intimate in these small theatres and the stage was not remotely placed at the end of a hall, as now, divided from it by a solid proscenium arch and walling. The Georgian stage protruded a long way into the small auditorium and the actor at the front of the stage was within the audience. He could shake hands with the people in the boxes closest to the stage.

This entire interior was constructed from wood and could be, and often was, readily fabricated within days to convert a bare empty building into a playhouse. Similarly, when a theatre ceased to be popular, it was no great effort to tear out the fittings and convert the space to another purpose. Indeed, in some cases the stage and proscenium were regularly dismantled between seasons enabling the space to be used for storage.

Whilst still playing the fairs, as of old, Jonas & Penley sought to establish regular venues by taking leases of available theatres in various towns. The year 1795 seems to be when the two brothers-in-law John Jonas and Sampson Penley became firmly established, buying the theatre at Henley-on-Thames from Thornton, a manager with an extensive circuit mainly in the Gloucester, Wiltshire and Berkshire area. The theatre, formerly outbuildings in the yard of the Broadgates Inn, comprised a stage built into a stable, and the pit formed from a warehouse. Jonas & Penley impressed the locals with their talent, being rated 'better performers than one would imagine.' The company placed £100 in the Henley Bank as a deposit against any demands made upon them, and the general conduct of the company indicated a better class of theatre than the locals had been used to from previous managers. The partners also contributed six guineas to the Henley-on-Thames list of donations for the Defence of the Country.

In May of the same year the company also arrived at Maidstone in Kent performing in a theatre belonging to Mrs Sarah Baker at the bottom of the High Street that was susceptible to regular flooding. Again Jonas & Penley made a good impression on the locals, a report stating 'their liberal and polite behaviour has excited the attention of the inhabitants.' As a result the partners intended to take a long lease on the building, dismantling and rebuilding the interior. However, Mrs Baker herself built a brand new theatre further up the High Street, well above flood level, thus rendering the Jonas & Penley plans superfluous.

Having failed to retain Maidstone, Jonas & Penley acquired a 21-year lease of the theatre at Lewes in East Sussex at £50 a year including adjoining tenements, which were let out for £8 and £10 a year respectively. This probably seemed a bargain to the partners but they were to find that Lewes was not such a good deal. The theatre, situated in a dank and insanitary area at the bottom of Star Lane in a place called locally Botany Bay, was not very old, having been built in 1789 by John Fox, a Covent Garden actor, who played in it during the off nights from his Brighton season eight miles away. He soon relinquished it, however, as there was a strong religious tendency in the town and he had not realised Lewes had a notorious reputation for being 'the worst town for theatricals in the Kingdom.' Presumably neither Penley nor Jonas was any more aware than Mr Fox had been, though Sampson Penley was never one for avoiding risky projects.

The Lewes theatre that Jonas & Penley held throughout a 21-year lease. The theatre had a cottage attached at either side.

Rapidly expanding their circuit, the brothers-in-law built a new theatre in Tenterden – reputedly the birthplace of William Caxton – in the Weald of Kent. Again, this was situated in a less than salubrious area down an alley behind houses in Honey Lane. Whilst the theatre is long gone the site is now a pleasant country lane of weatherboard houses some of which, standing in Theatre Square, are named Theatre Cottages.

Other venues that the Jonas & Penley troupe occupied around this time include Eastbourne – a recently built theatre that Jonas & Penley bought via complex mortgages over several years; Rye – an adjunct to a public house, the likelihood being Jonas & Penley paid an annual rent to the landlord; and Battle where the partners leased a plot of land for 28 years at seven guineas a year from Edmund Jupp, a local carpenter, who was no doubt the man chosen to build the theatre on it. The size of the plot measured a mere 57ft x 25ft indicating how tiny some of these country theatres were. From these few examples we see various methods employed by Jonas & Penley to secure the use of a venue. In larger towns, theatres were often built by local business men as limited companies with shared capital, these proprietors granting a lease by tenders from competing theatrical managements.

In 1798, William Penley – who never seems to have taken an active part in the management – and his wife Frances left the Jonas & Penley company to work for other managers in other parts of the country. This may simply have been to take advantage of better opportunities than the family business afforded. There can have been no dispute as the couple often returned, Mrs W Penley becoming the regular tragedy queen of the Jonas & Penley troupe for some years.

By 1801 the families had expanded greatly. Mr and Mrs Jonas now had seven children:
> Mary born about 1788
> John (9 February 1790)
> Joseph Charles (9 September 1792)
> Sophia born about 1794
> Maria (30 May 1796)
> Charlotte (10 June 1799)
> Charles Paul (18 August 1801)

Mr and Mrs Sampson Penley had five children:
> Sampson Jr (21 September 1792)
> Phoebe baptised on 18 January 1795
> Rosina (15 May 1796)
> Montague John Jackson (5 May 1799)
> William born in 1801

Mr and Mrs William Penley had three children.

It must have been a hard life for the three mothers. It cannot have been easy bearing and rearing children whilst constantly on the move, staying in one place for no more than a few weeks at a time before passing on to a new town, with a large family to clothe, feed and educate. In the early days the three wives also took part in the plays and, as all actresses had to provide their own costumes, a great deal of time must have been taken up with making and altering garments.

As the children grew older and developed, not only had they to be educated like other children, they were also trained specifically for the stage so they could each take their turn joining the company. The more family members that were able to take roles in the plays, the fewer outside actors need be employed.

As early as 1799 a playbill for *The Stranger* lists Master Penley, Miss Penley, Master Jonas and Miss Jonas in the cast. The eldest would be ten and the youngest four. The parts were, however, non-speaking ones, but gradually all the older children were regularly employed in comic dance pieces with titles such as *Caledonian Lovers*, *The Scotch Ghost* and *The Wapping Landlady*.

The circuit was thriving. Although regularly called 'Messrs Jonas & Penley', and there are extant early legal financial documents bearing both signatures, it looks as though Sampson Penley alone was really the manager, actors in their memoirs referring to 'Joining Sam Penley's company'. Jonas, whose name features on Jonas & Penley playbills more than anybody else, remains an enigmatic figure. Whether there was any official legal partnership between the brothers-in-law is doubtful in view of later financial travails, but henceforth the term 'J & P' will refer to the company, whereas the names Jonas and Penley will mean the individuals.

The partners had been visiting Mrs Baker's Folkestone theatre for some years. In 1774 she had built it on the Bayle, the ancient centre of the town that takes its name from the fortifications originally built there. It was a weatherboard building heavily tarred over with a roof much like an upturned boat. In front of the building was a rickety wooden shed that served as a stable. Containing the usual boxes, pit and gallery arrangement, the theatre also had an upper gallery (6d) where the spectators were crammed up under the roof like hens in a coop. It is estimated that the theatre would hold about 300. Mrs Baker was still advertising in 1794, so presumably had held regular seasons there up to that time.

However, at some time thereafter she sublet the theatre to J & P. On 28 December 1803, Sampson Penley wrote from Henley to say that they proposed to open the theatre in six weeks time but having left it too late to obtain a licence from the Quarter Sessions in Canterbury, sought permission from the mayor to allow it to go ahead. The postage on the letter was 1/4d, which probably includes the cost of a prepaid answer. It was very expensive arranging things in the years before telephones; in 1803 1/4d was equivalent to a labourer's daily wage. Prior to the penny post, introduced in 1840, letters had to be prepaid or paid for by the recipient according to mileage. The rates referred to a single sheet of paper which was sent folded and sealed with wax. An envelope would rank as a second sheet and double the price. Many letters were sent with continuation lines of writing crossing the page at 90° to the original, thus getting two pages for the price of one, though making for difficult reading. Until the penny post made corresponding throughout the country very cheap, it will readily be seen that actors and managers, who had to be constantly corresponding for business purposes, had yet another extraordinary expense compared to the average working man.

In 1804, J & P acquired a longer more permanent form of lease and petitioned for a licence after having 'enlarged and beautified' the Folkestone theatre. The provisions of licences granted under the 1788 act were very strict. Apart from the limit of a maximum of 60 days within a specified four months period, the performances were not to be within 20 miles of London, or eight miles of any patent or licensed theatre, within ten miles of the residence of His Majesty or 14 miles of the universities. Folkestone was to be a mainstay of the J & P circuit for many years and four offspring were either born or baptised in the town at various times.

An actor's life is precarious; there is never any guarantee of consistent employment. In Georgian times an actor was engaged for a season which in the case of the patent theatres could be as long as nine months but, on the other hand, in some country theatres as short as a week. It was commonplace for a theatre company to visit a town for the annual Race Week, playing every night with a different programme, often engaging actors especially. Surprisingly, the J & P company had a nucleus of actors who stayed many years. The Rackham family appear on its playbills from 1803 to 1813. Stackwood, Griffith, Mr & Mrs Dormer, Miss Watson and Mrs Beynon are names that crop up time and again over several years. Joint manager John Jonas figured prominently for 20 years taking on a great variety of parts though rarely playing leading roles. Even on his benefit night of *Hamlet* Jonas played the Gravedigger. Sampson Penley often played leads but later, as managerial cares took over, his name was sometimes missing from the playbills.

Many players came for but a short time. One such was a Miss Jackson, a seventeen-year-old whose father, a comedian in the Norwich company, had lately died. She joined J & P at Lewes and within three months had married the leading man Mr Holbrook at Battle, in Sussex. The Dean who married them wore enormous white wigs, and gave one as a present to the new groom. Afterwards when speaking of his bride,

Holbrook joked the wig was the best bargain of the two.

Mr and Mrs Holbrook soon moved on, had children and, after eight years of struggling, gave up the theatrical profession. Mrs Holbrook became known as the novelist Ann Catherine Holbrook recounting her early experiences as a professional actress in *The Dramatist; or Memoirs of the Stage* which gives a vivid look at the conditions of actors in country theatres during those years. Mrs Holbrook reveals that she and her husband worked for a weekly joint salary of £2.10.0, paid between 8/- and 10/- a week for lodgings and, in three months, travelled by post chaise a total of 280 miles costing £14.

The actresses in visiting theatre companies often made a romantic impression on local youths as they carried a whiff of the exotic compared to the girls of the town, and many a young man's heart would beat faster when the annual visit of the players was announced. How many fleeting dalliances developed into serious romantic attachments is impossible to say, as it is a fact that most young actresses married within the business. Many respectable people would not go to the theatre as the stage had a reputation for immorality and loose behaviour. In fact family-based theatre troupes, like circus and fairground travellers, were usually particularly strict in their moral code but, as we all know, true love conquers all.

Up to 1804 a stalwart of the company was Miss Esther Penley, the youngest of the Penley siblings. She played young lovers and pert maids and was always handy with a song. Alas, the company lost her valuable services when Esther married William Pepper, a twenty-five-year-old butcher and grazier from Folkestone. They were married on 2 October 1804 in Eastbourne, Esther being described as 'Miss Penley sister of Mr Penley, Manager of the Lewes Theatre.'

It is interesting that Esther Penley is not described as an actress. Whilst a manager was considered respectable, actors and actresses were still tainted with the idea of being rogues and vagabonds. In spite of the likes of Mrs Siddons, the greatest tragedienne of the day who carried enormous moral authority and respectability, and of whom Byron said he would 'as much sleep with the Archbishop of Canterbury as Mrs Siddons', many people regarded actresses as little better than prostitutes. This attitude lasted for many more decades, even as late as the 1880s *Punch* demanding 'Would any one of us wish our daughters to go on the stage? There can be but one answer to this. "No!"' No actress seeking respectability would ever publicly describe herself thus, she would be a musician, governess, teacher of elocution or of independent means –

anything but a despised actress. The stigma only disappeared at the end of the century when Sir Henry Irving – the first actor to be knighted – succeeded in elevating the position of the acting profession in society.

Esther Penley disappeared from the stage to become the respectable Mrs Pepper of Folkestone, going on to bear at least six children including sons Wlliam and Sampson – named after her acting brothers – who became respectively a sculptor and a woodcarver. There was clearly an artistic streak in the Penley genes, as will be seen as the story unfolds.

New Theatre, TENTERDEN.

By JONAS and PENLEY's COMPANY.

On SATURDAY Evening, May the 25th, 1799.
Will be prefented a NEW COMEDY, called

Wives as they Were,
A N D

MAIDS AS THEY ARE.

Lord Priory,	Mr. JONAS,
Sir William Dorrillon,	Mr. HOLBROOK,
Sir George Evelyn,	Mr. STREET,
Mr. Bronzely,	Mr. PENLEY,
Mr. Norberry,	Mr. HEALEY,
Oliver,	Mr. GRIFFITH,
Thomas,	Mr. SHERLOCK,
Lady Priory,	Mrs. HEALEY,
Lady Mary Raffle,	Mrs. GRIFFITHS,
Mifs Dorrillon,	Mrs. HOLBROOK,

End of the Play a favorite SONG by Mr. GRIFFITH.

To which will be added, (by desire) a Mufical Entertainment, called

My Grandmother,

Vapour,	Mr. PENLEY,
Sir Matthew Medley,	Mr. HEALEY,
Suffrance,	Mr. HOLBROOK,
Woodly,	Mr. STREET,
Tom,	Mr. SHERLOCK
Dicky Goffip,	Mr. JONAS,
Florella,	Mifs PENLEY,

BOXES 3s.——PIT 2s.——GALLERY 1s.
Doors to be open at SIX, and to begin at SEVEN.

☞ Nights of performing, Mondays, Tuesdays, Thursdays & Fridays.
⁎⁎⁎ Tickets to be had of Mr. Jonas, at Mr. Carpenter's, where places for the Boxes
may be taken.

Meff. JONAS and PENLEY beg leave, moft refpectfully to inform the Ladies and Gentlemen of Tenterden, and its Vicinity, that the Theatre is fited up in a neat and refpectable Manner, and that their Company confifts of Performers of the moft approved Abilities; and truft, the eftablifhed Reputation with which they have conducted the firft Theatres of Refpect, will entitle them to a Share of their Patronage, during their very fhort Stay.

An early playbill of the Jonas & Penley company.
The Miss Penley billed here is Sampson Penley's seventeen-year-old sister who gave up the stage on her marriage five years later.

SCENE TWO
1804 - 1806
THE JONAS & PENLEY CIRCUIT

A T THE START of the 19th century the Industrial Revolution was well under way and the nation's increasing prosperity was due to England becoming the most industrialised nation in the world.

It was a boom time for country theatricals. There was still a novelty value in a town having its very own new theatre, most having been built at the very end of the previous century. Also the country was at war and had been since 1792. (All the many Penley and Jonas children were born during wartime.) Parliament was pouring money into defences both at land and sea, labour was in short supply and wages were rising.

A third of Britain's total population lived in the south-east which was still predominantly an agricultural area although the south coastal and market towns that J & P included in its circuit had their resident populations much increased by the presence of militia men from distant parts of the country. There was a very real fear that Napoleon would invade Britain and platoons of soldiers were deployed along the lengthy south coast as no intelligence told of where Napoleon would launch his attack. The regular standing army was not large enough to guard the entire south coast, and county militias from all parts of the country were drafted in to aid the defence. Militias were civilians who, alongside their normal occupations, underwent some military training to be ready for local emergencies, similar to the later Home Guard and Territorial Army. It was heavily rumoured that Napoleon was ready, waiting for the first foggy night on which to launch his attack.

Whilst the situation was dire for the country, it did have some benefits for the theatre companies in the area, as soldiers and – at the ports – sailors were enthusiastic if undiscriminating playgoers. As the threat of attack lasted several years, and militias stationed for long periods, many playbills of the time carried announcements that certain officers had bespoken a performance, or that the military band would play.

In London, the war impinged less on the general public, and the sensation of the 1804/05 theatrical season was a thirteen-year-old boy known as Young Roscius – after Roscius the famous actor of the ancient world. William Henry West Betty was an Irish youth who first showed his desire for the stage at the age of eleven when his father took him to Belfast to watch Mrs Siddons in the role of Elvira in Sheridan's *Pizarro*. Betty's father introduced his son to the manager of the Belfast Theatre and the theatrical prompter William Hough, so he could direct, train and mentor young Betty. On his debut the boy brought in a large crowd; reports stating his performance was flawless and extremely well received. This led to further performances in which Betty precociously acted the lead roles in famous plays.

Master Betty's fame spread to Dublin, where his father did a deal for similar performances causing the citizens of Dublin to become so excited over Betty that the civil authorities extended the curfew an hour for those attending the theatre. Betty then toured Scotland and England where his performances sold out and earned a small fortune. Master Betty was now ready for London. On 1 December 1804, people started queuing at mid-day for the doors opening at six o'clock. Once the doors were open, crowds flooded inside to find seats, creating a huge disorder and chaos with fighting and fainting. Master Betty became the darling of the public, aristocracy and royalty. He broke all precedent by appearing at both the patent theatres Covent Garden and Drury Lane alternately, earning the colossal sum of £75 a night. The Justin Bieber of his day.

Sampson Penley tried to engage Master Betty for a night at Lewes, suggesting that he fit in the gig on one of his nights off work at the patent theatres. Lewes was less than 50 miles from London so he could easily travel down one day, perform in the evening, travelling back the next day arriving in time for his next scheduled show at Covent Garden. Unusually, Betty's father, the boy's money-grasping manager, turned the idea down stating his son needed to rest during his exhausting season. At a full house, the Lewes theatre only held £70 with nightly expenses of £12, so it is likely that even at inflated prices Mr Betty did not consider it worth the effort.

The prodigy caused such a furore that parents throughout the land were moved to thrust their own immature offspring into the limelight, and infant Roscia of both sexes and all ages sprung up all over the place – Master Benwell from Chester, Miss Fisher from Bath, the Ormskirk Roscius, Master Mori the Young Orpheus, etc, etc, *ad infinitum*.

Sampson, an established theatre manager being better placed than most parents, in July 1805 offered up his own twelve-year-old son Sampson Jr as a Young Roscius in the more modest locale of the Lewes theatre. His role was that of Young Norval in *Douglas*, the jewel in Betty's crown. This was followed by Frederick in *Lovers' Vows* – another Betty hit – making a total of three nights in Lewes. Sam Jr then gave an extra performance as the last night of the Tenterden season on 12 July. These nights were Sam Jr's stage baptism, but his career as a Young Roscius must have been as short-lived as Master Betty's for he disappeared again until reappearing in force at the age of eighteen as the leading man of the company. As will be seen, Sam Jr was to go on to greater things.

Mr. PENLEY begs Leave most respectfully to inform his Friends and the Public in general, that having brought his Son forward as a

Young Roscius

At the Theatre, Lewes, in the Character of DOUGLAS, which he performed three Nights with the most unbounded Applause, will make his Fourth Appearance on the Stage at this Theatre, in the Character of FREDERICK, in LOVERS' VOWS, and trusts he will meet the Approbation of an indulgent Public.

POSITIVELY THE LAST NIGHT THIS SEASON.
FOR THE BENEFIT OF MR. AND MRS.

PENLEY.

Theatre, Tenterden.

On FRIDAY, July the 12th, 1805,
Will be presented a celebrated Play, translated from the German of Kotzebue, and adapted to the English Stage by Mrs. INCHBALD, called

Lovers' Vows.

Baron Wildenham, — Mr. RACKHAM.
Count Cassel, Mr. PENLEY.—Anhalt, Mr. AINSLIE.
Verdun, (the Rhyming Butler) — Mr. JONAS.
Landlord, — Mr. GRIFFITH.
Cottager, Mr. MORETON.—Farmer, Mr. CLARKE.
And the Part of Frederick, by Master PENLEY,
Only Twelve Years of Age.
Agatha Friburg, Mrs. W. PENLEY.—Cottager's Wife, Mrs. RACKHAM.
Country Girl, Miss JONAS.—Amelia Wildenhaim, Mrs. KEYS.

Previous to the Play,

AN OCCASIONAL ADDRESS,

Written and to be spoken by Mr. SMYTHE.
End of the Play, a favorite Song, by Miss BARRY.
A Comic Dance, called The

VILLAGE FESTIVAL.

The Characters by Mr. M'Farland, Mr. Penley, Mr. Clarke, Mrs. Smythe,
Mrs. Jonas, Mrs. Young, and Mrs. W. Penley.
And a new PAS SEUL by Miss JONAS and PENLEY.

To which will be added, a comic Entertainment, called

High Life below Stairs.

Lovel, Mr. SMYTHE.—Freeman, Mr. MORETON.
Lord Duke's Servant, — Mr. AINSLIE.
Sir Harry's Servant, — Mr. PENLEY.
Philip, Mr. M'FARLAND.—Coachman, Mr GRIFFITH.
Kingston, Mr. CLARKE.—Tom, Mr. STACKWOOD.
Lady Bab's Maid, — Mrs. SMYTHE.
Cook, Mrs. RACKHAM.—Cloey, Mrs. YOUNG.
Mrs. Kitty, — Miss BARRY.
In Act the Second, a Mock Minuet by Mr. AINSLIE and Miss BARRY.

Boxes, 3s.——Pit and Slips, 2s.——Gallery, 1s.
No Admittance behind the Scenes.

Tickets to be had of Mr. PENLEY, at Mr. Banbroos.

Messrs. JONAS and PENLEY beg Leave to return their most grateful Thanks to the Ladies and Gentlemen of TENTERDEN, ROLVENDEN, and their Vicinity, for their Patronage and Support, and hope by continued Assiduity and Attention, to merit their Favors at a future Period.

WATERS, PRINTER, CRANBROOK.

Sampson Penley Jr made his debut as a twelve-
year-old prodigy in 1805.

24

Henley continued as one of the most successful towns on the J & P circuit and Mr and Mrs Jonas had another child, Esther, baptised on 5 February 1804 at Henley and Mr and Mrs Sampson Penley also had another daughter, Emma, born at Henley on 15 December 1805.

Things were going so well that Penley and Jonas decided to build a new theatre to replace the ramshackle one they had inherited. They engaged William Parker, a local builder, to design, plan and erect the new theatre. The hard-headed and practical approach of the brothers-in-law resulted in this building costing them just under £2,000. In October, they were able to announce to 'the Nobility, Gentry and others of Henley, and its vicinity, that they have erected, for their accommodation and amusement, a theatre, equal (if not superior) in convenience and decorations to any of its size in England. The painting by Mr Mortram of the Theatre Royal, Drury Lane'. The new theatre had two tiers of boxes, with the lower tier at the increased price of 4/-.

The entertainment offered by the J & P theatres was identical to that in all the similar theatres in the land. An evening's programme usually comprised a main play and an afterpiece, customarily a farce or 'musical entertainment'. It was not unusual to have *King Lear* followed by a pantomime. These main attractions were bolstered with at least one comic song or dance. Doors opened at six o'clock and the show started at seven. The final curtain aimed to be about 11 o'clock but was often later than that. The audience certainly got their money's worth whether in box, pit or balcony. It was customary to admit people at half-price around 8.30 pm, although for outstanding attractions such as guest artists of great repute half-price was suspended. When times were good there would be no half-price for anything, when business was poor it was, naturally, readily available. The term 'Second Price' with the reduced charges was used on playbills to denote this concession was available, and 'No Second Price' was the blunt statement when it was not offered.

The programme changed every night, hence theatre playbills were issued each day. They were not huge like present day posters but more the size of modern flyers printed on thin paper. They were ephemeral and hundreds of thousands must have been printed, of which only a tiny sample have survived. Earnest playgoers could buy copies of the playbill which were used as programmes as well as pasted up as advertisements. These playbills varied little from place to place or year to year. All over the country the play titles were the same, the typefaces and layout very similar, with the cast listed very formally eg: 'Mackbeth – Mr Rackham', with all the actors and their roles, followed by the actresses. This formality, usually lacking even an initial, makes it extra difficult in identifying players, especially when the surnames are common ones. If there are brothers and sisters who are actors in different companies the problem becomes infuriating when, for example, establishing which of the three acting Miss Penleys is present at any given venue.

As time passed, additional information came to be added and larger typefaces introduced. As most local newspapers were weekly publications, sometimes an advertised play might be changed at the last minute, and customers came to rely on the daily playbill regularly pasted up as an up-to-date source of information.

The playbill was also used for extra announcements such as special plays in preparation, and messages from actors to their public:

o   Repeat benefit of Messrs Atkinson and Moreton:
    In consequence of the unfavourable state of the weather on Friday last, and the receipts being inadequate to the expenses of the night, Messrs A and M feel grateful in acknowledging the liberality of the Managers in granting them another night, it being requested by several Respectable families.

o   Mr Dowton tenders his apologies that he is unable to fulfil his obligations as he is detained at Maidstone with a severe illness.

o   Doors to be opened at Six and to begin as soon as the races are over.

o   Mr Copeland has made arrangements with Miss Duncan to play for a few nights in Deal but she has relinquished it in favour of four more nights in Margate.

o   The future days of performing this week, will be Wednesday and Friday.
    NB: They are Moon-light nights.

One aspect often seen on these old playbills is the expression 'BY DESIRE'. This refers to a night when the play is a 'bespeak'. That is to say a person or group of people have especially ordered a certain play to be performed in exchange for patronage. Thus one sees the bills headed with:

o   By Desire of the Mayor

o   By Desire of the Young Ladies of Mrs Elliott's School

o   By Desire of the Master of the Hunt

and so on. Invariably a bespeak ensured either a fee up front or a guaranteed good house.

Usually a manager could persuade his patron to request a play that was currently in the company's repertoire, but it would be panic-stations if the chosen play was one not known by any of the leading players. One country manager was very quick-witted when a local lady of rank requested *Henry the Eighth*, replying that his company did not have the resources, but they could perform *Henry the Fourth* twice, which would come to the same thing!

In Georgian and Regency times the repertoire was fairly standardised, with the London theatres adding new plays which were then taken up in the provinces if they proved successful. Unless a failure, new plays in the London theatres were immediately printed, with copies available to buy by provincial managers. There were no copyright laws; if the company had the book the actors could learn their parts from it and mount the play. These plays were churned out over and over so that while the programme changed every night at one venue, when the company moved on to a new town they could bring them all out again. All the circuit companies presented the same repertoire thus enabling actors to easily move from one management to another, confident in knowing the fare to be produced was within their compass.

When an actor was contracted, the line of parts he was engaged for was understood, and he was expected to know those parts, or be able to learn them on demand. It was essential that an actor could learn 500 lines a day. With their regular workload how they found time to learn their new lines is astonishing, and it is no wonder that there were many complaints of actors being 'imperfect'. J & P, whenever possible, followed the practice of playing every other night. Though by no means sacrosanct, this routine would give the players two days to get up the next play. However, when playing a special week for, say, the local races or assizes, the theatre would be open every night to maximise profits. This is an example of an actual Race Week that J & P played at Mrs Baker's Canterbury theatre in 1812:

11 August	*Love Makes a Man* and *Turn Out*
12 August	*The Kiss* and *The Sleepwalker*
13 August	*The Boarding House* and *How to Die for Love*
14 August	*The Sons of Erin* and *How to Die for Love*
15 August	*The Wonder, a Woman Keeps a Secret*
17 August	*The Peasant Boy* and *Any Thing New*
18 August	*Douglas*

It was essential that touring companies visited towns when the maximum number of people was gathered. Not only was the above an arduous week in itself, but the company was split from the normal J & P company which was appearing elsewhere. In these circumstances, Penley would engage extra actors especially for this single week. Also, when visiting stars were engaged, they would send in advance the titles of the plays they intended to do, and arrive expecting the resident company to be fully rehearsed and competent to support them. There was seldom a proper rehearsal with a visiting star. However, the fact that a seasoned actor had his established line of parts meant he permanently had in his head, and thus at his fingertips, a whole host of roles that he could pull out as required. If that actor had agreed the roles before joining the company then his memory labour would be minimal until a new part was demanded of him.

The whole set-up is summed up by the story of the actor who was sent for urgently by a country company to replace an indisposed performer. Arriving just in time for curtain up, he entered the theatre demanding 'What's the play and where's the stage?' It was all he needed to know.

As a result of the mundane repertory, managements were eager to splash on the playbills such encouragements as:

- First time at this theatre
- Not seen here for seven years
- By special request
- By public demand
- A New Play performed with Universal Approbation at the Theatre Royal, Covent Garden

and similar blandishments. New hits from the London theatres were put into rehearsal as soon as the script could be acquired, and a brand new addition to the well-worn repertory was always to be welcomed.

More unusual attractions that Penley engaged included Mr Moritz 'exhibiting several astonishing Deceptions never before equaled, likewise various Feats of Strength and Agility in Balancing, a Wonderful Exhibition with Live Birds and a real Phantasmagoria'. This last was a forerunner to the Haunted House scene as, with the aid of a magic lantern — an early form of slide projector — ghosts and skeletons could appear and disappear at the twist of a moving lens. One has to admire the versatility of Mr Moritz, and wonder at the amount of equipment he was willing to transport by horse and cart.

Another star attraction was Mr Saxoni the celebrated rope-dancer 'just arrived from Paris whose extraordinary exhibitions on the Tight Rope, gave such universal satisfaction in this town a few years ago, and whose improvement is very considerable since his late tour on the continent.' This gentleman's extraordinary exhibitions included his 'original and surprising Hornpipe, and Flag dance, leaps over garters, manoeuvres with tables, chairs, hoops etc and a variety of novelties not yet seen in this town.'

There was, as yet, no division between the straight theatre, circus and what was later to be known as music hall. It was all entertainment, with even the patent theatres in London presenting spectacles with horses, fireworks and flowing water.

On one occasion at Lydd the main attraction was 'A Grand Exhibition of Two Transparent Paintings'. One depicted the king in his coronation robes receiving the Prince and Princess of Wales. The other showed the marriage ceremony of the Prince and Princess of Wales. These were probably large back-lit pictures on thin gauze-like material and, as the marriage had taken place in 1795, the pictures must have been touted round for years afterwards, and no doubt the man presenting them went on to visit other venues in the circuit.

A big coloured picture would have been a rarity; large paintings normally only being seen in grand houses, public buildings and churches. Collections of paintings open to the public were rare, relying on rich private owners occasionally opening their galleries for viewing. The first specific exhibition where owners loaned items was not held until 1805. The first permanent gallery was founded at Dulwich in 1814, the National Gallery in London ten years later. It is difficult for modern people, accustomed to being surrounded by huge advertisement hoardings, to conceive of the impact a large coloured picture would have on the people of those days.

Another attraction that Penley added to one programme in 1807 was described as 'a Grand Display of Transparent Fire-Works with Six Beautiful Changes'. This was another use of the magic lantern, the so-called fireworks being coloured patterns painted on glass slides projected on to a screen. By twisting the lens the operator could make them appear and dissolve. Again, to us a basic device, but to the Georgians a thing of wonder and delight akin to a giant kaleidoscope.

Mr and Mrs Jonas had another son, Henry, baptised at Folkestone on 9 April 1806.

By this time, J & P had a securely established circuit and were no longer visiting the annual fairs. It had been a struggle as there was much competition for venues in the south-east. Mrs Sarah Baker, the doyenne of Kent managers, had a circuit comprising Canterbury, Tunbridge Wells, Rochester, Faversham and Maidstone. She also owned Folkestone and Hastings theatres, but these were let on long leases to J & P. Mrs Baker had a comfortable relationship with Penley and at one point actually announced in the press that she was retiring and intended selling all her venues to J & P. Unfortunately that never came to pass, and in Kent our heroes had to be resigned to remaining in a lower league.

There were other managements too. Charles Mate had Dover, Margate, Deal and Sandwich in his circuit. Thomas Trotter had Hythe, Gravesend and Worthing. Samuel Jerrold had a small circuit of Sheerness, Lydd and Cranbrook. His theatre was not even in the town of Cranbrook itself, but was a barn in the hamlet of Wilsley, just outside. But people have to start somewhere and Jerrold's leading man at Cranbrook, John Pritt Harley, went on to be a popular actor at Drury Lane, while Jerrold's son Douglas became a playwright who wrote *Black-Eyed Susan* a hit play of 1829 that held the stage for many years and is still occasionally done today.

One Kent town that nobody obtained was Ashford. A company had established some sort of presence as early as 1750 but opposition was strong, the parish vestry in 1786 resolving to have plays visit only once every ten years. A bit different from the 24 hours non-stop entertainment piped into our homes nowadays! Neither J & P nor the formidable Mrs Baker ever managed to establish themselves in the town.

SCENE THREE
1807
A SEASON AT TENTERDEN

IN 1807, THE J & P CIRCUIT included the following towns: Henley, Lewes, Folkestone, Rye, Tenterden, Hastings, Bexhill, Battle and Eastbourne. The towns on the J & P circuit were not, of course, as we know them today. Eastbourne, for example, was a conflation of four villages, the present resort not being developed until the advent of the railway in 1849.

The venue at Bexhill was most likely a garrison theatre as what had been little more than a hamlet clustered around a church on a hill was increased in size by the arrival of a huge army camp. Most of these newcomers comprised the King's German Legion which had been formed from expatriate Hanoverians who had fled to England when Hanover fell to the French. As George III was also the Elector of Hanover, he formed all these displaced men into a legion within the British army. At its height the Legion contained some 14,000 as latterly men other than Germans were recruited – even French prisoners-of-war.

The largest ('holds £70') of the J & P theatres was at Lewes. As these theatres are long gone we cannot know exactly what each theatre was like. However, we do have some assistance. In 1805 James Winston, actor, manager, playwright, theatre owner and a founder of the Garrick Club, started compiling *The Theatric Tourist* a gazetteer in monthly parts of all the theatres in the country, illustrated with coloured plates. Unfortunately, his project fizzled out after publishing details of only 24 theatres. However, he had compiled notes on almost 300 venues with some sixteen significant circuits and these still exist in various archives. His self-painted illustrations are all exterior views. There are few illustrations from other sources, and interior views rarer still.

We know the exterior dimensions of some theatres and we are sometimes given an idea of the capacity by the expression 'holds £40' or similar. This indicates the takings from a full house. Because of the regular price structure and stability of admission prices it is often possible to deduce capacity from these figures.

But the principal source of knowledge of the typical small country venue is the existence of one remaining playhouse at Richmond in Yorkshire. This is the only surviving theatre out of the 300 or more that existed in Georgian times. Much research has been published based on this building, and it is open for all to visit. It is a working theatre serving the present community as well as a museum piece of great fascination. Theatres in large towns and cities were, of course, much larger even at the end of the 18th century, but the extant Richmond theatre is a paradigm of the country circuit theatre that flourished in the days of Jonas and Penley.

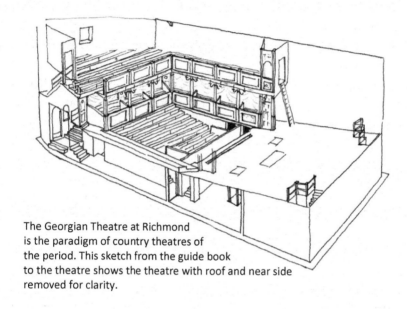

The Georgian Theatre at Richmond is the paradigm of country theatres of the period. This sketch from the guide book to the theatre shows the theatre with roof and near side removed for clarity.

The J & P theatres were visited regularly but not necessarily annually. Tenterden had a season from May to July, but only on alternate years. This was quite commonplace; the formidable Mrs Baker visited her newly-built Maidstone theatre only every other year. It was considered visiting more often would satiate prospective audiences.

Also it was not always possible to maintain a steady logical progress since a company, invariably chasing the chance of a larger audience, may in the middle of a run at, say, Tenterden break off and dash to Lewes for Race Week, then return to continue at Tenterden. Instead of several weeks season at a venue, it may be visited diverse times a year for short periods.

To see how the J & P company operated, this is an example of an actual season. In May 1807 the company arrived in Tenterden ready to open for a period of several weeks. On arriving, the players firstly went to their various lodgings, the wiser ones having secured these in advance. The less prudent had to spend their first hours trudging around the town looking for a place to stay. The average pay for an actor in the J & P troupe was £1 a week, and half of that would be spent on board and lodging. The Sampson Penley family stayed at Mr J Windsor's opposite the Bank. On the previous two visits in 1803 and 1805 they had stayed with Mr Bembrick or Benrigg.

When the company assembled, the building would not have been used for drama since they quitted it in July 1805 so would need at least cleaning out and making shipshape. May to July being mild months there would not have been too many problems with cold and damp, but at other times of year it was commonplace to see playbills announcing that the theatre had been well aired, or that fires had been continually burning for three days, and so on. It was also a regular feature to announce that the theatre had been totally redecorated. In this instance the playbill merely stated:

> Messrs. JONAS and PENLEY, beg leave to inform the Ladies and Gentlemen of Tenterden, Rolvenden, and Vicinity, they have neither spared Pains or Expence in providing a Company of the most distinguished Abilities, and getting up every Novelty in their Power for their Amusement, and most humbly Solicit the honor of that Patronage they have ever so liberally experienced.

The daily playbills for the Tenterden theatre were printed at Cranbrook – a town some seven miles distant – which must have been an added complication for Penley. The printer was Samuel Waters the parish clerk and school master who, it is said, used the table tombstones in the church-yard for spreading out his printed sheets to dry.

The J & P company was headed by Mr Rackham, who was leading man. Penley followed the policy of engaging married couples on the principle that a joint salary was cheaper than two separate ones. In addition there were, of course, the family members. Sampson and his wife regularly appeared, Mrs Penley taking small roles. Mr Jonas was always present in supporting roles. As on several of his children's birth registrations he describes himself as 'musician' rather than 'actor' or 'comedian', and later in life becoming a teacher of the violin, he might well have been also in charge of the music aspect of the shows, although none of the J & P playbills makes any mention of musicians.

Mrs W Penley is prominently present as leading lady. She was Sampson's sister-in-law, being married to brother William who, having successfully made a huge step up in his profession, was no longer with the

J & P family troupe.

We do not have a complete record of this season, but to give an idea of the repertoire, how varied it was, and how hard the company must have worked, the following is taken from the playbills that have survived for 1807. Feel free to skip to the end!

5 May	*The Soldier's Daughter*	*No Song. No Supper*
6 May	*Who Wants a Guinea*	*The Wedding Day*
13 May	*The Castle Spectre*	*Matrimony*
25 May	*The Iron Chest*	*Harlequin Everywhere*
29 May	*The Point of Honour*	*Fortune's Frolics*
30 May	*The Surrender of Calais*	*The Devil to Pay*
1 June	*The West Indian*	*High Life Below Stairs*
3 June	*The Sailor's Daughter*	*The Humours of Election*
5 June	*King Henry the Fourth*	*The Humours of Election*
8 June	*The School for Friends*	*Five Miles Off*
10 June	*The Curfew*	*The Shipwreck*
12 June	*The Honeymoon*	*The Highland Reel*
19 June	*Speed the Plough*	*Matrimony*
29 June	*The Curfew*	*Inkle & Yarico*
1 July	*The Busy Body*	*A Tale of Mystery*
3 July	*A Cure for the Heart Ache*	*The Weathercock*
6 July	*The Way to Get Married*	*The Spoil'd Child*

As the company was there for nine weeks, playing four nights a week for five weeks, and three nights for the remaining four, they presented a total of 32 different shows, the above list representing just over half of the season.

What is immediately apparent is how few titles are familiar to us today. *King Henry the Fourth* purports to be by Shakespeare, but was a bastardisation that had the alternative title of *The Humours of Sir John Falstaff*. In this production Master Penley, who was Sampson Jr and had done very little since his stint as a Young Roscius, was prominently billed as playing Hotspur. He had yet to attain his fifteenth birthday.

Some of the plays were very old: *The Busy Body* had been seen regularly for 100 years, *The Devil to Pay* dated from 1731, *High Life Below Stairs* was first staged in 1759. More recent works were *The Iron Chest* and *Inkle and Yarico*, both popular hits of the time by George Colman the Younger who, on later becoming Examiner of Plays, was far more censorious of other playwrights than his own works.

The Castle Spectre is the most famous play of Matthew G Lewis, known as Monk Lewis because of his predilection for gothic ruins, haunted abbeys and spooky things in general. First performed at Drury Lane in 1797 it had 60 performances during its first season and held the stage for 100 years. A hit by any standards! Lewis's own funeral was as bizarre as anything in his plays. Whilst on a voyage from Jamaica he died of yellow fever and was to be buried at sea. The coffin was lowered into the water, but slipped its weights and, instead of sinking, it simply floated away into the unknown.

Speed the Plough, first staged in 1800 at Covent Garden, was one of the biggest hits of its day and is an early example of the use of melodramatic language. There is an unseen character called Mrs Grundy, a sternly moralistic neighbour, and her name passed into common parlance in the expression 'What will Mrs Grundy say?' The author is Thomas Morton who wrote some 25 plays, of which this is the most well-known.

As there was no copyright system, old plays were often plundered and re-worked by authors desperate for an original plot. *The Spoil'd Child* was taken from a previous play called *The Romp*. It was transformed into a new version as a vehicle for Dora Jordan in 1790. The most up-to-date plays during this particular season were *The Sailor's Daughter* (1804), *The School for Friends* (1805), *Five Miles Off* (1806) and *The Curfew* (1807). Favourite plays from any time during the previous century were dragged out year after year by all theatre companies *ad nauseam*.

As the season approached its end, it was time for the members of the company to take their benefits. This was a system of payment hallowed by time. The principle of the benefit was that, after the expenses of the house had been deducted, the actor received all the takings for that one performance. This, in theory, should be a large amount and, in the position of star performers and local favourites, it was. However, in the case of lesser lights the benefit could actually cost them money as they had to guarantee the expenses of the house. Having been granted a benefit, the player would try to get the support of colleagues by asking if they would take part. It was a lucky player possessing a chum who was a popular favourite, as his friend's appearance would greatly enhance ticket sales. It was up to the player himself to sell tickets for his benefit and it was often a dispiriting business trailing round town trying to get the support of the gentry for this financially-crucial event. Some lesser players were granted a half-benefit meaning that two would share a benefit night. This, of course, meant they would only get half the takings, but the risk too was halved.

Actors lowly in the company's ranks were not entitled to benefits, giving rise to a traditional anecdote about parsimonious managements. Manager: 'The pay is 15/- a week.' Actor: 'Plus a benefit?' Manager: 'No benefit, but there is a practical meal in Act III'.

Actresses who sold tickets for their benefits often resorted to trailing their children round with them from door-to-door in the hope that the sight of their little offspring would touch the hearts of the householders and result in ticket sales.

Stars would descend on a provincial theatre usually working for a flat fee for so many nights plus a 'free benefit'. This meant there would be no deductions for the theatre expenses, these being borne by the manager. The J & P company could not attempt to engage star names for the tiny Tenterden theatre anyway. Mr and Mrs Jonas took their benefit as early as 10 June. Mrs W Penley on 12 June chose *The Honeymoon* and also offered a *pas seul* called *Caprice de Moment*. Mr & Mrs Rackham's benefit came next with a programme including Master Rackham dancing a sailor's hornpipe.

As the pecking order of the benefits makes clear, it will be realised the leading principals got in first, the public eventually tiring of benefit nights, and attendances faltering as the season petered to a close. The penultimate night was in aid of all the Jonas and Penley children who had taken part in concerted dance items and helped out in the roles of maids, pages etc, while the last night, normally a full house, was traditionally taken by Mr & Mrs Sampson Penley for their own benefit.

The season having ended, all the costumes, props and scenery were dismantled and packed for transit by hired carriers to Lewes, a distance of around 34 miles, where the season opened two or three days later. The actors were expected to make their own travel arrangements, those not further contracted leaving for elsewhere.

Of course things did not always run smoothly. Contracted actors may fail to arrive in time at the next destination and, over long distances on the poor highways, carriers' carts could suffer hold-ups or breakdowns. An unusual accident was reported in the press:

> A shocking accident occurred last Friday evening, at Eastbourne. As a carter, who had come with a team from Rye, to take away the theatrical luggage belonging to Messrs Jonas and Penley, was looking after his horses, he received a kick on his head from one of them, that dashed out his brains; although he was well acquainted with the vice of the animal, and had, in consequence, but a few minutes before he met the fatal accident, cautioned a stranger in the stable not to go near him.

SCENE FOUR
1808 - 1810
FAVERSHAM

BY 1808, THE THREAT of invasion by Napoleon was receding as La Grande Armée turned to conquering other European countries. To add to Britain's military woes Napoleon invaded Spain thus starting the Peninsular War, dragging our forces into further conflict when England allied itself with Spain and Portugal. It was also the year when the original Theatre Royal, Covent Garden built in 1732 was razed to the ground by fire. Neither of these events appeared to have had an immediate affect on the Penley family, but war eventually affects everybody in some way, both winners and losers, and the re-building of Covent Garden was to make a profound difference to the course of the English theatre.

Mr and Mrs Sampson Penley's final child, a son called Belville born in Folkestone, was baptised at Rye on 29 June 1808. This was the second child to be so named, a predecessor having been born in June 1804 also in Folkestone but buried within weeks at Eastbourne.

Mr and Mrs Jonas produced yet another son, Frederick, baptised at Tenterden on 30 September 1809.

The image of a theatrical troupe of close companions travelling together in a group from town to town in a steady progress throughout the year may have been accurate in Shakespeare's time and thereafter, possibly up to the end of the 18th century, but by the period when J & P flourished such a perception is no longer authentic. While the J & P company had a nucleus of family and loyal actors, many more players came and went for short periods as the exigencies of the company's activities required. These were more varied than a regular tour around a familiar circuit. Certainly regular seasons at rock-like venues still took place over a period of years, but equally certain towns had only spasmodic visits, while new and irregular seasons of various lengths were essayed at unaccustomed venues.

One has only to examine a compiled date sheet of known performances to realise that on many occasions the company was fielding more than one unit simultaneously. Sometimes the seasons over-lapped, the following venue opening some days prior to the previous one closing; often a theatre was taken for a short period such as a town's fair or race week necessitating the creation of an extra unit by engaging actors for a matter of a few days only. For example, looking ahead to a certain week in August 1812 J & P companies will be found appearing at both Eastbourne and Canterbury; and two extant playbills show that on 22 September 1814 one J & P company was in Peckham playing *Ways & Means*, while another was performing the very same play at the same time in Brussels.

Sampson Penley was not a man averse to taking risks. Theatres usually came available because the previous manager had failed and lost money; after all, a successful manager in a money-making house would cling on to it like grim death for his allotted 60 days, and such a theatre would rarely be unoccupied. Penley was prepared to take a chance on the misplaced assumption that he would succeed where others had failed. He was not alone in the belief, that was the attitude of most theatre managers of the time, hence the increasing prevalence of some venues going through a rapid turnover of managements.

The enterprising Mr Penley and the formidable Mrs Baker worked in professional harmony, each having their own circuit, though Mrs Baker was occasionally prepared to let some of her theatres to Penley for limited seasons.

In April 1810 the *Kentish Gazette* announced:

THEATRE, FAVERSHAM

Messrs Jonas and Penley beg leave respectfully to inform the Ladies and Gentlemen of Faversham and its vicinity, they have taken the above theatre of Mrs Baker and most humbly solicit the honour of their patronage and support; and hope that the Company they have provided, and the novelties they intend to bring forward for their amusement, will merit their favours.

This kind of fawning upon their prospective customers was standard procedure, the first week attractions were announced as:

Monday:	*Man and Wife*	*Hit or Miss*
Tuesday:	*Hamlet*	*Raising the Wind*
Thursday:	*The Iron Chest*	*The Young Hussar*
Saturday:	*The Young Quaker*	*Ella Rosenberg*

The history of the Faversham Theatre is quaintly unusual. This building had been Sarah Baker's original theatre at Margate, a wooden construction costing £500 hastily erected in July 1785. However, the manager of Dover theatre, Charles Mate, also had a theatre at Margate situated at the rear of the Fountain Inn belonging to Francis Cobb and, finding the competition from Mrs Baker too strong, after three months closed and decamped to

Dover. Mr Cobb, not only a landlord but also owner of Cobb's Brewery, was the local magistrate and responded by sending a petition with 900 signatures to parliament, receiving a royal patent for a theatre. This patent, with permission to run from 1 May to 31 October, gave a monopoly to Cobb and Mate in Margate. The licensee was also permitted to sell alcoholic drinks for 24 hours daily, a boon benefitting the brewer. A new theatre was built in Margate, opening on 27 June 1787. Because of the patent, Mrs Baker was forced to close and, dismantling her theatre into four sections, took it by boat round the coast to Faversham where it was re-erected, its size being 70ft x 32ft. Sarah Baker's own company visited the transplanted theatre only every two or three years, hence the lease to Penley in 1810.

The company was still there in June now having dropped Monday night playing. In *The Busy Body*:

> The part of Sir Francis Gripe, by MR W PENLEY of the
> Theatre Royal Drury Lane. End of the Play, a Comic Song,
> called "The Beggar in all Shapes," by Mr W Penley.

William was joining the family firm in his summer break from Drury Lane where he was now employed.

The season ended on 7 July with the benefit of Mr and Mrs Penley, the last press advertisement closing with the usual grovelling formula:

> Messrs Jonas and Penley beg leave most respectfully to
> return their sincere thanks to the Ladies and Gentlemen of
> Faversham and its vicinity, for their generous patronage and
> support, and assures them nothing in their power shall be
> wanting to merit their favours at a future period.

As 1810 drew to its close, Sampson Penley was now about to embark on a perilous venture. He acquired the lease of a London theatre.

SCENE FIVE
1810 - 1811
LONDON

LONDON THEATRES – being still controlled by the patent system introduced by Charles II – operated under totally different regulations from those in the rest of the country. Since the original royal patents granted to the theatres royal of Drury Lane and Covent Garden, only one more London patent had been granted. This was introduced because the two theatres closed in the summer months so a patent was granted to the theatre in the Haymarket allowing it to open from 15 May to 15 September. Between them these three had an oligopoly, no other London theatre being allowed to present straight plays.

London – a rapidly expanding metropolis providing for 1¼million souls – was the largest city in the world. Extensive housing developments had sprung up south of the river, and to cater for this new public there were now three theatres in the area referred to as the transpontine houses. Together with the other non-patent theatres that now flourished throughout London these were collectively known as the minor houses and, by law, were restricted to plays with music. They were limited to presenting operas, operettas, extravaganzas, burlettas, pantomimes, burlesques, vaudevilles etc. These various types of play had fine distinctions in their day, but the essence of them all was that music was paramount.

The minor theatres chafed under these restrictions with frequent transgressions occurring as managers pushed the permissible boundaries. Various ploys were used to get round the law – one wheeze was to offer a concert of music with an admission charge, then present a play *gratis* in the interval. Another tolerated scheme was to make all the dialogue in the form of rhyming couplets, with music playing at the same time. It was from struggling to present straight plays within these conditions that melodrama evolved.

Originally melo-drama – the word is a combination of melody and drama – the form eventually developed so that prose dialogue became permissible provided music was played as a background. As the actors had to speak above the music the style of acting broadened in the large London theatres so that melodramatic acting became associated with exaggerated or 'ham' acting. Actually, true melodrama still lives on in the modern cinema as most movies have virtually constant background music which manipulates our emotions as much as the spoken dialogue.

The other main difference between the major and minor theatres in London at this time was the minor theatres preference for long continuous runs of their successes, rather than the majors' policy of having a large repertory of works that they could bring out in short bursts, often for a night at a time.

It was announced The King's Concert Rooms in Tottenham Street had been converted into a summer theatre to be called the New Theatre. 'A considerable expense has been incurred in preparing this place for public amusement, and we speak without prejudice when we say that we never saw a prettier little theatre. . . . The Lyceum is a pig-stye compared to it.'

The building had been originally erected in 1772, later enlarged with a royal box for George III and Queen Charlotte, who were constant patrons. In 1802 the amateur PicNic Society rented the place as an exclusive club where aristocrats performed fashionable entertainments of music and drama. Each member was expected to provide a share of the entertainment and of the refreshments, with no one particular host. These antics were mocked mercilessly by the press of the day, and Gillray drew cartoons satirising the society. As the founder-members died off, interest in the society waned and the word picnic came into use as an *al fresco* meal.

This latest conversion to a proper theatre in 1810 was a venture by Mr S Paul, a gunsmith and silversmith in The Strand, whose wife fancied she had star quality for the stage. The public did not agree with her self-estimation and, in view of his rapidly diminishing bank balance, Mr Paul soon threw in the towel.

The theatre was a bijou affair seating around 500, much as the country theatres that formed the J & P circuit. The proscenium opening was only 21ft wide, and the distance from the front of the stage to the rear boxes no more than 38ft, with a pit no wider than 22ft.

The lease was acquired by J & P starting operations in October but, tied by the patent restrictions, unable to present the drama repertoire they had built up over the last 15 years. Penley's technique was one adopted by many minor theatre managers in those non-copyright times – he took the plot and dialogue of an existing straight play and interpolated music and songs. The opening attraction was the burletta of *Midas* plus *Don Juan* in which Sampson Penley Jr was 'spirited and interesting', the *Morning Post* reporting:

> As it was the first appearance in London with most of the actors who compose the present company, great allowances are to be made, and we hope at our next visit to see them much improved. . . . The scenery and dresses were splendid and appropriate, and the shower of fire in the last act produced an awfully sublime effect. The House was well filled.

On the *Morning Post*'s next visit the company must have indeed improved as we read that:

> Walter Scott's Poem of *Marmion*, which has been so much admired, has been dramatised at this Theatre in a manner highly effective . . . aided by some magnificently romantic scenery, and beautiful dresses, [it] possesses an interest we have seldom witnessed out of a Theatre licensed for the regular drama. The performers on this occasion exerted themselves with uncommon effect . . . all played with an energy and pathos that well deserved the applause they were honoured with. This piece, we predict, will have a very long run.

The play actually had 22 performances and it looked as if the venture was proving a success, though the only family members actually involved seem restricted to Sampson Penley, his eldest son, and daughter Rosina, the rest of the company being specially recruited. The regular J & P company led by John Jonas was maintaining the usual provincial schedule.

The intrepid managers surely looked forward to not only a bumper New Year but also a year of success and progress. Sampson Penley Jr was the mainstay of the company. The eighteen-year-old was outgoing and confident, and for his benefit the theatre announced 'a new Burletta, taken from the plot, incident, and diction of *Love in a City*, called *The Tom-Boy*.'

It was a full evening that also included a Hornpipe by Mr Roe; Master Ribbon, a musical phenomenon only four years old playing a grand military march, a rondo with double stops and a popular air; A Pathetic Tale, called *The Fisherman*, spoken by Mr Penley Jr; two dances by Miss Hart and Miss Mottram; a new burletta founded on the plot, incident, and diction of *The Weathercock*, and *Hamlet Travestie* which had first appeared the previous year. This farcical spoof was very popular and between 1810 and 1817 six printed editions appeared. In the text were facetious literary annotations purporting to be from Dr Johnson and other eminent authors. The farce, in rhyming couplets interspersed with songs, could be performed lawfully at the minor theatres that did not have a licence for legitimate drama. Penley Jr took the role of Laertes. The content of the play can be readily grasped from his opening entrance:

King: How now, Laertes, what's the news with you?
              You told us of some suit. –
Laertes: My Lord, that's true:
              I have a mighty wish to learn to dance,
              And crave your royal leave to go to France.
King: Your suit is granted.
Laertes: Sire, I'm much your debtor.
King: Then brush! the sooner you are off the better.

From Easter Monday 1811, for the entire week the company presented a Grand Oriental Melodrama *Ali Baba and the Forty Thieves* in which both Sampson Penleys appeared. It is unlikely that Penley would have been able to drum up a cast of 40. He probably got around casting problems with something on the lines of 'You two thieves follow me; you 38 wait outside.' All the London theatres made a special effort for the Easter holidays, producing pantomimes and light holiday fare, so it is pleasing to note that the New Theatre was 'exceedingly well attended . . . the numerous visitors were highly gratified.' *Ali Baba* ran for 9 nights, and toy theatre 'penny plain, tuppence coloured' sheets based on the production were produced. From this it can be deduced that Sampson played Ali Baba, Sampson Jr was Hassarack, and Rosina Fairy of the Lake.

One of the J & P playbills in the summer of 1813 at the Tenterden theatre advertising *Marmion* harked back to these days stating 'This piece was first produced at the New Theatre, Tottenham Street, under the arrangement of Messrs Jonas and Penley, and performed upwards of sixty nights with that approbation and success, that pieces of great sterling and merit always endure.'

However, in spite of these apparent successes Penley had, in fact, fared not much better than Mr Paul the silversmith, and in June announced the closure of the theatre. J & P had barely got eight months out of it, and the Sampson Penleys, father and son, retreated to the provinces from whence they came.

However, this bijou theatre was blighted for the next 30 years, changing its name eight times and having some 13 or 14 different managements over the three decades. It eventually succeeded under the Bancrofts who renamed it the Prince of Wales and instigated the 'tea-cup' plays of T W Robertson.

SCENE SIX
1811 - 1812
A BUMPER PERIOD

THE TWO SAMPSON PENLEYS were now free to join up with the main J & P company at Tenterden for the customary biennial visit. The tragedy *Romeo and Juliet* was presented, a rare event for Tenterden, where the audience preferred lighter fare. Sam Jr was Romeo, his father playing what must have seemed a rather elderly Mercutio. The fourteen-year-old Juliet was portrayed by the thirty-nine-year-old Mrs W Penley, Sampson's sister-in-law and Sam Jr's aunt, a woman who had given birth to seven children. Modern type-casting was unheard of in those days, rather casting by category.

Another rare tragedy, but more robust and melodramatic, was the old warhorse *Douglas* with Sam Jr as Norval, and Mrs W Penley in the more appropriate part of Lady Randolph his mother. The afterpiece was *Aladdin; or the Wonderful Lamp*; not a pantomime but rather 'a grand melodramatic romance as performed thirty nights by this Company, with the most unbounded Applause at the New Theatre, Tottenham Street, London.' One feels a sense of Penley, when drafting his playbill, consoling himself by saying 'So, there!'

At the end of June, Mr W Penley rejoined the company as usual, partaking of the opportunity of reuniting with his wife and earning some money during his summer break from Drury Lane.

The Tenterden season ended on 10 August 1811, the company then transferring *en bloc* to Canterbury where J & P had rented Mrs Baker's theatre for the annual Race Week, opening two days later with *The Honeymoon* with William Penley giving his Jaques, a part that was the mainstay of his Drury Lane reputation. The afterpiece was *Aladdin*, rescued from the ill-fated Tottenham Street theatre season. Although deficient in the customary numbers of nobility and gentry, the lesser folk attended the races in quantity that year. In spite of the competition from 'the ingenious Quantrell' and his firework displays, crowded houses for the week testified to the quality of the J & P company – considered of such excellence that it would have been extraordinary if the public had not supported it. Leaving Canterbury in a glow of pride and full money bags, the J & P troupe headed for Peckham, South London, opening on the 26 August with *The Honeymoon*. On this occasion Jaques was played by John Jonas, William

Penley not jeopardising his position by playing so near to Drury Lane.

Charles II had given permission for a regular fair to be held at Peckham, and a small theatre had been built to cash in on the crowds drawn to the fair. According to legend, this theatre attached to the Kentish Drovers pub was where Nell Gwynne started her career. For many years at the end of the 18th century the theatre was occupied by Flockton, the puppet showman who was a regular attraction at Bartholomew and other fairs. Flockton died a very wealthy man in 1794, and his theatre subsequently taken over by another fairground performer, a conjuror called Lane.

Mrs W Penley no longer appeared with J & P after the Peckham season. She was still under forty so we can only surmise about her absence; perhaps she rather enjoyed living settled with her husband which she would have been able to do during the Peckham season. This hard-working couple's careers are related in Act Two.

In October 1811, J & P attempted a season at Brighton. This made sense as Brighton is situated only eight miles from Lewes. This new theatre, reputed to seat 1200, had opened in 1807 with a successful season, but declined thereafter with a succession of failing managers. The existing management terminated its season on 26 October and J & P promptly moved in three days later. The Brighton theatre was under the patronage of the Prince Regent and admission charges were high for a provincial theatre being boxes 5/-, Pit 3/- and Gallery 1/-. In the usual grovelling manner, J & P's opening announcement was addressed to 'the Nobility, Gentry and Others of Brighton and its vicinity, likewise the Gentlemen of the Army'. Penley clearly had expectations of playing to an up-market audience so it was surprising he opened with *The Foundling of the Forest* a recent popular crowd pleaser. However, during the season *Hamlet, Othello* and *Romeo and Juliet* were all given, which seems as though J & P was attempting to appeal to a more intelligent audience than its usual ones.

The season ran until 13 December, closing with Mr and Mrs Penley's benefit and a bespeak by Colonel Palmer and the officers of the Prince Regent's Hussars.

The company then opened the following evening at Lewes with *The Royal Oak* and *The Romp*. It was intended to be a short season. There was a full house on the evening *Macbeth* and *The Highland Reel* were presented; presumably Penley specially arranged this all-Caledonian programme to appeal to an audience unaccustomed to visiting his theatre, as it comprised almost entirely of the military, mainly the Highland Regiment. In a stage box were privates of the 10th Hussars 'who conducted themselves with much propriety in their novel situation, and were in consequence, QUIZZED, with great good humour by their officers.'

The Lewes season carried on into the new year of 1812. An especially unusual bespeak took place on 13 January which was election day, with all the hotels serving dinners for the candidates' invited guests, numbering some three hundred people. There was a ball in the evening at the Star hotel, and the theatre was open gratuitously by order of some of Mr Shiffner's friends. The play offered some relief to the crowded ballroom which was packed to suffocation in the early evening, and again after the play until a late hour. The events passed off without any of the disturbances which were not uncommon in those days when electors were openly bribed by the candidates and voting was by a show of hands. Mr Shiffner's largesse paid off as he was duly elected as the local MP.

The Lewes season closed at the end of January with the final week including a bespeak by Colonel Sterling the Master of the Garrison Lodge of Freemasons, and the hope was expressed that other Freemasons in the town would also rally round and support the event – a benefit for no fewer than ten of the performers. The closing night was a bespeak by Members of the White-Hart Evening's Club for the benefit of Mr and Mrs Penley.

It is quite interesting to realise how much social activity was taking place in these small towns even in war time, and that normal life was proceeding in spite of barracks and army camps stationed on the periphery.

The prolonged war does not seem to have affected J & P other than by increasing its audiences. The managers did make frequent financial contributions to the war effort by holding special nights at their various theatres when all the proceeds, without deductions for expenses, would be sent to the Patriotic Fund set up to provide relief for men wounded in military action, to support the widows and dependents of men killed, and to grant honorary awards in recognition of bravery.

In March 1812 they contributed £10 9s 6d from a performance at Rye towards the relief of widows and families of men from *St George, Hero, Defence, Saldanha* and *Fancy*, ships lost during a Christmas Eve storm. The entire crews – totalling over 2300 – except for a handful of men were lost, these tempest-tossed losses being much greater than any war dead suffered at the Battles of the Nile, Copenhagen and Trafalgar combined.

A real-life tragedy struck the Jonas and Penley families too when Mrs Mary Jonas née Penley died on 24 April 1812 aged forty-three, far too

young even for those days. She must have spent half those years permanently pregnant, as John Jonas was left with ten children varying in age from
twenty-four to three, none of whom as yet had married. The fact that Mary
died in Folkestone may indicate that J & P were performing there at the
time.

But life must go on and Jonas threw himself into a particularly hectic
period for the J & P company which returned to Faversham in May for a
second season there. The leading man was again Sampson Jr; his brother
William, aged eleven, was singing comic songs while sister Emma, now at
the age of seven, was performing various dances including *pas de deux* and
double hornpipes with Miss Flemming.

This was the last season of J & P at Faversham as thereafter Mrs
Baker took back the theatre for her own use, but in 1812 the company
moved on to Canterbury where they performed again in Mrs Baker's
theatre for Race Week. Simultaneously, another unit was coping with the
season at Lewes and, astonishingly, this announcement appeared in the
newspaper at Windsor:

THEATRE ROYAL, WINDSOR

Messrs Jonas and Penley beg leave most respectfully to
inform the Nobility, Gentry and others, of Windsor and its
vicinity, this Theatre is Open for the Summer Season; that
they have spared neither Pains nor Expence in providing a
Company from the Theatres Royal, London and in bringing
forward every Novelty for their Amusement, which they trust
will merit that patronage they have so liberally experienced.

The J & P season at the Windsor theatre commenced on 3 August 1812,
the principal players coming from the London theatres. Sampson Penley
himself was praised for his excellent whimsical performance as Jerry
Sneak, the hen-pecked husband in Samuel Foote's 1763 war horse *The
Mayor of Garratt*. The subject of this farce is a traditional spoof election
held at the village of Garratt, now absorbed into London. The candidates
were always poor tradesmen, usually with a drink problem, and sometimes
with a physical deformity. The main qualification was a quick wit. They
assumed such titles as Lord Twankum, (cobbler and gravedigger), Squire
Blowmedown (a Wandsworth waterman) and Sir Trincalo Boreas (a
fishmonger). The most celebrated, Sir Jeffery Dunstan, was a second-hand
wig seller in the West End. He had knock-knees and a disproportionately
large head, and only grew to a height of 4 feet. The elections, held
annually, were attended by tens of thousands of people and became an
excuse for indulgence, licentiousness and drunkenness. The elections died

out in the early 19th century but the play survived somewhat longer.

Sampson was the only family member involved at Windsor – the rest were all needed elsewhere. The opening week's business was rated excellent and the boxes were crowded for the bespeak of the 'gallant Heroes of Talavera', the 29th Foot who had distinguished themselves in the fiercest battle of the Peninsular War, after which Arthur Wellesley was ennobled as Viscount Wellington.

Mrs Powell, a long established London tragedienne guested for a few days playing some of her well-known repertoire including Hamlet, a breeches part with a difference! During the short season a couple of managers appeared as actors for Penley – Mr & Mrs Jefferies his predecessors at the Windsor theatre, and Brunton, a man with fingers in many thespian pies whom Penley probably knew from Brighton.

The six-week season closed on 10 September with the verdict: 'The performances have been respectably and sometimes fully attended. The industry, attention, and punctuality of Mr Penley, will entitle him the support of the public at future seasons.' So what went wrong? Was it simply a matter of balance, the actors from the patent theatres too expensive? The productions over-costly in staging? For all his industry and attention, Penley did not return and was followed by other managers until the venue staggered to a halt to be taken over by religion.

Perhaps Penley realised that he could not function efficiently with J & P having three units operating at the same time. One wonders how Penley and Jonas managed to set up and cope with organising these. As playbills and press advertisements that have survived are so rare, it is often quite impossible to trace the travels of provincial theatre companies like J & P. Fortunately it is possible to establish something of their precise movements in the latter part of 1812. These prove awesome as the workload is mind-boggling:

January	Lewes **A**
February	Henley **A**
March	Rye **A**
April?	*Folkestone?*
18 May to 18? July	Faversham **A**
? to 24 July	Bexhill **B**
24 July to 5 August (Race Week)	Tenterden **A**
29 July to 11 August (Race Week)	Lewes **B**
3 August to 10 Sept	Windsor **C**
11 August to 18 August	Canterbury **A**

13 August to ?	Eastbourne **B**
24 August to 15 October	Peckham Rye **A**
16 November to 22 January '13	Lewes
12 December to 15 February '13	Brighton

The **A** company with the regular names Penley, Penley Jr, Rackham, Stackwood, Burton, and the females Watson, Lucas, Beynon, now joined by the seventeen-year-old Phoebe, played at Lewes, Henley, Rye, Faversham, Tenterden, Canterbury and Peckham Rye. The **B** company covered Bexhill, Lewes and Eastbourne, while a totally new **C** company was assembled from the London theatres to perform at Windsor under Sampson Penley. The Lewes and Brighton autumn and winter dates were taken by a company of mainly new names headed by Mr Jonas. Sampson Penley looks to be everywhere at once, and the travelling he must have undergone to supervise and organise these seasons is incredible. How on earth did he organise his A company opening at Tenterden on the same night as his B company closed at Bexhill? It is highly probable that Jonas was in charge of the B company and operated autonomously.

Detective work on the available playbills, press advertisements and press reviews indicates that Sampson himself did not go with his company to Tenterden and Canterbury for the short Race Week seasons, but must have left after Faversham closed, going to London to sign up players for Windsor, then on to that town to supervise and act in the season there.

After Windsor closed on 10 September, Penley re-joined his main company at Peckham where five of his children were already working. – Phoebe and Rosina as well as brother Sam Jr taking parts in the plays, with Emma forever dancing her hornpipe, and young William singing his comic songs.

The bewildering movements of Sampson Penley are entirely surmise. It would be a major effort even today with mobile phones and e-mail, so how did he manage his organisation when, apart from going in person, a letter carried by coach and horses travelling at ten mph was the only way to send messages?

The autumn of 1812 was, as customary, taken up with the usual visits to Lewes and Eastbourne. An unusual attraction was a character who became better known in the wider world. This was Signor Belzoni, the Roman Hercules who was 6ft 7in tall. Belzoni played English, Irish and Italian airs on the musical glasses, displayed several striking attitudes from antique statues and carried a group of seven men. His contribution concluded with his 'celebrated scene delineating Le Brun's *Passions of the*

Soul.' Le Brun (1619 - 1690) was court painter to Louis XIV and published a treatise with plates showing faces depicting admiration, anger, desire, compassion, rapture, scorn, etc. Presumably Belzoni copied these in a display of face-pulling. Unfortunately, Belzoni's performances 'did not prove so attractive as might have been expected' and he promptly disappeared off to Dover where he hoped for a better response.

Shortly after appearing at these southern venues, Belzoni toured several European countries, then went to Egypt where he excavated the colossal bust of Ramesses II, dispatching it to England where it still reposes in the British Museum. Today Belzoni is recognised as one of the great early Egyptologists.

Captain Shiffner and his friends were again very supportive during the season, bespeaking plays and giving their patronage. On 30 November when several Ladies and Gentlemen had requested *The Iron Chest* and *The Forty Thieves* the playbills announced that 'should the weather prove unfavourable, Post-chaises will be provided at the White Hart'. One would be hard-pushed in inclement weather to get even a plastic poncho out of a theatre nowadays.

The Masons of the Garrison also did their bit again by bespeaking *Douglas*, one of the few tragedies that J & P regularly performed. At the end, a Masonic Epilogue was recited by a Gentleman. It is certain that John Jonas was a Mason which may have provided a strong link as he was managing the Lewes season without Penley.

Another bespeak by Captain Shiffner and his Troop of Yeomanry Cavalry was *The Stranger* starring Mrs St Leger a star from Covent Garden, especially engaged to boost the regular company. There was scarcely a dry eye in the house at curtain fall. The audience perked up a bit when Maria Jonas as *The Savoyard* sang her song very prettily. Maria, now sixteen and specialising in song, was the most talented of the Jonas brood and would soon carve out her own career away from the family.

J & P was once more essaying a winter season at Brighton, the local newspaper expressing 'we heartily wish them better success than they experienced when they last tendered their dramatic services to the town.' A bit of a publicity downer in terms of encouraging audiences! This time they were running Brighton and Lewes in tandem, performing alternately at the two venues, so probably Jonas was based at Lewes, Penley in Brighton. Brighton ran from 12 December, opening with *Rich and Poor* and *Travellers Benighted* – perhaps not a good augury – ending on 16 February 1813.

An attraction that Penley engaged for four nights in Brighton was the celebrated performer the SIEUR SANCHES, who will make his next appearance this evening, when he will in the course of his performances, in the most extraordinary manner (never executed or attempted by any but himself) walk against the ceiling with his HEAD DOWNWARDS which wonderful feat he has performed to crowded houses every evening for these six weeks past at the Surrey Theatre.

Sanches then went on to Lewes where he did his stuff on the last night of the season, a bespeak by the Viscountess Hampden whose patronage filled the house, with the boxes especially brilliant in appearance. Unfortunately, in traversing the ceiling in his upside down walk Sanches fell, luckily not suffering any great hurt as, dusting himself down he carried on to his slack rope vaulting which astonished all present.

Having secured this wonderful performer, Penley made capital use of him, sending him round Eastbourne, Bexhill, Hastings and Battle theatres, performing two days at each. Sanches certainly earned his money as, apart from the upside-down walk and the slack rope, while upside down he balanced two boys in full swing on his rope, simultaneously discharging from his mouth a 'beautiful cluster of fireworks'. As well as all that, he did bird impressions and imitated several musical instruments by mouth alone, accompanying himself on the Spanish guitar. Which appears a bit tame considering his other feats.

The Brighton season, although longer than the previous year, was not a great success; the last night, *Wild Oats* and *A Mogul Tale* – for the benefit of Mr Penley – attracted a better house than at any previous night in the season. As a result of poor business, J & P did not return to Brighton, Thomas Trotter taking over the lease.

1812 had certainly proved a bumper year for the J & P company. It was not so good for Napoleon Bonaparte. At nearly half a million strong, La Grande Armée marched through Western Russia to capture Moscow but was forced to retreat during the severe Russian winter. Only 27,000 fit soldiers remained; La Grand Armée had lost some 380,000 men dead and 100,000 captured. Then Napoleon, abandoning his men, returned to Paris to protect his position as Emperor. The demise of Napoleon's ambitions was to have a profound effect on the J & P company's future.

SCENE SEVEN
1813 - 1814
THE END OF WAR IN VIEW

THE FOLLOWING YEAR, 1813, was less frenetically organised for the J & P company. Details of the early months of each year are particularly lacking, but it appears that in 1813 after the close of the disappointing Brighton season in February, J & P visited Eastbourne. This was quite different from the normal procedure which was to visit the town in August prior to, or after the Lewes race week. It was not a success.

Faversham had been lost and the season at Windsor was not repeated, another manager taking the theatre. The usual Tenterden season ran from 6 May to 30 July, and Lewes opened on 4 August for the customary Race Week, but Penley announced that the run would be until 17 August only, after which the theatre would be closed up until August 1814. Considering how much time had previously been spent at Lewes in former years, this is quite extraordinary. It would appear that J & P was performing for the Race Weeks only, and abandoning the usual winter season. Perhaps Penley had foreseen how things would be because in the event the theatre was 'miserably attended' except for the final night when Penley had booked Mrs Jordan to play Widow Cheerly in *The Soldier's Daughter*. For this occasion 'part of the pit was thrown into boxes'. This was often done for stellar attractions as that way the management could charge box prices for pit benches. It is not clear if this was physically done as, in Georgian times, the terms Boxes, Pit and Gallery seemed to be used as class distinctions as well as price differentials even when the auditorium was one level area. Possibly the front rows were simply cordoned off making them bookable unlike the normal pit, or perhaps low screens enclosed those rows in a manner similar to box pews in a church.

Mrs Jordan was indeed a star, in fact a figure of some notoriety. Reputed to have the finest legs on the stage, she specialised in 'breeches roles', which is dressing as a man. Several actresses in those far-off days were renowned for their breeches parts – they enabled actresses to titillate the men by showing a bit of leg. Many such actresses succeeded in capturing the interest of rich or influential patrons. There's a well-known story of the actress Peg Woffington – who lived openly with David Garrick and was notorious for her numerous affairs – coming into the greenroom after playing a character called Sir Harry Wildair saying

'By Gad, I do believe half the audience thinks me to be a real man.' Whereupon a bitchy colleague replied 'But, madam, the other half knows for certain that you are not.'

Mrs Jordan could command an unusually high salary, an outraged news item widely circulated in 1800 stating:

> Mrs Jordan is speedily to return to Drury Lane Theatre, at an increased salary of *thirty pounds* per night! – it is a matter of not unreasonable calculation, that this sum would furnish their daily allowance of soup to 7200 poor persons.

The top actors of the day would be lucky to get that amount per week. After some early affairs, Mrs Jordan (a courtesy title, she never married) became the mistress of William, Duke of Clarence. Settling down in domestic harmony like any married couple, setting up home at Bushy Park, together they had ten illegitimate children, all of whom took the surname FitzClarence. Mrs Jordan also suffered several miscarriages. Clarence was the third son of George III and had no role in life and no settled income; as a result Mrs Jordan's high salaries were very necessary to keep the family together. In spite of her many pregnancies she was not only a loving 'wife' and doting mother, she also worked non-stop. In 1811, after twenty years together, the duke realising that he was quite likely to become king started looking for an acceptable wife, and Mrs Jordan was ejected. She was given a yearly stipend of £4,400 (£278,000 in today's money), and custody of their daughters while the duke remained in charge of their sons. The allowance came with a stipulation that in order to continue receiving the money, and retain custody of her daughters, she must give up the stage. When a scapegrace son-in-law – one of her pre-Clarence daughters had married a Mr Alsop – became heavily in debt, Mrs Jordan returned to the stage to help pay off those debts. The duke, removing their daughters from her care, ceased her allowance.

At Lewes, Mrs Jordan, proving she was a big a draw as ever, attracted an over-flowing house. She also played another of her famous roles: Violante in *The Wonder* in which 'Young Penley played Don Felix very respectably'. This was the twenty-one-year-old Sampson Junior who had now been a leading man for three years.

As advertised, the theatre then closed, the company moving to Canterbury for Race Week.

The next venue would normally have been Eastbourne but J & P had visted in February and left the usual August slot to be taken by a rival Mrs Rhodes, whose very short stay engendered this terse comment from the local newspaper:

> Owing to the imbecility of the play-folk, or a want of dramatic taste in the inhabitants and visitants of East Bourne, the theatre presents a dismal appearance, the Sock and Buskin having, generally, to stalk forth to glimmering lights and *empty* benches.

Whether the managers were imbecilic or not, the results are plain enough: yet another case of miserable attendances. Why audiences should have suddenly plummeted at these two venues seems puzzling at first. But the obvious reason must be that with the recent defeat of Napoleon, the prospect of invasion was removed and many militia men withdrawn, leaving a much reduced and impoverished population. Parliament was debating the sending of militia men to Ireland, and to fight in the Peninsular War which was still going on. Since its inception the J & P company had prospered under wartime conditions, but the end of the wars looming imminently may not have been a good thing for Penley and Jonas. It would be ironic if the J & P company suffered hard times because of British military victories against the enemy.

As Brighton had also been relinquished, Penley could concentrate on his near London holdings. No doubt his actors were glad to move to Peckham on 30 August where it was advertised that the company would play every evening. Here the full forces of the J & P company were deployed, family members beginning to take major roles. Both Sampson Penleys maintained their position in the leads, daughters Phoebe and Rosina were regularly employed in ingénue roles, Emma danced and young William recited and sang funny songs.

From the Jonas family, John Jonas was his usual tower of strength playing an assortment of supporting roles, and his daughters Mary and Maria, like their cousins, were assigned ingénue parts with Maria coming to the fore as a singer both within plays and as a soloist. John's first-born son – also John – does not seem to have become an actor, but his second son Joseph was prominent both playing parts and in comic dances. Master Charles was called on for pages etc and even Esther, only nine years old, and little Henry at seven, had their place in the programmes which changed every night. This was a cracking pace to keep up for several weeks – a nightly change and open every night except Sunday. For the last three weeks Tuesday and Friday performances were dropped, the season ending on 13 November.

John Jonas was now around forty-seven years of age and a widower.

While his elder children were now adults and able to take care of themselves, he still had five children between the ages of four and fourteen, so it would hardly be surprising if he should have intentions of seeking out another wife, if only to provide a step-mother for his young children.

The J & P company moved on to Deptford where, creating a new venue in a building formerly used as a school, they played to packed houses. Ship building and victualling was a vital industry during the Napoleonic War and Deptford, a major port, was booming. The making of ships' biscuits was a universal cottage occupation in the town as not only Nelson's navy, but Wellington's army, were going through 44 tons of biscuits a day, and there is a family legend that Sampson Penley turned his hand to it. This must have been during the times he was not raking in money at the box office, as his theatres at both Deptford and Peckham were at this period playing to crowded houses.

Deptford turned out to have special personal significance for the Penley and Jonas families, and the start of the career of a new untried actor who joined the troupe on 13 December 1813. This was a youth of eighteen years who rejoiced in the name of Junius Brutus Booth.

On 16 February 1814, Mrs Esther Penley, matriarch of the Penleys, was buried at St Paul Deptford at the age of sixty-eight. Since ceasing to lead her own troupe she had toured with her son Sampson's outfit and was, no doubt, a tower of strength with both her personal knowledge of the business, and as a grandmother to the growing brood.

In contrast to the dismal business at Lewes and Eastbourne, Peckham and Deptford were thriving. The *Theatrical Inquisitor* of April 1814 reported that, at the theatre at Deptford, crowded audiences have 'testified their approbation of the company performing there. Messrs Jonas & Penley are very spirited managers, and many of our popular pieces have been produced in a manner highly respectable.' In a well-acted *Macbeth*, Mr Jonas made his exit as the Third Witch by 'throwing a back summersault'! The version of *Macbeth* then in current use was full of music with a chorus of singing witches, so a touch of acrobatics may not have been too out of place. The fact that Jonas, at his age, could still perform somersaults adds strength to the theory that he started out in show business as an acrobat.

SCENE EIGHT
1814
OVERSEAS

NAPOLEON, HAVING SUFFERED further defeats, limped back to Paris with the remnants of his army enabling the Allies to establish the British Army of Occupation in Flanders and Northern France. Cultural communications with the Netherlands were opened for the first time in 20 years. At this point Sampson Penley made an astounding decision. He closed the Deptford season and took the J & P company to Amsterdam. Why he did this is impossible to say. Admittedly his Sussex circuit was rapidly shrinking, but he was packing them in at Deptford and Peckham. Perhaps his idea was that, as the military had been providing much of his audience whilst guarding the south coast, he would go where the military was now deployed. The King's German Legion which had been stationed at Bexhill for several years had now decamped to Flanders, which must have been a major consideration for Penley.

Amsterdam had immediately swept back to normality, with imports of British goods and colonial produce brought by English ships jamming the port of Rotterdam.

> Many English settle among us, to sell in retail every kind of British merchandise, the excellence and cheapness of which draw an infinite number of customers; in short, great commercial bustle prevails in our city.

The British & Foreign Bible Society voted £500 to the recently formed Dutch National Bible Society, at which news being received by three of the wealthiest men of Amsterdam one shed tears, one seemed petrified with astonishment, and the third exclaimed 'The English are a pattern for all nations!'

J & P was the first company to cross the Channel since the outbreak of hostilities in the previous century and Sampson Penley and John Jonas had every reason to be optimistic about their venture. It was a major expedition with the entire Jonas and Penley families involved. The pioneering actors left on 6 May, in a Dutch ship filled with a cargo of treacle, the men occupying the hold, the only cabin being assigned to the women. It was a rough crossing and, for actors who had never previously left their native shores, sea-sickness was a novel experience. When at last in sight of land the thespians were appalled to realise the captain was not aiming for the coast. Many of the actors, unable to bear further discomfort trying to sleep on the boxes and barrels in the hold, demanded to be put ashore. The captain, being bound for Amsterdam, refused this request, but sent signals to the shore which resulted in a fishing boat putting out to the ship to take off such passengers as required assistance. A fee of ten guineas was demanded to cover the three miles. Much haggling got this down to two guineas before the disgruntled fishermen put the equally disgruntled actors on to dry land.

The company – the first from an English theatre to be seen in the city for many decades – eventually all assembled at Amsterdam on 12 May. There were three theatres in Amsterdam: the Dutch, French and German theatres. The German theatre, a private one built in 1791, had seating for 500. It was ideal for the English company who, on settling in, advertised themselves as 'Their Majesties' Servants from the Theatres Royal of London and Windsor'. This was a case of Penley exaggerating his rather weak credentials. J & P appeared from 18 May to 9 July 1814 performing for 22 nights which were well attended by the large Jewish community.

The playing troupe comprised: Sampson Penley, Sampson Penley Jr, Phoebe, Rosina and Emma Penley; John Jonas, Joe Jonas, Mary, Maria and Esther Jonas, plus a Master Jonas. Non-family actors were Booth, Burton, Franklin, Gutteridge (replacing McGibbon at Antwerp), Mountfort, Platt, Salter and Stackwood. Actresses were Miss Lucas, Miss Watson and Mrs Beynon

Mr Booth, the newest and youngest of the actors, kept a journal of the tour in which he complained that at the end of the first week he received only 10/- and not the promised 12/-!

The Amsterdam repertory comprised chiefly comedies, with domestic dramas, and single performances of *Hamlet* and *Romeo & Juliet*. The plays were enacted in English just as the company would do on their home ground. The list of the performances given at the German Theatre in Amsterdam is in Appendix II.

As the majority of the audience would be unfamiliar with the language, and the staging unconventional to the Dutch mind, it is difficult to assess how well the company was received. At the time of his two visits, some notes were made by a Dutch actor called Johannes Jelgerhuis who could not understand English. He enjoyed the comedies presented, considering them well acted, although he had reservations about the high shrill female voices. He also liked the rapidity of speech and action and the fact that the actors had good memories and did not use a prompter.

TOT SLUITING

Op verzoek van de Engelsche Kooplieden thans te Amsterdam verblijf houdende.

TEN BENEFICE VAN

Mr. P E N L E Y.

Schouwburg in de Amstelstraat.

ENGELSCHE TOONEELSPELEN EN VERLUSTPIGINGEN.

met toestemming van de bevoegde Authoriteiten.

Op aanstaanden Saturdag den 9den July 1814, zullen Hunner BRITTANNISCHE MAJESTEITS Tooneelspelers vertoonen het vermaard TOONEELSPEL getijteld:

LACH ZOO GIJ KUNNE

OF DE

GETROUWE NEGER.

(PERSONEN: als boven vermeld.)

Na het zelve eene bewonderde Aria, door Miss M. JONAS.

en

Een koddige Zang, door Mr. PLATT.

Daarna het Kluchtspel, getijteld: HET

SPROOKJE VAN DEN MOGOL.

(PERSONEN: als boven vermeld.)

TOT SLOT: DE VOLKSZANG

,, GOD SAVE THE KING."

Prijs der plaatsen: Balcon f 2:12. Loge f 2:4. Parterre f 1: 6. Gallerij f -:15.
Entrée-Billetten te bekomen bij Mr. PENLEY, ten huize van den Heer SCHMIDT, Kalverstraat, No. 38, en aan den Schouwburg, waar de Plaatsen te bespreken zijn, van Elf tot Twee Uren.

AMSTERDAM, bij HOLTROP, ZON, Boekseller, Kalverstraat, No. 36.

POSITIVELY THE LAST NIGHT.

By desire of the English Merchants now residing in Amsterdam.

FOR THE BENEFIT OF

Mr. P E N L E Y.

Theatre in the Amstelstreet.

ENGLISH PLAYS AND ENTERTAINMENTS

under the Authority of the Burgomasters.

On Saturday Evening July 9th 1814, their BRITTANNIC MAJESTIES Servants will perform an admired piece in three Acts entitled

LAUGH WHEN YOU CAN

OR THE

FAITHFUL BLACK.

Gossmer, Mr. PENLEY. Old Bonus, Mr. JONAS. Mordiner, Mr. SALTER. Delville, Mr. PLATT. Costly, Mr. BURTON. Farmer Blackbrook, Mr. MOUNTFORT. Charles Mordiner. Mssrs' JONAS. Waiter, Mr. BOOTH. John, Mr. FRANKLIN. Gregory, Mr. J. JONAS. And Sambo (the Black) Mr. PENLEY. Mrs Mordiner, Mrs LUCAS. Miss Gloomly, Miss BEYNON. Dorothy, Miss R. PENLEY. And Emily, Miss WATSON.

End of the Play the admired Air of ,, the Soldiers tir'd of Wait alarms,, by Miss M. JONAS.

And a Comic Song called ,, The Country Fair,, by Mr. PLATT. To which will headed a laughable Farce, called THE

M O G U L   T A L E.

The Great Mogul, Mr. PENLEY, Jr. Omar, Mr. PLATT. Zophaor, Mr. BOOTH. Selim, Mr. FRANKLIN. The Doctor. Mr. PENLEY. Johnny Atkins (the Cobler) Mr. JONAS. Eunuch, Sirve, &c. Irene, Miss PENLEY. Sophie, Miss JONAS. Zhenyis, Miss LUCAS. Beltrada, Miss M. JONAS. Zora, Miss. R. PENLEY. Fanny Atkins (the Cobler's Wife) Miss. WATSON.

Lower-Boxes f 2: 12. Upper-Boxes f 2:4. Pit f 1:6. Galley f -:15.

TO CONCLUDE WITH. THE NATIONAL SONG

,, GOD SAVE THE KING."

Tickets to be had of Mr. PENLEY at Mr. SCHMIDT, 38, Kalverstreet and at the Theatre, where Places may be taken from Eleven till Two.

The playbill for the last night of the J & P season at Amsterdam
9 July 1814.
On the European visits playbills were often double sided with
English/Language of the country

On his part, Sampson Penley sent a despatch home of his impressions of the city which centred on the cheapness of the food – Best Beef 5d a lb, Mutton 4½d, Veal 6d, Prime Hams and Bacon 5d to 8d and fish such as turbot, soles and haddock so cheap as to be hardly computed in the household budget.

The English Company moved on to Rotterdam, performing from 11 to 16 July, thence Antwerp from 22 July to 14 August. At some point during these seasons Sampson Penley returned to England to engage and prepare the company for Lewes Race Week starting on 3 August. It seems incredible that he should leave his company working in a foreign land; one would expect John Jonas to be the partner to return home and mastermind Lewes as he had done in previous years but he was with the continental company throughout. It is possible that the tour was actually Jonas's idea, and he may have had family connections on the continent as two of his daughters later married foreigners in Brussels.

On the last day of the Antwerp season, Mary Ann Jonas was born in St Paul Deptford, London, her parents being John and Mary Jonas. This is something of a conundrum as, apart from this entry in the parish register, we have no other knowledge of the matter. As John's wife Mary had died two years previously it would seem that he had married again, his second wife having the same name. Whatever the circumstances, it would be several months before he returned to see his new daughter.

The J & P company, including John Jonas, his son Joseph and daughters Mary, Maria and Esther, then went to Brussels, staying nearly four months. The Penley family was now solely represented by Sampson Jr and his sister Phoebe, Rosina and the others having returned to England. At first the troupe appeared at the Theatre de Monnaie, a huge place with five tiers of boxes and a pit paved with stone, but then moved to the smaller Theatre du Parc on 22 August. This much more suitable theatre had been built in 1782, closed in 1807 by decree of Napoleon, and now re-opened by J & P.

The defeat of Napoleon had produced a surge in favour of British culture, and Anglophile sentiments were the norm. The whole of the Netherlands was swept by this excessive admiration of English culture, and Brussels was the chief place of amusement abroad for the English upper classes, the ex-pat community numbering some 15,000 residents. These included the Duke & Duchess of Argyle, the Duke & Duchess of Richmond, Lady George Seymour and several other members of the nobility. The society was agreeable and elegant, encouraging many more English families, which arrived daily. J &P had every prospect of making a huge success.

The company (now billing itself as 'Messrs Jonas and Penley, their Britannic Majesties servants, from the Theatres Royal Windsor, Brighton etc.') consisted of the actors from Peckham and Deptford, but several guest stars were engaged from time to time. Mrs Jordan played for three nights enabling Sam Jr to repeat his Don Felix to her Violante almost exactly a year to the day since the pair packed the Lewes theatre. All Mrs Jordan's nights were sold out within hours and were attended by the Hereditary Prince of Orange. These must have been among Mrs Jordan's final performances as the following year, to avoid her creditors, she fled permanently to France, dying there in poverty in 1816, aged fifty-four.

It was a desperately sad end to a top luminary of the Georgian stage. Hazlitt celebrated her in the following panegyric:

> Mrs Jordan was the same in all her characters, and inimitable in all of them, because there was no one else like her. Her face, her tears, her manners were irresistible. Her smile had the effect of sunshine, and her laugh did one good to hear it. Her voice was eloquence itself: it seemed as if her heart was always at her mouth. She was all gaiety, openness and good nature. She rioted in her fine animal spirits, and gave more pleasure than any other actress, because she had the greatest spirit of enjoyment in herself.

Mr and Mrs Charles Kemble, stars from Covent Garden, arrived at Brussels in late September staying for three weeks during which Kemble elevated the usual programme of the J & P company by playing amongst his roles Hamlet, Richard III, Romeo, and Macbeth. Charles Kemble was the most respected actor of his generation and in old age became a national treasure. Mrs Mountain, a star singer from Drury Lane, also visited for three nights.

The Heredity Prince of Orange bespoke ('By Command' rather than 'By Desire') *The Castle Spectre* which Penley's playbill describes as 'the tragic play in Five Acts'. We would consider this old warhorse a melodramatic hoot as the play is full of ghosts, sliding panels and animated suits of armour, with a villain who has African attendants whilst living on the shore of Wales.

In spite of the presence of royalty, the English players were not highly regarded by the local authorities. They were locked out of the theatre one night as a ball was to take place there, with only members of the upper class organisation staging it being allowed in the building. Another night the actors had to play *The Iron Chest* and *The Village Lawyer* in modern clothes as they were unable to get at their stage costumes.

At one point the company's costumes were seized against a claim of a fifth of the profits. This would indicate that income was not exceeding expenses, and bills were not being paid. Salter, one of the leading actors, decided he had had enough and left, and Booth – who had started out playing bit parts – steadily progressed to larger roles as the company began to crumble. Mr Booth was not enamoured of his employers, a letter to his father dated 18 October saying 'Penley is a scoundrel'. The season rapidly coming to its end, *Othello* was chosen for Mr Jonas's benefit, the playbill being decorated with the compass insignia of the Masons, as was usual on his benefit nights.

Théâtre du Parc in Brussels where the J & P company
played from 22 August to 22 November 1814.

The company had performed exactly as they were accustomed to in England. This was very different from the French theatre and in many cases difficult to accept by the continentals. French plays were written to maintain the classical unities of action, time and place. The French – especially those with little English – baffled when the scene kept changing, thought the play had finished when it was only the end of the first act. One critic remarked that the scene-shifters worked as hard as the actors. In general the actors were thought good, with talent and reliable memories, but some thought them affected.

Few plays were repeated, but *Timour the Tartar* received three performances and the French critic was ecstatic with praise, saying no cost had been spared in costumes, sets, battles and props to contribute to the brilliant splendour.

> A young prince has a big part in this play and achieves a remarkable relationship with the audience. The part is played by a child of seven or eight with a charm that earns him enthusiastic applause. Miss Penley the Elder, the leading actress plays the Princess of Georgia, mother of the young prince, with both dignity and grace that, together, emphasise her beauty. The sensations of fear, terror, hope and joy that she expresses, one after the other, are performed with a zeal which proves this remarkable actress has a real talent and a profound understanding of her art.

This eulogy for Phoebe is very rare and all the more welcome as we have little on which to base an opinion of her prowess. The young prince was, in fact, the ten-year-old Miss Esther Jonas. The full list of plays presented at Brussels taken from extant playbills is in Appendix III.

As the season ended at Brussels, Sampson Penley Jr the leading man returned to England to seek a position at Drury Lane. His father, now also back home, was busy engaging the guest artistes and replacement actors for his continental troupe, and masterminding the seasons at Lewes (3 to 23 August) with Eastbourne following on 25 August. In addition, the regular Peckham season was announced:

> Messrs Jonas and Penley, have the honour to announce to the Ladies and Gentlemen of Peckham, Deptford, Camberwell and Vicinity, this Theatre will open for a short season this present evening Saturday August 27 1814.

With all the old regular players still abroad, Penley engaged a new set of actors for Peckham, with only daughter Rosina Penley and himself from the families. Amongst the new names was Mrs Kean, the mother of Edmund Kean – the new sensation and saviour of Drury Lane – who was said to 'resemble him astonishingly'.

Edmund Kean, a true mountebank first treading the boards as a child under the name of Master Carey, spent his early years touring fairgrounds and provincial theatres playing anything and everything from pantomime to Shakespeare. Indeed, an anecdote related in *The Guide to Knowlege* of 1837 links the young Kean and the early Penley troupe. While the Penley company was in the neighbourhood of Cheltenham, the celebrated Mrs Jordan appeared as a guest to play her famous role of Violante. On asking who was to play opposite her in the role of Felix, the manager indicated a dirty, scruffy small individual lurking in the wings, stinking of tobacco smoke and clearly the worse for carousing the night before. 'What! That little wretch to be my Felix! Never! I will never play to such a wretch! Take my name off the bills!' When Penley pleaded that no other actor knew the part except the little leading man, Mrs Jordan reluctantly agreed to play but flatly stated: 'Very well, if I have to play to such a hero, I must. But depend upon it, I shall never look at the wretch!' And that is how she performed her part opposite the unknown youth called Edmund Kean, keeping her word with religious fidelity. Years later, having witnessed his debut at Drury Lane, she went behind the scenes and, flinging herself abruptly upon her knees before him, said 'Can you pardon the injustice I did you! Will you blame my want of discernment, rather than any default of your own, that I did not, when I first saw you, feel and acknowledge, as I now do, the influence of your commanding genius?'

Edmund Kean as Richard III

The story is undoubtedly apocryphal, one of many that arose around Kean after he became a star, the only distinguishing feature being the person concerned admits she did not recognise his genius whereas most such tales are intended to show the narrator's acumen and foresight seeing in Kean what nobody else had espied. There is no evidence whatever that Penley employed the actor as an unknown.

After a long apprenticeship in third-rate provincial companies, Kean at last got his chance at Drury Lane. On 26 January 1814, the newcomer played Shylock to tremendous acclaim becoming an over-night sensation. Kean was immediately the biggest star in the theatrical firmament, being particularly known for his Richard III. Coleridge said 'To see him act is like reading Shakespeare by flashes of lightning.' Kean was not just a better actor than had gone before, he was a different sort of actor. He was also the daddy of all the hell-raising actors and pop stars of modern times, his carrying-ons being broadcast countrywide in the press of the day. He was the first actor intimately known to a public who never entered a theatre.

In spite of being addicted to drinking, whoring, and becoming increasingly unreliable, he is still regarded as one of the greatest actors of all time, and he appears many times in the story of the Penley family because in the theatre of the Regency era his presence was all pervading.

Along with Mrs Kean in the new Peckham company were Miss Kean, Mr and Mrs Darnley. Mrs Kean – who had abandoned Edmund as a baby – was actually Ann Carey, the granddaughter of Henry Carey of *Chrononhotonthologos* fame, and little better than a prostitute. Miss Kean was her daughter Phoebe Carey by an unknown man; Darnley was her son by a man of that name. All were regarded by Edmund Kean as his family after Ann Carey emerged from years of obscurity and destitution to sponge off her bastard son once he had become a star. As a result of his sudden elevation to stardom at the beginning of the year, and his poverty turning to plenty, Kean gave his mother an allowance of £50 a year and, by his new-found influence, helped her to find work as an actress. Hence they all ended up at Peckham working for Penley who, disliking to pay more than necessary for his players, may even have accepted a backhander to take them on.

Meanwhile, the continental company had left Brussels where, overall, the season had been only moderately successful, mainly because the English inhabitants of Brussels seemed to have had a preference for French language spectacles and operas presented at the French Grand Theatre. The J & P company's next assault was upon the town of Ghent where Booth remarked there were few English, but many Americans. This was of especial interest to Booth as his father, an ardent republican, had gone to America to fight for them against the English in the War of Independence. Booth was well accustomed to his father's ideas which included a picture of George Washington on the wall to which his visitors were expected to doff their hats and bow.

Apart from the Napoleonic War and the Peninsular War, the British had been fighting another American War since 1812. Once Napoleon no longer took the entire attention of the British forces, the American War became a major issue ending in December 1814 with the Treaty of Ghent, thus explaining the large American presence in the city.

The troupe opened at Ghent on 25 November proclaiming a visit of three nights only, but did not quit the town until 9 December in spite of paltry receipts. After which the company went on to Bruges where the town proved run-down and dirty, full of old ruinous buildings more like a poor English village than a large town. The troupe stayed from 12 to 31 December before travelling to Ostend.

There the intrepid band found the theatre was a wretched hovel. Poor as the venue may have been, the company was still there in March. Obviously, in spite of the conditions and the intimations of poor business that seemed to have dogged the enterprise, there must have been money to be made, otherwise Jonas would have called a halt to cut the losses, and returned the company to base much sooner.

The long tour finally ending, the actors drew lots for the order of their benefit performances. Booth tells us he chose *Richard III* for his night on 13 March playing to £25 with Jonas taking £12 for expenses. With that magnificent bonus of £13 in his pocket, Booth having left England playing walk-ons was now returning as leading man, arriving at Wapping on 3 April with the rest of the company.

He also returned with a three-months-pregnant woman. He was certainly a virile young man, having been involved in two previous paternity suits at the age of thirteen and seventeen!

Junius Brutus Booth, not yet twenty years of age, had, in under a year, compressed an entire apprenticeship from bit parts to leading man. It is thanks to his memoirs that we know much of the J & P continental foray. On his return to England his career rocketed and he was hailed, by some, as a rival to the great Edmund Kean himself.

In the absence of Booth's journal there is scant evidence of the next stage in Penley's continental ambitions. It appears that as Jonas and some of the actors returned home they overlapped with Sampson Penley coming out with reinforcements in the shape of additional actors. Over the next few years, whilst maintaining the home circuit, his company carried out continental visits establishing themselves in Calais and Boulogne where there were large ex-pat British communities.

The Penleys returned to Brussels to play another season at the Theatre du Parc, and 'actually performed at Brussels the night before Waterloo to a tolerably attended house'. As the Battle of Waterloo was fought on a Sunday, this means the company was playing on Saturday 17 June 1815, the eve of the battle. Belville Penley, Sampson's youngest child was, that night, at the age of seven playing a child's part clad in a regimental suit given to him by English officers. He was always to remember the triumphant return of the army and a subsequent visit to the battlefield.

SCENE NINE
1815 - 1816
THE NEW THEATRE ROYAL, WINDSOR

BACK IN ENGLAND there was no return to Deptford, the crowded audiences suddenly falling away; hardly surprising as Deptford, the centre of shipbuilding and victualling, booming during the Napoleonic War, immediately fell into rapid decline when peace was declared. The theatre there remained empty and unused for several years.

Before the next major development in the J & P saga, it must be presumed the company played the usual autumn visits, but there is actual evidence only for Lewes which opened on 9 August for a mere six nights, this being the annual Race Week. There was an unusual and disturbing incident on the night of the Race Stewards bespeak.

As the audience was milling forth at the exits at the end of the evening, a pickpocket used a sharp knife to cut his way into a man's pocket and abstracted his pocketbook while the owner's hand was actually resting upon it for safety. Of course, the man felt the theft, but the crook had darted off to be lost in the melee. The theatregoer thereby lost four £10 notes – a considerable amount for the time. Another patron had his pocket picked of £14. It is thought that the perpetrators of these outrages had visited the theatre the previous evening but, as the house was a thin one, had been unable to safely carry out any thefts. Considering the general lawlessness of the period it does seem rather foolish for men to carry such large amounts on their persons.

Business was reasonable but not crowded and, as the local newspaper pointed out, the season being so short and now being over, there was not much point in commenting on the qualities or otherwise of the actors. 'The Company are gone to Windsor, to open a new Theatre erected there by subscription, at an expence of between four or five thousand pounds.'

The first known theatre at Windsor was a barn set in a muddy field some distance from the centre of town, used between the years 1778 and 1793 as a playhouse. It was very small, only taking £20, but fitted up in a 'very neat manner' with two stage boxes, side and front boxes. Nevertheless, existing playbills grandiloquently refer to this building as the Theatre Royal, Peascod Street, Windsor.

The venue was acquired by Henry Thornton who was building up a circuit that eventually embraced some dozen theatres. He found Windsor not as straightforward as in most places, where being financially sound was the main requirement. As Windsor was the seat of the theatre-loving George III, the manager also had to have personal approval from the king himself. Realising that if the king were to attend his performances, a far superior more centrally located theatre was necessary, so Thornton set about constructing a new one in the High Street, with the king calling in from time to time to inspect the building's progress. The new theatre with a capacity of £70 opened in 1793 and the king and queen with their entourage were regular visitors

A description of the royal visits to this theatre at Windsor was provided in *Passages of a Working Life During Half a Century* a memoir by Charles Knight the proprietor and editor of the local paper:

> Tragedy was not to the King's taste. . . . "Was there ever such stuff as a great part of Shakespere? Only one must not say so! But what think you? What? Is there not sad stuff? What? What?" . . . One side of the lower tier of boxes was occupied by the Court. The King and Queen sat in capacious arm-chairs, with satin playbills spread before them. . . . With the plebeians in the pit the Royal Family might have shaken hands; and when they left, there was always a scramble for their satin bills, which would be afterwards duly framed and glazed as spoils of peace. . . At eleven o'clock the curtain dropped. The fiddles struck up *God save the King*; their Majesties bowed around as the house clapped; and the gouty manager, Mr Thornton, leading the way to the entrance (carrying wax-lights and walking backward with the well-practised steps of a Lord Chamberlain), the flambeaux of three or four carriages gleamed through the dimly lighted streets, and Royalty was quickly at rest.

Thornton – the manager who had sold his Henley theatre to J & P a decade previously – in 1806 sold the Windsor theatre which then lurched on via a series of short-stay managers. J & P had previously carried out one isolated summer season in Windsor in the old theatre, back in 1812, but other managers had taken over after that. In the good old days of George III, the theatre had been popular because the king was a keen theatregoer and the presence of royalty always attracted. However, since 1810 when the king's bouts of insanity became permanent all royal visits had ceased. Eventually the old theatre had been closed and the lease sold to a religious group who had turned it into a chapel. Although at the centre of royal activities, Windsor was essentially a country town of the narrowest minds, with many religious people opposing the theatre. There was little interest in the drama, so business had been poor during the theatre's limited openings.

However, a concerned group of citizens headed by Charles Knight, agitated for a replacement theatre. A new one was built by public subscription at a cost of £8000 – considerably more than the Lewes newspaper had estimated – and the lease granted to J & P. This opened on 21 August 1815 having being commanded to do so on that date by the queen, as it was her son the Duke of Clarence's birthday. The royal visitors, comprising the queen and three of her daughters, conducted over the new theatre at noon by Messrs Knight, Jonas and Penley, were highly pleased with the building, afterwards taking an airing through Slough in their carriages. In the evening Queen Charlotte gave a party at Frogmore House at which Clarence and his brother the Duke of Kent and their sisters were all present. None of the party attended the opening night of the theatre.

The new theatre unveiled at Windsor had two tiers of boxes, pit and gallery and was semi-circular rather than the old rectangular layout, a recent innovation in larger theatres to improve the sightlines. Slender cast-iron pillars supporting the tiers were said not to impede the view, although with an audience capacity of 700 there must have been a fair sprinkling of what today are designated 'restricted view' seats. In those days it was 'first come first served' except for the bookable boxes, hence doors opening an hour before curtain-up.

It was a gala occasion with a packed house greeting the new theatre and the new managers with enthusiasm. The evening commenced with an occasional address written by Mr C Knight and spoken by Mr S Penley of the Theatre Royal, Drury Lane before the main attraction *The School for Scandal*. Sam Jr was now a member of the company at Drury Lane which, having a summer recess, gave the actors freedom to work elsewhere.

Sampson Penley must have considered himself very fortunate to be granted the lease of this new theatre because of the royal connection. In Shakespeare's days, companies of actors could only function under the protection of a noble lord, being classed as servants of that lord and entitled to wear his livery. In those long-gone days acting companies were known as 'The King's Men', 'The Lord Chamberlain's Men', and so on. Under Charles II and his system of granting royal patents, actors at a theatre royal were authorised to call themselves 'His Majesty's Servants', and after acquiring Windsor Sampson took every opportunity to do so, styling J & P as 'His Majesty's Servants from the Theatre Royal, Windsor'.

Unfortunately, there was one great drawback at Windsor which had contributed to Thornton selling the place, and a lack of interest from other managements. This was a unique and peculiar condition: the theatre was not allowed to open while the boys of Eton College were at school. This meant that the theatre could only open during the school's summer and winter holidays, about five or six weeks in each case. There was one concession easing the restriction: the theatre could open for the annual Ascot Race Week in June, even though the boys would be attending school at that time. However, on the opening night, Sampson's new acquisition was splendid with its crowded house, and the drawbacks were pushed to the back of his mind.

It is believed that Shelley, who at the time was living at Bishopsgate near Windsor, may well have attended the opening night escorted by his friend Thomas Love Peacock.

The theatre and company were greeted with acclaim, with the abilities of Miss R Penley and Miss Lucas rendering them very deserving favourites. Mr S Penley of Drury Lane was 'spirited and elegant' as Charles Surface in *The School for Scandal* and in *The Stranger* 'evinced talents of the highest order such as will qualify him for the first walks in tragedy'. As Luke in *Riches*, 'he displayed the highest powers, his perfect conception of the character, his great command of expression. His simple and energetic action, and his clear and pleasing voice, marked this as a performance almost perfect. He occasionally reminded us of some of the peculiarities of Kean.' This excessive commendation of Sam Jr contrasts markedly with that he was to receive during his career at Drury Lane.

Running for barely five weeks, this highly successful first season closed on 16 September.

The Windsor winter season commenced on 9 December and, in recognition of the dark winter nights, the doors opened at 5.30 for a 6.30 start. Advertisements assured the public that the house was well aired, fires having been kept in the lobbies and other parts for the last three weeks. The season was five weeks, ending on 13 January 1816 when Sampson Penley came to realise the true significance of the contract he had signed. The boys were back at school at Eton and he had to cease operations. He grumbled publicly in the press that the theatre was thriving with good houses and it would be gratifying to the public if he could accede to their requests to prolong the season by a few days.

This was bad enough, but worse was to transpire. Some actors that Penley had dismissed were performing in a granary at Slough. The distance of this granary was no further from Eton than the Windsor Theatre was, and if performances at his theatre were hurtful to the discipline of Eton College, then the irregular performances at Slough must be even more offensive. Were the Magistrates giving permission for these performances? If so, they were acting illegally as no stage performances may be authorised within eight miles of a patent or licensed theatre. If they were ignorant of these renegade actors' performances then he respectfully begged the shows should be stopped immediately and, should they continue, he would go to law to protect himself without the fear of affecting his character in society.

Penley was correct in this as conditions attaching to licenses were very strict and eight miles was a laid down distance. This presumably put an end to the players in the Slough granary, but more was to come. The following notice appeared in the Windsor paper on 11 February:

A CAUTION
THEATRE ROYAL, WINDSOR

I, S Penley, Manager of the above Theatre, having been informed by several of my Friends, that a part of my Company, who were engaged for the Windsor season only, did stay at Windsor after the other part were gone, and have sent Petitions to several of the Inhabitants, stating, that they were deserted by their Manager without the least notice, and have thus imposed themselves on the Public by false assertions, – therefore hold it a duty incumbent on myself to stop such proceedings, and make Oath, that I have truly fulfilled my Engagements with the several Performers (eight in number) left behind; and that not one of them have any claim whatever upon me according to the nature of their Engagements.

S.Penley

Then followed a copy of the oath as sworn before two JPs at Deptford in Kent, restating the facts as above. Messrs Grant, Tuttle, Smith and Beynon were named as responsible for issuing the petition – a scandalous imposition as they had been paid all dues and demands at the expiration of their engagement. Furthermore, Penley had not made any charge upon them on their general Benefit Night.

The matter seems to have ended there, but it was an unpleasant hiccup in the first year of the new venture. We can be sure none of the renegade actors would be engaged by Penley ever again. The Mr Beynon involved must have been a relative of the widowed Mrs Beynon, perhaps her son, but the contretemps did not harm her own long-standing position with J & P as she was still appearing with the company up to 1822.

The next opportunity J & P had of opening the Windsor theatre was on 10 June 1816 for the annual Race Week when performances took place every night. This annual opening was not subject to the dictates of Eton College, and Penley managed to squeeze an extra three days out of it under the particular patronage of the queen. Then it was a matter of shutting up shop until the summer season.

The Eton boys having winged their way home for the holidays, the season opened on 30 July with Sam Jr back, plus other artistes from Drury Lane which like Eton, was closed for the summer.

Mrs Mardyn was the first guest star engaged during the opening week. She was followed later by Sam Jr as Gratiano and William Oxberry, a colleague from Drury Lane, as Shylock in *The Merchant of Venice*. Instead of Shylock taking his pound of flesh from the Merchant, in placing the knife in his belt, Oxberry sliced off the top of his finger resulting in blood gushing on to the stage. The actor soldiered on and when Portia said her line 'To have some surgeon lest Antonio do bleed to death', a man in the pit, thinking she alluded to the accident, exclaimed 'Here, mate, take my handkerchief, and I'll go for the doctor!'

The season closed on 14 September with the hope expressed in the local newspaper that Jonas and Penley would in future come up with a better selection of actors, disciplining them 'like a well regulated orchestra so that the inferior performers are never heard in dissonance with the most skilful.'

The difficulty was not unusual and easy to spot – it was one which affected all provincial theatre companies. Financial constraints on the manager meant that he was limited in the number of players he could engage for his troupe, and the policy of changing the programme nightly meant that those actors were called upon to play a whole gamut of roles, some of which they were suited for, others in which they were obviously miscast. It was not reasonable to expect perfection in every role as very few actors had the versatility to tackle a wide range of parts. Indeed, in the Georgian theatre there was a kind of type-casting by accepted categories; these were:

Tragedian/Leading Man, Second Tragedy, First Light Comedian, Second Light Comedian, Low Comedy Man, First Old Man, Second Old Man, Walking Gentleman. Actresses were similarly categorised as First

Tragedy, Second Tragedy, Fine Ladies, Singing Chambermaids, Old Women and Walking Ladies.

The leading tragedian was expected to play Romeo and Hamlet as well as Othello and Lear, irrespective of his actual age, while the leading tragic actress could be Juliet one night and Hamlet's mother Gertrude the next.

Actors in companies such as J & P had to be more versatile than at the patent theatres which had far more numerous personnel. Penley's light comedians were expected to undertake secondary roles in tragedies. Often the Low Comedian was needed to play, say, King Duncan in *Macbeth*, an impossible task for a man who, the previous few nights, had been desperately trying to raise mirth with broad jokes and comical antics.

The highest paid was always the leading man/tragedian, but in a country company this probably only meant 5/- or 10/- on top of the standard £1 a week. The Light Comedian was the most useful all-round actor as he could be cast in practically every play, his versatility being rewarded by coming next to the tragedian on the salary bill.

Of course, actors always moaned that they were underpaid and not cast in big enough parts. One actress in a provincial company complained to her manager that he favoured colleagues over herself. 'Notwithstanding your treatment, sir, I'll have you know that I have received a guinea a night in Dublin,' said she. Replied the manager: 'So you might, madam, but not for playing.'

Perhaps Penley had taken heed of the local editor's strictures for, when the winter season opened in December, Sam Jr and Oxberry were back, playing on nights they were not required at Drury Lane, and Rosina Penley, approaching her majority, having spent the summer months at the English Theatre at Valenciennes also returned. Her brother Montague was now on the acting strength and her fifteen-year-old brother William was also a regular on the bills with his assortment of songs.

The trump card, however, was the appearance of Edmund Kean, the biggest star in the land, who played for Oxberry's benefit at the penultimate night of the season. In spite of his appearance not being announced until 11am of the performance day, the box office sold out within two hours and even the queen's name could not procure a seat. Kean, who loved a lord, was entreated by Earl Harcourt to bless the local gentry with another night's performance, to which the great actor consented. He gave two of his famous non-Shakespearean roles – Sir Giles Over-reach and Sir Edward Mortimer – to packed houses. Severe flooding in the area did not deter people, and the business was a tribute to Kean's current phenomenal drawing power. At Drury Lane, Sam Jr was often in supporting roles to Kean so no doubt it was his persuasion as well as Oxberry's that induced the great man to condescend to visit Windsor. It was the custom of guest performers not to charge for their appearance at a benefit, and Kean was as much a soft touch for a good cause as a hard negotiator with managements. Though truth to tell, he would go anywhere for money, wenches and alcohol, not necessarily in that order.

In spite of Kean and his crowded houses, it was reported that overall the season had not 'repaid the manager for his exertions.'

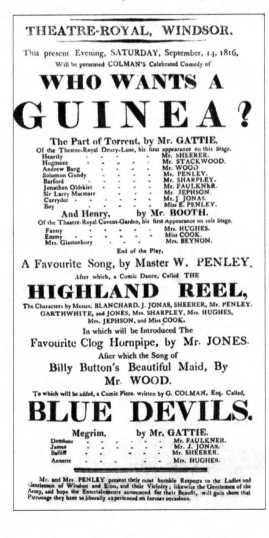

The final night of the 1816 summer season at Windsor with a benefit for Mr and Mrs Penley featuring Junius Brutus Booth, now of Covent Garden, on his first appearance at Windsor.

SCENE TEN
1817 - 1818
THE POST-WAR JONAS & PENLEY CIRCUIT

SOME 200 YEARS AGO the roads throughout the land did not provide easy travelling. The turnpike system of toll roads was meant to keep the main roads in good repair, but the conditions varied enormously. It was not until the next decade that the work of Telford and McAdam brought vast improvement to surfaces. Coaches and carriers carts often got bogged down in mud in winter, while hard uneven and dusty surfaces in dry summers brought jeopardy to undercarriages and wheels. One wonders how travelling players managed to get around as expeditiously as they seemed to have done. In 1817 the troupe at Tenterden had its last performance on Saturday night 31 May, and opened at Windsor for Race Week on Monday 2 June with a nightly change of programme. The stamina and fortitude of these players of old is astonishing.

Apart from the physical fitness required, mental agility also was a prerequisite. When one realises that the actor was in the theatre for four hours in the morning rehearsing, and five hours at night working, it is amazing when they found time to learn their lines at all.

It was unlikely that there would be more than one copy of the play, thus, for the actor attempting a new role, life was made even more difficult as he may have to write out his own part before he could learn it. This could be a help, in fact, as many actors found that writing out the part helped to fix it in their memory. There are many examples of prodigious feats of memory – actors getting a leading role at 4.30 and going on that night at 7.30 word perfect; others who, simply by reading the text through once, were able to play roles they had not acted for many years. There are even examples of actors who, unable to read, had to learn their part by having it read out to them. In such cases, they were able to memorise from a single reading. One is reminded of the story of the young Mozart who, having heard Alleghri's *Miserere*, went home and wrote out the entire piece from memory.

The Windsor summer season opened on 22 July with principal players Clifford and Jefferies. The last-named was a former manager of the theatre so had a good local following. It was quite commonplace for a manager to lose or relinquish his lease, returning subsequently as a mere actor. The qualities needed to be an efficient manager are not the same as those required of a successful actor.

Mr & Mrs Egerton of Covent Garden starred for four days with the company. In effect they were holding the fort for Oxberry and Sam Jr who, with Phoebe and Rosina, had been appearing at the English Theatre in Valenciennes where there had been a major contretemps with the eminent French actor Talma. The contingent from abroad arrived for the third week of the season, accompanied by an amateur – presumably an officer in the British Army of Occupation – who promptly essayed the role of Othello.

Of particular note during the season was the debut of Miss Jonas, the young lady who had inadvertently caused the difficulties at Valenciennes:

> The entertainment of *Rosina* followed, in which a Miss Jonas made her first appearance here as the heroine, and obtained a most flattering reception. She executed the different airs with a force, and at the same time a delicacy, of expression, not often exceeded.

This was Maria Jonas, the most talented of all John and Mary's children, who excelled by her singing prowess. In those days all actors were expected to be able to sing as so many plays, especially afterpieces, were musically based. Maria Jonas was, perhaps, more of a singer than an actress. Oxberry's benefit night, well saturated with singing, included several numbers by Maria and Oxberry himself.

Announcements proclaimed that Kean had been booked for three nights to open the 1817/18 winter season but surprise, surprise, the star attraction proved to be none other than Mr Booth! Indeed, the same Junius Brutus Booth who had started out with Penley no more than three years previously, playing bit parts at Peckham, and trailing through the Low Countries with Jonas and his diminishing band.

Since his return to England, Booth had spent a period with Thomas Trotter at Worthing and Brighton while persuading friends to make representations to the Covent Garden management on his behalf. Eventually, Harris the manager had succumbed by offering him a job at £2 a week playing bit parts. Now considering himself a leading man, this was not what the ambitious Booth had intended at all. So, after the end of the season, he returned to Trotter who upped his money from the previous £1.10.0 to two guineas, also promoting him to acting manager. Even this elevation did not satisfy Booth which, because of a quarrelsome relationship with Trotter, ended by his leaving and going to Windsor.

Presumably in his extremity he no longer regarded Penley as a scoundrel! However, at Windsor, Booth seems to have appeared only on 14 September in *Who Wants a Guinea?* being billed in large type as 'of the Theatre Royal, Covent Garden. His first Appearance on this Stage'. The season ending at Windsor, he crept back to Trotter who revenged himself by reducing Booth's salary to £1.5.0.

While Booth was at Brighton for Trotter, Edmund Kean – booked to appear as a guest star – failed to arrive; an occupational hazard when contracting Kean. Booth stepped in at the last minute with great success. As a result of this, influential people in the nobility and artistic world agitated for Harris to give Booth a proper chance at Covent Garden, to which he agreed. Appearing as Richard III to tremendous acclaim and deemed as good as Kean, Covent Garden offered Booth a three-year contract at £5 a week. Booth demanded £15 and, when the management would not budge in their offer, at Kean's behest Drury Lane swept in with a deal at £10 a week. Booth foolishly signed, and Drury Lane put him up for the first time as Iago to Kean's Othello. Kean stretched himself to the uttermost, acting the newcomer off the stage. Alas for Booth, the future parts on offer were not leading ones. Realising that he had fallen for a cunning ploy and that Kean would limit his opportunities at Drury Lane, he pleaded illness, retreating back to Covent Garden. The result was a messy court case over contracts, with Booth, patently in the wrong, pleading his youth and inexperience in business matters. Some people claimed he was actually under age, others saying that was not so as 'he appeared at Mr Penley's Theatre at Brussells three or four years ago and has been married about three years.' The fact of the matter was that Booth, soon after returning from his continental tour with the disintegrating J & P company, had married his pregnant inamorata on 17 May 1815 and, having just turned nineteen at the time, would not be twenty-one until 1 May 1817. The end of it all was Kean triumphant against all comers, and Booth settling down to a more normal sharing of major roles with Charles Mayne Young, the Garden's principal tragedian.

Booth, having a physical resemblance to Kean, modelled himself on the great man, delivering broader versions of the well-known Kean roles. In London he was never really taken seriously as a tragedian, but he had star status, and toured the country raking in large payments guesting with provincial companies, including a prodigious day on 19 April 1817 when he played Sir Edward Mortimer in three different towns for the sum of £30 – 11am at Cirencester, 4pm at Gloucester and 8pm at Cheltenham.

Now Booth was to open the 1817/18 winter season at Windsor – in place of Edmund Kean – for his erstwhile employer Sampson Penley. It must have given great satisfaction to Booth as Penley billed him as the 'Celebrated Mr Booth of the Theatre Royal, Covent Garden' and increased the prices of the Upper Boxes to the same as the Lower Boxes. Billed for one night only, Booth played Sir Giles Overreach in *A New Way to Pay Old Debts*. Then Penley puffed on the bills that, due to Booth's success and by public demand, the star was retained for a further two nights, next playing Macbeth with Phoebe Penley as Lady M. The extra two nights did not, in fact, take place. Booth, in his account book, records his takings at various venues using two columns, one for the receipts and one for his share – Booth's contracts being mainly sharing deals. His account book has several entries where his share is given as £0.0.0 and on other occasions in its place the word 'gratis' is used, and sometimes 'ingratitude'. These entries refer to another actor's benefit, as it was the custom for actors to appear free of payment at fellow players' benefits on a mutual reciprocal basis.

Booth's account book states the Windsor date as a benefit for Penley, and in the shares column the single word 'meanness'. There is clearly some skulduggery involved here. Neither the press advertisement nor the playbill says it is Penley's benefit, which would be very unusual in any case being the opening night of the season. Without further evidence, it looks like Penley pulled some sort of fast one on Booth; perhaps it was a sharing deal and there was a dispute about the split (Booth's listing it in his account book as a benefit for Penley being heavy sarcasm). Whatever the financial shenanigans, Penley probably tried to make up for it by persuading Booth to do two more nights resulting in Booth – not known for his meekness and docility – throwing a wobbler and storming off into the night. Perhaps to Sampson, Booth at only twenty-one was still much the same gullible youth whom he had started in the business, rather than the major star the actor now considered himself. To Booth no doubt Penley remained a scoundrel. Booth's place in *Macbeth* was taken at short notice by Mr Palmer-Fisher who had been due to play Macduff.

Four years later, Junius Brutus Booth, the son of an ardent republican, was to abandon his wife and son, running off with a flower girl to America where he fathered a new family while living in rustic isolation in relatively primitive conditions.

As the season approached its end, the verdict was that the public support was not commensurate with the exertions of the managers putting on the shows, and there had been too many empty benches.

As a last fling, Penley announced Kean himself as Othello on the final Wednesday, and this great draw gave much delight and admiration. Kean was expected to give his Hamlet on Friday, but when 7.30 arrived and Kean had not, Mr Creswell the acting manager went on to request the audience's indulgence by waiting a little longer. After another 15 minutes had passed, Cresswell returned saying there was no sign of Mr Kean and no message from him, so he was therefore forced to abandon all hope of his arrival. 'Mr Creswell stated that he had been present at the engagement between Mr Kean and Mr Penley, that it left no apprehension of such an unfortunate result; that Mr Penley must stand acquitted of all blame.' *The Beaux Stratagem* being substituted, Creswell then offered money back to anybody who chose to leave, but there was little disapprobation and few took up the offer. Kean's peccadilloes becoming commonplace, no doubt audiences had ceased to be surprised or angry.

But two 'no shows' by two different stars in one short season did not give audiences confidence in their local theatre.

In 1818, once again the J & P troupe dropping everything at Tenterden, made haste to Windsor for the Race Week. There had been quite a change in the personnel of the J & P company, losing some long-standing names whilst gaining newer ones that seemed to have some staying power, and Mr Salter was back heading the company. Salter, it will be recalled, was the first to flee the continental J & P company in 1814 and now held a strong position as a reliable provincial leading man. Rosina played Juliet to Salter's Romeo as she was now an essential part of the company, as were sister Phoebe and brother Montague.

A special attraction from Drury Lane was Miss Clara Fisher who was engaged for two nights to play Richard III and Shylock. Should these be thought unsuitable parts for a female to play, how much more inappropriate for a seven-year-old girl! The child was the latest in a succession of infant prodigies who had followed on from the Master Betty craze of 14 years previously. She had made her debut as recently as December 1817 at both the patent theatres and was widely admired, even sceptical reports saying 'although not very warm admirers of precocity of talent, we cannot but consider this infant a great prodigy' and similar sentiments. Clara, the youngest of three sisters who all appeared in the plays, was now cashing in on her reputation as the 'admired Lilliputian actress' by taking well paid visits to theatres throughout the land, just as Master Betty had done long before Miss Clara was born.

Whereas Master Betty retired at the age of seventeen to attend college, making two abortive come-backs and two failed suicides before enjoying his great wealth at leisure, Miss Clara Fisher continued her infant prodigy career very successfully, progressing to a full acting career as an adult. At the age of sixteen she emigrated with her family to America, becoming a big star. She married, had seven children, and she and her husband opened a theatre in New Orleans. Retiring with a large fortune that was dissipated by an expensive life-style and bad investments, she returned to the stage. Dubbed 'the oldest living actress' in the USA, she continued acting until the age of seventy-seven, finally retiring in 1888 and dying some ten years later.

The winter season at Windsor opened on Boxing Day with Phoebe Penley and Salter in *George Barnwell; or The London Merchant*, a tragedy that follows the downfall of a young apprentice due to his association with a prostitute. The most famous work of George Lillo, first performed 85 years previously, it is remarkable for its early use of middle- and working-class characters, becoming one of the most popular plays of the century. Rosina, who might have played the part of the prostitute had she been available, was not in the Windsor company having flown the family nest to become leading lady at the prestigious Bath theatre.

Business was not booming at Windsor and to bolster the last week Penley engaged Miss Matthews from Covent Garden to play and sing in *She Stoops to Conquer*. But all was of little avail and the season closed on 16 January with Penley's exertions to attract the public something of a failure. The population was pre-occupied with other pleasures during this period, and the local press opined Penley would do better to reserve his strength for a more propitious occasion when his losses may be made up by 'that future patronage which his unwearied exertions and liberality deserve.'

It is not surprising that business was poor. Windsor was a country area and, in the period following the end of the Napoleonic War, the agricultural industry passed from prosperity to extreme depression. Many farms were given up and notices to quit became commonplace. Large tracts of land were untenanted and uncultivated, their tenants having fled. Bankers pressed for their advances, landlords for their rents, tithe-owners for their tithes, tax-collectors for their taxes, and tradesmen for their bills. Insolvencies, seizures, arrests and imprisonments steadily increased.

Going for a night out at the theatre was becoming no longer a viable prospect.

SCENE ELEVEN
1819
COVENTRY

SAMPSON PENLEY WAS in a quandary. Apart from Peckham, his circuit comprised country and coastal towns. His new Henley theatre – opened with such a flourish in 1805 – had closed eight years later and converted to a chapel, becoming a school in 1816. At its other theatres, having lost a major section of their audiences as the militia men returned to their homes, and the former agricultural workers fleeing the depressed countryside to seek work in the manufacturing towns, J & P now could only face the possibility of vastly reduced seasons. Windsor, itself, was suffering from markedly reduced attendances.

Penley, reasoning that if the country population was shifting to industrial towns there must be better pickings there, made the bold move of opening a new theatre in Coventry. The population of Coventry at that time was 21,000, half of whom were employed in the silk trade. The theatre was built by Sir Skears Rew, a plumber and glazier by trade, who had recently served as mayor. As he had no connection with the theatre profession, it is difficult to see why he embarked on the venture.

A typical town circuit theatre with a house attached, the building measuring 96ft x 34ft, was estimated to have seated around 800. Penley, with his company billed in the now customary style 'His Majesty's Servants from the Theatre Royal, Windsor' opened on Easter Monday 1819 with *A New Way to Pay Old Debts*. The theatre immediately began to attract good audiences, it was said, of 'beauty, elegance and fashion'. The playing strength comprised the regulars from Windsor including Salter, Burton, and all the Penley children (except, of course, Sampson Jr) – even Master Belville being roped in to do the odd page and servant role.

When the annual Race Week season opened at Windsor there were few of the familiar faces to be seen as they were all at Coventry. A newcomer Barton from Liverpool headed the troupe with Rosina, taking leave of absence from Coventry, as leading lady. Oxberry and Sam Jr also played during the week which fortunately was extremely well attended.

While Sampson was busy wooing a new audience, in the wider world the simmering discontent of workers in Manchester erupted into the massacre called Peterloo, and the future leaders of the country at Eton College were up to clandestine shenanigans as this press report reveals:

> The Masters of Eton, having discovered that many of the senior scholars had employed most of their time in Theatrical studies, and that they performed plays two or three times a week, have given positive orders that they shall be discontinued; in consequence of which two very neat theatres have been pulled to pieces, containing some expensive scenery.

Did Sampson Penley know anything about this? Probably not, and as the college authorities were able to dictate opposition to his theatre, Penley had to tread warily at the best of times.

It appears that clandestine performances of plays at Eton have a long history going back to pre-Puritan times. A revival came in the mid-18th century when a secret drama society was set up in Long Chamber where the 70 scholars lived and worked. It is reported that they were locked in there after dark, so plays became a way to alleviate boredom. They had costumes, props, special effects, scenery, and the plays continued as an open secret, tolerated by the authorities. Eventually the Oppidans, fee paying boys, set up rival companies and theatre at Eton flourished. A letter dated 13 May 1818 talks of a 'Revival of the theatre, describes new scenery and the potential actors among the boys, and future productions.' A painting dated c1815 by the drawing master at Eton shows the stage in Long Chamber, therefore the masters were fully aware of the 'secret theatres', but they were not to be public knowledge outside Eton. When these activities began being talked about in Windsor and London, the Head Master banned the productions, as reported in the newspaper.

At the conclusion of his regular Windsor summer season, Penley placed an advert announcing no winter season was to be held, but an Easter opening instead which had not previously been tried.

The entire company then hot-footed it down to Eastbourne, opening on 20 September with *The Belle's Stratagem* and the farce *High Notions*. They played until the end of October then moved on to Lewes – for the first time after several years omission – opening on 2 November.

Back at its old stamping ground J & P carried out a thorough repair and redecoration of the premises, long neglected by varied occupants and non-usage. The auditorium was repainted by Montague Penley who also provided new scenery, including a particularly pleasing front drop. Montague, who carried out a double life as actor and artist, was in the future to lean more towards scenic artist and management than acting. The scenery and costumes for *The Miller and his Men* were especially beautiful.

Under the auspices of a respectable but anonymous individual of the town, Sheridan's *Pizarro* was enacted. This play about the conquering of Peru was inordinately popular during the period, and Rolla was a part that was expected of leading men just as much as Othello, Macbeth or Hamlet. Salter, in the role, was accorded the highest praise. Phoebe played the Sarah Siddons role of Elvira.

Rosina was becoming the leading lady of the family company, though often sharing leads with her elder sister Phoebe. She played Lady Teazle in *The School for Scandal*, the eponymous Jane Shore in Rowe's 1714 tragedy, and Violante in *The Wonder* the role made famous by Mrs Jordan. For the Misses Penley benefit they chose *Macbeth* as the main piece, and Rosina performed *The Actress of All Work* a comedy *tour de force* in which, playing six different roles, she was greatly and deservedly applauded.

For their joint benefit Salter and Burton offered *Richard III* after which Burton sang a new song called *Dandies and Dandyzettes* mounted on a velocipede, this early form of bicycle substituting for the singing of songs on an ass, which had previously been regarded as a comic attraction. It did not seem to diminish an actor's credibility to perform such stunts after a serious play. Perhaps a present day audience might be encouraged to visit a Shakespeare play if they thought Sir Derek Jacobi would do an encore on a skateboard singing a comic song.

John Jonas's benefit play was *A New Way to Pay Old Debts* which was followed by a pantomime *Harlequin Captive*. The press comments on this are enlightening:

> In the latter, the veteran Jonas, as Clown, exhibited specimens of agility, that would have done great credit to any performer in that particular line, of the present day, less stricken in years.

This is additional evidence that John Jonas is likely to have started his show business career as an acrobat. We have no evidence of his date or place of birth but, working back from the age given on his death certificate, he must have been around his mid-fifties at the time of this production.

The last night of the season concluded with a final address from Penley. The Lewes season closed on 30 December having lasted two months – a major innovation after neglecting the town in recent years.

The company moved on to Rye, opening there on 5 January 1820.

SCENE TWELVE
1820
THE ACTING PENLEY FAMILY

O N 29 JANUARY 1820, George III died. He had been king for nearly 60 years, although for the last ten years totally incapable, his son the Prince of Wales acting as Regent. It was a sad end, and the theatre lost a great patron who had found it one of his chief pleasures in his younger days. The Regent became king as George IV. He had had very tempestuous relations with both his father and his wife Caroline of Brunswick whom he had been compelled to marry in 1795, and made strenuous efforts to divorce her. He was an extravagant man with debts at the time of their marriage equivalent to £50million in today's money. They had parted the year after the wedding, and in 1814 Caroline left the country.

Piecing together the movements of the J & P company at this time is not easy as evidence is scant. Dating is complicated by the fact that sometimes there is more than one unit operating at a time, with extra players brought in. Regrettably, out of the 240 located surviving playbills of J & P there are few disparate venues, almost half being for the Tenterden theatre, but there is in the Rye museum archive a run of 16 of the 1820 season from January to March. This enables the strength of the J & P company at that time to be seen in its entirety.

The Sampson Penley family now involved comprised Mr Penley (Sampson), his sons Mr M Penley (Montague), Mr W Penley (William), Master B Penley (Belville) and his daughters Miss Penley (Phoebe), Miss R Penley (Rosina) and Miss E Penley (Emma).

The Jonas family is more debatable. There were five sons and five daughters in John's family and apportioning their roles is fraught with difficulties. Mr Jonas (John) the father and his daughter Miss Jonas were the only members of the Jonas family billed as appearing. Which of his daughters was this particular Miss Jonas? The usual one was Maria, famed for her singing, but there are several playbills listing a host of musical items and this Miss Jonas is only singing in the occasional quartet. In any case, Maria had gone on to the Surrey Theatre company at this time. Judging by the parts she plays, this Miss Jonas could be Mary (32), Sophia (27) Charlotte (21) or even Esther (16).

Usually the eldest daughter is simply Miss Jonas, with younger sisters being Miss M Jonas, Miss C Jonas and so on, so it is most probably Mary – the eldest Jonas daughter – appearing at Rye. The main non-family members are still Salter, Burton and the ever faithful Mrs Beynon.

A particular feature of the plays presented in this season at Rye is the amount of music. *Guy Mannering*, a comic opera based on the novel by Sir Walter Scott with music by Henry Bishop, was very popular, having played upwards of 100 nights at Covent Garden. Another Scott novel *Rob Roy* was also transformed into a comic opera that played successfully at Covent Garden. The Rye audience must have enjoyed music and song as Messrs Brett and Minter were engaged for three special nights and they were singers presenting solos and duets in musical interludes between the plays, but not taking part in them.

When Jonas's benefit night arrived he chose *Hamlet* in which Salter was the Dane, Jonas played Gravedigger and Phoebe was Gertrude. As on all playbills and advertisement extant for Jonas's benefits, Masonic insignia is placed at the head. The farce was *Tom Thumb* with Belville Penley playing the lead. He was now twelve years old and presumably still on the small side.

The Misses Penley benefit was Mrs Inchbald's elegant comedy *Wives as They Were and Maids as They Are* – a staple of the J & P company since it was first performed in1797 – and *The Miller and his Men*. When nowadays we are used to our self-opinionated actors pontificating on all kinds of matters out of their own sphere, it seems abject grovelling by the sisters to read 'The Misses Penley, with the most profound respect to their Friends and the Public in general, hope the Entertainments selected for their Benefit will merit their generous patronage, which it shall ever be their study to deserve.' But as Dr Johnson said in 1747:

> *The drama's laws the drama's patrons give,*
> *For we that live to please must please to live.*

The projected Easter season at Windsor does not seem to have taken place, the next opening being as usual for the Ascot Race Week. Mr Bromley of the Theatre Royal, Haymarket, headed the troupe, and a singer of comic songs called Mr Hammond appeared. He was to figure greatly in Rosina's subsequent career.

Sampson now embarked on his second season at Coventry, opening on 2 June, somewhat later than the previous year. Rather oddly, the theatre was advertised as having been re-decorated. This was a common enough ploy to attract custom, but the theatre was only a year old. The summer was a particularly hot and sultry one, certainly not good weather for theatre going.

Penley's advertising appears to have suddenly taken a whimsical turn similar to the fashion adopted by the London minor theatres. For the Two Miss Penleys' benefit night, *Don Giovanni* was heralded as 'a Comic, Heroic, Operatic, Tragic, Pantomimic, Burletta Spectacular Extravaganza'. The scenery described as 'having most of it appeared before, has been (of course) already received with unbounded applause, and will be repeated as often as the Managers can get up Pieces to introduce it.' The dresses 'are as good as the Proprietor can possibly afford, and the properties are of very little use to any but the owner.'

Fortunately this spoofing (all too often very near the truth) was confined to this one occasion and may well have been the Penley girls' idea to jolly-up their special night. Subsequent playbills reverted to the standard prosaic formula.

The season ended on 28 July and all the regular company members present – Misses Penley, Salter, Burton *et al* – sped to Windsor where the summer season opened on 31 July.

William Oxberry, a regular visitor at Windsor during his summer break from Drury Lane, was in the opening play with Mr Knight, a newcomer to the troupe, also from Drury Lane. The season was no sooner under way than the Duchess of York, wife of the second son of George III and thus sister-in-law of the king, died on 6 August aged fifty-three after a long illness. George IV was reported to be residing at his cottage in the grounds of Windsor Castle. The theatre was closed for a few days in respect; a blow to the performers as they did not receive any income when not working.

Leaving Windsor to run under Jonas, Penley and Rosina travelled down to Lewes to open the season there mid-week on 9 August with a company headed by Bromley from York and Mordaunt of Drury Lane supported by unfamiliar names. Oxberry also followed a few days later to be the star attraction for the end of the very short season, just two weeks, concluding on 22 August. Performances were advertised to be every night, but in fact seem to have taken place on nine nights out of the 12.

The company moved on to Eastbourne as was its wont, but it appears Rosina did not go as she had returned to Windsor, being on the playbill at Windsor on 21 August. It seems remarkable in those days of coach-and-horse transport how much activity took place between the J & P companies and the towns where they played, with performers nipping back and forth as readily as in the later heyday of the railway system. Eastbourne opened on 24 August for two weeks only. It is significant that Penley was now playing every night compressed into two-week seasons and he, himself, was more frequently on the acting strength rather than confining himself to a strictly managerial role. It was rather like stepping back 25 years to when J & P had first started, before its circuit had developed.

Back at Windsor, the season had jogged on after the enforced closure, with the last week scheduled to have performances every night from 4 September when Oxberry, too, returned to give his Shylock in *The Merchant of Venice*. The Penley sisters gave way on this night to allow Miss Chester – a local actress who had played Portia for several nights at Drury Lane – to reprise her efforts at Windsor. The afterpiece was *Perouse*, a play where a chimpanzee is a crucial character. The role was played by Master Jonas. Again, there are five Jonas sons to choose from but it must have been one of the two youngest – either fourteen-year-old Henry or eleven-year-old Frederick.

Each evening being by desire or under the patronage of the usual supporters such as army officers, local MPs and eminent locals, the season closed on Saturday 9 September. However, a reprieve was granted as, to compensate for the loss of performances due to the death of the Duchess of York, another week was added 'under the immediate and gracious patronage of His Majesty'. It looks as though Sampson had been round to George IV's cottage to do a bit of unctuous pleading. Since the new theatre and Penley's regime, the main royal supporter had been Princess Augusta, George III's second daughter out of his 15 children. She had been born in 1768 so was much of an age with Mr & Mrs Sampson Penley and Mr Jonas, and had never married. It is likely that any links with the king would be via this sister.

The bonus week commenced with His Majesty's Servants performing *Macbeth* with Salter as the Thane and Phoebe as Lady M, William played Seyton, and Master Belville was Fleance. Jonas played Second Witch (did he still do his somersault?), Mrs Beynon as Third Witch. Miss Jonas and Miss E Penley were Singing Witches. In those days *Macbeth* was invariably presented with music by Matthew Locke, Charles II's royal composer, and featured 'The Pit of Acheron, with a Fiery Cauldron, a Grand Solemn Incantation and a Dance of Witches'.

On the following evening Mr Salter was Othello, Iago being played by a Gentleman Amateur, with local lady Miss Chester again putting Phoebe's and Rosina's noses out of joint by playing Desdemona. A couple of years hence Rosina was to replace Miss Chester as the leading lady at York when that voluptuous lady went on to greater things.

The Windsor winter season opened on 26 December with *Jane Shore*. This tragedy in Shakespearean mode by Nicholas Rowe had Rosina playing the lead role. She was not to know it then, but not too far in the future it was a role in which she was to make a mark in France. Now developing into a tragedy queen, just as her Aunt Frances (Mrs William Penley) had done, Rosina was regularly tackling parts such as Isabella in *The Fatal Marriage*, and Virginia in *Virginius*.

The audiences were disappointing but the inclement weather offered an excuse. After the end of the short winter season, the theatre was reopened for one night only at the command of Princess Augusta.

> The house was crowded by all ranks of the neighbourhood, anxious to pay a tribute of respect to a Princess so universally beloved. Indisposition, we regret to say, prevented her Royal Highness from being present. The performances were *The Poor Gentleman* and *Raising the Wind*. In addition to the usual strength of the Company, Mr S Penley displayed those talents, which on former occasions have made him so great a favourite with the Windsor audience.

Sam Jr had not appeared in recent years at Windsor, leaving the field clear for his Drury Lane colleague Oxberry. However, his link with Windsor was far from over; he would be seeing much more of the town in the future.

At some point during the year Sampson Penley had acquired another addition to his circuit: the lease of the Dover theatre. Charles Mate, the long-term manager of Dover had long retired and his theatre passed on to other managers. Robert Copeland had held Dover and Margate since the turn of the century, dying in 1816 leaving the properties to his son. William R Copeland, who had interests elsewhere, disposed of the circuit, with most venues being taken over by Saville Faucit, though Sampson Penley acquired the Dover theatre. The fact that Dover, being next to Folkestone, fitted the J & P circuit more satisfactorily than Coventry – which does not seem to have been as successful as everybody expected – may have been a deciding factor. Though, with the seasons in the towns of Lewes, Eastbourne and Rye being curtailed, it does not seem a propitious time to launch an additional venue on the South Coast.

SCENE THIRTEEN
1821 - 1822
DISASTER!

PENLEY OPENED HIS third season at Coventry on 23 February 1821. He had tried April in 1819 and June in 1820, so whether this was because it had to fit in with visits elsewhere, or whether he was desperately trying to find the right time of year to drum up the best business, cannot be ascertained. Penley does not seem to have attempted to introduce guest stars at Coventry, a ploy often resorted to for boosting attendances. On this occasion he ran it for exactly a month, closing on 23 March. It was then announced that Penley was selling his interest in the theatre to Robert William Elliston, a popular and versatile actor who had recently acquired the lease of Drury Lane. The avowed purpose of this after such a short venture was, according to the press, that Penley intended to take his company to Hanover to present English plays there under royal patronage. This is particularly intriguing as we know how Sampson, having something of a pioneering spirit, was the first after hostilities to cross the channel in 1814. The former Prince Regent, now King George IV, was also King of Hanover and proposed visiting his kingdom for a coronation. It reads as though Sampson was hoping to latch on to this event.

Meanwhile, having made 'special arrangements', Penley attempted a few days at Windsor during the Easter holiday, but this was not very successful and was in line with theatrical enterprises throughout the kingdom, many of which were in the doldrums. M Alexandre, a ventriloquist appeared for two nights, Mrs Glover, a mature actress who had been around for many years at Drury Lane, Covent Garden and other theatres, being the principal attraction on the other nights. The local newspaper ventured the hope that success may 'in some degree compensate Mr Penley for the serious losses of his Winter Season.'

The theatre was open again for the annual Race Week when 'the performances have been respectable, and the company genteel and numerous.'

George IV's coronation took place on 19 July 1821 and J & P's Windsor summer season opened on 2 August with a free performance in honour of the event comprising *The Way to Get Married* and *The King and the Miller of Mansfield.* Phoebe and Rosina were both back in the company, as was Jonas, Miss Jonas and the faithful Mrs Beynon, though most of the company were newcomers to Windsor. Oxberry, the regular visiting summer star, had remained in London where he now had a chop house and bar frequented by theatrical folk and, whilst keeping his place at Drury Lane, had ceased touring to concentrate on his writing and publishing ventures.

According to the local press 'Messrs Jonas and Penley have wisely abandoned the old stock plays with which everyone has been satiated, and got up some interesting melodramas in a style of superior excellence.' They then went on to do *Oroonoko* which had been around since 1695, and *Obi; or Three-Fingered Jack*, a favourite for 20 years and still so popular with the Windsor public it was performed four times. So much for satiation!

During the final week *The School for Scandal* (1777) was presented with Rosina as Lady Teazle, a part that she was to play many times, with many different actors in the role of her husband, and *Wives as They Were and Maids as They Are* (1797) a staple of the J & P repertoire since it was written. The policy of abandoning the old war-horses looks to be simply a figment of the reporter's imagination or, more likely, a PR attempt to boost attendance figures.

More obvious stratagems to draw business included the added attraction of Mr Wilson on the tight-rope. He not only somersaulted over the orchestra but, accompanying himself on the castanets, also danced a fandango which had been specially composed for him by the First Violin of the orchestra of the Theatre Royal, Madrid in the form of a Tambourine Rondeau. No doubt very rhythmic, but likely to be short on melody one feels.

In the early days of the 19th century when business started to slump, managers would try anything, and circus-type acts would be included along with the drama. Plays with horses and dogs in prominent roles were often extra money-spinners even at the major theatres. When a playwright delivered a new play *The Caravan; or The Driver and his Dog* to the debt-ridden Drury Lane it proved a great success, chiefly because of a live dog that was trained to save a child from drowning by leaping from a rock and plunging into real water. When the manager burst into the greenroom asking 'Where is he, my guardian angel?' He was told the 'The author has just left,' to which the manager replied, 'I don't mean the author, I'm talking about the dog.'

The Windsor season closed with this verdict from the local press:

> The success of the season has certainly not been consider-
> able, although the Managers have made every exertion to

produce the most attractive novelties. But when we consider the depressed state of theatrical speculations throughout the kingdom, we cannot expect that Windsor should be an exception to the general want of encouragement for dramatic entertainments.

Penley made his living by putting on plays. His only source of income was the takings at the box office, so he had no chance of earning whenever his theatre was closed. This explains why, in spite of poor business, again Penley tried stretching his legally permitted time at the theatre. For decades, theatre managers throughout the land had relied on race weeks to boost the size of their audiences. Whilst Ascot races had long enabled an annual week's opening in June, Penley now approached the Duke of York – the steward of the near-by Egham races – and gained his permission and patronage to open the theatre for a week to coincide.

Egham races had a long history, taking place at Runnymede meadow alongside the River Thames where the Magna Carta had been signed. The course was described as 'an oval course, short of 2 miles by 66 yards, and nearly flat.' Egham races continued until 1886 when they moved to Kempton Park.

There is no record of how this extra week fared, and one senses a whiff of desperation about it.

As regards Hanover, the king and entourage left Ramsgate for Calais on 25 September, progressing via Brussels to Hanover arriving on 8 October. He stayed in the state until 25 October, arriving back in Ramsgate on 8 November. A large obelisk in Ramsgate Harbour commemorates the occasion. Nowhere is there any mention of an English theatre company, although that does not mean Penley's troupe did not go there. Perhaps it did, and proved an expensive flop not to be reported upon. Conceivably Sampson had every intention of visiting Hanover, but more likely it was an excuse for selling his Coventry lease after such a short time. What really happened is something very different from that original bluff press announcement.

The last play that John Philip Kemble attended before leaving England to retire on the continent was *Hamlet* at the Dover Theatre with Salter in the name part. Kemble, renowned for his Hamlet, afterwards sought out Penley to shower praise upon his leading man. It was a rare highlight in the occupancy of his recently acquired venue.

On 15 November, Sampson Penley was arrested for debt at the behest of one Charles Selby and others, and imprisoned at Dover. Two days later, having found sufficient money, which was in excess of £100, he was released by agreement with the plaintiff's agent.

Unfortunately, Penley's troubles went deeper and on 26 November he was arrested again, this time at the behest of W B Blenkinsopp for a much more alarming debt of £918. 18. 7 – in today's money about £73,000. Then on 29 November along came John Clements with another £16 (£1200) owing to him. Penley's position was dire, debtors were not treated kindly in those days.

As we know from Dickens, even later in the century, a man who could not pay his debts could be incarcerated indefinitely, often resulting in entire families spending years in jail. Prisons were privately operated and a prisoner was expected to pay 'Garnish' and 'Chummage' on being admitted, a bizarre idea presuming that a man facing imprisonment because he had no money would have sufficient to pay these imposts. Garnish was a payment of 5/6d which gave access to cooking facilities and hot water, and chummage was a ticket which allocated which room you were to sleep in. By paying 2/6d a week a prisoner could send his room chums out and have the room to himself, the outcasts having to find somewhere else to go. The only people who escaped payments were prisoners so destitute they subsisted on a small pittance granted by the authorities or charitable hand-outs, and were thus confined to the most mean and squalid part of the prison.

Not a great prospect for a man of business who had had thousands of pounds pass through his hands and employed scores of actors and the services of many artisans. Fortunately, there was one escape: under the relatively recent Insolvent Debtors Act of 1813, debtors could request release after 14 days in jail by taking an oath that their assets did not exceed £20, (£1,500) but if any of their creditors objected, they had to stay inside. Even after a lifetime in prison, the debt remained to be paid.

At this point it must be wondered why Penley alone was responsible for the debts if J & P was a business partnership. Certainly there are archive papers extant showing their joint dealings regarding mortgages and leases with both signatures, so the position seems inexplicable. Perhaps at some past juncture Jonas had ceased to be legally and financially involved although playbills were still headed as Messrs Jonas & Penley.

Penley wrote a desperate letter to Charles Knight the leading freeholder of the Windsor theatre, his distress reducing his writing to a scrawl which makes some words unreadable and his sentence structure awry.

Charles Knight Esq.

Dover Jan 4th 1822

Sir

I this morning rec'd yours and at your request send the lease
of the theatre as you wish it, tho under present circumstances
there could be no cause for it. I have rec'd a paper of a
demand for rent etc. Mr Jonas has likewise rec'd one, but
cannot tell what it means, as I have mentioned to you in a
former letter the occasion of my confinement and that I have
no other means to clear myself than to take the Act and leave
my several estates in the hands of my creditors – I now beg
to inform you, that I cannot be from this Place till the 27th
inst. after then I with all speed wait upon you at Windsor and
trust that you will intercede with the gentlemen to let me
have the theatre again and I doubt not that the arrears will be
paid after a little time – you and the other gentlemen must be
certain of the ill success we have had during the Kings illness
and the absence of the royal party. The last season, if the
princess had been at Windsor would have no doubt that her
patronage would have enabled us to made everything clear
and as I have <u>her</u> promise do all in her Person to serve me
and family I think that her attendance will enable me to make
amends to every one at Windsor – as I said before I trust
some friends will come forward to assist me when I get from
this and I hope you will not make any arrangement till I have
the pleasure in seeing you.

I am sir yours etc

S. Penley

P.S. will esteem it a favour if you will send the enclosed as
directed and one of [?] papers on Sunday

Penley was obliged to surrender his leases, and no doubt raised sufficient
money to pay his debtors at least a percentage of the amount owed. If he
could keep at least one theatre he could continue in business, but all had to
go if he was to 'plead the act', which is what he was obliged to do to avoid
a long imprisonment. He was released on 3 February 1822 by the
Insolvent Debtors Court.

The advantage of the 1813 act was that a man could not be re-
arrested for the same debt even if that debt remained. Even so, Penley was
now penniless with a wife and children to support. It was a time to take
stock. No doubt he, himself, could have obtained work in other
companies; it was commonplace for theatrical managers to go bust. There

was no disgrace, everyone in the early days of the 19th century knew they were in a precarious financial position and had to be prepared for boom or bust conditions. Even in the 21st century, 92% of the acting profession is out of work at any one time, fortunately cushioned by modern social security methods unknown to Penley and his colleagues.

It is a fact that most theatre managers in the 17th and 18th centuries died in impoverished circumstances. Unlike businesses today, they did not cream off profits in good years and bank them, but ploughed them back into their companies and carried on. As a result they never seemed to realise when they were losing money until it was too late, assuming it was merely yet another dip and business would pick up again. One of the few successful managers of the time was the formidable Mrs Sarah Baker who, when she died in 1816, left theatres and other investments totalling £15,000, roughly a £1million in today's money.

So what was Penley to do now? Fortunately, Sampson Jr was off his hands and doing well at Drury Lane, and Montague, too, was making his own way as scenic artist, actor and painter. He was still responsible for William, now or shortly to be twenty-one, Belville not yet fourteen and his three unmarried daughters Phoebe (27), Rosina (26) and Emma (17). He must have thought it regrettable that his elder daughters had not yet found husbands so that he was no longer bound to support them. In fact, they were not a liability, but one of Penley's remaining strengths as both were competent actresses capable of playing leading roles and, as such, obviated the necessity of hiring actresses from outside the family.

For Penley was not giving up his profession as actor-manager. Just as in 1814 he ventured on to the Continent, he did so again. Since the peace, English actors had travelled back and forth over the Channel and there is reason to believe that J & P had carried out an amount of business previously at Calais and Boulogne, both possessing run-down theatres. A guide called *Sketches of Ancient and Modern Boulogne* published in 1826 states: 'The Theatre of Boulogne is a most wretched building.' Both towns had large ex-pat populations – some 1800 English in the latter town – largely because the cost of living was much cheaper than in England. It was also a time-honoured method for people with financial problems to flee to France where they could not be touched. Penley fought on!

SCENE FOURTEEN
1822
PARIS

AN INTRIGUING ITEM in the *Literary Gazette* of 20 July 1822 carried the news that Mr Penley, who had successfully tried a similar experiment in Brussels, Calais, Boulogne etc, was the projector of a plan to present a series of performances of plays in Paris by an English company which would be patronised by the British Ambassador at the French Court. Actors said to be engaged included Dowton, Knight and Miss M Tree, negotiations pending with others including Charles Kemble and Oxberry.

As far back as 1814, when Penley had established his company in Brussels, there had been clamours for an English Theatre to be established in Paris as, like Brussels, many ex-pats were residing there. However, at that time a published letter from France had printed this warning:

> So long as the number of English visitors to this capital shall continue as great as it is at present, an English Theatre may succeed; but . . . can only look to the British for support. . . . a Frenchman cannot be expected to enter it; . . . to revolt their bigoted attachment to the unities, and their equal abhorrence of anything strong, or of any thing low . . . of any thing natural. . . . What dramatic author have we who may claim the notice and patronage of a people, who possess in their own language, and in their own taste, such writers as Corneille and Voltaire, Moliere and Racine?

French intellectuals were wedded to the works of Racine and Corneille who penned classical tragedies written in alexandrines that observed the unities. Most had never heard of Shakespeare, the few who had, following in the steps of Voltaire, who decreed 'he was a man who wrote coarse and barbarous plays that would not be tolerated by even the lowest rabble in France' and 'Shakespeare is a savage with sparks of genius which shine in a horrible night.'

Parisians had never really seen Shakespeare at all, very few attempts at French versions had been tried; indeed, English plays in general were not widely known, especially during Napoleon's regime when he controlled the theatres, often by closing them altogether. Although the French were ignorant of our English theatre, there was a constant traffic in the reverse direction with French boulevard comedies and melodramas translated into

English for new works in London. The traffic was all one way, thus Penley's was truly a pioneering venture and a landmark in both English and French theatre. No English theatre company had visited a Paris theatre since 1603 when Elizabethan players, touring the continent, offended Parisians by performing plays in a venue other than the only theatre in the capital at that time.

In 1819, M Merle the manager of the Théâtre Porte-Saint-Martin in Paris had visited London as a tourist, and English managers also often visited Paris, so it is curious that, although a French company had been established in London for many years (from 1821 to 1828 occupying the very same Tottenham Street theatre that had been Penley's nemesis) nobody seems to have attempted to set-up an English company in Paris. Merle, having been to London, became quite an Anglophile, introducing to his theatre boxers, cock fights, jugglers and other British imports, but never actors in an English play. He never stopped extolling the wonders of London to his friends. Merle thought that English actors and their plays had much to offer the French, and would be appreciated by Anglophiles.

Thus in July 1822, when Sampson Penley sought to appear in Paris, Merle, full of enthusiasm for English theatre, agreed to engage his troupe for six performances providing he received permission from the authorities. Penley wrote to the British Ambassador Sir Charles Stuart respectfully requesting that he intervened on Penley's behalf to solicit the necessary authorisation. Penley pointed out the respectability of his players, and the fact that his company was regularly patronised by the royal family at Windsor. He did not, of course, mention that he had just lost the theatre there, together with all the rest of his leases. Permission was granted providing he notified the chief of police and furnished details of the works to be presented.

One of the successes of Talma, France's leading actor, was in a rare French version of Shakespeare's *Othello*, so Sampson Penley must have thought he was on to a winner when he planned to open with that play. On 31 July, long before the opening of the box office at the Théâtre Porte-Saint-Martin, a large impatient busy crowd gathered, and soon the vast auditorium, packed to the gallery, was far from able to admit all those who demanded entrance. The first night was a sell-out with droves of disappointed customers turned away. No doubt Penley was rubbing his hands together at the sight of the money flowing into the box office after his recent disastrous experiences, but in his wildest dreams could not have anticipated what was to happen.

Penley used the form of words he had always used abroad: 'By His Britannic Majesty's most humble servants will be performed the tragedy of *Othello* in five acts by the most celebrated Shakespeare.' This was unwise billing as to the French it was a double provocation to call Shakespeare 'the most celebrated' and to flaunt the patronage of the English king.

It acted as a red rag to a bull to the poets. They – providing tragedies for the Théâtre Français – thought that should this Shakespeare man be admired, their own work may be shown up as facile and feeble. A mutinous faction was assembled for the express purpose of driving the foreigners off the hallowed stages of France. The French writer Stendhal claimed 'a set of noisy fellows were seen moving about in the crowd before the opening of the doors, saying: "we must take care what they are about here. This Shakespeare, who wrote the play which is to be acted tonight, is one of the Duke of Wellington's *aides-de-camp*, and is protected by the Bourbons."'

Penley had not reckoned on the political passions which were flourishing everywhere in a continuing war with the English – lost on the battlefield – but now fought with the pen of the journalist.

The cast was billed as:

Othello

The Duke of Venice	Mr Penley
Brabantio	Mr Rutherford
Gratiano	Mr Papham
Ludovico	Mr Clifton
Montano	Mr Heathcot
Othello	Mr Barton
Cassio	Mr Juston
Iago	Mr Bromley
Roderigo	Mr Rothemberg
Antonio	Mr Wyatt
Lorenzo	Mr Bradshaw
Desdemona	Miss Rosina Penley
Emilia	Miss [Phoebe] Penley

Les Rendez-Vous

Quake	Mr Jonas
Captain Bolding	Mr Rothemberg
Smart	Mr [Joseph?] Jonas
Simon	Mr Wyatt
Lucretia	Miss N Gaskill
Sophia	Mrs Bromley
Rose	Miss Gaskill

Mr and Mrs Bromley, Wyatt and Clifton had all been recently at Windsor. Barton was 'a man of peculiar but considerable talent' from the Dublin theatre. Except for the family, the other names are new recruits. Rosina and Phoebe had played their respective roles previously at Windsor and elsewhere. The afterpiece *The Rendezvous* was a recent one-act operetta by Richard Ayton in which the principals are the three women. Neither of the Miss Penleys were singers, something of a handicap to a rising actress's career when so many afterpieces were musical. The role of Smart, which is little more than a bit part, was played at the premiere at London's English National Opera House by Mr Salter, J & P's ex-leading man. Here, in Paris, the part was assigned to Mr Jonas, probably Joseph, who for the past four years, had been employed at the Surrey Theatre in musical roles.

As soon as *Othello* started, hisses and whistling arose. Cries of 'Speak French! We will have nothing but French spoken here!' followed by interruptions and jokes. Abuse levelled at Barton, as Othello, completely stopped the piece, yet the actors struggled on towards the third act, the noise becoming unbearable. Fighting broke out in various parts of the pit, the actors cut the entire third and fourth acts to get to the smothering scene and the end; finally the stage was invaded and the actors forced to beat a retreat in chaos, followed by mayhem and riot.

Théâtre Porte-Saint-Martin in Paris which Penley thought would be his salvation but turned out to be another disaster.

In the circumstances it seems foolhardy that a further attempt should be made but Sampson, ever the optimist, proposed *The School for Scandal* for the second night. The idea being that a comedy, and not by Shakespeare, was thought likely to be more acceptable. Merle decided that if the prices of the seats were increased it would keep the rowdies away and they would have a more select and quieter audience purged of troublemakers, but, of course, the opposition took their tickets at any cost so they could once again go on racketing, booing, shouting, whistling and throwing things.

The School for Scandal was received no better than *Othello*. All sorts of projectiles – potatoes, eggs, coppers and clay pipes – were thrown at the unfortunate actors. Miss Gaskill was well-nigh blinded by one of the weighty copper two-penny pieces thrown at her with such force that she fainted.

Merle was not, however, totally unprepared on that second night and no sooner had the play and trouble started, the manager came out and asked if he had to continue the representation. Whereas on the first night that request had been answered with 'Oui', so the cruel persecution could continue, now the reply was 'Non, Non! Down with the English' from the outraged audience. Consequently, it was announced that two favourite French comedies would be given by French players in place of the advertised programme. French satisfaction and the honour of the country were safe. But that was not sufficient as, even after the English players had withdrawn, rioting broke out again preventing the French actors, too, from proceeding.

The audience was not only against the poor English actors, but were themselves in two rival factions, Bourbon supporters clashing with the Buonapartists. A squad of gendarmes that Merle had prudently standing by was then drawn up on the stage, whereupon they were assailed with broken seats and benches, the audience preparing to storm the stage. The officer commanded his men to prime and load, threatening to fire should the tumult continue, thus eventually bringing the rioters to their senses.

Even after all that, Penley was willing to subject his company to another attempt, which indicates the state of desperation he must have been in. The Chief of Police advised that before a third attempt be made the prices should be raised yet again, the attendance limited to a third of the capacity, and increased surveillance introduced. However, the minister who had given permission for the English company, ignoring this advice, banned further performances.

When news of the debacle filtered back to England the press were outraged:

> We should rejoice that no British Actor ever endeavoured to display his professional talents upon the Parisian boards; but this speculation having been tried and defeated by these shameful proceedings at the Porte Saint Martin, . . . degrades

still more deeply that contemptible, inhospitable, and ungrateful mob, who have so rudely carried their base passions into a public theatre; at the same time displaying an infamous disregard of their own country's reputation, and a cowardly spirit of insult to strangers.

Our readers will have perused with some surprise, and perhaps not without some emotions of indignation, the treatment which a company of English actors has experienced in Paris. This, too, among a people who call themselves the most polished of any in Europe! . . . London swarms with French and other foreign artists, of every kind, who are allowed to exercise their talents in whatever way they like, and where they prove that they have talents, reward and patronage are sure to follow. We hope this distinction will long continue, or at least that it will only cease by our example being adopted by our neighbours.

This horrifying and dangerous event must have been far worse than anything Sampson could have imagined or had endured previously, yet the following day he sent a letter to a Parisian newspaper claiming that the opposition to his company was by no means general, and the disorder caused by a minority prevented the remainder from assessing the quality of his company. He then did what managers have always done, and still do, in these circumstances; he claimed that he would engage stars for his future programme.

Of course, this was all whistling in the wind. After the fiasco, no London stars would risk their reputations, even if Sampson could afford them. So, rather than flee the city as is generally thought, Penley, driven from the Théâtre Porte-Saint-Martin, applied for permission to use a small private theatre in the Rue Chantereine. This application threw the whole French Cabinet into a dilemma and the point was debated at several meetings during which Sampson and his company had to cool their heels for a fortnight in expensive Paris hotels. Having been deprived of profits from the aborted season, and now with these extra unlooked-for expenses, they were in a beggarly position.

Le Miroir said: 'Sir Penley's company or any other must give up any idea of gaining a hearing in a public theatre in France.' The directors of the Théâtre Porte-Saint-Martin wrote to *Le Réveil*:

In making arrangements with the director of the English company for six performances of British dramatic masterpieces we thought that we would please the public; we were mistaken. Our one aim, our first responsibility being to please it, we had to halt the performances as soon as public opinion showed itself overwhelmingly. The ensuing events were out of our control.

Respectfully, Desserre and Merle, Joint Directors

Penley, having burned his boats in England, risking his all in France, was not going to be told by any insolent froggies that he must give up! In spite of all the bureaucracy, obstacles and indifference of the authorities, eventually Penley was given permission to open at the Théâtre Favart – a huge opera venue four times as large as required, and ruinously expensive to fit up. It appears this theatre was owned by the brother-in-law of the Minister of the Interior who wished to profit from the rental. However, another minister pointed out that the central situation of the Favart might attract further riots and disturbances, thus the pleadings of the English Ambassador were heeded and permission was granted to use the little private theatre. It is incredible to our modern ears that this matter should be considered worthy of government discussion at all, much less the amount of time devoted to its deliberation. However, this was the body that ruled that top French actor Talma must not walk about with his hands behind his back in a classical tragedy, because that was a typical stance of Napoleon!

So Penley rented the *salle* or hall in the Rue Chantereine where the performances were arranged on a private subscription basis, somewhat in the manner of what today we would call a club theatre. The season opened on 20 August.

> The Vandals have disappeared; the representations in the Rue Chantereine are now attended by true Frenchmen, and never will it enter into the imaginations of Frenchmen, that is, of men belonging to the most civilised, the most generous nation in the world, to stone actors and actresses to death, because they say 'heart' instead of 'coeur'; and 'love' in place of 'amour'. . . . The actors of Mr Penley's Company are very superior to what they were at first supposed; to be convinced of this, it is sufficient to listen to them with attention, and to consider all the disadvantages of the circumscribed space in which they represent pieces which would require continual changes of scene.

The *Gazette de France* reported on the opening night:

> An audience more select than numerous, could only afford Mr Penley a moderate return, in a pecuniary point of view; but he was indemnified by the contrast which this assemblage of distinguished persons, the true representatives of French urbanity and politeness, presented, to the band of stupid,

contemptible persons, who displayed their *patriotism and national spirit* in the pit of a Porte St Martin. The performances for this night are, Sheridan's comedy of *The School for Scandal*, and the comic opera of *Rosina.*

The room was cramped and lacked the most indispensable accessories, making difficult the performance of plays that required involved sets, yet the troupe somehow managed to present the Shakespearean tragedies *Romeo and Juliet*, *Richard III*, *Macbeth* and *Hamlet*, Rowe's tragedy *Jane Shore*, melodramas *The Castle Spectre* and *Guy Mannering* and several comedies, including the classics *The School for Scandal* and *The Taming of the Shrew*, plus *The Honeymoon*, etc. with a dozen different afterpieces. Lacking the normal facilities to be found in the theatres of the time, the performances were probably nearer to true Shakespearean conditions, 'two boards and a passion' or concert performances.

The Parisians really eager to learn about English drama, especially Shakespeare, were regularly present, but in small numbers, while the English fans were even more rare. Stendhal, the French writer who championed Shakespeare against Racine and Corneille, loudly encouraged these performances, and the usual audience, consisting largely of men of letters, did not fail any occasion to applaud the actors. Of all the company, Rosina Penley, proving to be a hit with the intelligentsia, became a favourite with the French.

It remained a struggle in the wretched little *salle* in the Rue Chantereine, as all the better class of Parisians – more likely to support the venture – left town for summer, a winter season would have fared better. By the end of August, with audiences building, *La Réveil* suggested that in time the English players may become a vogue. Even though the conditions were primitive, the performances continued until 25 October. Penley then requested an extension of stay and permission to give two performances a week in the Louvois room. It was not the desertion of his audience that closed Penley's English theatre, he fully intended to carry on through the winter. The request unfortunately coincided with a clamp-down by the stern and over-zealous censors on all cultural activities, including newspapers and booksellers; Penley's request was not granted.

Sampson's company, even though performing as a subscription theatre, was closed down. In spite of great difficulties, they had managed to present a representative repertoire of English theatre for several weeks. The resolute Sampson Penley had struggled along suffering all the *merde* thrown at him by the French but, as he was dependent on the authorities' express permission, he was compelled to throw in the towel. One can only admire and wonder at his dogged spirit; it can only be that from a child touring with his mother he had had a lifetime of struggle, and had, in his time, battled against greater odds.

It is unfortunate that Rosina could not have remained in Paris to expand on her obvious success, as a less gifted but more beautiful actress was to do a few years hence.

Five years later an English company of players from Drury Lane and Covent Garden was established at the Théâtre Favart attracting audiences from the highest social and literary circles, briefly becoming the fashion of intellectual Paris as Charles Kemble followed by a succession of London's top stars came in turn. A third-rate actress from Drury Lane called Harriet Smithson, was promoted to leading roles, becoming a major star on the strength of her beauty and her mad scene as Ophelia. The modish and the chic adopted the fashion called *à la folle*, which comprised a black veil and wisps of straw woven into the hair, and Miss Smithson became the toast of Paris, to be wooed and won by the composer Berlioz. The fashion for English theatre – lasting all of ten months – petered out as soon as our major stars declined to fag across the Channel. A further attempt was made by Macready in 1846 which again was briefly fashionable, but was not allowed to continue more than a few weeks.

It is true that the English style of acting was so welcomed that it completely overturned the moribund classical French declamatory method, and it may have been the company headed by Charles Kemble and Harriet Smithson that eventually popularised English theatre in France, but it was undoubtedly the pioneering ramshackle Jonas & Penley Company of Comedians who first introduced it to modern Paris.

That was not much consolation to Sampson Penley in 1822. All he knew was – irrespective of the quality of his company or lack thereof – he was not given a fighting chance, and the bigoted Parisians were simply taking revenge on the English actors for the success of the English army at Waterloo. Penley's Parisian adventure thus ended in ignominious failure.

Sampson Penley returned to Calais where a bigger blow awaited him. His son William had fallen prey to that 19th century scourge of young adults – tuberculosis. Starting his showbusiness career as a boy singing comic songs, William had progressed to playing young men roles alongside his brother Montague in the family troupe, his singing – no longer confined to comedy material – continuing to be an asset. The fact that William was not included in the cast in Paris was ominous. William died of 'rapid consumption' and was interred at Calais on 28 October 1822 aged 21, three days after the last Paris performance.

It had been truly an *annus horribilis* for Sampson Penley. But the year was not yet over, and Penley launched a short season of plays in Calais. It is not clear when the season opened, but an extant playbill for 8 November 1822 indicates that Jonas, Mrs Beynon, Phoebe and Rosina, together with the players from Paris were still resolutely plying their trade in the old warhorse *Wives As They Were and Maids as They Are*. The season ended on 20 November with *Isabella; or The Fatal Marriage* for the benefit of Penley and his daughters, followed by *Raising the Wind* with, somewhat surprisingly, the lead role of Jeremy Diddler played by Montague Penley – 'his First Appearance at this theatre.' Why he should suddenly appear out of the blue on the last night of the season is inexplicable, unless he had come to assist in getting the company back to England.

For while there is little concrete evidence that Penley or Jonas appeared on a stage in their home country ever again, two isolated press advertisements from the archives of the *Kentish Express* indicate that this was so. Though in his parlous financial position it appears hardly credible, Penley returned to England to re-open the Dover theatre. On 19 November it was announced:

THEATRE, DOVER
MR PENLEY
RESPECTFULLY announces to the Inhabitants,
Visitants, and public in general, of the vicinity, that
he returns from Paris for the purpose of OPENING the
above THEATRE
On SATURDAY next, the 23rd instant
when will be performed, the popular Comedy of
THE WONDER;
with an afterpiece, translated from the French, entitled
THE SECRET
Or, Hole in the Wall.
The Theatre will continue OPEN every EVENING
during the period of the FAIR ONLY, and will be
produced in succession, a selection of the most popular
Plays, Farces, Melo-Dramas etc;
Boxes 3s – Pit 2s – Gallery 1s

As no further information has been found, it must be assumed that this short season during the fair took place. The company closed at Calais on the 20 November, and the Dover fair season opened on 23rd, so it is almost certain that the entire troupe returned home to fulfil this limited engagement.

A further advertisement was carried in the newspaper on 24 December using the same formula 'Mr Penley respectfully announces to the Inhabitants, Visitants, and public in general, of the vicinity, that he returns from Paris for the purpose of opening the above theatre,' this time for a season opening on 26 December. The implication is that Penley had been back to France after the fair, returning to launch a proper season in Dover. The plays to be given on the opening night were *Jane Shore* and *Perouse*. All of Penley's daughters could have been in the company as there is no trace of them elsewhere at that time. *Jane Shore* was Rosina's big success in Paris.

SCENE FIFTEEN
1823 AND AFTER
FAREWELL

THERE HAVE BEEN many gaps in relating the story of Jonas and Penley, but always ahead some thread waving in the breeze has been found to tie up the preceding loose end, enabling a coherent narrative to be given even with the numerous omissions. The previous year was full of painful events, but now we are faced not with gaps, but a huge void. There are no journals or letters – rare enough in the heyday of J & P – no new playbills. Only very isolated hints to be gleaned from a handful of different sources indicate that Sampson Penley survived.

Other than the two Dover advertisements to contradict the assumption, Sampson Penley looks to have gone out of business. That is until we get another glimpse of the man back in France. Penley was still roaming the continent in November 1823, a report in *Le Diable Boiteaux* stating 'The troupe of English actors, which was so unpopular a year ago at the Théâtre de la Porte Saint Martin, is now giving performances at Dunkirk. M Penley is still the director of the strolling actors.' The link with the Paris debacle was going to cling to Penley for some time.

A playbill dated 17 November 1823, proclaiming the second night of the season, advertises Penley's troupe appearing at Dunkirk in *She Stoops to Conquer*. Penley himself is playing Hardcastle, the irreplaceable Mrs Beynon plays his wife, and Jonas is the awkward servant Diggory. Miss Jonas is also in cast, but which one of Jonas's several daughters cannot be categorically stated. The other names are all new. Phoebe is not in the company, neither is Rosina who was engaged throughout most of 1823 on the York circuit.

In 1862, at the age of seventy, two years before he died, Thomas Colley Grattan, prolific author, intimate of great men, confidant of foreign royalty, and former diplomat to the USA, wrote his memoirs in which there are two references to the Penley family. He was at Valenciennes in 1816 when the 'charming actresses' the Penley sisters and Miss Jonas were appearing at the English theatre there, and he was living in Boulogne in the summer of 1824 when we next hear of Sampson Penley.

Grattan had a surprise visitor in the shape of his old friend the eminent actor Edmund Kean who, after holidaying in Paris with his wife, was waiting for the signal for the departure of the ferry home, their baggage having already being taken aboard.

'While he hastily gave me this sketch of his situation, an old actor, Penley, well-known in France and Flanders, who was at that time, with his company, proving their *familiarity* with Shakespeare by taking considerable liberties with him in Boulogne, rang at my door having traced Kean to my house.' After this rather snide remark, Grattan goes on to tell how Penley, moaning about his misfortune and ill-luck, many hardships etc, besought Kean to act for them, offering half the receipts. Kean pleaded fatigue, but Penley pressed and beseeched until Kean, who had a soft heart, agreed to stay the night. No doubt Sampson played on the fact that his son Sam Jr was a colleague of Kean in the Drury Lane company. The town was papered with advertising, and that night Kean played Shylock to double prices and a packed house. The receipts 'staved off Penley's misfortune and helped his company for many days to come.' Kean did not even take his payment, dividing his share of the profits between the rest of the company. Kean was quite cavalier about money. Although screwing inordinate sums from managers, he was lavishly generous to drinking pals, and a soft touch for charitable causes. Once when accosted by 'a half-starved Negro', the famous actor sought through his pockets for money and, finding none, handed the beggar his coat.

Grattan does not appear to have connected Penley, the old impoverished actor, with the charming actresses he had admired at Valenciennes in 1816. Neither does he date the event more clearly, making all the more tantalising a paragraph in the *Theatrical Observer* announcing the plays and cast at Boulogne Theatre for 9 August 1824, which were *The Wheel of Fortune* and *Rosina*. Among the company are Mr Penley, Miss M Jonas and the J & P stalwart Mrs Beynon. The stage manager is Serle, presumably the same Serle who was in the Windsor company for Sampson Penley in 1820. 'The whole under the direction of Mr Smithson' the brother of Harriet Smithson the actress who, in 1827, was to beguile all Paris. We cannot be sure of which Mr Penley we have here, but it is almost certainly Sampson himself as he has clearly lost the Boulogne venue to Smithson.

Even more intriguingly, in Oxberry's *Dramatic Biography* – in a eulogy of Miss Smithson – is reproduced a playbill for Boulogne for 9 October when the actors are: Williams, Barry, Roberts, Clifford, Colepoys, Hives, Smith, Penley, Jones and Barton. Actresses: Miss Emery, Miss Walpole, Mrs Beynon and Miss Jonas. Visiting stars from Drury Lane are Wallack and Miss Smithson.

Oxberry states: 'Some of the persons, whose names appear in it, belonged to the company that Penley took to Porte St Martin.' The only names that fit that statement are Penley himself, Barton – the Othello on that occasion – and Mrs Beynon. Clifford and Clifton may be the same man, as the two extant playbills for Penley's Calais company have a Mr Clifford on one and a Mr Clifton on the other. Barry was not in the Paris company, but was in Penley's Dunkirk troupe.

For a manager to give up his company to another, and then be found included on the acting strength of the new subsequent company was by no means rare. In the coming years it happened constantly as more and more actor-managers found the managing part not only onerous, but financially disastrous. If Penley resorted to this tactic, he was only one of many who sloughed off financial cares, settling for ekeing out a living as a £1-a-week actor.

That the same troupe from Boulogne and Calais also appeared at Brussels is clearly shown when Serle, making his debut the following year as Hamlet at Covent Garden, – 'almost the only thing not wanted at this theatre' – was billed as 'from the English theatre at Brussels, first time in an English theatre.' It was not, of course, as he had appeared at Windsor five years previously, but it was no doubt not politic to draw attention to that. Serle was following exactly the same path as Sam Jr ten years previously – and probably for much the same reason – using the status as leading man abroad as a lever to gain acceptance in London, as we read in the *Theatrical Observer*:

> Boulogne English Theatre – Mr Smithson, the proprietor of this Theatre, has conducted it with great spirit, although he has not been so successful as he deserved. Mr Wallack and Mr J Knight have been acting here, and the charming Miss Smithson engaged for a few nights. Many of our best Comedies and farces have been respectably acted.

From now on it is a land of surmise, speculation and conjecture, for the last concrete evidence of Sampson Penley is this remarkable item in the *Times* of 22 December 1825:

> A delicacy for the breakfast-table, which is exhibited for sale at most shell shops in town, denominated Isle of Wight potted shrimps, is prepared at Calais by Penley, the actor, father of the individual of that name at Drury Lane Theatre. The traffic in this fresh stimulus for English gourmands is, we understand very considerable.

Though Penley is still described as an actor, it looks as though he is now chiefly in the catering trade, and with this bizarre statement the trail goes stone cold.

At some point Mr and Mrs Sampson Penley must have returned permanently to their native land as, on 10 April 1832, Sampson Penley died and was buried at Gravesend. He was sixty-seven years of age. In the spring of his days this indomitable man had chosen one of the most exacting of professions – that of a country actor-manager. Not for him the settled existence of belonging to a London company like his brother William, with a permanent home and a life like normal people. His life-style meant he was constantly on the move, staying in one place for no more than a few weeks at a time before passing on to a new town, accompanied by a wife and large family to clothe, feed and educate. With his close relatives he built up his theatrical company and, for a number of years, had a circuit of theatres that provided entertainment on the doorstep of the many country people who could not, in those days, readily travel to large towns. With his children flying the nest, and times changing, Sampson had too many hard years, and one's heart goes out to him languishing in Debtors' Prison, emerging to face the struggle to keep his company going. The picture of his begging Kean to appear for him at Boulogne is pathetic. No doubt he should have quit much earlier than he did; no doubt he should have emulated Mrs Baker and salted money away in the good years. Perhaps he was stubborn, and thought he could succeed where others had failed, a common showbusiness belief that persists to the present day.

Was Sampson a good actor? Probably not. As he rarely played leads there are very few words about his prowess, but no doubt like brother William he could turn in a reasonable father or guardian and light comedy performance. He seldom acted at all in later life until times became tough and money tight. Was he a good manager? Probably not. The Jonas & Penley company was praised in the early days, being 'better performers than one would imagine' at Henley, gaining commendation for depositing £100 in the local bank for any claims against them, and 'their liberal and polite behaviour' excited the inhabitants of Maidstone. But as time progressed, it is likely that Sampson may have turned into one of the 'lovable rogues' that seem to blight the theatre world in all periods, with a trail of unpaid bills, Booth calling him a 'scoundrel'.

But his forays on to the continent immediately after the evacuation of Napoleon deserve credit for pioneering, and his attempt to bring English theatre to Paris for the first time should be recognised as a landmark in both English and French theatre history.

His widow Mrs Sampson Penley née Lucy Finch departed this life on 5 December 1836, 'after a lingering illness endured with patience and resignation'; she was sixty-five. One can only conjecture what kind of woman she was, to live with a husband whose profession as a travelling theatre manager must have been one of the most precarious of professions, even in those unsettled days. She gave birth to at least eight children within 16 years, all born while the company toured its circuit of country theatres in the south-east, bringing them up whilst constantly on the road. Her husband never attained the status of a London actor like his brother William, and she must have been very relieved when her eldest son became a regular in the company at Drury Lane. Sampson, at the end of his life, lurched from crisis to crisis as he tried to keep his company together. One imagines Lucy resignedly packing up, time after time, as the Penley troupe moved on in search of a new audience. As the family grew up and branched out, one wonders if she yearned for them to find a more settled respectable career, for, as we shall see, when she died all her surviving children were still active in the theatrical industry.

And what of John Jonas? The partner and brother-in-law of Sampson Penley went through all the vicissitudes of an actor-manager, yet remains a person in the shadows. His name appears on many existing J & P playbills, but is rarely on press advertisements except under the expression 'Messrs Jonas and Penley beg leave most respectfully to announce . . .' because he seldom played principal roles. He lost his wife far too early, and we can only conjecture that he found love a second time.

John Jonas probably retired from acting and managing after the Paris debacle, becoming a teacher of the violin and, when he died suddenly of bronchitis on 11 March 1847 at Walham Green at the age of eighty-one, his death certificate listed that as still being his occupation.

RIP

Sampson Penley 1765 to 1832

Lucy Penley c1770 to 1836

John Jonas c1766 to 1847

Mary Jonas 1769 to 1812

The most famous person buried at Gravesend – in the chancel of old St George's church which burned down in 1727 – is the Indian princess Pocahontas. The graveyard surrounding the rebuilt parish church of St George had become full by the latter part of the 18th century, and in 1788 extra ground was acquired for an extension known as Woodville. It was there where the grave and headstone of the Penleys could be found.

However, the whole of the St George's graveyards were closed for new burials in 1855, and Woodville was turned into gardens. Now in the 21st century, this garden area has been altered again to form the paved Civic Square in front of the Civic Centre. The remains of Pocahontas are long lost, but skateboarding youths must be exercising their skill over the bones of Mr & Mrs Sampson Penley and their daughter Phoebe. It is fortunate that a transcription of the gravestones was made in 1913:

> HERE REST THE REMAINS OF SAMPSON PENLEY WHO DEPARTED THIS LIFE APRIL 10TH 1832 AGED 67. ALSO OF LUCY HIS WIFE WHO DEPARTED THIS LIFE DECEMBER 5TH 1836 AGED 65. IN WHOSE MEMORY THEIR AFFECTIONATE CHILDREN HAVE CAUSED THIS HUMBLE TABLET TO BE RAISED. RECORDING LIKEWISE THAT OF THEIR SONS WILLIAM PENLEY WHO DIED AND WAS INTERRED AT CALAIS OCTOBER 28TH 1822 AGED 21. ALSO SAMPSON PENLEY WHO EXPIRED SUDDENLY AT PARIS MAY 27TH 1838 AGED 44. WHERE HIS REMAINS ARE DEPOSITED. AN ANGELS ARM CAN SNATCH US FROM THE GRAVE, LEGIONS OF ANGELS CAN'T CONFINE US THERE. TO THE ABOVE REMAINS ARE ADDED THOSE OF PHEBE PENLEY, DAUGHTER OF SAMPSON & LUCY PENLEY WHO DIED ON THE 17TH OF JUNE 1842 AGED 46 YEARS.

The story of the Penley actor-managers continues as the lives of their children are successively revealed, but first we look back at the same time span already recounted, from the very different aspect of the parallel career of Sampson's brother William Penley and his wife. For many years William was an actor in the Drury Lane company; his family was granted an unusual boon by the Queen of England and, compared to the average actor of the time, he died a rich man of property.

ACT TWO

MR W PENLEY

'high in the estimation of the town'

and

'that deserving actress'

MRS W PENLEY

SCENE ONE
1798 - 1801
EXETER AND WEYMOUTH

IN LATE 18TH CENTURY Oxford there was a movement to clear the streets of untidy, messy and unsavoury market stalls which offended contemporary sensibilities, and provided an effective barrier to traffic. These street markets, dating from medieval times, were finally condemned in 1771 to be replaced by a new market in the city for the sale of meat, fish, poultry, herbs and vegetables.

William Penley, younger brother of Sampson, was born in Market Street, Oxford Market on 28 May 1773, but not baptised until 12 March 1788 at St Marylebone, London.

In 1791, at the age of eighteen, William married Frances Mary Anne Saulez. She was nineteen, daughter of an English mother and a French father, and does not appear to have been an actress prior to marrying William, although she surely had talent – as will be seen. The newly-weds joined the Jonas & Penley Company of Comedians. William and Frances's family soon expanded with three children:

William Henry Saulez Penley (born on 4 August 1793)

George Frederick Penley (19 May 1795)

Frances Mary Ann Penley (16 March 1797)

The earliest J & P playbill extant shows Mr W Penley and Mrs W Penley playing leading roles at Henley-on-Thames on 16 January 1798 in *Everyone Has His Fault* and *The Irishman in London*. But later in the year, leaving the family concern, they secured an engagement with Mr Hughes's Company of Comedians on the Exeter circuit. They must have expected this to be a more favourable engagement than the one they had just left, but they could not possibly have seen that the Queen of England herself, stepping into their family affairs, would actively promote the future of one of their small sons with an astonishing boon that could never have been dreamed of by a pair of itinerant actors.

Hughes led a respectable company from a theatre he had built some ten years previously, a pleasantly situated pretty red brick building with a columned portico running the full width of the front. Hughes had been a button-painter in Birmingham, given that up to become an actor and scene painter at Coventry and, by good fortune, ended up at Plymouth Dock where he married the daughter of the theatre owner. On his father-in-law's death, Hughes took over the Exeter circuit which also included Salisbury and Weymouth, building up a powerful provincial presence and becoming part-owner of Sadler's Wells in London. On 17 May 1799, he also became the father-in-law of Joseph Grimaldi when his daughter Maria married the eminent clown.

George III, an unadventurous king, dutifully married a German princess, Charlotte of Mecklenberg-Strelitz, meeting her for the first time on their wedding day. Charlotte had never been to a theatre, and after George introduced her to Drury Lane she immediately became as keen a theatregoer as her husband. The couple became regular visitors to the seaside town of Weymouth, first visiting in 1789, and every year thereafter until 1805. George was very popular with the locals who, to mark the fiftieth year of his reign, in 1810 erected a statue at the end of the Esplanade which is there to this day. Unlike most statues, this one is painted in bright colours and, while George appeared to be a solemn sort of chap, he did have a childlike wonder about many things, and a painted statue seems singularly appropriate.

George loved the theatre wherever he was and regularly visited plays in London, Windsor and, when on holiday, at Weymouth. Hughes had great respect for the king, not least because his presence was always a boost for business. The actors loved him too, and George regarded the lowly thespians kindly.

An especial favourite of the king at Weymouth was the low comedian Mr Goddard. George's taste in humour was not very elevated. Towards the end of the season, as was the custom in theatres throughout the land, each of the leading performers took a benefit in turn. The time had come for Goddard's benefit but, unfortunately, the king had to leave that day to return to London to open Parliament. Goddard was distraught, as the absence of the king would have a devastating effect on the numbers attending and mean a heavy loss for him. With great misgivings, Goddard sought an audience with the king, which was granted. George, in his kindest manner, told the comedian not to worry, he would remain and attend. The king saw the show, afterwards travelling through the night rather than disappoint a poor country actor.

It appears travelling through the night was not unusual, although it seems very odd for a king in the days when roads were bad and lighting non-existent, but one press report detailing the annual trip to Weymouth states:

> Their Majesties and the Royal Family, in their journey to Weymouth, on Sunday night next, will stop at Hartford Bridge, and take a repast by way of supper; after which they will continue their route to Weymouth, where it is expected they will arrive soon after nine on Monday morning.

The king and queen saw a lot of Mr and Mrs W Penley during their summer holiday in Weymouth, as they went to the theatre three or four times a week. They graced William's benefit night in October 1798 when the pieces given were *The Jew* and *The Purse*. Between the two, William gave a dissertation on *Hobby-Horses* describing every hobby, which all characters ride through life, concluding with his own hobby. Mr Fisher gave an address on Nelson's victory at the Battle of the Nile. The band of the Berkshire Militia played *God Save the King*, in which the full company joined, followed by *Rule Britannia*. A transparency of Britannia trampling Anarchy and Rebellion underfoot was shown, and oak and laurel wreaths were worn by the Royal Family, nobility and 'even the comedians'. It must have been quite a gala occasion celebrating the kingdom's victory at sea.

The Penleys were back the following year 1799 when, for their benefit at Weymouth, the queen commanded the play *The Way to Get Married* and the farce *My Grandmother*. The assumption, in the lack of concrete evidence, is that the Penleys were also re-engaged by Hughes for 1800. Some time around then Frances gave birth to her fourth child, a daughter the couple named Catherine. She was more fortunate than her employer's daughter, as on 18 October Maria Grimaldi née Hughes died in childbirth; by 1805, from his large family Hughes was to lose three of his daughters.

The Penleys were certainly re-engaged by Hughes in 1801, when his principal players were Mr Sandford and Mr Liston. Sandford was a local favourite who had a long career without leaving the south-west circuits. John Liston had made his first appearance on the stage at Weymouth, showing a humorous personality that encouraged him to specialise in old men and country bumpkins. He was soon to go on to better-class work than Mr Hughes could offer, becoming a big star for many years, but back in 1801 he was merely a local favourite. Hughes himself rarely performed, confining himself to management, though, with the assistance of other artists, he still painted scenery, and his productions were noted for their backcloths.

Hughes's company started the circuit at Exeter, running from the beginning of the year until the middle of April. Many country managements relied on spicing up their long seasons by introducing guest artistes from London and the major provincial patent theatres. Hughes was no exception, and for several weeks the famous clown Dubois – with his apprentices – was engaged. For Dubois's benefit, he and his pupils gave 'Wonderful Performances consisting of Extraordinary Manoeuvres of Strength and Agility called *The Polandric Exercises.*' If that were not excitement enough, Master J Bland gave a display of Extraordinary Feats on the slack-rope 'which excel all other Exhibitions of the Kind ever offered to the Public' followed by a new pantomime ballet dance called *The Woodmen of the Alps* in which Mr and Mrs Penley took part, and a blindfold Dubois did a hornpipe in wooden shoes upon a stage bestrewn with eggs avoiding breaking any. This was a popular stunt of the period.

One night in February another Penley was brought to the stage. *The Stranger* with Mr Penley as Peter and Mrs Penley as Charlotte, also had Master Penley as the five-year-old Son of the Stranger. William and Frances Penley had two sons, and this one, being only slightly over the correct age, would most likely be their second son George Frederick. The boy's role is a non-speaking part, but young George must have been particularly beguiling in view of what happened a few months later. The play was followed by more feats on the slack-rope by Master J Bland, the whole show ending with a new pantomime called *The Witches of the Rocks* with Penley as Harlequin, Mrs Penley as Columbine. The Penleys were nothing if not versatile.

Though by no means amongst the first-rank principal actors, the Penleys were well thought of by their employer, and used to advantage in a whole host of varied supporting roles. As the season approached the end, the evenings provided one benefit after another as each of the company took their turn. Unusually, the company turned to Shakespeare for Mr Sandford's benefit, that gentleman playing the lead role in *Hamlet* with Penley in the small role of Osricke. It is clear that William preferred, or was cast in, comedy roles rather than dramatic ones.

Penley's own benefit followed and, whereas all the previous players had announced that their benefit play had been bespoken by some patron, the statement heading William's advertisement does seem to have a whiff of pathos clinging to it:

> Mr Penley presents his duteous Respects to the Ladies and Gentlemen of Exeter, and its environs, hopes (as he has not had the Honour of gaining any particular Patronage) the pieces he has selected for his night will meet their

Approbation and Indulgence, and assures them, that nothing in his power shall be wanting to render the Evening's Performance agreeable.

In *The Jew and the Doctor*, William gave his Abednego the Jew, with Mrs Penley as Emily. Then came 'An occasional Prologue written by Mr Dryer to be spoken (for this night only) by Mr Penley riding ON AN ASS.' Mr Dryer being William's landlord, he probably supplied the ass as well as the text. Both Penley brothers seem to have thought that speaking while sitting on an ass was hilarious, as they turned to this ploy on more than one occasion. William was certainly giving his audience its money's worth as he now offered a musical farce *The Apparition*, concluding with 'a whimsical Pantomimical Entertainment as performed upwards of fifty nights at Sadlers-Wells Theatre called *Blue-beard, Black-beard, Red-beard and Grey-beard; or Harlequin Skipper.*' Penley was Harlequin Skipper, Mrs Penley his Columbine.

Whilst a leading actor at a major theatre could specialise in tragedy, the comedy of manners, or even low comedy, the lesser lights in country venues had to be able to turn their hand to whatever was required, be it Shakespeare, Congreve or pantomime. At the very time William was showing off his prowess to the good folks of Exeter, a ten-year-old boy called Master Carey appeared before George III after being summoned from his usual surroundings of a fairground booth while at Windsor. His mother and his manager were in despair as the boy had no suitable clothing to wear before his monarch and, it being Sunday, all the shops were closed. Fortunately, finding a Jewish clothier open, they were able to buy a suit and the decently clad Master Carey duly appeared at Windsor Castle. The king kept the lad reciting for two hours, then despatched him clutching two guineas. As the boy grew up learning his craft, he became renowned more for his acrobatic Harlequin than his Shakespeare, but achieved final fame as the eminent tragedian Edmund Kean.

The Exeter season came to an end on 20 April 1801 and the last night was Frances Penley's benefit. It was not unusual for the lesser lights in a company to have to be at the end of the queue as, with the public's support for benefits waning as they progressed, the top dogs wanted to get in first. However, normally the very last night was reserved for the manager who gained a full house and made a closing speech peppered with grovelling compliments to his patrons. It would appear that Mrs W Penley was more highly regarded than her husband, as the local newspaper carried this paragraph a few days prior to the event:

> After a long and, we trust, not an unprofitable season, the
> Exeter Theatre closes with a Play and Farce, for the benefit of
> that deserving actress Mrs Penley, on Monday next. . . .
> Among those whose endeavours to please the public have
> been particularly conspicuous; we cannot hesitate to say Mrs
> Penley stands foremost – her exertions in every department
> of Theatrical Representation, have been unremitted, and with
> a private character strictly unblemished, she does credit to the
> Patronage she has received, and we doubt not but her benefit
> on Monday will amply compensate her for the constant
> attention she has shown to please a candid and liberal
> audience.

The benefit was 'Under the patronage of the Ladies of Southernhay Place'
and comprised *First Love; or the Female Emigrant* followed by William
repeating his comic song *The Country Club* 'and by particular desire of
several Ladies and Gentlemen who were present at Mr Penley's benefit he
will repeat the Epilogue spoken on that night Riding on an Ass.' (When in
doubt sit on an ass!) The whole evening concluded with *Fortune's Frolic; or
the Ploughboy Made a Lord* with Penley as Robin Roughhead, and Frances as
Dolly.

It is interesting to note that the newspaper considers that Mrs Penley
should gain support not only for her unremitting exertions, but for a
strictly unblemished private character. One would think that with four
young children and a husband permanently at her side the opportunities to
be blemished must have been very limited.

With the troupe's arrival at Weymouth, timed by Hughes to coincide
with the king's annual visit,

> Their Majesties honoured the theatre with their presence; the
> house was full of company, and the comedy of *Speed the
> Plough*, and *Fortune's Frolic*, were well performed; in the
> play Mr Penley as Farmer Ashfield, and Mr Purser in the
> character of Evergreen, received much applause.

No doubt the choice of play – a new comedy in old rustic vein – hit the
mark with the king. The Royal Family honoured the theatre again when
they went to see *The Battle of Hexham*, a historical play wherein Master
Penley performed the character of the Prince to great applause.

On 9 September, the king and queen, after a pleasant excursion on
the water, went to see *A Bold Stroke for a Wife* and *The Devil to Pay* in which
Mr Bannister exerted his comic abilities and Mr Penley performed the part
of Simon Pure, for which he was applauded. Bannister was a leading
comedy actor of some repute. Hughes ensured he engaged some of the

king's favourite players during his stay, and established stars like Munden and Quick often guested for several days. As the king laughed and rejoiced in these well-known mirth-provoking faces he had seen many a time before, in Windsor and London, he would cry 'Bravo, Quick!' or 'Bravo, Suett!'

Although the country was at war with France, some holiday resorts continued developing, those patronised by royalty being the most favoured. Weymouth was becoming so popular it was bursting at the seams and a new development of 'forty-nine capital houses' called the Crescent was added to the east end of the Esplanade. This extended to the Pier, forming one of the 'most beautiful walks in the kingdom' being 2400 feet in length, with a chain along the inner side, and faced with Portland stone next to the sea.

Along with the parades along the promenade, pleasure cruises and theatre visits, on 1 August 1801 Queen Charlotte gave a fête at Radipole, a village on the outskirts of Weymouth which had a lake. This is now a nature reserve within the borough of Weymouth. The entertainment was arranged by Princess Elizabeth who went in advance of the royal party so that when they arrived their way would be 'strewn with flowers by Mrs Taylor and Mrs Penley the comedians, dressed as Country Girls'. The amusements commenced with Mr Taylor dressed as a sailor singing a sea-shanty, after which the comedians assumed the characters of gypsies seated under a hedge singing sprightly songs round a camp fire.

The royal family then enjoyed a sumptuous dinner in an elegant marquee, while six more tents were occupied by 200 members of the nobility tucking into a 'most elegant dinner, served up in a superb style.' While dining, Robert William Elliston the noted actor and a current favourite, in the character of a monk, announced the victory over Napoleon's Invincible Army, and songs and panegyrics were delivered. A military band struck up patriotic tunes, the National Anthem was sung, and the king's health toasted.

The royals then toured the fair which comprised milliners, toy shops, libraries and lottery offices. The king put into the lottery, and all the nobility bought something. The comedians, along with Elliston – now dressed as a naval officer – then delivered an exordium on British loyalty ending with Mr Taylor singing *Rule Britannia* and *God Save the King* (again). And where was William Penley in all this? 'A Mr Penley in the character of a Merry Andrew, rode about the fair seated on an ass, and his humour excited much pleasantry.' Well, if the ass routine has worked twice before why not use it again? A Merry Andrew is a kind of jester.

Princess Elizabeth had relied greatly on the services of Mr Hughes's Company of Comedians for the singing and entertainment aspects of this royal fête, and her mother Queen Charlotte must have been very grateful for the performers' contribution to the success of the event. Perhaps the queen thought some kind of bonus was in order? Perhaps she took pity on Mrs Penley having to labour on the stage with four young children in tow? Perhaps Frances confided she was pregnant again as another child was growing within her. Whatever the reason, the queen appears to have been particularly taken with the six-year-old George. What exceptional attributes this little boy gave forth is impossible to say; perhaps he was stunningly beautiful, perhaps she had wept to see him as the orphan child seeking his father in *The Stranger*? One wonders what especial charm George exuded to appeal to the queen to warrant him becoming her protégé. However, the little tot must have won the lady's heart, as a very unusual benefaction was granted by Queen Charlotte who, taking the little boy under her protection, placed him at the King's Grammar School, Sherborne to be educated with the sons of gentlemen. Why the nine-year-old William was not the one selected for this boon is a mystery, but what an amazing endowment this must have been to a pair of itinerant actors.

Sherborne School originated in the 8th century in connection with Sherborne Abbey, but the public school as known today was founded in 1550. The term 'public school' often baffles foreigners as they are the antithesis of that, being exclusive very expensive fee-paying boarding private colleges chiefly frequented by the great and good of the land. Pupils at Sherborne, Eton, Harrow and other public schools were the sons of the upper classes – often nobility – destined to be future officers and administrators of the British Empire. It is said that Waterloo was won on the playing fields of Eton. This may be an exaggeration, but we have seen how Eton College was able to dictate to the manager of the Windsor theatre when he was allowed to open and close.

One has to wonder how a small boy of theatrical parents was likely to thrive in such surroundings. Also one has to wonder about the contradiction within Queen Charlotte. Although loving the theatre, she naturally disapproved of her son the Duke of Clarence openly living with the popular actress Mrs Jordan. Her attitude to that was to remain aloof, but how could she ignore her own grandchildren, even if illegitimate, yet foster a child of an unknown actress?

SCENE TWO
1802 - 1805
RETURN TO J & P; and LIVERPOOL

In 1802, William and Frances returned to the family J & P company, probably in Folkestone during March, as there they had a fifth child, a new son, baptised in the name of Robert on 19 March. In the days before reliable contraception, it was an occupational hazard for actresses to cope with childbirth at regular intervals during their career. The great Mrs Sarah Siddons bore seven children, outliving five of them. The notorious Mrs Jordan bore 13 illegitimate children – ten with the Duke of Clarence – during her acting career, and Frances's sister-in-law Mary Jonas bore ten children during the 24 years she trailed round with the J & P company.

Present day actresses adopt the principle of carrying on working 'until it shows' but that was hardly economically possible in Georgian and Regency times, so audiences became used to seeing Juliets great with child, and similar nonsenses. Giving birth was a hazardous procedure even for well-off women in comfortable surroundings; Jane Austen lost four sisters-in-law to childbirth. How much more danger lurked for women in dubious lodgings with scant medical care, at a time when childbirth posed the greatest risk to a woman's health, and was the single most common cause of death with a known 20% mortality rate for the mother.

The death rate for children was double that, 45% of children dying before the age of twelve. It was a veritable triumph for one's sons and daughters to attain adulthood, but even then many young adults were slain by tuberculosis.

Tragically, the birth of Robert Penley was swiftly followed by the death of the two-year-old Catherine who was buried on 29 March also at Folkestone.

Later in the year, the seasons at Lewes and Eastbourne followed, where they were joined on a flying visit by George III's favourite actor John Quick. He had served for 30 years at Covent Garden creating many new roles including Tony Lumpkin in *She Stoops to Conquer*. On this occasion he gave his Scrub in *The Beaux Stratagem*, a part he had been playing for 25 years. In the afterpiece *Animal Magnetism* Quick's Doctor and Mr W Penley's Le Fleur 'kept the house in continuous laughter'.

The rare appearance of an acknowledged favourite star invariably boosted the audience figures, but a manager had to balance whether the increase in takings actually covered the extra salary demands of the star in question. Such problems were a regular headache for brother Sampson, but did not concern William as he was never part of the management, merely a hired actor.

The J & P company, as customary, moved on at the end of December and it was at Rye that the nine-month-old baby Robert was buried. Two babes lost within the year must demand great stoicism, especially when the mother has to carry on facing her public on the stage. That is what Frances did, because she had no option. At a charity performance of *Richard III* on the 4 January 1803 Mrs W Penley acted Lady Anne. William was not in the play, but gave one of his comic songs and took part in the afterpiece.

Battle followed in March, before the J & P company took up residence at Tenterden in May for several weeks. Mr W Penley was described as from the Theatre Royal, Weymouth, as were Mrs W Penley and Mrs Keys.

Mrs Keys stayed, but at the end of May William and Frances moved on to Liverpool where they were engaged in the company opening the newly built Theatre Royal there. A fine stone building with an elegant curved facade, it contained a horse-shoe shaped auditorium that held almost £400. This was a theatre for a modern city and a far cry from the tiny Tenterden theatre the Penleys had just left. The Liverpool lease had been acquired at £1500 per annum by Lewis and Knight. The season was arranged in an unusual manner: the summer months were headed by stars from London when the prices were 4/6, 2/6 and 1/6, after which the stars departed, leaving the resident company to perform in the winter months at reduced prices. Similarly, the wages paid in summer went as high as £4 a week, but only half that in winter.

Thomas Knight chose *Speed the Plough* for the opening of this brand-new theatre on 6 June 1803. Penley, although not in this play, played a leading role in the musical afterpiece *No Song, No Supper* being billed as 'his first Appearance on this Stage'.

William and Frances were chiefly employed in the afterpieces for the first couple of months, and as performances were usually on alternate evenings they were not over-worked. Their work load increased as the season wore on and the managers realised they needed to reduce their expenses. William had a few up-market roles in the main play from time to time – Scrub in *The Beaux Stratagem*, Verges in *Much Ado About Nothing* and Fluellen in *Henry V* for example – but he was destined for low-life and comedy parts.

William took second place to Charles Mathews the First Low Comedy man, but gained a reputation for considerable humour and original merit, his playing of 'Dr Ollapod, Scrub, Tandem, Caleb Quotem, Isaac Mendoza, Spado, Ralph, and Frederick Willinghurst raising him high in the estimation of the town. . . . Mrs Penley plays a variety of business, is an excellent dancer, and has taken the leading characters in serious and comic pantomime.'

After the London stars had gone, business fell off even at the lower prices and, with the audience now comprising mainly gallery and pit, takings were often under £100. The clerks who frequented the pit had a habit of going out after the main play to buy veal pies, causing the afterpiece to start to a near empty pit, the clerks noisily clattering in again with greasy mouths when the farce was well under way.

As lesser lights, the Penleys had, of course, to take their benefit in the winter season. They divided the main play and the afterpiece with an 'Address by Mr Penley, *sitting on an ass,* that he has delivered twice before Their Majesties'. William was not a man to let go of a good thing. Even at lower wages, a season of 10 months was not to be sneezed at, especially as when it closed on 16 March Frances was very great with child once again.

Under the circumstances the Penleys remained in Liverpool, and on 1 May 1804 were blessed with the birth of another daughter whom they christened Esther. Their timing was impeccable on this occasion as the new season, for which they were both retained, commenced on 4 June.

The new theatre at Liverpool where Mr & Mrs W Penley took part in the opening season

Frances must have made a good impression with her employers as there was a marked upturn in the characters she was now given. Celia in *As You Like It*, Zorayda in *The Mountaineers* and Lady Percy in *Henry IV* all came her way. In October, the visiting star was Young Roscius, aka Master

Betty, on his tour immediately prior to his sensational London debut, and Frances had several supporting roles during his stay. The precocious youth was already coining it in before he reached London, his takings at Liverpool becoming legendary, drawing houses of £300 a night for two weeks, he himself cleared £1520 – around £133,000 in today's money.

The annual benefit round was a crucial event that gave a better idea of a player's actual pulling power. At the end of the 1804/05 season, Young – the resident leading man for several years – had two nights that brought in £162 and £290, Mathews took £238. Mr Penley's 'failed materially, in the amount which his services and merits entitled him to expect'. Out of 25 performers only five pulled in lower amounts than William, who managed to scrape in just £93. The *Liverpool Advertiser* urged its readers to make up the deficit by attending the benefit of the 'pleasing and very meritorious Mrs Penley' who had distinguished herself by the propriety of her demeanour and her assiduity. The 'very chaste agreeable actress and elegant dancer' pulled in £123. William does not seem to have had much luck with his benefits; still, between them a sum in excess of £200 was not to be sneezed at, especially as another child now had to be fed and clothed.

It is not known if they were able to visit their son George at his school in Dorset, or if during his vacations he joined them wherever they were working. In the *Salisbury & Winchester Journal* of 3 September 1804 there is a report of an evening at the King's Grammar School, Sherborne when, before 50 distinguished guests, a list of named boys recited passages from Virgil, Homer etc. The now nine-year-old George Penley is on the list but, true to his parents' calling, he gave a speech of Rolla from Sheridan's popular tragedy *Pizarro*. Good for George! Regrettably, George Frederick Penley now disappears into apparent oblivion, but he will emerge again with another boost from his patron Queen Charlotte.

The following year saw the William Penleys back again with the family firm. William's roles were usually supporting ones, often men of quality, mainly in comedies or melodramas, whereas Frances's tended to be leading lady parts in dramas and tragedies, although she occasionally offered a 'favourite *pas seul* called *Caprice de Moment*' and played Columbine in a pantomime. In *Mackbeth* Frances was naturally Lady Mackbeth to Rackham's Thane, but William played First Witch in a production that, as was then customary, relied greatly on the music composed by Matthew Locke.

SCENE THREE
1806 - 1811
DRURY LANE THEATRE

FRANCES – ALWAYS BILLED as Mrs W Penley – was now the leading lady of the J & P company in play after play, week after week. Yet, whilst at Rye, she gave birth to a son Aaron on 20 May 1806. It is pleasing to report that not only did this child not die in infancy, but grew up to achieve a greater fame that eluded all the other members of the extended Penley family.

However, compared to his wife, William is rarely featured on J & P playbills after August 1806, due to having made a great leap forward in his career, something that most provincial players fail to do. He had been accepted into the resident company at Drury Lane Theatre, a major step up in his profession.

The Theatre Royal Drury Lane was the chief theatre in the land, but not the same building that had been granted the patent by Charles II in 1663. That had been destroyed by fire in 1672. The replacement, purportedly designed by Sir Christopher Wren, opened in 1674 and had lasted over 100 years when Richard Brinsley Sheridan bought the theatre in 1778. Sheridan was a playwright, orator, MP and one of the foremost figures in the country. His comedies *The Rivals* and *The School for Scandal*, two of the very few plays of the period that have survived, are now classics constantly revived.

In 1791, the old building, which seated around 2000, was in such a parlous state that Sheridan and his partners decided to demolish it and create a brand-new state-of-the-art theatre which opened in 1794. Seating 3600 with five tiers of boxes, it was a vast place and greatly disliked by the actors who were used to the old theatre. The stage of the new theatre was huge: 83ft (25m) wide and 92ft (28m) deep and could have housed the old building in its entirety on its boards. No wonder that Mrs Siddons called it a 'barn of a place' and she and John Philip Kemble left in 1803. It was the largest theatre in Europe and, except for churches, it was the tallest building in London.

Thus the theatre that William entered was only 12 years old, and the great size must have been alarming to an actor used to the intimacy of the homely theatres of his brother's circuit.

William made his London debut on 13 September 1806 as Jaques in

The Honeymoon, the *Morning Chronicle* remarking two days later: 'A Mr Penley appeared, for the first time on this stage, in the part of Jaques, which Collins used to play, and was very well received.' Though some hankered after his predecessor in the part:

> The successor to the lamented Collins, in this mock-heroic, is a new performer Mr Penley, who had an arduous task in following such an actor as Mr Collins. He was well received, though he does not possess all the genuine comic humour of his predecessor.

The role of Jaques is by no means a leading one, the character appearing in only two scenes. It is a cameo part, consisting of a servant deputising for his aristocratic master, the humour coming from the lowly man aping his boss and uttering home truths. He reappears in the final scene as himself, making asides to the audience when the nobleman and his friends untangle the plot which has a passing similarity to *The Taming of the Shrew*.

Flimsy though the role may be, William was to make this part his own and played it for many years. In fact, in spite of playing many roles and creating parts in many new plays, he never achieved a similar success again.

The Honeymoon was the first play by John Tobin to be approved. He submitted over a dozen works to the patent theatres, but all had been rejected. Eventually in 1804, *The Honeymoon* was accepted but Tobin, suffering from tuberculosis, was advised to go and live in the West Indies. He died on the first day of the voyage out and his body returned to be buried at Cove near Cork, thus he never saw the great success of his play which held the stage for the next 50 years.

William's debut was followed five days later by Quick's old role Scrub in *The Beaux Stratagem*, but there may have been some resentment against the engagement of William, as this paragraph appeared in the press just a few days after making his debut.

WICKED FORGERIES

> We some time since cautioned our contemporaries against the designs of some mischievous persons, who are in the habit of sending abusive letters, with forged signatures, to the Editors of Papers, for the vile purpose of gratifying private malice by calling forth unmerited resentment against inoffensive individuals. – A letter of this description, with the forgery of the name of Mr Penley, of Drury Lane Theatre, was a few days since sent to the Editor of an Evening Paper, who naturally commented upon what he considered to be an unmerited reflection upon his conduct; and thus was the author of the forgery gratified by the temporary accomplish-

ment of his wicked design. Mr Penley has since come forward, and made affidavit before the Magistrates at Bow Street that 'he was neither directly nor indirectly concerned in writing the note alluded to.'

Following the runaway success of *The Honeymoon*, and after rejecting him for years, the management could not get enough of Tobin, so rummaged in the rejection pile and came up with *The Curfew* set in France at the time of the Norman Conquest. Penley was cast as Walter, the Toller of the Curfew, a tedious old man appearing only in the first act, another nice cameo for William. The play had 20 performances but, according to Miss Pope, an actress in the company, Sheridan the manager halted further representations because the deceased Tobin's relatives were entitled to an extra benefit after 20 performances which he was not prepared to give.

Throughout the 1806/07 season William Penley made regular appearances in a great variety of work, most often occupied in the afterpieces. As the programme changed nightly in those days, William was beavering away night after night in supporting roles, only heralded by his name on the playbill for that day.

Drury Lane was licensed for the winter season only, usually late September to early June, thus enabling the players to appear elsewhere in the summer months. At the end of the season, in the summer break, William had the opportunity of rejoining his wife in the J & P company on their regular circuit of Tenterden, Lewes, Eastbourne etc.

There was a coach service between London and Maidstone, with a link onwards to Tenterden. The 57 mile journey taking some 13 hours, William is unlikely to have come back and forth very often, other than for paid work.

William's family was fragmented, with husband and wife apart for much of the year. Their eldest son William Jr was at Alton in Hampshire where his mother's younger brother Georges Saulez ran a French-speaking school; George, by courtesy of Queen Charlotte, was at school in Dorset. Presumably daughters Frances, now aged ten, and Esther along with baby Aaron were with their travelling mother, rather than settled in London for most of the year with their father.

William was a comparatively humble but valuable member of the Drury Lane company returning for the 1807/08 and 1808/09 seasons. In the summer break between these two years William and his wife were at Brighton under the managers Brunton & Fields. A press clipping remarks: 'Mr W Penley's Lissardo, in the play, was a treat to his old friends,' which would indicate that William had appeared at Brighton previously.

In October 1808, the afterpiece *Blue Beard* surfaced after five years absence. It contained a great deal of pomp and glitter as fresh as when it first appeared but, of all the players from its original production, only Mr Bannister and Mrs Bland were left. Unfortunately, on the day of the revival Bannister's mother died and he was unable to appear, Penley stepping in at the last minute to play the part. 'Miss Gayton's admirable dancing was the only thing that merits particular commendation.' So no brownie points to William for saving the situation.

In December, Penley created the role of Benedetto in a new play *Venoni; or the Novice of St Marks* by Monk Lewis. Adapted from a French original, it concerned the intercourse of nuns and monks in Venice. The first two acts were well received, but the audience found the third act risible as the scene depicted the monk hero and nun heroine separated by a thick wall, unbeknownst to each other, speaking some 30 alternate monologue speeches. By the third night Lewis, realising he would have to alter this, rewrote the third act, but the original act is printed in the play book. It was done 18 times.

On 24 February 1809, Drury Lane Theatre burned to the ground. Not only a blow for William personally, in his third season there, but a national calamity, this being the premier theatre in the country and renowned throughout Europe. This was the theatre that, a mere 15 years after opening with such grandeur, was overnight razed to the ground. Sheridan, seen drinking a glass of wine and watching the conflagration, when challenged if he were not distraught stoically replied 'Can't a man have a quiet drink by his own fireside?'

Nothing daunted, arrangements were put in place to move the Drury Lane company to the Lyceum Theatre for the remainder of the season. The Lyceum, having just been rebuilt by S J Arnold, was not licensed for legitimate plays. It was created as an English Opera House, but it was legally decided that the famous Drury Lane patent could be transferred temporarily, with the company, until such time as its own theatre may be rebuilt.

Actors in the theatre of that time usually established a range of parts for themselves regarding these as sacrosanct, only giving way begrudgingly to other players. This is one reason why actors and actresses often played youthful parts well into advanced years. As recently as 1939 Sir John Martin-Harvey was still playing the role of Sydney Carton in *The Only Way* at the age of seventy-six – a part he had been playing since taking it up forty years previously. As the crux of the play depends on Carton clandestinely substituting for the young romantic lead, one wonders if the actors playing that role had to age alongside the star!

William Penley gradually added new characters to his repertoire but nothing was to equal his Jaques in *The Honeymoon*.

The fecund Frances Penley gave birth to yet another son on 6 April 1809 at 6 Red Lion Passage – presumably William's home in London. Baptism followed at St Bride's, Fleet Street, on 21 May and the baby was named Edmund. Alas, he died exactly three months later.

In May there was a record crowd of £800 at a performance of *The Honeymoon* when uproar arose because of one of William's speeches:

> The late Drury Lane Company performed at the Opera House on Monday night, to one of the most brilliant and crowded audiences that ever graced its walls. The play was *The Honeymoon*. Mr Penley, in the Mock Duke, was admirable. His soliloquy, which concludes the second scene of the third act, produced an extraordinary effect. Meditating upon his short-lived elevation he says 'It will be rather awkward, to be sure, to resign at the end of a month – but, like great men in office, I must make the most of my time, and retire with good grace, to avoid being turned out.' The audience immediately caught these words, and interrupted the Mock Duke with a thousand bravos, and an enthusiasm of applause from every part of the House. It was some time before the uproar subsided, and Mr Penley was able to finish the sentence, which runs thus – 'As a well bred dog always walks downstairs, when he sees preparations on foot for kicking him into the street.' Here the applause revived, and continued for some minutes. Among those who witnessed the scene was Mrs Clarke.

Mrs Clarke was a well-known courtesan and mistress of the Duke of York the commander of the army. She had just published her indiscreet memoirs in which it was revealed that she had been selling preferences to promotion, which the Duke of York had ensured. On a parliamentary enquiry, the Duke had promptly resigned, denying all guilt, saying he had made no benefit. However, Lord Castlereagh, also accused, admitted that he had gained personal benefit, but would not resign. This caused public uproar, one manifestation being the scene at the theatre described above. Alas, this seems to be the only lengthy good review that William Penley ever received.

Again, as the Lyceum closed for its summer recess, William travelled down to Kent to play with brother Sampson's company. At Lewes

> the Theatre, under the management of Messrs Jonas and Penley, attracted numerous audiences on Thursday and Friday; and on Saturday patronised by the Stewards, the house was overflowing in every part. The play was *The Honeymoon*, in which Mr W Penley represented the Mock-Duke, with his accustomed excellence; and the performance altogether deserved and obtained the general plaudits of the audience.

William was now established in a regular pattern of work. His contract with Drury Lane was annually renewed, and in the summer recess he went down into Kent to join the J & P family company. In the summer of 1811, Sampson started billing William in slightly larger type than the others as 'Mr W Penley (*of the Theatre Royal, Drury Lane*)'. For any actor to be able to claim 'from the Theatre Royal Drury Lane' or 'from the Theatre Royal Covent Garden' meant money in the bank, as such a performer could usually gain a premium, no matter how small, from the association with the two greatest theatres in the land.

William Penley, a small part player in a major theatre, seemed content to play supporting roles in his brother's company. When they worked in the provinces, many lesser London actors seized the chance to play leading roles normally denied them, so perhaps William was cautious by nature, knowing his limitations.

This regular pattern of work was suddenly shattered, as after 1811 neither Mr nor Mrs W Penley appeared with the J & P company ever again. It is possible that Sampson and William fell out over a family or professional issue. Some Penley descendents thought William lost money putting it in Sampson's failed London venture at the Tottenham Street theatre. This may be so, the date being right, but it can only be conjecture. It may simply be, with their family growing up, William and Frances were fed up with living apart for great chunks of the year. William, settled in the Drury Lane company, had a regular income for nine months of the year. His salary is not known, but the two major London theatres paid far more than the provinces. It is difficult to reconcile wages as they fluctuated with a performer's current popularity. The most popular performers of their day such as Munden, Fawcett and Quick received £14 a week. Often new performers came on the basis of a three year contract paying, say, £4 the first year, £5 the next and £6 the last. The salary list ranged from as low as £1.10.0 per week, up to 17 guineas. William was likely to be at the bottom end of this sliding scale, probably no more than 4 guineas at best.

SCENE FOUR
1812 - 1816
THE NEW DRURY LANE THEATRE

THE DRURY LANE COMPANY had been fully three years occupying the Lyceum while the new theatre was being built in Drury Lane. At last a new building had arisen from ashes of the old. Already on the shakiest financial ground, Sheridan, ruined entirely by the loss of his building, had turned to brewer Samuel Whitbread – an old friend and fellow MP – for help. Whitbread agreed to head a committee that would manage the company and oversee the rebuilding of the theatre, but asked Sheridan to withdraw from management himself, which he did entirely by 1811. Debts on the destroyed theatre amounted to over £400,000 and Whitbread persuaded many of the old shareholders, including the Duke of Bedford – owed for unpaid rent – to waive their claims. But it was still essential to raise the enormous sum of £300,000 to erect a building free of encumbrances. The new theatre was designed by Benjamin Dean Wyatt on behalf of the Committee comprising 13 members including four noblemen. Samuel Whitbread, really the leader of this rather amateurish band, was the only one with much idea of how to run the place. S J Arnold, from the Lyceum, was appointed manager and had to report to the Committee – all novices in the business of running a theatre. This method was chosen in an attempt to stop debts escalating out of control, as they had in Sheridan's time.

The new Drury Lane theatre made a slight concession towards intimacy, seating 3,060 people, 550 fewer than the destroyed building, though it measured 66ft from the front of the stage to the centre box with a pit 56ft wide. The stage itself was 46ft deep, exactly half the depth of its predecessor, and 6ft wider at 77ft, but quite large enough to house any one of brother Sampson's entire theatres. As Coleridge remarked, 'Our theatres – Drury Lane and Covent Garden – are fit for nothing; they are too large for acting and too small for a bull fight.' One peculiar feature of the new building solved the long-standing antipathy between King George III and his son the Prince of Wales by having separate entrances and separate boxes at opposite sides of the auditorium. On one occasion when the father and son had met in the foyer of the previous theatre a fight had ensued, their respective supporters having to drag them apart.

The new Drury Lane theatre opened with a company of principal players comprising Elliston, Ellis, Dowton, Palmer, Lawson, Wrighton, Bannister, Wrench and Wewitzer. The last named was a veteran low comedian and the last survivor of David Garrick's company.

The actresses were Mrs Glover, Mrs Edwin, Miss Duncan, Miss Kelly and Miss Mellon. William Penley was not classed as a principal, but he was retained in the new company.

On 10 October 1812, the opening production was *Hamlet* with Robert Elliston in the title role, William being one of the Gravediggers. William now played David in *The Rivals*. This role is merely that of servant to Bob Acres a rather buffoonish countryman, so not exactly a plum part for William, and something of a comedown as he, himself, had played Acres shortly after joining Drury Lane. He did somewhat better in *The School for Scandal* when he was cast as Crabtree.

The Drury Lane Theatrical Fund – supposed to support retired players who had fallen on hard times – had been somewhat neglected. In the days prior to old age pensions and social security hand-outs, this type of fund was set up on a voluntary basis, with workers paying a modest amount from their weekly wages. William Penley was one of the committee men who administered the Fund. One beneficiary was the afore-mentioned Wewitzer who, specialising in funny foreigners, had a career lasting 44 years. His salary, starting at £2 a week, gradually increasd until he attained £7, which he maintained until old age when it declined rapidly to £3. After retirement he eked out his life on an annual stipend of £65 from the Fund before dying in 1825. It is said he had mastered over 400 different parts during his career.

One of Penley's fellow committee members, John Bannister, the best low comedian of his day and a former manager of Drury Lane, organised a big benefit production to raise money, even persuading Mrs Siddons to appear, considered a coup as she had retired the previous year. By Bannister's efforts, the grand sum of £983 was raised, and the Fund committee awarded him a diploma and the title Master of the Fund. Although William was not high in the pecking order of actors, he must have been considered a person of probity and repute to serve on such a committee.

Genest, on summing up the first season in the new theatre, said: 'The company was numerous but not efficacious, there were too many middling actors and too few good ones – it is evident from the bills that few of the plays were strongly cast. The company was not strong, but in many instances the plays were not cast to the best advantage. He suggested that it would have been a better policy to cast each play afresh – as we do today – with no performer claiming any character as his right.

Having acquired a range of parts, actors were reluctant to give them up. This system worked well with comic roles, and star comedians known for a certain part would be engaged for a lifetime playing the roles they had made famous; audiences would be disappointed if they did not. Nowadays we would balk at an over-ripe Hamlet or Romeo, but as late as 1948 in his film of *Hamlet*, Olivier was forty years old, and Eileen Herlie playing his mother was twenty-eight!

During 1812, William's second son George Frederick Penley, having attained his seventeenth birthday, left Sherborne School where he had been placed through the munificence of Queen Charlotte. Her Majesty's interest in the boy did not wane as she then persuaded her Vice-Chamberlain Colonel Edward Disbrowe, a descendent of one of Cromwell's officers, to provide 300 guineas to fit George out for a commission in the East India Company army. The first page of George's multi-page application papers reads:

> The humble petition of George Frederick Penley sheweth that your petitioner is desirous of entering the Military Service of the Company, as a Cadet for the Bombay Infantry Establishment to which he has been recommended by the Lord Viscount Melville at the Request of the Queen.

One can hardly get more up-market than that, and incredible for the son of an actor. The Viscount Melville mentioned is the second one, succeeding his father in 1811, MP for Hastings in 1794 and Rye in 1796, and First Lord of the Admiralty from 1812. Is it too fanciful to think that the Viscount knew William of old from Hastings and Rye – two places on the J & P circuit?

The nature of George's education is given as 'Classical and Arithmetical'. He was unable to produce an entry in a parish register to prove his age, but swore an oath that to the best of his knowledge he was born at Sevenoaks in Kent on 19 May 1795. His father wrote a declaration to this effect on the application, and glued in was a copy of George's baptism entry – also for Sevenoaks, on 14 December 1796 – signed by the vicar and witnessed by the churchwarden. The authorities seemed very keen to know that the applicant's parent had not paid money or other valuable consideration to any person for furthering his son's application, a statement that William signed. A similar statement that had to be signed by the sponsor is crossed through, and written alongside are the words: 'Upon my honor I do not think it would be quite delicate to ask the Queen to sign this statement. John Melville.'

The interest the queen took in this lowly-born boy is extraordinary, especially when he was of an age with her own illegitimate grandson – also the son of an actress – George FitzClarence, the eldest of the ten childen that Dora Jordan bore with the Duke of Clarence, a youth whom Queen Charlotte totally ignored.

George Frederick Penley had before him a very different life from the one of an actor like his father, though not very different from George FitzClarence, as they both ended up in the Indian army. One has to wonder how a decade of mixing with the upper classes as confrères affected his developing personality, compared to his siblings who had lacked those advantages.

William Penley returned to Drury Lane for the 1813/14 season and was cast, with Elliston, Oxberry and Miss Kelly, in a new comedy *Rogues All; or Three Generations*. A farce reported as 'replete with nonsense and vulgarity, destitute of ingenuity in the plot, or humour in the dialogue.'

In a theatre struggling against a mounting debt, on 26 January 1814 a miracle happened. Edmund Kean made his first London appearance in the part of Shylock in *The Merchant of Venice* and English theatre was never the same again. Though the house was only a third full, the spectators were connoisseurs of acting who had come to see not the play, but the new actor. John Philip Kemble the leading actor of the day was dignified and impressive, his method of acting declamatory, much in the fashion of the French tragedians. Kean was a revelation; not having the natural attributes of Kemble, he had to play his parts in a completely different way. Kean's impulsive and passionate manner was hailed as 'natural', and overnight a new star was born. He was the right man at the right moment. The new theatre was mired in debt, and this little man arrived in time to set the tills ringing. In his first season he played Shylock 15 times, Richard III 20, Othello 10, Iago 8 and Hamlet 10, creating a box office profit of £20,000 and making over £1000 at his own benefits.

William, playing afterpieces and bit parts, did not have much opportunity to bask in the shadow of the new genius, but appeared as the cook Furnace in *A New Way to Pay Old Debts*, and Trapland, a lecherous old scrivener in Congreve's *Love for Love* – both plays starring Kean.

While brother Sampson had to be content with his minor country theatre at Peckham Rye as the nearest thing to a London venue, William, during the summer recess, was able to perform in other London theatres. He made an appearance at the Lyceum Theatre – now relegated to a minor musical theatre again since the re-opening of the new Drury Lane – in *The Shipwreck* a musical entertainment with music by Dr Arnold. This was a well-known piece of the time but, the cast excelled themselves, including:

> Mr Penley as a sailor, Harry Hawser, displayed abilities which we really did not think he possessed. In all his parts he has always deserved the praise of correctness and respectability. No fault could be found, and no superior excellence pointed out. He had probably not yet entered the line in which his particular talent lay, and in which he now will no doubt continue to shine. As a sailor, he displayed that forcible expression of blunt, honest feeling, with the easy transitions from despondency to joy, from melancholy to thoughtlessness, which distinguish our tars. In spirit and manner he recalled Bannister in his best days, to our remembrance, and lost nothing in the comparison.

William was ahead of his time. Some 16 years later T P Cooke, creating the archetype British tar in *Black-Eyed Susan*, made a small fortune. However, there is no evidence that William Penley pursued this line of parts. Perhaps he should have, for another review said: 'The admirable acting of Mr Penley in Harry Hawser, has retrieved the reputation he had lost by his repeated and vulgar buffooneries. In this line of characters, he promises to excel his dramatic contemporaries, as much as he himself is excelled in almost every other department of exertion.'

During the 1814/15 season William was still at Drury Lane playing his regular old parts and creating others in new plays such as *Fair Cheating; or The Wise Ones Outwitted* in which two old misers Coiner and Discount (Lovegrove and Penley), wish to marry each other's daughters, in order to save a fortune of £20,000. Of course their plans are foiled by the machinations of the misers' servants, daughters and their beaux. Another new role was Old Snaps, another guardian part, in a new afterpiece *Past Ten O'clock and a Rainy Night* which was pretty successful, being acted 27 times. So much for his vulgar buffooneries!

From February there was another Penley at the theatre, as William's nephew Sampson Penley Jr joined the company under the billing 'Mr S Penley', William remaining as he had always been at Drury Lane – simply 'Mr Penley'.

Though both Penleys were re-engaged for the 1815/16 season they seldom appeared together in the same play, as William was more often in the afterpieces than the main attraction. Sam Jr was given every opportunity to shine in principal roles. William had never been more than a supporting player specialising in fathers, old dukes and ancient buffers in general, in spite of still being only forty-two. Did he regard his nephew proudly, or as an upstart? We shall never know.

As the finances of the theatre were habitually shaky, the Drury Lane company had been fortunate to have the new star Edmund Kean bringing in the customers at the box office. At the end of the season, as a token of esteem from his colleagues, and gratitude from the managers, a cup valued at £300 was presented to him in the names of all the acting company at Drury Lane including 'S Penley Jun and W Penley Sen'. The only actor who did not subscribe was Munden whose parsimony was proverbial: 'You may praise Kean all you like, but don't expect Joe Munden to pay for it.'

After this it must have come as a shock for William to read in the press that he was to retire along with several others. No doubt some of these players were genuinely retiring or voluntarily resigning; but not William, he was definitely pushed. He immediately wrote to the management committee asking them to reconsider their verdict. This letter was ignored and, after a reasonable time spent waiting for the postman each day, he sent a further letter imploring to keep his job:

The Gentlemen of the Committee
Wᵐ Penley
30 Augᵗ 1816
Gentlemen,

 Having been anxiously waiting for an answer to a letter I wrote at the close of the season, may I take the liberty now to request one, I hope gentlemen you will take into consideration that I have been eleven seasons in the theatre during which time I have never incurred the forfeiture of a shilling, that some few years since I played Mr Bannister's and Mr Mathew's business (during their long illnesses) with much success, that I am still but a young man for the characters I undertake, with a voice capable of being heard in every part of the theatre, that the parts I have lately had given me, some of them very indifferent ones, I have taken without a murmur and endeavoured to make the most of them by strict attention to dress (many of them from my own wardrobe) and always have been perfect, that I am in possession of a great many characters in most of the acting pieces which gentlemen of greater abilities would not play and those of less might not give satisfaction in, that the salary I have offered to return at is but a mere trifle, and that I have ever been considered a quiet and respectable member of the company.

Waiting your determination

I am Gentlemen,

Your Ob^t hum^b serv^t

Wm Penley

August 30th 1816

55 Rathbone Place

William, pleading for his livelihood, exaggerates his service slightly as he made his debut 10 years previously on 13 September 1806. The remark about 'forfeiture' means he has never been fined for any misdemeanour – actors were liable to fines of all kinds – for being late at rehearsals, refusing to play as cast, drunkenness etc. The use of the word 'perfect' denotes he has always remembered his lines. Finally he states he has offered to return at what is obviously a reduced salary. All this pleading was in vain and the committee did not relent. Trying to rescue something from this disaster he deemed a benefit performance for himself would be in order, but finding that the Drury Lane theatre was barred to him for that purpose, had to arrange for the use of the Haymarket theatre:

> Mr Penley (late of the Theatre Royal, Drury Lane), who, after ten years of the strictest attention to his profession, has this Season, by the reduction of the Establishment, been deprived of his Situation in the service of the Public; and who, from recent regulations, cannot avail himself of the powerful aid of his Brother Performers of the Theatre Royal, Drury Lane, who readily offered their friendly assistance, begs to announce to his Friends, that it is his intention to take a Benefit at the Theatre Royal Haymarket (by Permission of the Lord Chamberlain), on Monday next: when will be performed the favourite play of *A Cure for the Heart-Ache*; the Interlude of *Sylvester Daggerwood*; the favourite Farce of *Of Age Tomorrow*; with a variety of popular songs, aided by several distinguished Actors, from the Theatre Royal, English Opera. Tickets to be had of Mr Penley, 55 Rathbone Place, Oxford Street, where places for the Boxes may be taken.

It must have been a bitter blow for William but, while he was a competent performer, there were plenty of others who could play his roles. Whether the recent introduction of Sam Jr into the company had some bearing is impossible to say, but it may have called attention to his uncle and how long he had been in the company, perhaps latterly not pulling his weight or giving value for his salary. Ten years is quite a time for an actor of no special merit.

Although he was only in his early forties, it does not appear that William attempted to get a place with any other theatre. Apart from the odd appearance in old colleagues' own benefits, William Penley looks to have disappeared from the theatre world.

William's wife Frances — so long the leading lady of the J & P company — must have also given up the buskin as she too placed an advertisement in the *Times*:

> MRS PENLEY (wife of Wm Penley, late of the Theatre-Royal Drury-lane, who, after ten years of the strictest attention to his profession, has this season, through the reduction of the establishment, been deprived of his situation in the service of the Public), begs to inform the Ladies in general, she has for their inspection an ELEGANT ASSORTMENT of MILLINERY and DRESSES, at her residence, 55 Rathbone-place, where ladies bringing their own materials may have them made in the most unique and fashionable style.

The couple, outraged at William losing his position, must have both become disenchanted with the theatrical profession as a mode of life. They certainly discouraged their children from treading the boards as, unlike their cousins, none of them became actors. William, retiring from acting, went into business as an upholsterer, cabinet maker and undertaker.

William Penley Jr, the eldest of William and Frances's children, now twenty-three, somewhat unexpectedly married Margaretta Callaghan on Christmas Day 1816. The rest of the family, ignorant of the proceedings and expecting him home any time, were kept waiting for their dinner. When William Jr turned up with his new bride in tow, his father, not knowing the cause of his absence until he returned, congratulated him and said he hoped he had enough to provide a suitable establishment for his new wife as, seeing he had not been consulted, he would have nothing to do with it. William Jr had 13/- in his pocket at the time, but managed to keep his head above water until establishing himself as a drawing master. William Jr remained a drawing master all his life, and he and Margaretta were to produce eight children.

SCENE FIVE
1817 - 1835
THE EX-ACTOR

SOON WILLIAM JR was at his own establishment at an address in Shouldern Street, Brompton Square where he was involved in another food related incident. On 8 June, three villains stole 7lb of beef, value 3/-, and 2lb of bread, value 6d, the goods of William Henry Saulez Penley, drawing master. The culprits aged sixteen, seventeen and twenty-one were all transported for seven years. The Penleys lived in harsh times.

William Sr was now a full-time dealer in second-hand furniture, auctioneer and undertaker, his acting days firmly behind him. A strange echo tied his present life to his former one in the shape of a 'Remarkable Theatrical Coincidence'. Three years previously, on 21 September 1814, the Drury Lane company had their annual dinner at the Ship Tavern, Greenwich. It was usual before the dinner to take a ramble in the park where, amongst their merry-making and gambols, a pretend duel was fought. The loser in the duel, feigning death, was Mr Raymond the stage manager of the company. They held a mock funeral and William Penley, playing the part of the undertaker, led the whole party of rollicking thespians to a mimic place of interment. After these larks the company fell to their dinner. Now, three years later, Mr Raymond had actually died (not in a duel!) and at his funeral nearly the whole party that had taken part in the Greenwich dinner attended him to the grave, at St Paul's Covent Garden. The undertaker was William Penley. Having only a few months previously quitted the stage, he found himself now employed professionally to do the last duties to his late lamented stage manager.

On 16 March 1818 William and Frances Penley's only surviving daughter Frances Mary Anne Penley – like her siblings, having been kept away from the stage – married Joseph Astor, a scion of the famous American family. They went on to have 11 children.

William, from his second-hand furniture warehouse at 33 Rathbone Place, advertised that he would buy every article for ready money, and sell quickly and cheaply for a small profit. He boasted of rosewood tables, sets of drawing room and parlour chairs, piano-fortes, bedsteads and mattresses. He also hired out rout chairs, seats and tables, and jogged along, with occasional advertisements for special pieces on offer such as four elegant rosewood loo-tables of large dimensions and superior make, inlaid with buhl work (tortoiseshell and brass marquetry). Loo was a popular card game of the day. He also advertised an elegant rosewood six-octave cabinet piano. Another bargain was some sheets of plate glass. In addition to these offerings, he also appears to have gone into the business of property dealing as, calling himself an appraiser and house agent, he advertised a small cottage for sale or rent.

On 17 November 1818, Queen Charlotte died. She had not only produced 15 children with her husband King George III – still alive but blind and insane – but had also assisted the little son of the itinerant players William and Frances Penley back in 1801. That little boy was now an officer in the Indian army, and his mother, herself, had only three months to live. On 26 Feb 1819 at Rathbone Place, London, Frances Mary Ann Penley née Saulez known professionally as Mrs W Penley, the former tragedy queen of the Jonas & Penley company, died. She was forty-seven years old.

Two days after his brother Sampson had to finally abandon the performances with his troupe at the modest *salle* in Paris, on 21 October 1822, William Penley remarried. His second wife was Susannah, widow of G S Young late of Pentonville. This lady, of similar age to William, had considerable property left to her by her first husband.

William and his first wife had produced children who had nothing to do with the acting profession. William Jr, having married on Christmas Day without his father's knowledge, had established himself as a drawing master, at one period occupying a position at his uncle Georges Saulez's academy at Alton. There, young gentlemen were boarded and educated for 25 guineas per annum, and lessons were conducted in French.

Aaron Penley, William's youngest child, also became a drawing master, going into partnership with big brother William Jr as stationers at Portsea, as well as building up a teaching practice there. Aaron married Caroline Turner of Sheffield on 10 March 1830 and, according to the *Dictionary of National Biography*, they went on to produce 18 children, of whom only two survived to adulthood.

In December 1831, William Jr and Aaron, 'at the urging of several friends' expanded their stationery business in Portsea to include a new circulating library. This promised 'all the popular, new and standard works;

together with Magazines and every periodical publication of merit.'

All through the early months of the following year the brothers placed advertisements in the local newspaper for their new circulating library and reading room. The brothers also sold books, stationery, art materials, plus music, harp and guitar strings. They also advertised that miniatures could be painted – from one to 20 guineas – with likenesses guaranteed.

In July 1832, William Henry Saulez Penley and Aaron Penley were declared bankrupt. In fact, the library had been far from profitable, and those friends who had suggested that it would be a valuable adjunct to the brothers' stationery business were probably friends no longer. The library had lasted barely six months. By September, the entire stock-in-trade of the bankrupt brothers, including the library of '1,400 first-rate volumes as one lot' was advertised for sale, plus the entire household furniture of the bankrupt William. The lots included eight mahogany chairs, circular loo table, brass fenders and fire irons, valuable paintings, rich cut glassware, Japan and French bedsteads, ivory handled cutlery etc. William Jr had built himself up into a man of some substance after marrying with only 13/- in his pocket.

As a result of this debacle the two brothers, returning to their artistic pursuits, went their separate ways. William Jr remained in the Portsmouth area for several years working as a teacher of drawing, offering his Drawing Academy at Miss Davis, High Street, Gosport, and at his own home in Portsea, fees being one guinea per quarter.

Aaron went to live at Sheffield, presumably because his wife came from there, also taking on pupils at a guinea a quarter. In 1835, Aaron Penley made his public breakthrough as a professional artist by exhibiting three portraits in the Royal Academy Exhibition that year. He also moved from Sheffield back to Southampton, where he advertised himself as 'Painter in Water Colours to Her Most Gracious Majesty the Queen, by Special Appointment' and, once more in connection with his brother Mr W Penley of Portsmouth, gave lessons in drawing and miniature painting.

SCENE SIX
1836 AND AFTER
FAREWELL

IN JANUARY 1836, William Penley's second wife Susannah, died. They had managed 14 years together, and she would never have known life as an actor's wife, William having withdrawn from the stage long before meeting her.

William Penley, ex-actor, now auctioneer and man of property, himself died on 23 March 1838, aged sixty-five, at Connaught Terrace, Hammersmith, London.

When their father died, William's and Aaron's situations drastically changed. William Jr, having resided at Portsea and run a drawing academy for 15 years, announced he was giving up the business, not surprising as, in his father's will, he had been left a dozen various properties including houses, stables, grassland etc in Northampton, Battersea and Hampstead. William moved to London, and the 1841 census states he is living at Mornington Crescent with his wife Margaretta aged forty-two. He moved to Reading in 1842 advertising himself as a teacher of drawing again, which seems odd for a man of property, especially as he sought a school for his two sons and two daughters where he himself could teach. William and his wife had eight children, and at the time of the 1861 census he was retired and living in Islington. He died on 27 January 1866.

Ex-actor William's middle son George Frederick Penley of the Indian Army was bequeathed two houses with stables and coach houses, with an earnest wish that, were he to die without issue, these should go to his brothers and sister, or their children. George, making his entire career in the army, would seem to have had little contact with his family members. He married Elizabeth Walters on 21 June 1823 at Lambeth, and was gazetted a commission in HM Army in the East Indies on 28 June 1838, later becoming a major in the Bombay Native Infantry, and in 1855 was promoted to Lieutenant-Colonel. After his retirement he lived at Croydon, dying on 14 May 1869 aged seventy-three.

Mr & Mrs William Penley's only daughter Frances Mary Anne Penley, who had married Joseph Astor in 1818, died on Jersey on 3 May 1839 closely followed by her husband on 24 August. Alas, far too short a time to benefit from her father's will.

Aaron was left a leasehold house in Connaught Terrace, next door to one of those left to his brother, another in Howland Street and a third in Goodge Street, all in London. Aaron joined the New Society of Painters in Watercolours in 1838, most of his future work being in that medium. He was to show over 300 works at the Society's annual exhibitions, his paintings being reviewed many times over the coming years.

At one exhibition Aaron's portrait *Major Penley* was given a bit of a kicking:

> Portrait of a pair of epaulets would have been a better title; portraiture and subjects are surely at a low ebb nowadays. Mr P would do better to remain at his miniatures.

That may have been a one-off failure as in 1841 Aaron painted Prince Albert, having seven sittings throughout late February and early March. The queen and Prince Albert expressed themselves much pleased with the likeness. A watercolour portrait of Queen Victoria by Aaron Penley is now in the National Portrait Gallery.

In 1843, Aaron was a teacher at Cheltenham College, Bath, and in 1849 the assistant professor of civil drawing at the East India Company's college at Addiscombe. No doubt brother Major Penley facilitated this appointment. Aaron was considered an innovative teacher, introducing lessons in the new art of photography. He was promoted to senior professor in 1855, moving in 1861 to the Royal Military College at Woolwich.

Aaron wrote several books on the technique of painting, and introduced into Britain new colours such as viridian and aureolin. He also took out a patent for a new form of drawing board. While he was obviously regarded as a good teacher, there was less universal praise for his work as an artist, *Blackwood's Magazine* stating: 'Mr Aaron Penley is still wedded to an ancient manner pertaining to a period now gone by.'

Examples of work by Aaron Penley are in the British Museum, the Victoria and Albert Museum, the National Portrait Gallery, the Tate Gallery, and several provincial galleries. In the National Portrait Gallery there are three photographs of Aaron Penley taken 1860-62.

Dying in retirement at Lewisham in 1870, Aaron is the only Penley of the two generations covered by this book to gain the eminence of an entry in the *Dictionary of National Biography*.

William's sons greatly benefitted financially from their father's death. It would seem, in retrospect, that it had been betterment for William to give up the stage in 1816. However, that was a very reluctant farewell as he was forcibly retired, and his wealth was a boon coming from his marriage to his second wife. From what can now be deduced from his theatrical career, William was no more than a jobbing actor rarely playing leading roles even when with brother Sampson's company. But not everybody can be a hero; most of us are required to stand on the pavement to cheer as the hero passes by. The best that can be said of William is that he was at the edge of the kerb.

None of William's offspring had ever had any theatrical connections, though three generations further on came the most famous actor of all to bear the Penley name.

It was necessary to run forward in time to conclude the story of Mr and Mrs William Penley and their artistic children. We must now return to the year 1814 and pick up the story of Sampson Penley's children, who all became actors, managers – or both.

ACT THREE

Mr SAMPSON PENLEY Jr

'he spares neither trouble nor expense in catering
for the amusement of the public'

SCENE ONE
1815 - 1819
DRURY LANE THEATRE

AT THE END of the J & P season at Brussels in November 1814, young Sampson Penley Jr, leaving his father's company to sink or swim on the continent, eagerly returned home to look forward to a more exciting step upwards in his career. He had been a leading man since the age of eighteen but, of course, always in his own father's company. He had learned a lot in the five years he had been playing principal parts and had a store of roles in his repertoire equal to an actor twice his age. Many actors were content to remain in the world they knew, but players of ambition, both men and women, knew that true fame and success could only come from London.

Sam Jr had tasted the delights of London theatreland early on, when he and his father were the principals at the Tottenham Street theatre. But that was one of the more insignificant minor theatres – not even the status of the Adelphi, Surrey or Olympia – and his dad had lost a lot of money on that venture. The two patent theatres Covent Garden and Drury Lane were the only ones that mattered and he, Mr Sampson Penley Jr, had a contract for Drury Lane.

It was not unusual for actors from the provinces to get a chance at the two major theatres. They were always after novelty of both play and player, trying out many a leading man or lady from the provinces, most proving unsatisfactory. All over the country, provincial managers and knowledgeable cognoscenti with the ear of the London managements recommended performers from personal experience, and emissaries were always being sent thither to assess the suitability of names offered to them.

Back in 1776, Mrs Sarah Siddons, herself, at the age of twenty-one had been talent-spotted and hastened to London to take up the opportunity offered to her by David Garrick to play in his final season at Drury Lane. Unfortunately, she blew her chance and, mortified, returned to the provinces. She earned a second chance in 1782 when she was welcomed back to Drury Lane by Garrick's successor Sheridan. This time she was not only a success but became the wonder of the age. Although she retired in 1812, Mrs Siddons was still around, a figure of awe, the queen of tragedy.

Now he, Sampson Penley Jr, was going to tread those same boards that had nurtured Garrick and Siddons of the previous generation. That an actor from the provinces could still make it big in London had been proved only the previous year when Edmund Kean, a small, slight, unknown pale-faced man of twenty-six from the Dorchester theatre, appearing for the first time at Drury Lane on January 26 1814 in the role of Shylock, had become an overnight sensation. Kean was now the town's biggest attraction, heading the roster of actors that Sam Jr was about to join.

Although with a modest position, Sam's uncle William was a long-standing member of the Drury Lane company, and it may well be he was able to facilitate his nephew's opportunity. Because his uncle had been billed for years as Mr Penley, Sam made his debut on 28 February 1815 as 'Mr S Penley from the English Theatre at Brussels. First Appearance.' He was twenty-three years old.

Reviews are singularly lacking but the *Caledonian Mercury* said:

> A Mr Penley made his *debut* last night in the character of Young Norval. – His voice is good, his countenance expressive, and his person of middle size, and well proportioned. His performance was received throughout with rapturous applause.

The part was one that Sam had first played at the age of twelve at Lewes when his father had thrust him forward as a Young Roscius, and he had played it several times since, often with his aunt Mrs W Penley as Lady Randolph.

Written by John Home, *Douglas* is a tragedy that observes the classic unities. Old Norval, a shepherd, brings up as his own son a child whose true mother, now Lady Randolph – full of ill fortune, luckless love and melancholy – presumes to be dead. Young Norval, revealed to be the heir to Lord Douglas, is reunited with his mother, only to be killed by Lord Glenalvon the villain of the piece. In despair, Lady Randolph throws herself off a cliff. On the first night of this play in Edinburgh an excited voice cried 'Where's your Wullie Shakespeare the noo?'

The New Monthly Magazine was more fulsome in its praise of Sam Jr's debut:

> Feb. 28.— Mr Penley from the English theatre lately established at Brussels, was introduced for the first time to a London audience, in the character of Young Norval, and was received with universal applause. He appealed, on the 7th of March, in Belcour, in *The West Indian*, and justice compels the admission, that a more successful *debut* has seldom been

made by any candidate for the first walk in elegant comedy.

A critique that passed into more permanent form than ephemeral reviews can still be found in the *Biography of the British Stage*:

> Mr S Penley: This gentleman has been on the Stage from his infancy and at that early period of his life we imagine he must have acted pretty nearly as well as he does now. He was transplanted from some Provincial Theatre to the Boards of Drury Lane where he made his first bow as Young Norval in *Douglas*. He personates fops and pert servants with some ability and can boast of a fine figure and finer teeth which are seen to great advantage from the Dress Boxes and the second Tier.

Sam must have been pleased to have played to rapturous applause, knowing full well that the London audience could be particular to the point of cruelty. London playgoers firmly believed they had the right to dictate to the players.

Sampson Jr, although simply a jobbing actor, was certainly no fool. He knew he was not going to make an impact like Kean, a once-in-a-lifetime genius. Kean was a tragedian even though compelled to play all sorts of parts in the country theatres; actually in the provinces he had been better known for his Harlequin than his Shakespeare. J & P actors had to be versatile, and Sam Jr had played everything thrown at him, so was ready to be tested.

After his debut he was given the chance to show what he could do with a varied range of important principal roles such as Mercutio in *Romeo & Juliet*, and Bolingbroke in *Richard II*. At a benefit performance for the Drury Lane Theatrical Fund, Mr S Penley was chosen to deliver a specially written address. So everything was looking rosy for Sam Jr in his new position, although as Hotspur in Shakespeare's *Henry IV*:

> Mr Penley, as Hotspur, has contrived to do away the credit he obtained in *Douglas*; never was any thing more lamentable. The character, as represented by him, is an awkward, vulgar, noisy boy; his legs seem to have entertained a family feud, and are perpetually running from each other, as if they intended to bestride the stage. His voice is weak and thin; his action is altogether without grace or dignity; he does not even for a moment bear the least affinity to a hero; he is for ever capering about the stage as if bitten by a tarantula.

The Drury Lane season ran from September to June so in the summer break Sam Jr went down to his father's new theatre at Windsor. Starring as 'Mr S Penley of Drury Lane', the Windsor audience and critics proved much more kindly disposed.

Sam was re-engaged for the new Drury Lane season. However, prior to the 1815/16 season opening, there was an appalling sensation when Samuel Whitbread, the main man on the management board, was found with his throat cut. Whitbread admired Napoleon and his reforms in France and Europe, and hoped that much of these would be implemented in Britain itself. When Napoleon abdicated in 1814, Whitbread was devastated and began suffering from depression, and on the morning of 6 July 1815, he committed suicide by cutting his throat with a razor. The inquest revealed that he had been suffering from a brain tumour. The rest of the Board was thrown into turmoil as Whitbread had been the strongest personality, the others sheep-like followers, and there was doubt that the theatre could afford to reopen at all.

Fortunately for Sam Jr and the rest of the company it did open, with Kean once again the glittering star attraction. Unfortunately, no sooner was it under way than Sam Jr got stabbed with a sword. He was playing Roderigo in *Othello*, and in the sword fight with Cassio received a wound on the knee which put him out of action for several days. Receiving minor wounds was an occupational hazard in the days when many plays had duels, and the ability to fence was a necessary accomplishment for any actor. Today such scenes require the hired expertise of a 'fight arranger'. Neither was it considered necessary to have official understudies. Apart from new plays, it was almost always certain that another member of the company would be able to take over the role, many of the lesser lights having played leading roles in the provinces. If the worst came to the worst, an actor would read the part, but that was rarely necessary.

Sam Jr got a rare chance to appear with his Uncle William in yet another revival of *The Honeymoon* as William was, as usual, playing Jaques, his personal part for the last nine years.

> We never saw a theatre more crowded. Oxberry in Lampedo, Penley in Jaques, and, more especially, Knight in Lopez were each highly laughable in their way. But it was too much to expect, that we should do more than tolerate the assignment of our gay and eccentric favourite Rolando to the unfledged ambition of Mr Penley Junior.

The *Times* did not much care for Mr S Penley. As Sparkish in *The Country Girl*:

> The coxcombry of Mr S Penley, however promising, is not altogether to our taste.

As Lord Foppington in *A Trip to Scarborough*:

> We think this actor may improve his performance, which is quite sufficiently listless and affected, by varying, here and

there, in a small degree, the mode of puppyism that he has adopted. At present he is too laboured and monotonous. Still it is his best attempt.

But in a new play called *Accusation*:

S Penley was the unprincipled servant of Valmore; he was active, subtle and forcible throughout.

Hurrah! Praise at last from the *Times*. But, alas, the *Theatrical Inquisitor* merely said: 'Mr S Penley grinned and shewed his teeth as outrageously as ever.'

On 12 January 1816, to great acclaim, Edmund Kean played Sir Giles Over-reach in Massinger's *A New Way to Pay Old Debts*. The role of the overwrought Over-reach – a malicious villain – provided Kean with one of his best parts. People had even fainted at his malevolent portrayal.

Sam Jr appeared as Tom Allworth, in love with the villain's daughter who, despite the father's machinations, marries her in a happy ending. This production was a solid hit playing for 26 successive performances – a rarity for a straight play – and boosted anew Kean's reputation which, after being all-conquering, was sagging somewhat from his unreliability, erratic performances and off-stage antics.

Sam Jr, retaining his part as Allworth in the many showings of this popular work, was to appear regularly in Kean's supporting casts. A painting of a scene from this play is in the Garrick Club. As Allworth his costume is described as 'A light mixture kersey-mere jacket and trunks, trimmed with pink galloon, narrow black ribbon and plated buttons; white silk pantaloons; pink satin vest, trimmed with light blue, and plated buttons; russet shoes; lace ruff' which nowadays sounds as camp as a row of tents.

Following the dismissal of his Uncle William from the company the year after Sam Jr joined, Sampson Penley Jr was thereafter known simply as Mr Penley and billed thus on subsequent playbills, a fact not always recognised by former historians who have often conflated the two men. Sam Jr was certainly thought of as a major asset to the Drury Lane company, returning each year after the summer break which he usually spent as a guest star at his father's theatre at Windsor. In the summers of 1816 and 1817 he also went with his Drury Lane colleague Oxberry to Valenciennes to play in the English theatre where his sisters and cousin Miss Jonas were appearing.

On 1 April 1818, Sam Jr showed the world another string to his bow.

Not content with being an actor and stage manager, he now burst forth upon the world as a playwright. It was the custom for a playwright to read his play to the assembled cast in the greenroom, and after reading his tragedy one tyro author confessed there was nothing he knew more terrible than reading his work before such a critical audience. 'I know one thing more terrible,' said a witty actress. 'Having to sit and listen to it.'

So how was Sam's play received at its debut? After yet another performance of *The Beggar's Opera* at Drury Lane, the afterpiece was '*The Sleeping Draught* a farce by Mr S Penley the Drury Lane comedian'. This première drew forth a letter to the editor of the *Morning Post* complaining that it was a rip-off of a farce called *Love and Laudanum* lately successfully produced at the Woolwich theatre. The author stated:

> Towards the latter end of December last I lent the farce of *Love and Laudanum*, then called *Who's the Murderer?* to a gentleman equally the friend of Mr Penley and myself, at that time resident in Windsor. I cannot at this moment aver that it was seen by Mr Penley, of Drury Lane, but am prepared to prove that it was placed in his brother's hands for perusal, who returned it with comments, at the same time signifying his warmest approbation of the very incidents which have so soon found their way into his brother's piece. If I be incorrect in my statement, it is in the power of Mr Penley to come manfully forward, and as an author to clear himself from the unpromising charge of gross plagiarism in his first production.

This calumny was answered the following morning by Sam Jr loftily protesting he had not been to Woolwich for many years and never to the theatre there, thus did not know the author or of his play. He pointed out the incidents of the play were lawful game as they were taken from 'Boccace', a source common to all.

In fact, the farce, completely taken from Boccaccio (Day 4 Novel 10), had been dramatised previously as *The Narcotic*. Though critics said Sam Jr's play was 'poor', the afterpiece was repeated several times during the season, published, and as a piece of theatrical comedy it was greatly appreciated by players and public alike, being brought back many times and holding its place on the nation's stages for many years.

The main role of Popolino was played by John Pritt Harley. Six years older than Sam Jr, he had started his career in 1806 as an eighteen-year-old with Jerrold in the country town of Cranbrook in Kent, at much the same time as the twelve-year-old Sam had been with his family company seven miles away at Tenterden. Harley had made his debut at Drury Lane six months after Sam, but soon rose to far greater stardom. There is a picture of Harley in the role of Popolino in the National Portrait Gallery.

> [The play] is one of the drollest we have seen for a long time past. It makes no pretensions to wit or character; but all the fun depends on the situations and equivoques, which are extremely well contrived. We do not recollect any farce that has so striking and complete a conclusion. The whole weight of the piece lay on Mr Harley, who played most exquisitely.

> Without any great abundance of material, Mr Penley has contrived, not by pungency of wit, or breadth of humour but by pleasant equivoque, and ludicrous situation, to produce one of the merriest farces which we have lately seen. The writer of the critiques at the bottom of the play-bills (a gentleman whose veracity is, now and again, a little questionable) may, with great truth, state, "that the new farce was received with shouts of laughter". He may add, "even critics laughed" and it is certainly impossible to compliment Mr Penley more highly.

Shortly afterwards, the newly published playwright attempted another work. As the previous one was a re-jigging of a classic work, Sam Jr clearly thought he was on to a good idea, though not an original one as many of the so-called 'new' plays at that time were re-workings and borrowings from previous successes. However, in this case, whether he knew it or not, Sam Jr was offering a significant moment in the history of English drama.

On 24 April, came *Marlowe's Celebrated Tragedy of the Jew of Malta in five acts with considerable alterations and additions by S Penley, Comedian.* This was most likely the first time that Marlowe's play had been performed since 1633 when it was first published. After Marlowe's dodgy death and disgrace, his plays had disappeared into limbo. Whilst over the years many of the works of his contemporary Shakespeare had been seen, albeit in truncated and bowdlerised form, Marlowe was a distinct novelty.

Kean played the lead role of Barabas, a part very much up his street as the Jew is an out-and-out villain. Unfortunately, the new version was not considered an improvement.

> The alteration performed on this evening was made by S Penley, Comedian. As usual in these cases, he has inserted too much of his own, and omitted too much of the original. He has injudiciously left out all that relates to the poisoning of the nuns; in his third act, Abigail leaves the stage apparently in perfect health, a short scene of thirty-five lines

ensues and then she is discovered on her death bed, though it
is impossible to divine what can have occasioned her death in
so short a time. The manner of Barabas's death is altered.

It takes a bit of nerve to tinker with a 200-year-old classic, but Marlowe
was not revered, never performed at this period, and Sam Jr was not
known for lacking brass neck. *Blackwood's Magazine* gave a very lengthy
review of the unusual event of which this very brief extract conveys the
tenor:

> . . . a long and tedious scene between Lodowick and Mathias
> at the commencement, . . . very uninteresting and intrusive
> people at best; . . . the play, upon the whole, greatly injured
> by the alterations, and see no reason for any of them, . . . The
> performance flags very much during the second and third
> acts, and is not likely to become a favourite with the public.

The play was performed 12 times and published but, being coolly received,
was soon laid aside. It is said that the production so offended Jewish
patrons they boycotted the theatre for the rest of the season. As at this
time Jewish people were great theatre-goers, and may have formed a
considerable portion of the regular audience, that could possibly have
confirmed the decision to withdraw the play.

As the 1817/18 season approached its close, the principal actors of
the Drury Lane theatre company were called to a meeting with the
managing committee. They were informed that the situation at the theatre
was financially dire with debts having reached £80,000.

London salaries were considerably more than in the country theatres
and, naturally, star names could command much larger pay than the also-
rans. It was proposed each performer who had a salary of over £4 a week
take a reduction by a graduated percentage. Unless the proposal was
agreed the theatre must close. 'Then let it close!' cried Dowton. 'I will
never consent to abandon a single farthing. I am, myself, proprietor of
many theatres, by some of which I lose £40 a week, but I should blush to
call my performers together on such a question as the present. I will never
consent to this.' Dowton, a popular comic actor specialising in crusty old
buffers, was the son-in-law of Mrs Sarah Baker who had died the previous
year leaving him her long-standing Kent circuit. As with Dowton, several
actors in the patent companies also controlled theatres elsewhere. Elliston
owned the Olympic theatre, controlled the Birmingham theatre and had
interests in other provincial cities. Even Sam Jr was involved in his father's
theatre at Windsor.

The cost-cutting measures at Drury Lane being howled down by the players, the season lingered on for another 30 nights, but even Kean could only pull in a paltry £87 a night at the door. A full house brought in around £700, with nightly expenses exceeding £200. The Drury Lane committee, though comprising men of public stature, were amateurs at running a theatre and their dealings had been less than business-like, with some members making arrangements and agreements without the consent of others. Apart from the main committee there was a sub-committee and, as in many such situations, all the work and responsibility fell on a few conscientious members, while others rarely bothered even turning up to meetings. There was much in-fighting between the two committees and blame apportioned when flops occurred and money drained away. The Drury Lane amateur management had staggered on for six years in a haphazard fashion, incurring insurmountable losses.

The truth of the matter was that the new theatre had cost so much to build, plus debt interest to pay, with the large size making it expensive to run. Also there was much more competition from other venues, London now having a dozen theatres and, whilst none of them was licensed for straight drama – only the three patent ones still having the oligopoly – these minor theatres were constantly flouting the law, and actors such as Kean himself were appearing at them. The patent trio made attempts to crush these upstarts, but times and attitudes were changing, many actors now contracting for limited appearances rather than seasons, allowing them to take work for varied managements.

The committee's immediate solution was to invite Stephen Kemble to undertake the management. Stephen, a brother of John Philip and Charles Kemble, was a man of gross physical proportions which made him a successful Falstaff. He had considerable experience at managing theatres having been in control of the Newcastle circuit for many years. A further remedial attempt to balance the books was a reduction in admission charges from Boxes 7/- and Pit 3/6d to 5/- and 3/- respectively.

The new manager also brought in his son Henry Kemble from Bath, who made his first appearance on 12 September as Romeo, his Mercutio being Sam Jr. On 20 October, Farquhar's *The Recruiting Officer* was revived, Sam Jr playing Kite. 'With the exception of Stanley as Plume, the rest were shamefully imperfect'. It was not repeated, and was not a good omen for the new management.

Reviewing Bickerstaff's opera *Lionel & Clarissa*, the *Times* critic was still sniping at Sam Jr: 'Penley failed entirely in Jessamy, an event that might have been predicted.' The *Theatrical Inquisitor* also weighed in with

'Penley's Jessamy, was a most disgusting piece of surcharged affectation.'

Theatre business was not helped at the very end of the year when a week of dense fog settled throughout London causing drivers to dismount to lead their horses on foot, pedestrians to stumble around unable to discern the road from the pavement. There was much shrieking as horses loomed unexpectedly from the fog, and people calling for guidance as to their whereabouts. Most of the shops closed for fear of accidents, and in the auditoriums of the theatres the actors could be but barely discerned on the stage. Needless to say, there was a marked increase in crime during those days, perhaps the most brazen being the rascal who stopped a cart, cut the traces, mounted the horse and road off into the dark.

The only real success of the season was a new five-act tragedy *Brutus; or the Fall of Tarquin* which was to become John Howard Payne's finest work. Again, Kean was the star, Sam Jr playing Aruns, Tarquin's youngest son. In spite of the play being repeated 52 times, when the 1818/19 Drury Lane season ended it was with a thumping loss.

The position after Stephen Kemble's attempts was even more parlous than before; the committee – once again seeking for desperate solutions – closing the season early on 8 June. As a direct result the actors, pleading poverty, petitioned the Lord Chamberlain to allow them to use the Haymarket. Having a summer licence, permission to use the theatre was granted for a season which ran from 17 June to 10 July.

Drury Lane Theatre as it would have been when giving regular employment to William Penley (1812 – 1816) and Sampson Penley Jr (1815 – 1826)

SCENE TWO
1819 - 1820
A NEW REGIME AT DRURY LANE THEATRE

AT LAST, REALISING they were amateurs at the game, the Drury Lane committee decided to lease out the theatre building.

Out of four proposals, the man chosen was Robert William Elliston. He had been an actor since 1791, a member of the Drury Lane company for many years and, of course, an experienced manager, having at various times had the Surrey, the Olympic, and the Theatre Royal, Birmingham. In Leamington Spa he owned not only the theatre, but the circulating library and other property.

As an actor, he was better in comedy than tragedy, but versatile enough for both genres and always welcome to his public. Jane Austen said he was her favourite actor. Like many actors of the time, Elliston drank to excess and, depending on his mood and his friendship with the actor in question, could be both parsimonious and over-generous when arranging contracts.

Years of excessive drinking did not affect his prodigious workload. His daily correspondence was inordinate; he personally drew up the playbills and advertisements; attended rehearsals; dealt with all managerial affairs and still appeared in leading roles 60 nights each season. His provincial interests meant frequent travels from London, and the wonder is that he could manage a tenth of all this when for days at a time he was often incapable through drink.

Yet out of the four options, it was certainly the wisest choice, and a great relief to Sam Jr as Elliston, in spite of shedding 40 employees, chose him to be part of the new 1819/20 company:

Tragedy: Kean, Pope, Holland, Powell, Foote, Thompson, Mrs West, Mrs Robinson, Mrs Egerton, and Mrs Knight.

Comedy: Elliston, Dowton, Munden, Harley, Oxberry, Knight, Russell, Butler, Gattie, Hamblin, Barnard, Penley, Mordaunt, Hughes, Meredith, Elliott, Keeley, Mrs Glover, Miss Kelly, Mrs Edwin, Mrs Mardyn, Mrs Harlowe, and Mrs Orger.

The comedy contingent was particularly strong, the first six names probably all the top comedy actors of the time. Without Kean the tragedy team was weak.

Elliston opened on 4 October 1819 with *Wild Oats*, Elliston as Rover, one of his star parts, and Sam Jr as Harry Thunder. The box office took £638 at the door, a vast improvement on the sickly returns under the previous management.

Elliston, hero of the hour, promised his audience that they would have legitimate drama, Shakespeare and writers of genius, plus all the old favourites of the public appearing in turn. He ended by telling them that Mr Kean would resume his engagement in early November. The new regime looked very promising indeed.

Robert William Elliston
the
Manager of Drury Lane

Another new play rescued from the Tobin slush-pile called *The Fisherman's Hut* surfaced with a cast headed by the company's best comedians, with Penley and Hamblin in the leading roles of two rival suitors. Penley was the villain:

> Mr Penley offends us at all times by serious personation, and in *Durazzo,* corroborated our belief of his utter unfitness for that department of the drama.

It was given three times before withdrawal by public demand.

When Kean joined the company Shakespeare took its place in the repertoire. Sam Jr's role in *Hamlet* was Osricke, one of his compendium of fops. Horatio was played by 'one Hamblin, a wretch – a very scarecrow disreputable to the company.' This was rather an unfair comment as, three months later, when the advertised actor of Hamlet was indisposed, Hamblin agreed to step in at extremely short notice though never before having played the part. He did very well and 'promised future excellence', Elliston stating he would reward his assistance with a small piece of plate. A very small piece – a gold tooth-pick!

In January 1820, Kean acted in a revival of *Coriolanus*, and Sam Jr was cast as Tullus Aufidius, the strongest supporting part. However,

> Mr Penley's Aufidius was endued with a most pragmatical sternness; and this rough warlike soldier was so coxcombical that we could only wonder how, with such a hero at their head, the Volscians had stomach to fight at all, or could resist any attack.

It was not the custom to take a curtain call with the entire cast at the play's end, as we invariably see nowadays but, at this time, the fad of calling for the leading actor to come forward at the end of the play was becoming quite regular. This had mainly arisen via Kean's followers, a sort of fan club called the Wolves. Many people, including the general public and the actors themselves, disliked this new fashion. The *London Literary Gazette and Journal* thundered:

> The applause, on the second night, was extremely partial; but at the end, when Penley came forward to announce the next performance, some dozen 'voices' raised the shout for Kean, who had just been carried off the stage in a very painful position, with his head hanging down. It is strange, that this senseless cry should ever be listened to; if the imagination has been affected by the performance, it destroys the vision; and the best that can be done with regard to these injudicious friends of a tragic actor, who do him real injury by their favour, when they insist on such a call, is for the public to treat them with the obloquy and contempt bestowed upon *other resurrection men.*

After the curtain had fallen, Sam Jr had come forward to announce the following night's play but after two successive attempts to speak he was defeated by the many cries for Kean:

> Ultimately Mr Kean appeared, and taking the other performer's hand in his, gave out the play for repetition, amid thunders of applause. The shouting and waving of hats continued a minute or two after they had retired.

Today, an actor, especially a leading one, would feel cheated if he were to be deprived of his curtain call. Sir Donald Wolfit's calls were a one-act play in themselves!

The death of George III on 29 January at last enabled *King Lear* to be seen on the boards. It had been diplomatically banned during the years of his illness; now he was safely dead the play could be resumed. Edmund Kean, eager to be the first to act the role again, had been much taken with the 'storm at sea' he had seen at the Eidophusikon. This was a miniature theatre with a stage opening eight feet wide and six feet high that had been created by Philippe de Loutherbourg, a former innovative scenic designer at Drury Lane, to display spectacular effects in miniature using coloured lighting and moving scenery. De Loutherbourg had changed the face of English theatre during Garrick's regime at Drury Lane, bringing in perspective in a series of cut-out pieces rather than painted on one flat canvas. Garrick spent £290 on scenery during his first season at Drury Lane; after hiring De Loutherbourg at the colossal sum of £500 per annum, the scenery bill for Garrick's final season had soared to £1674. De Loutherbourg gave up work in the real theatre to create his Eidophusikon at his home, the miniature theatre becoming a London attraction for many years.

Kean wanted these miniature storm effects re-created on the large Drury Lane stage. Elliston, at much trouble and expense, mounted an impressive new production to flatter Kean's whim. Unfortunately, the spectacular lighting and storm effects were splendours that Kean, feebly trying to make himself heard, struggled against. Rae played Edgar, the 'wretched' Hamblin was an excellent Edmund, and Sam Jr, playing against type, was the sadistic Duke of Cornwall who puts out Gloucester's eyes. The first night could have been filled three times over and the delighted public flocked to the play for 26 performances even though it was not considered one of Kean's successes.

Sam Jr now offered a third work from his pen, a five act comedy *Gallantry; or Adventures in Madrid*. This caused particular interest, attracting a large house and several full reviews in the newspapers. However, there was little dispute in the verdict of critics and audience:

> The whole comic strength of the house was brought forward to support it, but not all the amusing petulance of Dowton, the comical contortions of Munden, the florid animation of Elliston, and the playful frivolity of Harley, sustained by the efforts of Mrs West, Mrs Edwin and Miss Kelly, could procure it a favourable hearing . . .
>
> . . . a storm of exprobation; hisses, and cries of *off, off,* came hurtling with the sterner thunders for the manager's apology.
>
> . . . it met with a decided and deserved condemnation; and the manager . . . ventured to hint that the difficulty of judging between a good comedy and a bad one was rather above the comprehension of the audience on a single representation.

Elliston did not endear himself to his public when he made that suggestion, the response being 'we cannot think that those to whom he addressed himself, had any right to complain of being placed in a situation of difficulty on that occasion.'

The play was not helped by malcontents acting the giddy goat with their applause. It was sport for a large portion of the audience, but death to the hopes of the author. It was inevitable that the play was promptly withdrawn on the fall of the curtain.

In March 1820, both the patent theatres staged dramatic versions of Scott's recently published novel *Ivanhoe*. As there were no copyright laws at that period, Sir Walter Scott's latest novel was always eagerly anticipated and immediately turned into various dramatic versions by sundry expeditious hands. Covent Garden offered a version by Samuel Beazley with Charles Kemble as Ivanhoe, while Drury Lane had a version by Alfred Bunn with Sampson Penley Jr in the title role. Ivanhoe, though not actually the main character in the play, was certainly a larger role than Sam Jr was normally given and as, apart from Kean, Kemble was the leading actor of the day, pitched him against a player from a higher division than he normally inhabited. The *London Gazette* said the Covent Garden version was

> A magnificent spectacle, extracted from a portion of the novel, commencing after the tournament, and concluding with the burning of Front de Boeuf's castle . . . Charles Kemble as Ivanhoe is a noble picture . . . The scenery is of the highest order, and the decorations superb. The trial scene one of extraordinary beauty.

However, it spent eight times the space to say how awful the Drury Lane version was:

> A miserable piece, in five acts . . . utterly unintelligible, and unutterably tiresome. In our lives we never witnessed a sadder hotchpotch. . . . one dull uninteresting scene follows another . . . Mr Penley strutted and straddled like a thing of gilt gingerbread, as Ivanhoe.

William Hazlitt wrote an essay on the two rival versions in which he said: 'the sound of the trampling of the champion's steed, who comes to rescue her from destruction, which is, however, nearly ruined and rendered ridiculous by Mr Penley's running in with armour on from the farthest end of the stage, as fast as his legs can carry him.' It had eight showings during the season, which sounds to have been seven more than it deserved.

The season closed on 8 July with Madame Vestris in *Giovanni in London* for its 29th performance. Madame Vestris had become a major new star in a very short time, and her breeches role as Don Giovanni one of the sights of London. The entire season of 199 nights had averaged takings of £220 a night – much better than under the previous regime – and resulted in Elliston, in spite of brow-beating his audiences, being once more regarded with favour.

SCENE THREE
1821 - 1822
THE ACTING MANAGER ON TOUR

IT SEEMS CURIOUS that Sam Jr, consistently receiving poor reviews, was re-engaged year after year at Drury Lane. The *Times* was regularly vitriolic, but it was not the only newspaper to carp about Sam's lack of abilities. Perhaps no great shakes as an actor, Sampson Penley Jr was regarded as a solid company man and a good manager as, in the summer of 1821, he was acting manager on a tour for Elliston round his Midlands circuit.

One of the actors said 'Mr S Penley, of Drury Lane, was the manager, and a more gentlemanly young man, or one more calculated to conciliate the good will of a company of actors, it would be difficult to find.' Sam Jr's younger brother Montague was also in the company playing Second Light Comedy roles.

On one occasion at Coventry, whilst preparing for the show, the company was placed under arrest and told not to leave the premises, while manager Penley was hauled off to see the mayor. The dispute concerned an interpretation of the Licensing Act, Penley maintaining that he had a right to play 60 nights spread over a period, and the magistrates insisting that the 60 nights, to which the licence extended, must be played consecutively, excluding Sundays, which they contended was the meaning of the Act of Parliament. The curtain eventually rose about half-past-nine that night when Sam returned, but the theatre was subsequently closed.

As Sam's father had run the place for the previous three years before giving up the lease to Elliston, Sam should have known what he was about, and his interpretation was the one generally adhered to and accepted throughout the country.

George IV's coronation on 19 July 1821 was a magnificent and expensive affair, and Elliston's grand facsimile of the coronation parade was his great money-spinner of the 1821/22 season. He got much mileage from this procession and for many nights at Drury Lane he presented the same bill of fare: *Geraldi Duval*, a musical offering, *Coronation Procession*, and a farce *Monsieur Tonson*. Elliston held a small party to celebrate the 100th performance on 17 January 1822, some of the committee men sending in bottles of champagne, Madeira and sherry, while Elliston himself rustled up a few biscuits and oranges.

This popular attraction was the despair of serious theatregoers who complained that it clogged up the stage of the national theatre, preventing serious work being performed. Elliston's copy of the coronation procession on the Drury Lane stage was such a great success he subsequently sent the show around his provincial theatres starting at Northampton. Sam Jr impersonated the king, which Elliston had done at Drury Lane, and Montague Penley was Prince Leopold. The parade took 45 minutes to pass across the stage with actors playing several roles, tearing off one elaborate costume, running round the back scene, to don another and cross again. When the company arrived at Coventry, this production was mocked and howled down, as the town was then the most radical in England. Perhaps all these kinds of annoyances and interferences at the Coventry theatre may well have been contributary to Sam's father relinquishing his lease to Elliston.

Sam Jr was back at Drury Lane again for the 1821/22 season:

> *Richard III.* Richard Duke of Gloster – Mr Kean (his first appearance this season) Duke of Buckingham – Mr Penley (who is re-engaged at this theatre)

Elliston obviously thought highly of Sam, as Buckingham is generally accepted as the second lead, and it is surprising that an actor from the comedy – rather than the tragic – strength of the company should have been assigned the role.

When a blazing comet such as Edmund Kean became flavour of the month, his repertoire was constantly offered. Audiences could not get enough of his Richard III; however, the version of *Richard III* that was common in Georgian times was not, as you may guess by now, as Shakespeare wrote it. The play was actually a hotch-potch concocted by Colley Cibber in 1700 which – using only 800 of the original lines – ran under two hours. Cibber dragged in lines from other Shakespeare works and wrote additional material himself including seven new soliloquies for Richard. This version held the stage for 150 years because it omitted several minor characters, sharpening up the main role to provide a vehicle for star tragedians. Macready tried to restore the original in 1821 but soon reverted to Cibber, and in 1845 Phelps restored much of the proper text. However, the public did not see the complete Shakespearean text acted until Irving produced it in 1871. Lesser actors still clung to the familiar, often proffering their own pastiche of the two versions. Even Olivier in his famous film of the play stooped to include the odd line of Cibber.

Sam Jr was usually cast as Buckingham, a part that no actor need be ashamed of playing. Unfortunately, not all the critics agreed with Sam's suitability for the role. The *Theatrical Observer* was increasingly outraged, commenting in successive issues:

> Mr Penley, who is re-engaged at this theatre, made his first appearance as Buckingham, which he presented in a spiritless manner. This gentleman makes a tolerable fop, but for any other part we do not think him highly qualified.

> It is with regret we enter into a decided protest against the performance of the Duke of Buckingham by Mr Penley. He is as unfit for such a part, as Mr Powell is for that of Harlequin. Mr Penley may play the walking gentleman, or the soft-pated fop, but to attempt the political tool Buckingham is folly in the extreme.

> We greatly regret to see Mr Kean so badly supported by the very indifferent Buckingham of Mr Penley, who is just as well calculated for that part as any of the scene-shifters.

Nobody seemed to want Sam to extend his range, refusing to accept him in anything other than the pert servants and fops he had been assigned when first coming to the Lane.

The management may have taken notice of these strictures as Sam Jr was dropped from the role and instead given Richmond, the hero who comes on at the end to slay Richard, becoming Henry VII. However, he was soon re-instated in the former role. One wonders if he was a drinking pal of Kean, a notorious toper. It was probably in the time of Kean that the following anecdote arose, which has been applied to many famous names. Kean enters as Gloster and is decidedly incapable, 'Sir, you're drunk!' shouts a man from the audience. Kean replies 'If you think I'm drunk, wait 'til you see the Duke of Buckingham!' It would be a pleasant fancy to think that Sam Jr's place in theatrical history was perpetrated in that anecdote.

As Cassio to Kean's Othello, the kindest thing the *Theatrical Observer* could say was 'Mr Penley's Cassio is not amiss.' Another review stating 'in Mr Penley's hands Cassio is not the man we took him for.' But Elliston still regarded the young man with favour, as in Kean's *Hamlet* Sam was promoted from Osricke to the more important role of Horatio.

In December, Penley played Lord Glenarvon in a new vehicle launched for Madame Vestris. This was an extravaganza opera called *Giovanni in Ireland* which was hoped and expected to emulate her current success *Giovanni in London*. The music was cobbled from Irish airs, and the main reason for mounting it was another grand parade, this time of the Installation of the Knights of St Patrick. Elliston thought combining the essence of two previous hits would be a guaranteed success; in the event it was greeted with some derision, only staggering on for five performances and, in spite of the enormous expense and time spent producing it, the play was withdrawn. So much for Elliston's promises of 'legitimate drama, Shakespeare and writers of genius'.

The theatre may have been lacking writers of genius, but it was mounting new plays by contemporary writers, and on 28 January, while his bankrupt father was languishing in Dover Jail, Sam Jr's latest opus *Owen Prince of Powys; or Welch Feuds* was mounted with Kean in the title role, and Sam himself as Tudor a serf.

Owen, a young Welsh Chieftain, is enthralled by a fair nymph, but leaves her in charge of a faithless friend who threatens that, if not marrying him, she will be thrown into the sea. She chooses death rather than marriage, and his servant is ordered to drown her. In defiance of orders, the servant preserves her, making the villain believe that she is dead. Owen hears the false tale that his lady has fled away, and also that his old father is killed and his castle burnt to the ground. Going to the castle of his faithless friend he discovers the treachery, but is disarmed by his foes and about to be put to death, when his living lady, rushing in, frightens the villain by his belief that she is a ghost. Thus the lovers escape, but there are further assaults, sallies, and re-takings, in which all the three – Owen, his lady, and their foe are slain.

The plot was clearly a load of old tosh, but then a lot of Shakespeare's plots are limp in themselves. There is more to a play than the plot. So what was the verdict on Sam's latest venture?

> The language was in general either feeble or turgid, overrun by metaphor, and full of sentiments more remarkable for their truth than their novelty. (*New Monthly Magazine*)

> We do not complain of want of zeal or exertions, but of a miserable lack of judgment, which, combined with other defects, rendered the whole quite contemptible. (*Literary Gazette*)

> The play may be performed a few nights to thin houses, but it has produced no impression which can give it the slightest chance of a long existence. (*Morning Chronicle*)

Although the situations of the plot are pure melodrama, they were probably no worse than other plays of the day, and the play might well have succeeded in another production. The actors, clad in a motley selection of costumes of all ages and nations, did little with the material. Kean, in a chain mail shirt, took a long time a-dying 'in such a style of throes as no man ever died from a stab which he survived sufficiently to walk about delivering speeches'. Penley, playing the role of Tudor in a doublet of black and white goatskins ('all over goat'), was accused of appearing out of character in the scene of the supposed drowning of the heroine.

Interestingly, in considering Sam's writing talent, there was one particular speech which many reviewers seized upon:

> there was one very vivid and appalling picture in the account given by the vassal of the pretended death of the lady, where he described her as clinging to the ivy after she was hurled from the rock, and told how it crumbled and broke in her eager grasp for existence. If the author can do more like this, let him go on: there is nothing else in the play to justify his writing more tragedies, though there is quite enough to shew that he can do many other things well. The stock of imagery and the copiousness of language, which will do very little for a tragedy, may adorn twenty essays, and set up an orator for life!

But another review of this speech commented:

> There was one very vigorous description given by Tudor of the pretended death of Theodora, but the subject was too horrible to permit us to listen to it with unmingled pleasure.

Obviously this particular speech was the highlight of the play, but received with varying emotions by the reviewers. Perhaps the remarks on this speech were the inspiration for Sam to consider himself a future expert in oratory? No further dramatic works by Sam appeared on the stage and he had to be content with his very first effort *The Sleeping Draught* remaining as his sole testament as a playwright; many years after Sam Jr's death it was still being performed.

Elliston's acting manager James Winston implies that the failure of *Owen Prince of Powys* was because of Kean not learning or performing his part adequately. Kean was always a law unto himself. If he had not been idolised by the masses, much of his behaviour would never have been tolerated; frequently drunk, often absent, he was a constant thorn in the side of many managers. It was only his extraordinary pulling power that gained him huge salaries and the toleration of his appalling professional and personal misbehaviour. He claimed 'I always take a shag before the play begins.' Kean was a flagrant lecher who had visits to his dressing room by, not only trollops, but also women in the company, Winston reporting that he often had three women to 'stroke' during performances.

So, for Sam it was back to his familiar roles, with the occasional new part to test his mettle. In *The Suspicious Husband*

> Penley played the part of Jack Meggot. It was a 'sorry sight.' Harley was wont to perform the character, and ought to retain it.

> Mr Penley's playing Jack Meggott is a mistake in the casting. Honest Jack is a whimsical, eccentric, pleasant fellow. Harley used to do the part; and it is in his way certainly more than in Mr Penley's.

But the *Morning Chronicle* said: 'Mr Penley's Jack Meggott was one of the best things he has yet attempted'. You pays your money and you takes your choice, it all depends which paper you read.

During the summer closure, Elliston had the interior of the theatre entirely gutted and remodelled by Samuel Beazley at a cost of £22,000. The auditorium, never working properly since it was built in 1812, had received various tinkerings in the interim, but this was a major project which basically enlarged the stage, widened the proscenium and narrowed the width of the auditorium. When the new Drury Lane season opened on 16 October 1822 with *The School for Scandal*, Sam Jr was back again to be denigrated by the critics: 'Mr Penley always looks like a footman and therefore seems tolerably at home as Trip.' He was also a 'tolerably good Fag' in *The Rivals* – a pert servant again. But Elliston still persisted in giving Sam the roles of Buckingham in *Richard III* and Harry Thunder in *Wild Oats* as well as retaining him as Allworth in *A New Way to Pay Old Debts* which had many showings.

Penley played Oswald in *King Lear*, a new production in which it was trumpeted that the original fifth act would be restored. Shakespeare's *Lear* had long been superseded by the Nahum Tate version which had a happy ending with Cordelia marrying the Duke of Kent. This was the customary version, thus the restoration of the original was a decided novelty.

In the event, when Kean – a small man – as Lear was required to carry on the dead Cordelia, played by Mrs West, he could only manage with the utmost difficulty, staggering about the stage in danger of dropping the poor woman which, according to Genest, 'set the audience in a laugh until the drop of curtain.' Not quite the desired end for a tragedy!

SCENE FOUR
1823 – 1826
MANAGER OF THE THEATRE ROYAL, WINDSOR

WHEN SAM'S FATHER Sampson was incarcerated in Dover prison for debt, the only way to extricate himself was by surrendering all his theatre leases and fleeing to France. This left the Windsor theatre without a tenant for the first time. Knight put the building out for tender, and in 1822 a manager named Smith provided a season. However, by 1823 Sam Jr had obtained the lease and he announced the season would be opening on 28 July 'under the direction of Mr S Penley of the Theatre Royal, Drury Lane'. This was a good move on Sam's part as the family connection with Windsor was strong, his father having provided the shows there since 1815, Sam Jr taking prominent roles in the past. He could justly claim to be a local favourite. Windsor was convenient for London, being only 25 miles distant. Several coach firms plied between London and Windsor, it was a popular route. The fastest was probably Matthew Milton's coach that left twice daily from the Angel Inn in the Strand at 7.15am and 4.15pm taking 2½ hours to reach Windsor. The fare was 7/- inside and 4/- outside, luggage carried free. Of course, Sam may well have had his own horse, or hired one in preference to a public coach. He will not have tried to emulate the man who carried out this bizarre event for reasons known only to himself: garbed only in a belted flannel jacket and worsted pantaloons, he started on foot from Hyde Park Corner with Moody's coach, keeping pace with it all the way to Windsor. When the coach stopped to change horses, the runner also stopped but took little refreshment. Running barefoot all the way, he arrived before the coach. The likelihood is that he did it for a bet, as betting on various unusual endeavours was endemic at the time.

Sam Jr could manage matters at Windsor while continuing his Drury Lane acting career. The added advantage of the main season taking place during the patent theatres' annual summer break – which this particular year was extended to 1 October – enabled Sam to appear in person and engage actors from Covent Garden and Drury Lane. The orchestra was conducted by Mr Day of Drury Lane, and the whole company – comprising actors from the London theatres – ensured an ensemble 'far superior to any ever before assembled on the Windsor boards.' Which seems a bit of a slap in the face for Sam's poor old dad.

The first week comprised entirely comedies: *Laugh When You Can*, *Man and Wife*, *How to Grow Rich*, and *The Suspicious Husband*. The latter two were advertised as never having been previously acted at Windsor. Some dramas followed including *Guy Fawkes*, *The Iron Chest* and *King Lear* with Sam playing Edgar in a manner 'vigorous and easy'.

As was customary at Windsor, the last week was taken up with bespeaks by various regiments and local worthies including the two MPs who represented Windsor. Here occurs one of those felicitous connections that brings an unwarranted sense of gratification to the historian. One of the MPs from 1823 to 1826 was Edward Cromwell Disbrowe the son of the Colonel Disbrowe, vice-chamberlain to Queen Charlotte, who was deputed to come up with the 300 guineas necessary to launch Sam's cousin George on his career in the Indian army.

The closing night was crowded, and Sam 'displayed the versatility of his abilities to great advantage.' The audience had obviously liked what they had seen during the season, and a general feeling of bonhomie and satisfaction washed over the premises with approbation for the exertions of the new manager. Sam did not undertake a winter season at Windsor, presumably his work at Drury Lane precluded his doing so effectively, and Smithson from Boulogne was the manager with Barton – the Othello from the Paris debacle – as his leading man. At times the theatrical profession must have seemed like a village with actors and managements forever meeting and parting, and no doubt a large amount of 'horse-trading' took place.

Sam Jr was, of course, occupied in the 1823/24 Drury Lane season, and it was not long before the critics were attacking him again in a review of Sheridan's *A Trip to Scarborough* with these damning words:

> Of Thompson and Penley, in Colonel Townley and Loveless, we had rather not say anything. Two such miserable representatives of men of fashion and gallantry we have rarely beheld, and most ardently do we wish that we may never be compelled to witness such a sight again.

In October, William Charles Macready made his first appearance at Drury Lane, choosing for his debut the lead role in Sheridan Knowles's tragedy *Virginius* in which Penley played Caius Claudius. Macready, educated at Rugby school, was not destined for the stage but, when his theatre-manager father was jailed for bankruptcy, took over the company at a very young age. Making his London debut in 1816 at Covent Garden, within three years he became an actor of the first rank and rival to Kean. He possessed a dour personality and, after the death of Kean, became the leading tragedian of the age. Macready's reputation was much later sullied in the USA by a riot at the Astor Place Theatre, New York in 1849 arising from the jealousy of the American actor Edwin Forrest and his fans. The disorder resulted in the deaths of 23 persons and the injuring of a further 36, who were shot by the militia summoned to quell the disturbance.

But at the time of Macready's Drury Lane debut he was still jockeying for position with Kean. In spite of Elliston raising Kean's salary from £30

William Charles Macready
as Virginius

a week to £20 a night, he refused to act with Macready, as he was fully aware of the new man's abilities and must surely have been conscious of his own failing powers. He knew Macready was not an upstart like Junius Brutus Booth whom he could crush; the new tragedian was a man he feared, correctly as it turned out, who would command a large following and eventually oust him. To add to Kean's apprehensions, Macready came trailing an aura of heroism. During a recent visit to Birmingham, on his way to his lodgings after giving his Hamlet

'when he approached a small cottage in flames, surrounded by a concourse of people, as usual, eager to look on and loathe to assist. The flames were bursting out of the front door and a cry of distress was heard from within; he instantly threw off his coat, waistcoat, and hat, and with the agility of a harlequin, sprang into the parlour window, from whence he soon issued with an infant in his grasp: the flames had caught his clothes, which, however, were soon extinguished, and the infant received by the speechless mother in an agony no words can describe. The hat, coat, and waistcoat, of the adventurous hero were gone, and he darted through the crowd as he was towards his lodgings. The papers teemed with this exploit, but no one could tell the name of him who had so gallantly ventured his life, and a pecuniary reward of considerable amount was offered to the "unknown" by a committee of gentlemen.'

Macready, however, was thwarted in his anonymity when a low fellow was apprehended selling a fine coat in which was Macready's name. The papers now praised his modesty more than his intrepidity, and his next appearance at the theatre resulted in thunderous applause before he had even opened his mouth. At his benefit he had a packed house and afterwards received a £10 bank note with a note saying it was a tribute to his humanity and courage in rescuing the cottager's child from the flames. Promptly going round to the unfortunate couple, he handed them the money saying he had only been the mean instrument in the hand of God in procuring it for them.

In November, with both actor and author hoping to repeat the success of *Virginius*, Macready starred in a new play *Caius Gracchus* by Sheridan Knowles in which Penley was cast as Licinius. It was withdrawn after seven performances.

Not all was Roman tragedy though, and Sam played his usual multiplicity of parts as required. He even achieved some commendations, in *The Merry Wives of Windsor* 'Mr Penley was also a very good representation of the easy Mr Page.' This was not Shakespeare, but an opera by Frederic Reynolds, a prolific author of some 100 works, a noted amateur cricketer and husband of Elizabeth Mansel, sister of Robert Mansel manager of York Theatre where Rosina Penley was currently employed. Of Reynolds's latest work Genest said 'this evening he reached the acme of dramatic infamy, by degrading the best comedy in the English language to an Opera.' This version that Genest despised achieved 24 performances.

Penley's Rosse to Kean's Macbeth was judged 'very good'. But in *The Lord of the Manor* 'Penley's Young Contrast was the essence, not of frivolity, but of vulgarity: it possessed not a single feature of the eccentric man of fashion.'

One of the hits of the 1823/24 season was 'a Grand Drama of Action and Spectacle (founded on an ancient custom of the Hindus) called *The Cataract of the Ganges; or The Rajah's Daughter*'; a spectacular melodrama with military bands, dancing girls, a massacre, real horses, fire and tons of water. This afterpiece in two acts had 14 scintillating scenes painted by Stanfield and other leading scenic artists of the day. It was played 54 times throughout the season, with Penley as Iran, a young Hindu Warrior.

It would be tedious to relate all the roles Penley played in so many long-forgotten plays, but he was certainly an important member of the company and used well.

In the summer, Sam operated Windsor theatre, opening it for a Race Week in June and a summer season of half-a-dozen weeks when the boys of Eton College were dispatched hence on their annual vacation. He had made some renovations in the building during its closure, with re-embellishments and decorations 'at considerable expense'. The seats of the boxes and pit were covered with crimson cloth, and the fronts of the boxes and gallery 'ornamented with subjects from the antique.' The whole interior was described as painted in warm pinks in a tasteful manner. Sam's brother Montague was responsible for all this and he was to remain all the season as actor, scene painter and box office manager. Sam trumpeted that his company comprised players from the London patent theatres, which was certainly true but they were not stars. At the season's end Sam Jr was made aware of the same problems that his father had to face:

> The vacation of Eton College terminated on Wednesday. Unfortunately the theatrical seasons are here so short, that before the public are adequately acquainted with the merits of a company, their endeavours to please are brought to a conclusion, and thus the manager is deprived of the fair reward for his liberality and exertions. We fear this has been felt on the present occasion.

October 1824 saw the start of a new Drury Lane season with Sam immediately receiving more abuse for his appearance in the opera *The Marriage of Figaro*: 'The gay, the gallant Count Almaviva was consigned to Mr Penley. It was a piteous sight. Why did not Elliston rescue the opera from utter contempt, by taking the character himself?'

Elliston, trying to repeat the success of *The Cataract of the Ganges* came up with *The Enchanted Courser; or the Sultan of Curdistan* 'a Grand Oriental Tale of Magic taken from the *Arabian Nights*,' a regular source for finding plots. The star attractions of this spectacle were 'Mons Ducrow and his Troop of horsemen in Equestrian Evolutions', closely followed by the scenery. When the rehearsals began, the horses were present but no Ducrow. When sent for, he arrived waving his contract which he said was for the horses, but not for their trainer, thus Elliston was obliged to arrange a separate payment for the services of Ducrow. Elliston was not the only one to play craftily to his financial advantage! In the spectacle, Penley played the Prince of Persia. Elliston, surely expecting this to pack them in like *The Cataract of the Ganges* and his *Coronation Procession*, had crammed the show with magnificently costumed processions, but the play was hardly a success achieving no more than 11 performances.

The press asked why the national temple of the drama was putting on spectacles aimed at children. One answer was that Elliston was desperately trying to fill his seats. Spectacles were expensive to mount but, as he had proved, were popular with the public. But in the theatre there is no such thing as a sure-fire success, and just because the public flocked to one procession, it did not mean they wanted to see more. The heroine escaping on horseback riding up the cataract with water pouring on to her and fires blazing all around was a great novelty, but to try and pull off a similar – now lacklustre – stunt immediately afterwards in the following play was surely tempting fate.

Elliston's costume and scenery bills were mounting at a time when his box office takings were falling. His answer was to pay more and more money out by engaging stars for a few nights work, rather than employing first-class, but less starry, actors at a moderate seasonal salary. Wallack was offered £500 for 40 nights' work, Booth was paid £140 for eight nights, and Miss Stephens settled for 25 guineas a night.

Shortly before Christmas, towards the end of *Guy Mannering* in which Sam Jr played Colonel Mannering, a stage weight of 3 cwt fell striking all before it as it crashed on to the stage. A large piece of timber struck Miss Povey who, seriously injured, had to be carried off home in a coach. Stages can be dangerous places.

Theatre Royal, Drury Lane.
This Evening, the Tragedy of KING
Richard the Third.
King Henry, Mr ARCHER,
Prince of Wales, Miss C A R R,
Duke of York, Master J. CARR, Blunt, Mr Harrold,
Duke of Gloster, Mr KEAN,
Duke of Buckingham, Mr PENLEY,
Lord Stanley, Mr POWELL, Tressel, Mr Younge,
Duke of Norfolk, Mr THOMPSON,
Lord Mayor, Mr TURNOUR, Dighton, Mr HOGG,
Earl of Richmond, Mr WALLACK,
Earl of Oxford, Mr W. H. WILLIAMS,
Tyrrell, Mr RANDALL, Forrest, Mr PLUMSTEAD,
Sir William Catesby, Mr MERCER,
Sir Robert Brackenbury, Mr Y A R N O L D,
Sir Richard Ratcliffe, Mr WEBSTER,
Elizabeth, Queen of Edw. the 4th, Mrs W. WEST,
Lady Anne, Miss SMITHSON,
Duchess of York, Mrs K N I G H T,

After which, a Melo Drama, called
TEKELI;
Or, the Siege of Montgatz.
Tekeli, Mr PENLEY, Wolf, Mr ARCHER, Conrad, Mr TERRY,
Count Crafts, Mr HARROLD, Captain Edmond, Mr MERCER,
Bras-de-fer, Mr HARLEY, Maurice, Mr BROWNE,
Isidore, Mr KNIGHT, Frank, Mr HUGHES,
First Dragoon, Mr WEBSTER, Second Dragoon, Mr KING,
Hungarian Officer, Mr HOWELL, Officer, Mr MAKEEN,
Alexina, Miss L. KELLY, Christine, Miss CUBITT.
In Act II.—The Ballet from Philandering, in which will be introduced
The Provençal.
By Mr & Mrs NOBLE, Mr & Mrs OSCAR BYRNE.
To-morrow, The Merry Wives of Windsor, with Spanish Gallants,
after which, Love, Law, and Physic.

Sam Jr was a very busy actor, often appearing in both the main play and afterpiece on one night.
This playbill from 22 March 1824 shows he played the second lead of Buckingham in *Richard III* and the lead in *Tekeli*, a part he had been playing since 1811.
In spite of all that he did not even rate a mention in the *Theatrical Observer* review!

Early in the new year, Edmund Kean made his first appearance of the season, directly after a sensational court case where he was accused of criminal conversation (ie adultery) with an alderman's wife. The box office took a record £720 that night; the public had not come to support Kean, but to shout at him. It mattered little how feeble Penley's Buckingham was, with the audience making such a racket in protest about Kean's private life that the whole play passed in dumb show. It must have been harrowing for Penley and the others having to suffer this indignity through their star's private follies now made public. This was the turning point in Kean's career as the darling of the gods; always unpredictable, often irresponsible, it was his private life rather than loss of talent that proved his undoing. At his next appearance in *Othello* the clamour was taken up again, and once more Penley, as Cassio, and his colleagues had to plough on through a continuous racket.

The following day Kean made a grovelling apology in the news-papers, and at his next appearance in a performance of *A New Way to Pay Old Debts* there was only a small faction of opposition, most now support-ing Kean, perhaps mainly because of the harsh excoriation he had suffered from the public press.

By the following week, things were back to normal, except Sam started getting some praise – although one self-opiniated critic proclaimed 'Browne, Archer, Penley etc nightly outrage character, language and conception' – in his old part of Young Novall the fop in *Fatal Dowry*, he 'rendered it very effectively.' *Faustus* with Penley as Enrico ran a successful 24 times: 'Mr Penley deserves our favourable mention for his performance as Enrico which is spirited and good'. *Othello*: 'Mr Penley played Cassio extremely well.'

> We feel great pleasure in having again to speak most favourably of Mr Penley's Cassio; in fact this gentleman is a very valuable member of the company, and shows a great deal of ability upon many occasions.

One feels like cheering on Sam's behalf.

As the season drew to its close, a new play appeared that was an excuse to stage yet another spectacle. Elliston, like many a theatrical impresario, was always confident that he was right and knew his public. This time the show was based on the French coronation. The journey across the Channel was depicted by an un-rolling panorama. A special ramp was created circling the pit at the side of the dress boxes enabling the procession to leave the stage, walk round the auditorium, regaining the stage at the opposite side. This only took five minutes and it was considered that, whilst conceding the accuracy of the representation, the whole thing was disappointing compared to our own coronations because our peers and royals wear much more showy outfits, and many more personnel are involved. Penley's part was that of garbing the 'king' in his boots – back to a servant role!

During his usual summer break masterminding his season at Windsor where brother Montague was also now taking a leading part, and the outstanding show was *Der Freischutz*, a fortunately rare incident occurred. The press advertisement says it all:

> WHEREAS I, JOHN HEXELL, did, on the Evening of Tuesday last, cause a Disturbance at the Theatre, by throwing an Onion at Mr. S. Bennett, then performing on the Stage, thereby subjecting myself to a prosecution; and Mr.Penley having kindly agreed to forego any further proceedings, on condition of my publicly apologizing, and paying the costs thereof: I do hereby humbly ask pardon of the said Mr. S. Bennett, and of the Audience generally.
>
> JOHN HEXELL,
>
> X his Mark

Sam was back at Drury Lane for the 1825/26 season playing all his stock parts. Few new plays were mounted, and prior to the new season it was announced that both the patent theatres had agreed to pay a maximum of £20 a week to any player, no matter how eminent. Times were getting hard, competition giving way to collusion once more.

Well accustomed to supporting the erratic Kean, and also by now the rather stolid and solemn Macready, Penley was called upon to support Junius Brutus Booth in the latter's special three night engagement. Booth, who had gone to America some time before, where his ranting style was more appreciated, returned to England when he heard that Kean was departing for America in the wake of the sexual scandal. In fact, they met as they passed each other at Liverpool. Booth, having made his career from imitating Kean, without having the latter's talent – much less genius – was engaged for three nights only at Drury Lane where he played three of Kean's top roles.

The first play was *Brutus*, in which Sam Jr played his usual role of Aruns, little more than a walk-on part. It must have rankled with Sam, having to support Booth, now a star whereas, 11 years previously in Brussels, Sam had been the leading man and Booth a mere beginner; a common situation that often occurs in the theatre world.

The *Times* remarked that Booth was given a great welcome, but having seen him play decided he had not improved during his four-year absence, and that any £6 a week actor in the company could have done as well with a fortnight's rehearsal. At the end, there were calls for Booth, but he declined to be so honoured. The newspaper declared this was a good thing as this offensive custom, started by the sycophantic followers of Kean, should not be allowed in this country. When Booth declined to respond to the call, Wallack came forward to apologise. He explained that Mr Junius Brutus Booth, who had been so favourably received in the character of Lucius Junius Brutus, was unable, through the fatigue of playing Lucius Junius Brutus, to come before them, but Mr Junius Brutus Booth should be apprised of their complete satisfaction with his rendering of Lucius Junius Brutus, and that Mr Junius Brutus Booth would repeat the character of Lucius Junius Brutus on an early occasion.

Whether this gentle spoofing was actually delivered by Wallack, or whether the newspaper reporter was being satirical, the intention was surely to deflate the pretensions of the star.

In *Richard III*, Booth played the first three acts with a degree of tameness bordering on apathy, then made up for it by going over the top, with his death scene being eminently ridiculous accompanied by such gasping, plunging and face-making, as the *Times* had never before witnessed on the stage. Sam Jr, playing Buckingham as he had often done with Kean, did not warrant a mention in the review.

Othello was presented, and the *Times*, who had no love for Junius Brutus Booth, reported 'we have never seen it more inefficiently performed within the walls of a Royal theatre.' Booth was feeble and spiritless, Wallack's Iago was a meagre effort and took liberties with the text, and 'Cassio was personated by Mr Penley, who sustained this, as he does almost every other character, in a very unsatisfactory manner.'

That being the full extent of his London comeback, Booth then embarked on a lucrative tour of the provinces, paying a flying visit to Amsterdam to perform four nights at the German theatre where he had appeared as a tyro with Penley in 1814. Back for a final three nights at the Coburg minor theatre, Booth then returned to America, with the English press reports of *his* sexual peccadilloes resounding round his ears. He spent the rest of his life in the New World, becoming the doyen of American actors and siring ten children with his London flower-girl. In 1846, his legal wife, learning of her husband's second family, left England for the United States to confront him. After years of unsuccessful attempts to break up his relationship, she divorced him in 1851 whereupon he legally married his paramour. Among his children were three actors – Junius Brutus Booth Jr, the famous Edwin Booth, arguably USA's greatest actor, and John Wilkes Booth the infamous assassin of Abraham Lincoln.

The time was gliding by for Sam; as one Drury Lane season closed he moved himself to Windsor for the summer. During 1826, he advertised that the season would be six weeks only, and that the theatre would remain closed for the rest of the year. Presumably winter business was so poor it was not worth other managements taking it on. Sam was once again staunchly supported by brother Montague, and when the season ended, the local newspaper asserted it had been 'a golden season to the manager.'

Then in October, he was back at Drury Lane to play his old roles supporting Elliston, Kean and Macready. Years of excessive drinking caused Elliston medical problems with lapses of memory and hallucinations. He suffered a stroke, losing the use of his hands, turning into a decrepit old man overnight, but soldiered on.

He actually attempted a new role – that of Falstaff. On the first night he gave a more than adequate performance, but at the next showing it was a pitiful sight. There is a great difference between acting the drunk and being one. The audience could only reach one conclusion, and when finally Elliston collapsed in heap and had to be carried off by Wallack playing Prince Hal, the booing and fruit projectiles were considered well justified. On many occasions in the past, Elliston had brow-beaten his audiences, now the man was down it was a chance for a good kicking. How much was drink and how much illness is debatable, probably a combination of the two. But he was also in arrears of £5500 rent, the Drury Lane committee demanding that this be paid, or the lease be forfeited according to contract.

Elliston, protesting that he had spent some £30,000 improving and re-decorating the theatre, including a new portico designed by Sir John Soane, considered he was entitled to some leniency in the matter. However, his finances were in a sorry state and the committee, fearing he would build up further debts if allowed to continue, cancelled Elliston's lease and advertised the theatre to let. Elliston had to relinquish his interest in Drury Lane and on 10 December 1826 was declared bankrupt.

Mr Penley, unable to rely on Elliston anymore, was not retained by the new management.

SCENE FIVE
1827 - 1829
MARRIAGE AND HONEYMOON

SAMPSON PENLEY JR now had to take stock; like Othello, his occupation was gone. He had had a good run at Drury Lane lasting over a decade and was still only thirty-four years old. It might be thought that with his Drury Lane reputation he could easily have sought a position in a good-class provincial company such as Edinburgh or Bath, but there is no evidence that he did that.

Neither was he called upon by his old boss Elliston who, remarkably, bounced back from his medical and financial afflictions and obtained the lease of the Surrey theatre where he acted up to six times a week, had a tremendous hit with *Black-Eyed Susan*, and died in harness in July 1831. Until the end of his days, in his cups, Elliston blamed the Prince Regent for his misfortunes saying the prince had urged him to spend £20,000 on unnecessary lavishments to the theatre. There is no evidence that Sam Jr worked in another London theatre after leaving Drury Lane. It is impossible to say how Sam occupied himself and kept body and soul together at this period unless he had other work besides Windsor that has not come to light.

He had been running the Windsor theatre for the last four years and continued to do so with renewed vigour. Firstly the annual Race Week where several regulars were back including Mr Dodd a perennial favourite at Windsor, who played low comedy roles such as those made famous by Liston, Dowton and other star comedians.

> Our Theatre has been opened during the race week with considerable success. The audiences were very select and the performers better than those generally congregated for so short a season. A new melodrama of *Luke the Labourer*, was particularly well supported; and the manner in which it was got up reflects the highest credit on the manager, who upon this, as on all other occasions, has evinced that he spares neither trouble nor expense in catering for the amusement of the public.

It was necessary for this isolated week to be well supported as the profit-margin must have been small, especially when a new production was mounted. Sam Jr had a better chance of making money in the summer season of six weeks but, of course, there were not the inflated racecourse crowds to draw upon.

Fortunately, the 1827 summer season was highly successful with excellent business enhanced by command performances of the faithful Princess Augusta, and bespeaks by the local MPs and officers of the military stationed in the town. Sam, eschewing booking London names, relied throughout on his permanent company. On the final night – Sam's benefit – the house was packed, thus going a long way to tiding him over to the next season.

Sam did not attempt winter seasons at Windsor and, when the 1828 Race Week came again, the local paper suggested that 7 o'clock was too early a start and an hour later would be more suitable, bringing in more people and an increase of money to the exchequer. The suggestion was not adopted.

When the summer arrived Sam had no family support, both Emma and Rosina having retired. Again he relied on a resident starless company with Younge shouldering all the leads and Dodd the low comedy. Sam, himself, rarely playing leading roles, was in the main piece every night carrying on in the line of parts he had maintained at Drury Lane – in Shakespeare: Osricke in *Hamlet*, Gratiano in *The Merchant of Venice*, Mercutio in *Romeo and Juliet*, Prince Hal in *Henry IV*. When Younge played the Kean role of Sir Edmund Mortimer in *The Iron Chest*, Sam gave his Wilford as he had done so often before at Drury Lane. Taking a hint from the local press, *Virginius* was played on three occasions, another chance for him to reprise his old role of Icilius. Two new parts that he would have had to learn were Macduff and Charles Surface, as previously they would have been too high a flight for him at Drury Lane. A week before the season closed, sister Rosina came out of retirement to return to the fold to play four nights. Her return and the usual bespeaks meant a strong end to the season.

On 2 October 1828, Sampson Penley Jr married Katherine Wickey Taylor at St Martin-in-the-Fields, London. Miss Taylor was aged twenty-five and Sam ten years older. Sam had met his future wife whilst walking in Barnstaple, falling in love on sight, and found out she was the daughter of the postmaster. It was a very short courtship prior to marriage. The newly-weds went to Italy on a prolonged honeymoon funded by the rare-book dealer Thomas Thorpe, a great friend of Sam. Thorpe, who claimed descent from Shakespeare's publisher and was the leading book dealer of the day, commissioned Sam to scour Italy for certain antiquarian works. On returning, the newly-weds lived at 12 Sloane Square where their first son Lionel Banks Penley was born on 17 July 1829.

Sam was back at his theatre at Windsor for Race Week opening on 2 July that year with one night devoted to 'Two Amateurs well known in the fashionable world' when one 'celebrated Amateur' played the lead in the play and the other 'celebrated Amateur' headed the farce. Sam had complied with the suggestion of delaying curtain up until 8 o'clock to ensure a select and fashionable audience, but it had not boosted takings at all. The regular troupe including Younge and Dodd were back again, and a special night 'under the immediate patronage of His Majesty' (George IV) featured the Rainer Family of Tyrolese singers – precursors of the Von Trapp family.

On the closing night of Race Week an unfortunate incident occurred at the theatre when one of a party of officers in one of the boxes, using a switch or horsewhip, touched the bonnet of a lady seated in the pit. Her husband remonstrated with the officer who protested it was an accident caused by his trying to swat a playbill that had fluttered down from above. The words led to an argument that developed into a fracas, with supporters of the outraged husband trying to drag the officers out of the box. Fortunately, some impartial gentlemen were able to smooth things down, and the disturbance was brief. However, the newspaper report of the affair stated that, while it assumed the matter had been caused entirely accidentally, the theatre cannot be turned into a bear garden at the caprice of any obnoxious person's ill-conduct and, if there is any suspicion that such an affront was deliberate, henceforth they would hold up any offender as being an object of public contempt and disgust.

Sam Jr, now a family man, was joined by Emma and Rosina – now both back in harness after their short-lived retirement – for the summer company which was again headed by Younge. The season opened with three nights starring French group Le Trois Troubadour who sang but 'not to crowded audiences'. In *Othello*, Younge played the title role while Sam essayed Iago. With 237 more lines than Othello, Iago is the fourth longest part in all Shakespeare. The character was not in Sam's normal repertory and this was probably the first time he had been called upon to play it. As *Othello* needs two tragedians of equal stature, at Windsor Sam Jr remained as the only competent choice. Not being a tragedian, and the part new to Sam – he had been playing Cassio for years – it was a lot of hard graft just for one night as it does not appear that he ever played it again. He was certainly back playing Cassio when Kean visited during a later season, Iago taken by Ternan the leading man.

Again, one boggles at the apparent ease with which an actor could play other than his accustomed role. It was commonplace in those times for a leading tragedian to have both Othello and Iago in his repertory, often alternating them with another actor.

The Bottle Imp was a new afterpiece by Richard Brinsley Peake, derived from a folk tale found in Grimm's Fairy tales, currently a hit in London. The local critic found the production superior to the one he had recently seen at the English Opera House, and he was perturbed that the playbill said it was the last night of the play. The production was of such excellence it deserved to be seen by far more people before its withdrawal.

The Windsor newspaper declared that the season had been profitable, the performances attractive and the *Corps Dramatique* of a superior class. On the last night Sam gave 'a very feeling and appropriate speech.'

The following year, Race Week was reported to be 'uncommonly dull' with a diminished attendance, blame being attributed to the cost of accommodation, a guinea a night for a bed being considered moderate. Fortunately for Sam, the theatre was well attended, and an intimate glimpse of the Windsor Theatre during that Race Week of 1830 is provided by Edward Stirling, at the time a lowly wandering actor, who obtained an engagement:

> I found a temporary engagement at Windsor, with Sam Penley of Drury Lane, as manager. It was Race week. Eton boys were admitted for two shillings and sixpence each from six until eight; the signal for their departure was the ringing of the college bell. A pretty game they had, laughing and talking to the actors and actresses during their performances, shooting peas at the heads of the unfortunate fiddlers, sliding down pillars from gallery to boxes, etc. Penley, however, made money by this, and his regular audience came at eight from the races.

These jolly japes by upper-class hooligans were bound to end in tears, as will be seen later.

The summer with Sam, sister Emma, the regulars Younge, Butler and the low comedy favourite Dodd got off to a slow start. The usual assorted programme of favourites, pot-boilers and new productions had a minimum of classics, though in both *Macbeth* and *The Rivals* Phoebe Penley made an increasingly rare appearance.

On 21 August Sam threw open the theatre free of charge to celebrate the birthday of William IV who had succeeded his brother George IV on 26 June, but overall the season proved disappointing:

> Our theatre will close tomorrow, after a season which we are
> sorry to say has not proved so successful as the manager
> (from the extraordinary exertions he made in catering for the
> amusement of the public) was led to hope for and expect. The
> performances, from the commencement, have been extremely
> creditable to the establishment; and we sincerely hope, that
> on the next visit of Mr Penley to Windsor, he may meet with
> that liberal encouragement to which his well-known good
> taste and zeal so fully entitle him.

The local newspaper was always supportive because the owner and editor
Charles Knight, was the theatre's principal freeholder. If the shows were
ever strongly criticised then they must have been very bad indeed. Knight
went on to greater things, but the paper's reporters remained supportive.

While a bachelor, Sam may have been able to coast along getting by
with his income from Windsor. Now he was a married man, with a family
and establishment to maintain. His only financial life-line was diminishing;
he would have to look for further sources of income.

He put pen to paper to write a 25-page booklet *Observations respectfully
addressed to the nobility and gentry on the existing importance of the ART AND
STUDY OF ORATORY* which was sold by his friend Mr Thorpe at his
premises in Covent Garden. It can hardly have brought in much money
and read as though nothing more than a plea for oratory to be studied
under an expert – like music, dancing and painting. The author urges MPs,
lawyers, clergymen, and even ordinary people who read aloud to friends, to
study oratory like the ancients.

The point of all this may be deduced by the introduction in which the
author 'respectfully submits his offer of instruction upon a novel and
effective system not theoretically devised but emanating from the practical
advantage of many years' experience and observation.' A footnote adds
'Additional particulars may be obtained of the Professor, Mr S Penley, at
his residence No 199 Oxford St.'

No mention of being an actor or playwright, Sam is now a Professor
of Oratory, and the pamphlet is actually a sales gimmick touting for
students. The whole thing is couched so discreetly that the message is
easily missed and was probably not a success. There is no evidence
elsewhere of Sam proclaiming himself as a Professor of Oratory, though it
was quite commonplace for actors and singers to advertise private lessons
while they were resident for a season in a town.

SCENE SIX
1830 - 1835
RICHMOND, NEWCASTLE, AND LEICESTER

SAM'S ANSWER TO a diminishing income was to lease another theatre, and this he acquired at Richmond, Surrey. A manager called Klanert had held the theatre for many years, running a four-month season from the end of July until November, and in the past Sam Jr and Oxberry had appeared as guest artistes. Klanert retired in 1829, Sam taking the theatre in 1830. A letter published in *The Era* of 26 November 1881 avers that 'Edmund Kean took over what remained of Penley's lease – the grievous manager. This was in 1831. I have John Lee's letter to Penley making the proposal,' From this it is certain that Sam's sole season was not a great success but there is no documentary evidence of the season anywhere, apart from the fact that Sam and Katharine's second son Francis Thorpe Penley was born in the town on 20 November 1830. Kean famously had the theatre and adjoining house from 1831, dying there in 1833. After that short-lived venture, Sam needed to find another venue.

For the best part of a century much of the provincial theatre had depended upon the Circuit System, but these were rapidly disappearing, the major circuits concentrating on their original base theatres, whilst shedding most of the other lesser venues.

Sam originally thought his acquisition of the lease of the Theatre Royal, Newcastle-upon-Tyne a good thing. His sister Phoebe had been in the company there three years previously and it may have been via her encouragement that Sam took on the lease. Though since Phoebe's stint at the theatre, business had gone downhill, the previous manager becoming ill and in debt, £380 in arrear with his rent, and announcing he was 'a ruined man and could pay nothing'.

The theatre in Mosley Street, built in 1788, had been leased by several managers, the most notable being the avoirdupois-challenged Stephen Kemble who held it for 15 years. It was a large house seating some 1500, half in the exceptionally capacious gallery. Though not daunting for Sam, who had been used to years in the 3000-seater Drury Lane, still somewhat distanced from the cosy country theatres of his father's company where he spent his youth. It was stated to hold £135, the main season being several months in winter with extra weeks for the assizes, races and fair.

Sam's brother Belville, now twenty-two and participating in management, was despatched to complete the formalities, and the season was scheduled to open in early December, but preparations were delayed as the entire auditorium was re-painted, a new ceiling installed and a new chandelier hung. The grand opening was on 15 December 1830 when *The School for Scandal* and *Teddy the Tiler* were the attractions.

Sam gave a gracious speech praising the proprietors for their consideration of his suggestions, stating his watchwords were respectability and attention, the good conduct of his actors giving a zest to their abilities. And so his new venture was launched.

The old Newcastle theatre
built in 1788.
Stephen Kemble was the
manager from 1791 to 1806

Sam Jr acquired the lease in
1830

The leading ladies Miss Cleaver and Phoebe Penley were returning, both having been there three years previously under the former manager. Miss Sidney, an agreeable actress, 'was not troubled with much vivacity or power of expression.' The leading man was Ternan – 'forcible and reads well' but considered over-the-top. However, this did not stop him from becoming a popular favourite in Newcastle, and a future rival. Mr Hay the low comedy man 'cuts a poor figure'. 'Mr Penley is himself a good actor of volatile fine gentlemen, though rather too old looking.' Sam, still playing his line of fops and pert servants, perhaps should be going for more mature roles as he was now pushing forty. Perhaps the responsibility of a family as well as two theatres was getting him down.

A Miss Field 'from the Liverpool theatre' possessed a voice of considerable compass, trilled beautifully, singing with ease and self-possession. Belville Penley was the Box Book Keeper and this pair will be coming to our further attention shortly. It is a shame that Montague, wearing his scene-painter's hat, was not involved, as the scenery – taken over from the previous incumbent – was wretched and shabby.

The large resident orchestra under Charles Miller was a feature of the theatre, and Sam Jr carried on the engagement of the maestro and his men from the previous tenant.

The journal of one John Waldie gives us a glimpse of on-the-spot opinion of the first weeks of the season. Newcastle-born Waldie kept a series of journals wherein he made private comments about theatres and actors both in this country and on his many travels in Europe. With his excessive theatre-going and varied experience it can be presumed he had some idea of what he was talking about.

On a visit to his home town, Waldie, taking the opportunity to see what was happening at the theatre where he used to serve on the board, made notes in his journal. His comments about Sampson and his sister Phoebe are often not very complimentary. It would seem, even after all his years at Drury Lane, Sam still retained the attitudes of a country actor.

> 7 January 1831: Penley's Windsor Company. *Man and Wife* was the play – dull and humdrum – the farce was *Free and Easy*. Penley is a good actor in light comedy, tho not elegant, and his sister in tragedy may be tolerable.

> 12 January: We had a new farce, *A Husband at Sight*, very comic and taken from the French. Miss Penley in the young lady disguised as a man and married against her will to a soubrette, or young peasant, who had been attracted in the eyes of a young baron, was good.

> 21 Jan 1831: *The Way to Get Married*. Miss Penley made nothing of Miss Clementine, which should have been done by Miss Cleaver. Penley is boisterous but so-so in Tangent

> 24 Jan 1831: [*Richard III*] Penley blustered in Richmond and tried to look like Charles Kemble.

> 11 February 1831: [*Black-Eyed Susan*] It is all in bad taste – but the pantomime of Mr Penley was good in the serious part. In the early part he was boisterous and vulgar. Miss Penley as Susan – very dull and uninteresting.

Waldie was, no doubt, more accustomed to the actors at the patent theatres which he attended regularly, and the top actors in the foreign capitals he had visited but, with his journals covering many years and countries, he was eager to see any theatre, wherever he may be.

All-in-all not a wildly enthusiastic welcome for Sam's company, but once played in, it was acknowledged that it was the best ensemble for some years. It was a tradition in Newcastle that Fridays were 'fashionable night' and the proprietors of the theatre inserted an advertisement suggesting that soirées and parties be not arranged for that night, allowing it to be the regular theatre night for the gentry as it had been previously.

The season ran until late May 1831 and was reasonably successful, with regular bespeaks that filled the place. Ternan as leading man was very popular as his robust acting style suited the Geordie audience. Sam himself played light comedy leads and second tragedy roles like Macduff and Prince Hal as he always had. There was some criticism that plays were repeated too often; obviously Sam was reluctant to venture out of his own comfort zone.

Sam announced that he was limiting his season to four winter months plus the odd couple of weeks in summer. The previous manager had tried to open the theatre all year round. The Newcastle Race Week in June included Emma Penley in the company, as sister Phoebe and brother Sam had returned to Windsor to head the cast for the annual Race Week there, which took place at the same time.

The Windsor company was considered sub-standard and was received with ill grace. Every piece presented was completely murdered and, apart from the Penleys, not one player was deemed fit to even grace the boards of a fairground booth. It is likely that four months of Newcastle audiences had dulled Sam's perception of the quality of actor demanded in Windsor. It was stated that if Sam did not bring a better company next time his business would suffer markedly.

In summer 1831 they were joined by Miss Field who 'sang with her accustomed fascination', and local favourite Dodd with all his 'humour and vivacity'. Otherwise the company was mundane, but praise was heaped on Phoebe and, to a lesser extent, on Sam.

Sam, emulating his father's attempts at empire building, now captured yet another venue as he took the lease of the Leicester theatre, instigating a thorough overhaul and redecoration of the place, together with a complete set of new scenery. Sam also ensured that the Leicester public was made aware that Her Royal Highness Princess Augusta had recently honoured him with a command performance at Windsor which was 'brilliantly attended, and had gone with great éclat.' Sam opened at Leicester for the race week in September 1831 with 'a *corps dramatique* as clever as has been known here for some years past' which included Phoebe, Dodd, Dry, Miss Field, and Miss Cleaver (all from Windsor) as well as himself.

Sam looks to have attempted some sort of personal PR, as among the gobbets of information carried in the local paper it mentions he had made his debut with Harley 'with whom he frequently performed upon the more exalted boards of Drury Lane'. Stating Penley was a versatile performer, it was clear he 'had profited from the lessons of Elliston: a better master he could not have had.'

> The classical taste, spirit, and enterprise, of which Mr Penley has given such a conspicuous proof in the decoration of the theatre, are equally evinced in the practical business of the stage. The pieces already produced prove him to have a proper regard to the claims, value, and importance of the legitimate drama; yet, with a due sprinkling of more light amusement. His company is . . . of well-disciplined veterans, who have hitherto proved themselves, in all respects, competent to sustain their parts with credit to themselves, and satisfaction to the audience.

The company was working every night during Fair Week, mainly taken up with nautical dramas including *Black-Eyed Susan* wherein 'Penley's William was a faithful and animated portrait of this singular and amphibious class of mankind.'

As the short season ended, the local paper opined 'Few weeks exhibit such a variety of performances, and much fewer their exquisite delineation.' It is difficult to see what can have gone amiss because, in spite of the lavish praise bestowed upon Sam's company, he did not return. The reason for a company quitting a venue is invariably poor business. The following year the Leicester theatre had the company of Mr Parker Cooke.

1831 had been a full year for Sam, playing at Newcastle from January to May, Windsor from June to September and Leicester in September and October.

When the time had come to open for the Assize Week at Newcastle Sam had demurred. He had told the proprietors that it would be wise to close from Race Week until December to which they agreed. Then when December arrived Sam said they should not open because cholera was rife throughout the city. This was a major epidemic that struck several towns in the country but was particularly virulent in Sunderland and Newcastle with 40 to 50 persons dying daily. Nationwide, 20,000 were to die before the contagion was halted; the committee agreed to a month's delay.

It is certain that Sam did not want to return to Newcastle, claiming the distance from London was impossible for him to operate efficiently. The journey by coach from London to Newcastle took 32 hours. Also it is likely he did not wish to risk cholera! However, persuaded to continue with his contract, the situation was resolved by sub-letting the theatre to Mr Coleman Pope, with the even more splendidly named Mr Cooper Stinnett to carry out the on-the-spot managerial functions.

Sam thus remained in the south and back in Windsor. Heeding past strictures of underwhelming actors, Sam launched his Race Week in 1832 with three nights of Edmund Kean who gave his Othello, Shylock and Sir Edward Mortimer. Alas, Kean did not attract and the result was empty benches. It is unlikely that the extra expense of engaging Kean was covered by the takings.

Sam brought Ternan, now the leading man at Edinburgh, to lead the Windsor company in the summer of 1832 and, notwithstanding any loss on Race Week, booked Kean again for three nights to open the season. Kean, who was dying in public, still worked prodigiously. At Windsor he performed Tuesday, Thursday and Saturday, while appearing at his own theatre at Richmond on Monday, Wednesday and Friday during the same week. The *Theatrical Observer* of 25 July 1832 remarking:

> The Richmond Theatre...will open on Monday next, under the management of Kean, who is to perform there three times a week, at Windsor twice, and at the Haymarket every Monday during the season; pretty sharp work that for a man with a shattered constitution.

In *Othello* Kean had the title role, Ternan played Iago, Sam his usual Cassio and Rosina as Desdemona. The *Morning Post* said Kean played to 'very fashionable and crowded houses' whereas the local Windsor press begrudgingly called them merely 'tolerably good houses.'

Sam resumed duties in person at Newcastle for the 1832/33 season with himself, Rosina and James Anderson as principals. But things were not going well there, and in March Sam protested his difficulties to the proprietors' committee, claiming the opening of a circus had destroyed all his best efforts. Cooke the celebrated equestrian had erected a temporary wooden pavilion in West Gate and opened for a season on 28 January with a stud of 21 horses. The circus was hugely popular and crowds of all classes flocked to its shows. A sour dissenting letter was published in the *Tyne Mercury* ostensibly comparing Cooke's circus unfavourably to that of Ducrow who had visited the town on a former occasion. However, in his tirade the writer, rubbishing the circus, said people should prefer the theatre as, more educational and beneficial, it was a school of morality as well as an entertainment.

As a riposte to this statement the *Newcastle Journal* made the point of quoting several plays recently presented – crude melodramas and low-life comedies – and sarcastically enquired where the morals were. The editor further stated that the circus was no competition to the theatre as it attracted a different audience and, in any case, Penley's company had been playing to empty benches long before the circus even appeared. Sam Jr, who played no part at all in this wrangle, was dragged in and excoriated. It must have been an added insult when the Mayor and other upper-class patrons gave their annual bespeaks to Mr Cooke's circus rather than to Sam's theatre.

In May, Sam Jr shared in the national calamity that was the death of Edmund Kean. Almost to the end Kean had been working, his finances in a precarious state having made and spent several fortunes. He needed to keep working to eat, and he could only keep working with the aid of incessant glasses of brandy. He played no fewer than 14 performances at Drury Lane of which eight were as Othello to Macready's Iago. The performances drew the town as it was the first time the two foremost tragedians of the age had acted together. The pair hated each other, and it was only his contempt for his rival that kept Kean going.

Kean worked when and where he could, each performance a nightmare. At Brighton he was taken so seriously ill that he was forced to step down halfway through the performance, allowing his secretary the actor John Lee to take over. But he rallied again and asked Drury Lane, where he was committed for future performances, to advance him £500 which was refused. Affronted by this rebuff from a theatre to where he had brought thousands, ignoring his legal commitments, he signed to perform at Covent Garden opening – to great acclaim – with Shylock. He was announced as Othello with his son Charles playing Iago – the first time London had seen father and son on the same stage. A great crowd assembled for the event, but the older man struggled through three acts before collapsing in his son's arms with the words 'O God, I am dying. Speak to them for me.' He was borne unconscious from the stage.

Two months later Edmund Kean was dead, aged forty-five. That wayward genius, who spent a career letting people down through drunkenness and irresponsibility, was still a star name and had brought a lot of money to the coffers of Drury Lane. Penley Jr had often supported him and, as a manager, employed him in his latter days. The funeral was a huge affair with extra coaches and steam boats taking the mourners out to Richmond, where Kean was to be buried. The pall bearers of ex-colleagues were followed by Kean's son Charles as chief mourner, supported by eight more mourners. Heading the following procession were the entire 12 members of the Drury Lane Theatrical Fund Committee, including Sampson Penley Jr (who had replaced his uncle and still served), then actors from each of the London Theatres in order of precedence, members of different professions, and lastly citizens of Richmond.

> On the 15th May, 1833, expired the celebrated tragedian, Edmund Kean. He first appeared in London, as Shylock, in the *Merchant of Venice*, January 25th, 1814. It has been calculated that, during a period of nineteen years, he realized more than £150,000, by the exercise of his powerful talent; yet he died poor, and, from the wreck of his fortune, a few of "Honours baubles" only were preserved to his son, not as the inheritance of his father's wealth, but as memorials of his father's fame. A single page would contain the names of all the actors who have died in the possession of their acquired riches. – A volume might be filled by those whose delinquencies have led them scarcely wherewithal to purchase the "nails for a coffin."

In June the Newcastle Race Week company was headed by Ternan, with only Sam himself from the family. In August Sam requested the rent be reduced from £300 to £200; on the grounds of the unfair competition he had suffered from Cooke's circus, the proprietors countering with a demand for £250. Sam was so worked up about all this that he had been corresponding with Mr Lamb the Under Secretary of State because the Newcastle magistrates declared themselves unable to do anything about it as the law currently stood. Mr Lamb hoped a remedy for such situations could be included in Mr Bulwer's Theatrical Performances Bill which was currently before parliament. The hope was not realised.

For the 1833 season at Windsor Sam brought the twenty-two-year-old Scottish actor James R Anderson down from Newcastle as the leading man, and both Phoebe and Rosina were seen during the summer. Anderson and Rosina left before the end of the season to go to Leicester where Anderson and Belville Penley had formed a partnership to run the theatre there.

During the last two weeks of the season, Sam was ill and unable to perform, which seems to have 'operated much against the success of the establishment.' He would not have given up his duties lightly – even today, actors struggle through if humanly possible – and it emphasises how, in addition to other qualities, the Regency actor had to be supremely fit.

Fortunately, Sam was back before the last night of the season, which was his benefit and under the patronage of the two local MPs. The attraction was *Henriette, the Forsaken* in which the lead role was taken by Mrs Penley. Another little puzzle here as this, presumably, was Sam's wife who was not known as an actress. The role was an arduous one for an amateur to undertake, and it is not apparent why Mrs Penley should have chosen it for this rare event, even if she did wish to support her husband.

In view of the financial problems up there, Sam returned in person to launch the Newcastle 1833/34 season. Younge, Anderson, and Rosina were all back in the company and Charles Miller was once more leading the large orchestra. Cathcart was the new leading man, and a Miss Stohwasser was particularly delighting the audience.

The 1834 Race Week at Windsor did not include any family members, but the summer season thrived as, due to the presence of the Court, Windsor was becoming a resort. The town's attractions included a terrace, with the finest military bands in the service, hourly water excursions, drives in the parks and forests, and other delights including

> our Theatre, too, under the direction of that spirited manager, Mr Penley, with a selection of artistes from his establishment in Newcastle, offer a nightly treat certainly not to be surpassed in any provincial Theatre.

It proved to be an unusually prosperous season with many houses full to overflowing. This was attributed to the fact that many old favourites such as Younge and Dodd, Sam and Rosina, were back after what the local paper disparagingly called three or four years of miserable substitutes by 'Bartholomew Fair heroes'. Anderson and Miss Stohwasser, 'our little favourite', Miss Mayoss and Yarnold were all popular performers. Phoebe appeared once only during the season in an afterpiece for her sister Rosina's benefit.

The patrons at Newcastle were welcomed back in December to a newly decorated and embellished auditorium, and an orchestra of 23 musicians under the direction of Charles Miller the long-serving Newcastle conductor. The principals were the same as the previous year, Miss Stohwasser inevitably alongside Anderson, though it was Rosina, in her first appearance of the season, who appeared as Juliet to Anderson's Romeo. Dodd from Windsor was a new addition, though he had been a Newcastle stalwart some ten years before for the previous manager.

During the season a rather unpleasant incident occurred which shows Sam Jr at his best. The local newspaper told the story succinctly:

> Two missiles, a stone and a piece of iron, were thrown into the orchestra from the gallery, by which two of the performers were struck with considerable violence. Mr Penley, with that promptitude and proper spirit which ever actuate his conduct, immediately directed one of the performers to announce from the stage, that he would give a reward of £5 for the apprehension of the offenders, who were soon after taken into custody. On Wednesday they underwent an examination before the Mayor, when Mr Penley attended, and expressed a desire that further proceedings should be stayed, as he believed the young men had received a caution which would prevent them from offending in similar manner in future. The chief magistrate complied with the request of the manager, and discharged the prisoners, having previously given them a severe admonition, and pointed out to them that by a perseverance in such conduct very serious consequences might ensue, and that, in fact, they might subject themselves to be tried even for their lives. The worthy manager, we think, acted in this instance with culpable lenity.

A manager had always more to deal with than simply putting on plays. Whether this was a straw that broke the camel's back one cannot say but, at the end of the season, Sampson threw in the towel at Newcastle and the lease passed to his brother Montague. No doubt the success of the previous summer at Windsor had bucked Sam up no end and he could now forget about that horrible place in the north-east.

SCENE SEVEN
1835 - 1838
FAREWELL

FOR WINDSOR RACE WEEK in June 1835 Sam offered himself, Rosina, Miss Crisp and Mr Dodd as the principal players, and produced 'several new and popular pieces'. Unfortunately, they were not all that popular as audience numbers were sadly lacking.

Nothing daunted, prior to the summer, Sam went to some trouble and expense in fitting out and newly decorating the auditorium. The old chandeliers were replaced with handsome new ones, and a new drop scene by Grieves of Covent Garden depicted Richmond Bridge, river and a neat histrionic temple to the memory of Edmund Kean. The company was rated excellent and Penley strenuous in mounting a succession of novelties. A newcomer to the troupe was Miss Parsloe, an effervescent young lady who liked flashing her legs at venues throughout the land. Windsor rated her dancing as easy, graceful and pleasing.

That old stand-by Sheridan's tragedy *Pizarro* was produced with Younge as Rolla

> displaying great powers; his address to the Peruvians - itself a master piece of eloquence was delivered with much dignity. Miss Penley's personation of the unhappy Elvira was an admirable performance, and fully justifies our former opinion of her powers, but Dodd was sadly out of his place in Orozembo; however, in his serious part he gave as much satisfaction as the remembrance of his low comedy characters would allow.

This highlights the perennial problem with small country companies. From time to time there were not sufficient actors to obviate personnel playing out of their accustomed line of parts. Dodd, a great favourite in low comedy roles, no doubt habitually resorted to bodily contortions and funny faces in his efforts to elicit laughs. Called upon to play a straight part in lieu of a spare actor, no doubt just the sight of him standing there dressed as an Inca chieftain was enough to set the house a-ripple.

Closing with a series of bespeaks, the latter end of the season was well attended, though whether financially it made up for what had been a disappointingly slow start only Sam would know. Having suffered almost continuous condemnation for his acting prowess during his ten years at Drury Lane, it must have been pleasant to read the regular paeans of praise showered upon him by the local press: 'The acting was generally speaking very good, particularly that of Mr and Miss Penley'; 'Mr Penley's perform-ance of Tom Cringle was admirable'; 'Of Mr Penley himself he is the very *beau ideal* – if we may be allowed to apply the term – of a sailor. It seems to be with him a perfectly natural character and one that he is peculiarly fitted to assume.'

Sam, having relinquished control of Newcastle to Montague, was professionally in contact with his brother, and at the conclusion of the long Newcastle season actors from there returned to Windsor for the 1836 summer season. Rosina, Mr & Mrs Cowle and Moulton were prominent, repeating their roles in the Newcastle success *The Jewess*, a play by Planché based on a French original by Eugene Scribe. Sam pulled out all the stops in mounting this far-famed play, excelling with the splendour of the dresses, the parade of armed knights and the banquet scene. The scenery was by Mr Willett of Drury Lane assisted by Mr F Fenton, one of the actors; costumes, machinery and decorations by Messrs Spray, Hogg, Monro, Wyatt etc. all of the acting company, so it looks as though Sam's lesser players were expected to turn their hand to more than simply mastering their roles. Rosina was 'as usual in such characters, extremely effective' in the lead role, and Cowle, new to the Windsor audience, augured well regarding his ability in Shakespearean characters.

When *The Dream at Sea* was announced, Sam's fans expected he would be offering them another example of his ideal sailor, however, at the last minute the role was taken by another actor. Sam had stood down on the advice of his doctors who barred him 'from engaging personally in his profession'. This would indicate some medical crisis that bode ill for the future, if it was necessary to curtail his more strenuous activities. This, too, may be the reason why brother Montague had taken over the reins at Newcastle. Sam continued as manager at Windsor, but he never acted again.

As usual, bespeaks occupied the last week with the patronage of the MPs, and the ever faithful Princess Augusta with her annual command, and Queen Adelaide herself commanding *The Belle's Stratagem* and *The Merry Mourners*.

Having relinquished all activity elsewhere, Sam was concentrating exclusively on Windsor, yet the June Race Week of 1837 did not have any Penley family members in the company.

When the summer season opened, the familiar names included Rosina, but no Mr Dodd. Once again, as had now become habitual, the season got off to a poor start, only picking up half-way through the five-week run. Victoria, the new queen who had ascended the throne two months previously, commanded an evening – on which occasion the orchestra was considerably augmented and the audience very numerous.

The arrival of the eighteen-year-old queen heralded a major shift in the attitudes of the nation. The Georgian and Regency periods with all their licentiousness were past eras; Victoria's subjects were becoming more serious in their tastes, leading to the increased popularity of learned lectures in theatres and public halls. Art, literature and frivolity were giving way to science, knowledge and business. The age was becoming genteel, and middle-class people would no longer tolerate drunken, wenching actors like Edmund Kean. The leading actors were now the po-faced Macready (who kept his excessive drinking off the stage) and Charles Kean, Edmund's priggish son who was righteous and devout, and whose future ponderous productions were noted for their supposed historical accuracy of decor and costume.

The new young queen was a devotee of many entertainments including the USA lion trainer Isaac Van Amburgh 'The Brute Tamer of Pompeii', famous as the first man to put his head into a lion's mouth. Victoria saw him seven times over six months, no doubt the sex appeal of Mr Van Amburgh – rather than his prowess with animals – attracting her.

The sex appeal of the new queen herself seems to have excited one Edward Butter Hunnings who tried to gain entrance to Buckingham Palace, saying he had been invited to dinner. On another occasion, when prevented from accosting the queen, he had fled and plunged into the Serpentine Canal to avoid pursuit. He now followed her to Windsor, going about the town 'in an eccentric manner wearing an enormous broad-brimmed hat, riding a curiously-coloured pony.' Going to the theatre in a drunken state, Hunnings refused to leave when requested, causing Penley to summon a policeman who forcibly removed him. Hunnings, then returning 'with a female of dubious character', tried to force his way back into the theatre. His conduct was so violent that Penley had him taken to the police station where he was kept prior to appearing before magistrates. Yet another unlooked-for problem for the theatre manager, on top of the perennial ones of attracting audiences and engaging actors as cheaply as possible.

Sam's friend Thomas Thorpe, the book dealer who had funded his prolonged honeymoon in Italy, had taken out a large loan for which Sam stood guarantor. No doubt this friendly gesture was simply considered as a formality as Thorpe was in a big way of business. He was famous for taking a classified advertisement in the *Times* which occupied three of the four columns on the front page. However, in early October 1837, with the deadline for repayment looming, Thorpe was unable to meet his obligations and his creditors turned to Sam who had stood surety. The usual way to deal with such matters in those days was to flee to France out of harm's way until all blew over. Like his father before him, Sam duly whisked his wife and three small sons Lionel (eight), Francis (seven) and Godfrey (four), precipitately off to Paris.

Sam, with his wife and family, remained in Paris at No 7 Rue du Colysèe until May of the following year when, the financial matter that had driven him abroad having been settled by Thorpe, the Penley family was safe to return. On 28 May 1838, Sam went to the English Embassy to obtain passports and, whilst untying his boots on returning home, fell to the floor calling 'Kate! Kate!' He died shortly afterwards, the cause given as apoplexy. He was forty-nine and is buried at Montmartre.

Sampson Penley Jr was a thorough man of the theatre. Having been a leading man since the age of eighteen, he obviously knew the job inside out, and colleagues like Elliston regarded him as a good man to have around as acting manager.

He took over managing chores from his father, and the Windsor season carried on year in, year out, in spite of many vicissitudes. He is commended over and over for putting on excellent fare that was unappreciated by the townsfolk. It is not easy running a theatre company and he failed in Leicester, Newcastle and Richmond. But it was a time when few managers were able to make money, and he failed no more so than they.

We are told, as an actor on his Drury Lane debut, that he specialised in fops and pert servants but, as he got older he, like his father, was willing to tackle anything. Judging from the various critical comments it appears that he was always regarded as a 'country actor', a somewhat derisive term used in London which had connotations of barnstorming and ham acting. Whatever the critics may say about his acting abilities, the fact is he played leading supporting roles to the biggest stars of the day, Buckingham and Richmond to Kean's Richard III, Cassio to his Othello, Gratiano to his Shylock. He provided similar support to Elliston, Macready and Booth, and he never stopped working, night after night, often in both main play and afterpiece in a single evening. He tackled classic roles such as

Mercutio, Cloton, Hastings, Count Almaviva as well as melodrama and comedy. It is certain that he was regarded as a reliable and staunch support, and that his name meant something to the public. Classified advertisements say: 'Tonight – *Richard III* Gloster Mr Kean, Buckingham Mr Penley'. The Penley name must have stood for some attraction to be the only one mentioned alongside the star.

As an actor, the impression of Sam in later life is of a man unwilling to tackle anything outside his comfort zone, and could be criticized for always repeating his established repertoire. It is difficult to form a picture of the man from the scanty notes of his appearances on the stage. At Drury Lane he was accused of being boisterous and vulgar, rattling and skipping about on stage, grinning at the upper boxes, whereas at Windsor he was considered a first-class light comedian and second tragedy player. To other actors he appeared a gentlemanly young man, so it comes as something of a surprise to read in the memoir of his son L B Penley 'My father died when I was nearly nine years of age . . . I believe he was rather a taciturn man . . . tall, spare and bald.' Perhaps Sam Jr was a considerably better actor than people realised.

Sam's widow had a small stipend from the Drury Lane Theatrical Fund that her husband had helped administer for so many years. Katherine remained in Paris supplementing her pension by giving lessons, only returning to her home town of Barnstaple in 1847 to set up a school for four female boarders. She specialised in the French language, having resided ten years in Paris as tutor to the children of a French nobleman. She preferred girls between the ages of eight and ten as at that age 'their morals and manners are more easily formed.' Her terms were 30 guineas per annum and there was only one holiday – five weeks at midsummer.

Her three sons were educated in France and Germany, before returning to England where Godfrey died in Norfolk at the age of nineteen, while Lionel and Francis, after going to university and taking holy orders, became schoolmasters.

It is now time to consider in greater detail what Sam Jr's sisters and brothers were doing. They have been occasionally mentioned in the foregoing but they all had lives and independent careers quite apart from the work they did with, and for, their father and brother.

ACT FOUR

Miss ROSINA PENLEY

'truly a great actress and accomplished tragedienne'

and her sisters

Miss PHOEBE PENLEY

'so great a favourite in this city'

and

Miss EMMA PENLEY

'on the high road to the highest honours of her profession'

SCENE ONE
1805 - 1817
FROM CHILDREN TO ACTRESSES

SAMPSON PENLEY, LIKE King Lear, had three daughters. Unlike Shakespeare's play, where the trio are effectively differentiated, two centuries after their decease it is often difficult to distinguish between the three Penley sisters. When they acted together in the J & P company there is no problem, as the eldest – Phoebe – was known as Miss Penley, Rosina as Miss R Penley, and Emma was Miss E Penley. Difficulties arise when the sisters go their own way and appear in other companies without their siblings. When there is only one Miss Penley in the company there is no need to refer to her as other than Miss Penley. Oftentimes there is the problem of accurate identification. We must do the best we can with the material available.

Phoebe was born 'at some place in Kent' about 1794/5 and baptised at Minster on the Isle of Sheppey on 18 January 1795 which presupposes the J & P company was performing there, although no record has been found. Rosina was born on 15 May 1796 and baptised at St Nicholas Church, Sevenoaks on 14 December 1796. Interestingly, her baptism was on the same day and place as those of William Penley's son George Frederick (the one who went to be a soldier), and her cousin Maria Jonas (she of the beautiful voice, also born in May) – the three siblings William, Sampson and Mary having their respective offspring 'done together'. Again, the likelihood is that the J & P company was in town at the time, although no evidence of Sevenoaks comprising part of the circuit has been found. At this very early period, J & P may have been playing at local fairs or barn fit-ups on an *ad hoc* basis.

Young ladies in Jane Austen's time, for that is the period of the Penley daughters' childhood, were brought up to read and write, draw and paint, stitch and sew, sing and play. An upper class lady would value these accomplishments for their own sake, but for many working women they were a necessity. Working women in those days were not all servants and labourers who could get through life with a minimum of education. Some were actresses where reading, writing and a phenomenal memory were essential for the conning of new roles, the ability to adapt and transform clothing a prerequisite, actresses being obliged to provide their own costumes, and any musical ability giving them a great advantage in obtaining work, as no theatre evening was ever without music and song. It would be very unusual if Lucy Penley did not ensure that her daughters were not provided with the practical talents necessary to take their place in the J & P company.

The earliest evidence for any of the sisters appearing on the stage appears on playbills for 1805 where Miss Penley and Miss R Penley, with Jonas cousins, perform an Allemande – a German dance that anticipated the waltz. Come 1807 Phoebe and Rosina, aged twelve and eleven, were regularly taking part in the entertainments, although as dancers rather than aspiring actresses. At this stage they appeared with the Jonas children in a succession of comic dance pieces with titles such as *The Scotch Ghost*, *The Wapping Landlady*, and *Little Peggy's Love*. They were also used for walk-on parts such as the Ghosts of Murdered Children in *Macbeth*.

It was not until 1811 that Phoebe was cast in young adult parts such as Anna the confidante to Lady Randolph in *Douglas*. The following year she was joined by Rosina, both girls taking an assortment of supporting young women's roles, the more experienced Miss Watson and Miss Lucas – both long-standing members of the J & P troupe – taking the leads. Around this time they were joined onstage by the third sister, six-year-old Emma, who is forever dancing a solo hornpipe in a multiplicity of various programmes.

The Peckham season of 1812 shows all the Penley family (except Montague) pitching in as required. Sampson Jr is leading man, Phoebe being the eldest girl takes on most of the ingénue roles, though Rosina also has a fair sprinkling through the season. Emma is still dancing away and taking small roles such as fairy attendants in pantomimes, eleven-year-old brother William is there reciting and singing comic songs, and even little Belville does his bit as Tom Thumb.

Travelling as a family unit was advantageous but, as father Sampson spread his theatrical empire, it became necessary to utilise his children in the most economical way. Phoebe and Rosina, only a year apart in age, could play similar roles in different companies. This became necessary when Sampson undertook his pioneering tour of Flanders in 1814 while a company remained at home to fulfil the regular circuit engagements.

In 1816 and 1817 Phoebe, Rosina and their cousin Maria Jonas were engaged at the English Theatre at Valenciennes. The British Army of Occupation was stationed there following the retreat of Napoleon and time hung heavy on the hands of resting soldiers. Not only did the theatre provide a pleasant diversion, but some of the officers were encouraged to get up their own amateur dramatics. Though there were some wives present it was not seemly for them to strut their stuff on the stage so for the fortnightly productions the professional services of Mrs and Miss Dawson, Miss Penley, Miss R Penley and Miss Jonas were called upon. These actresses 'of full average merit, and moreover every one extremely good looking, more than one of great personal attractions' must have stirred many a manly heart in a soldier's chest. Beauty is said to be in the eye of the beholder, only five years later Rosina was often considered to be lacking that very quality.

Drury Lane theatre, where Phoebe and Rosina's brother Sam Jr was now gainfully employed, closed – as usual – during the summer, enabling Sam and his colleague William Oxberry, a comedian with a diffident and eccentric personality who also turned his hand to writing, journalism and editing plays, to travel to Valenciennes in 1817 to appear as guest stars with the resident English company.

However, Talma the noted French tragedian, arriving late with his own company on the previous evening to perform *Manlius Capitolinus* by Fosse, the English company was compelled to give way to the French one, as there was only one theatre in the town. Oxberry and Penley, waiting the whole of the following day, expected some apology from the French manager for his conduct to them and the English company of comedians. Not receiving such a thing, a letter was sent to Talma, who on reading it, replied to Mr Oxberry that he was ignorant of the whole proceeding, wished him a good morning, declared nothing would give him greater pleasure than to see him at Paris, and that he would there show him what a grateful recollection he entertained of the hospitable and generous conduct he had experienced in England.

This dismissive reply enraged Oxberry who then, blowing the whole thing up out of proportion, wrote to the English newspapers about the affront to the English players. He and Mr Penley were so sufficiently assured of their talents they could smile at every slight cast upon them, but far worse was the insult offered to a lady of no mean talent and of an irreproachable moral character. The performance that had been so cavalierly cancelled was for the benefit of Miss Jonas who 'in England such a character is entitled to, and received the protection and support of every liberal mind.' Oxberry, then slinging a remark about the decline of the boasted French gallantry, ended by saying his story will not be credited when he gets back to the greenroom of Drury Lane.

Flames were fanned, claims and counter-claims professed, ancient rivalries dusted off, with Oxberry blustering only his respect for the fair individual – ousted without the slightest apology – was the reason for his warmth in complaint, and Talma shrugging his shoulders over an affair he knew nothing about and which was, self-evidently, entirely unintentional.

It was all getting rather silly; Oxberry himself, after saying again it was the spirit of the Englishman protecting an oppressed country-woman in a foreign land, and that he would have done the same for any woman of any country, had no wish to prolong the discussion of what was a trivial matter, but Talma must have known what was happening and the 'young and meritorious female', anticipating the profits from her benefit enabling her to return to her home country, had her hopes blighted.

It was truly a storm in a teacup as, when all the dust had settled and Talma gone, the English players continued performing – including the postponed benefit for Miss Jonas. Oxberry and Penley appeared in some of their favourite characters

> and if applause may be considered approbation, they have no cause for complaint. The rest of the company, with few exceptions, comprises a 'scum of Britons, whom their o'er-cloyed country vomits forth to desperate adventures and assured disgrace.' . . . the elder Dawson was originally a painstaking butcher, and, for his own credit's sake and that of the state, it is to be wished he had confined his butcheries to Whitechapel, and not obtruded them upon the drama. We have three young ladies, however, possessing great ability – Miss Penley, Miss R Penley, and Miss Jonas, whose talents would do credit to the London boards.

The 'scum' quotation is from *Richard III*.

After all the hurly-burly in Valenciennes in July, during August and September both Sam Jr and Oxberry joined father Sampson Penley's company at Windsor with the talented Misses Penley and Miss Jonas also returning to the family fold. It was regarded as a particularly strong company at that theatre:

> We have now a company of comedians superior to any I have ever seen exhibit here . . . *The School for Scandal* was performed on Thursday in which Miss Penley and Miss R Penley sustained the characters of Mrs Candour and Lady Teazle. The acting of the former was truly respectable, and the latter gave a chaste, elegant, natural, and impressive portraiture of the titled lady.

It is not often that the receipts of benefit nights are published, so it is invaluable when they are, as they were at the end of this season. We can see the amounts gained by even players of lowly status: Mr Oxberry £76, Mr Bengough £27, Mr Jefferies £30, Mr S Penley £30, Performers £32, Mr Penley, Miss R Penley and Miss Jonas (jointly) £56. Oxberry was a popular London star who was on £8 a week at Drury Lane hence the big turn-out for his benefit, Sam Jr was less than half as popular in spite of all his appearances at Windsor. Rather oddly, Sampson Snr, Rosina and Miss Jonas seemed to have shared a benefit, although this could be a misprint and the recipients should read Miss Penley, Miss R Penley and Miss Jonas, the trio of young actresses who had been working together for the last two years, which would have been more natural, Sampson normally taking a solo one on the last night.

An unsuccessful benefit night at a typical country theatre.

As the performer taking the benefit had to guarantee the expenses of the house for his evening, it was not unusual for the poor chap to end up out of pocket.

SCENE TWO
1818 - 1820
WINDSOR, BATH AND COVENTRY

S AMPSON, OPENING WINDSOR for a short winter season while the Eton boys were on holiday, employed Phoebe, Rosina and Miss Jonas again. Phoebe and Rosina were also in the J & P company at Windsor for the annual Race Week opening on 8 June 1818 when the attractions were *The Belle's Stratagem* and brother Sampson's new farce *The Sleeping Draught* playing to 'unbounded applause at Theatre Royal, Drury Lane.'

The summer season followed on 28 July, opening with the regular favourite *The Castle Spectre* with Phoebe as the ghost, Rosina as the heroine Angela. During the season Rosina played Juliet to the Romeo of Mr Salter, the actor who left the J & P company back in Brussels before the end of the season, but had now returned to the fold as leading man. In *She Stoops to Conquer*, Rosina was Kate Hardcastle to Salter's Young Marlow. In *The School for Scandal*, Rosina played Lady Teazle to her father's Sir Peter Teazle. Sampson Sr, himself rarely treading the boards by this time, is content to let Rosina become his leading lady. Already one has the impression that Rosina is a better actress than Phoebe, or at least, a more popular one. The roles she is taking at this period are ones calling for humour and vivacity, rather than heavy tragedy.

It would be foolish to say that the Penley sisters had a sheltered life – no actress in the pre-Victorian theatre could possibly claim that – but they had always had the security and comfort of living and working in the family environment. Even when abroad at Valenciennes the three girls were like a family unit, especially when joined by brother Sampson Jr. One wonders how soon they hankered to break away and test themselves in the harsher world of the competitive theatrical milieu.

When the winter season at Windsor opened on Boxing Day, Salter and Phoebe were both back there, but Rosina was not in the company.

Undoubtedly the most talented of all Sampson Penley's children, Rosina was the first of the sisters to venture into the wider world when she obtained a contract at the Theatre Royal, Bath for the 1818/19 season. In former days, Bath had been the most important of all provincial theatres. Apart from Edinburgh, it was the first theatre out of London granted a patent in 1768. Bath, being a fashionable Georgian resort, attracted the best actors and often proved the last stepping-stone to a London reputation. Mrs Siddons was the Queen of Bath from 1777 to 1782 before wooed away to Drury Lane by Sheridan. The small theatre that attracted playgoers from London especially to see La Siddons was replaced by a larger one in 1806, built in only ten months. It was in this theatre that the twenty-three-year-old Rosina made her debut, opening the season on 31 October, in the part of Donna Violante in *The Wonder, a Woman Keeps a Secret!* Mrs Centlivre's old war-horse, first written over 100 years previously and dedicated to George I. The role had been Mrs Jordan's most successful, and requires an audacious actress.

Pre-publicity heralded Rosina in this manner:

> Miss Penley (daughter of the manager of the Windsor Theatre) is highly spoken of; this young lady has been particularly regarded by the Princesses, and has frequently had the honour to recite both at the Castle and at Frogmore; and having also been complimented by the notice of the most distinguished persons about the Court, she is said to have acquired an habitual assumption of fashionable manners, which renders her comedy more polished than that of any other lady since the days of Miss Farren.

Hazlitt described Elizabeth Farren as having 'her fine-lady airs and graces, with that elegant turn of her head and motion of her fan and tripping of her tongue'. She had retired in 1797 to marry the Earl of Derby.

Rosina was no Elizabeth Farren and was not a success. She was considered by many to be very young and inexperienced and, whilst contracted to play principal roles in both comedies and tragedies, was not competent in either realm. This opinion was not held by all, and correspondence in the local press flowed from both detractors and supporters. The *Bath Chronicle* stated:

> Miss Penley has played in *Three Weeks After Marriage* and *The Honeymoon*. This lady does not possess the requisites for genteel comedy; she has much to unlearn, before she can expect success in that walk.

A month later the same newspaper was gracious enough to say of Rosina's performance in *The Hypocrite* 'Miss Penley represented the young Lady Lambert very respectably; and in parts requiring similar talents she will be very useful.' In other words, she was not up to anything major but was quite acceptable in ingénue roles. Nowadays, when teenage actresses are major film stars, it seems odd to modern eyes that Rosina should be excused as being 'very young' at twenty-three. However, it must be said that the pre-flaunting of her habitual hob-nobbing with the royal family and vaunting her toffee-nosed manner cannot have endeared her to her future audience. Class was paramount in Regency times and everybody knew actresses, no matter how well respected, were working women who aped their betters on the stage. They were only counterfeit ladies and gentlemen up there , and whilst men were much more free and easy mixing classes with sporting and drinking associates, ladies were more censorious at women who tried to be 'better than they are'. One hopes it was the theatre management's idea to boost Rosina's credentials in this way, and not the actress herself; if the latter she soon learned her lesson.

The record of that season at Bath is sparse and it is impossible to name all the parts Rosina played. Even so it is clear that she was not over-taxed with a profusion of roles. On New Year's Eve she played the prostitute Millwood in *George Barnwell*, a role within her compass. Over the Christmas holiday week the theatre had booked Il Diavolo Antonio an acrobat and wire walker to appear betwixt play and afterpiece 'for the special entertainment of the juvenile classes'. But those poor children had to sit through long evenings of turgid tragedies as well.

During January, Rosina was Lady Grace in *The Provoked Husband*, Helen McGregor in *Rob Roy* and Volumnia in *Coriolanus*. This latter role is the mother of the hero, requiring a mature tragedy actress in the Mrs Siddons manner, proving a daunting task for such a young actress as Rosina. She was not mentioned at all in the review of the play. The following month in *Brutus; or the Fall of Tarquin* she was cast as Tullia, wife of Tarquin, another tragedy mother with grown up children. In this instance the review mentioned none of the players at all, devoting itself to outrage at the sentiments of the play and rubbishing it in general. This in spite of the fact that the play with Kean – and Rosina's brother Sam playing his son – was a big hit at Drury Lane, taking an average of £250 a night for the first 30 performances.

Rosina was being pushed into roles beyond her capabilities, cast in unsuitable maternal parts; they were not giving the poor girl a fair chance. Another young actress Miss Jarman a regular at Bath was, like Rosina, branching out in the early years of her career. The local newspaper, describing her as youthful, interesting, deserving and improving, had to admit that her benefit had failed, and in some recompense the manage-ment had given her the privilege to 'issue tickets for her advantage for Saturday night'. In other words, Miss Jarman had been granted a certain amount of tickets to sell and keep the proceeds herself.

In *The Ethiop; or The Child of the Desert* Miss Jarman had the breeches role of Orasmyn the desert child, while Rosina played the lesser role of his sister Cephania in this romance of Bagdad by William Dimond. It is interesting to see how Miss Jarman progresses as she keeps appearing from time to time during the relating of the Penley sisters story.

The Bath season normally ended at the end of May though Rosina must have left early, probably by several weeks, as she was in the J & P company when it opened the new theatre at Coventry on Easter Monday in April 1819. After being a source of public argument, Rosina was probably glad to get away and back to the bosom of her family, though it was not to be the last she saw of the Bath theatre.

Many of the regular J & P performers were present at Coventry, but a detachment including Rosina was required to pop down to Windsor for the annual Race Week where she was now billed as 'Miss R Penley of the Theatre Royal, Bath'. Her Windsor fans were not to know she had been something of a failure there. If she had been used wisely at Bath, it could well have been a stepping stone to a higher level of work. But the theatre is full of 'if only' occasions so Rosina, putting it down to experience, buckled down to the task in hand. Sampson, pulling the stops out for this one week season, had recruited his son Sam Jr and Oxberry from Drury Lane as well as Rosina, the bulk of the regular J & P players – including Salter – being still occupied at Coventry.

Coventry had closed when the Windsor summer season opened on 3 August 1819, so both Phoebe and Rosina were on hand with leading man Salter. Brother Sam Jr and Oxberry, on holiday from Drury Lane, again made appearances. During the final week, as customary, benefits were held for Salter and Sam Jr, but there was a composite one for 'the performers'. Family members of the company comprised Sampson Penley (rarely appearing), daughters Phoebe, Rosina and Emma, sons Montague and William, John Jonas, Miss Mary Jonas and Miss Charlotte Jonas. The old comic dance *The Scotch Ghost* was dragged out for the occasion; all the former juveniles now well into adulthood.

Windsor closed on 11 September, then it was all down to Eastbourne where the season there opened on the 20th with Salter, Phoebe and Rosina in *The Belle's Stratagem*.

The same play opened the next stand at Lewes on 2 November 1819. A feature of the repertoire was now a melodrama *Ella Rosenberg* which was to become one of Rosina's regular offerings in future years. Rosina gave her Lady Teazle in *The School for Scandal*, but on this occasion Mr Bennet, rather than her father, played Sir Peter; Phoebe was Mrs Candour. Both sisters were 'everything the author could have wished.' Rosina essayed the tragic role of Jane Shore, another role that she gathered unto herself for the future. Surprisingly, in *Pizarro* Rosina played a lesser role allowing Phoebe to take on Mrs Siddons's famous role of Elvira. No doubt family pressures held as much sway as professional casting in a close company such as His Majesty's Servants from the Theatre Royal Windsor.

Rosina played Donna Violante, the role she had opened with at Bath, with Salter as leading man. For their joint benefit night the two sisters chose *Macbeth* along with *The Actress of All Work* a new comedy by Oxberry in which Rosina played six different characters. This slight piece was based on the plot of an actress trying to obtain an engagement with the theatre manager father of her lover. She interviews the father in several different extreme guises so she can, at the end, reveal her versatility and prowess as an actress. Oxberry stole the idea from the actor Charles Mathews who, specialising in a one-man show, had a male version of the plot. This sketch became a favourite piece for Rosina's future benefit nights.

Goodbye Lewes on 1 January – hello Rye on 5 January 1820. The season opened with *The School for Scandal*. The Penley family were out in force for this season, with even the twelve-year-old Belville taking part, older brothers William (19) and Montague (21) now playing major roles, Emma, now fifteen, acting servants, maids and gipsy girls. Following this circuit of small southern towns since the children were born, the Penley family would have felt at home in all of them, rekindling old friendships and settling into familiar surroundings.

SCENE THREE
1820 - 1822
COVENTRY AND PARIS

THE SECOND J & P Coventry season ran from 2 June to 28 July 1820 and, as Windsor Race Week commenced on 29 May that year, Rosina remained at Windsor to lead the company which relied on visiting actors from the London theatres. She played Mrs Haller in *The Stranger*, another role which became a fixture in her ever widening repertoire. A newcomer to the company was Mr Hammond singing a comic song. This may be when he and Rosina first became acquainted. In future years she was to work with him a great deal. At the end of the week she re-joined the rest of the regular company in Coventry.

The summer season at Windsor opened on 31 July enabling the entire J & P company to return from Coventry. Oxberry, becoming a regular summer guest, headed the company with Salter and the two elder Misses Penley in strong support.

The company then split: Phoebe remaining at Windsor and Rosina going to Lewes to open the season on 9 August with *The Stranger*. The Lewes season was remarkably short – running only until 22 August with performances every night. For his benefit on the last night, Sampson himself appeared playing Sir Able Handy in *Speed the Plough*.

Most of this unit then moved on to Eastbourne, opening on the 24 August with Oxberry playing Sambo in *Laugh While You Can*. It does not look as though Rosina went with them as she is advertised as being at Windsor on 21 August in *The Steward*. On September 4 Oxberry was back at Windsor to play Shylock with the unit there.

What a prodigious amount of travelling these players undertook, and what complicated logistics must have been involved organising which actors should be engaged on what dates in which venues. Sampson lived a life of constant shuttling back-and-forth between his companies and theatres. How he organised everything by letters via the expensive post system is something of a miracle!

The short Windsor 1820/21 winter season, running from 26 December to 13 January, saw both Phoebe and Rosina in the company with brother Montague. Hammond was also there again singing his comic songs. Rosina was now developing as a tragedy queen playing Isabella and Jane Shore yet again. As the only other J & P regular was Mrs Beynon, there must have been another unit elsewhere. The local newspaper, lamenting that audiences had not been in proportion to the attraction of the performances, blamed the inclement weather.

J & P's third Coventry season opened on 23 February 1821 with both Phoebe and Rosina in the company. The repertoire was the usual familiar fare, but the auditorium was vastly changed as major alterations had taken place; plainly the design of this new theatre had left a lot to be desired. The season closed on 23 March. The seasons in most of the J & P theatres were becoming markedly shorter, a sign that audiences were diminishing. Penley often now opened for two weeks playing every night, rather than staying in a venue for a month playing alternate nights. He was even back to playing roles himself – a saving of a salary.

We have seen how, in 1822, the J & P company came to a calamitous end in this country and how Penley's attempts to survive were quashed by his disastrous foray into a hostile Paris. Yet, once the English players had established themselves at the modest *salle* in the Rue Chanteraine their performances were appreciated by the *cognoscenti*, a newspaper stating that one of the Penley ladies 'deserves to be distinguished by a spiritual diction and modest grace which combines perfectly with what we would call in our actresses une gentille gaucherie.' That lady was Rosina. *Jane Shore*, the tragedy by Nicolas Rowe, caused great enthusiasm for both the work, and how it was played. In the critic's opinion it was a tragedy equal to the first masterpieces of Shakespeare. As for actresses:

> Miss R Penley has shown a genuine sensitivity, an extraordinary energy, a natural demeanour, and is truly a great actress and accomplished tragedienne. Her playing drew tears from the whole audience.

Rosina struck a chord with the Paris intelligentsia, Stendhal himself pronouncing Miss Rosina Penley a first-class actress who made a strong impression as Juliet and Jane Shore, giving as proof of her acting skills that, lacking beauty, she relied on her talent, not her looks, to portray the parts. Talma and French leading actress Mlle Mars also applauded Rosina in these roles. *Jane Shore* was obviously to the Parisian taste as two French versions were mounted in the following six months. Both proved flops, presumably due to the lack of a French equivalent as talented as Rosina Penley. Stendhal concluded that everyone agreed the success of Miss R Penley kept growing. Rosina would have been highly pleased at these comments, but probably had never heard of Stendhal, much less read his works. She surely read the encomium of the *Le Miroir*:

> Miss Penley, who until the present has shown herself simply as a graceful and intelligent actress, proved the evening before last, while playing the role of the guilty Jane Shore, that she does possess genuine sensitivity, remarkable vigour, a naturalness which avoids vulgarity, nobility without affectation; she impressed us as a gifted tragedian. Her touching pantomime . . . wrung tears from the whole audience. Frequent applause made it plain to Miss Penley that in France talent always finds unbiased appreciation and enthusiastic admirers.

Although the general opinion was that the English company was weak, Rosina herself won the plaudits of the connoisseurs of drama, Stendhal even venturing to suggest that she was responsible for changing the face of French theatre. It was her performances that showed the French what Shakespeare could be like, paving the way for greater actors to be welcomed in Paris. After two months of performances, further activity was suppressed by the censors.

Rosina had cleverly elided into a tragedy queen and, whilst continuing to play comedy roles, she was increasingly regarded by managements as a leading lady in the Mrs Siddons repertoire. Once the J & P company no longer existed, on her return to England she became her own mistress and sought work in other respectable companies.

SCENE FOUR
1823 - 1825
ROSINA ON THE YORK CIRCUIT;
PHOEBE AND EMMA AT CHELTENHAM

ROSINA WAS ENGAGED on the York circuit for the 1823 season. In the previous century, from 1767 to 1803, the York circuit – under Tate Wilkinson, one of the best-known names in theatre management – had been the premier circuit in the country. It was Wilkinson who obtained a royal patent jointly for the York and Hull houses in 1769, an achievement preceded by only Edinburgh, Bath and Bristol in the provinces. After Tate's death, his son John Wilkinson took over the theatre, but its fortunes fluctuated until 1821 when Robert Mansel became the manager. Mansel, the son of a clergyman and nephew of the bishop of Bristol, as a young actor had appeared with the J & P company billed as 'Mr Mansel from the Theatre Royal, Covent Garden'. In fact Mansel, having failed at Covent Garden, was doomed to the provinces thereafter, but progressed, becoming a popular player at York from 1812, and the manager there from 1818. When he acquired the lease, the *York Herald* was pleased to point out his talents as an actor, and his good quality and manners as a man. Praised for his fine taste and discrimination, he was keen to purge the drama of its impurities. These attributes would be welcomed, as the conduct of some recent performers and the character of their performances 'estranged persons of delicacy.'

He recruited a strong company which included an actor with the splendid name of Frederick Baltimore Calvert. This tragedian, specialising in Shakespeare, spent almost all his career on the York circuit no matter the various managers who came and went. A familiar name was W J Hammond, the singer of comic songs at Windsor, who, developing into a fine comic actor, had played three seasons at the Haymarket. Coleman said of him that 'He had wigs of all kinds and costumes of every description, but he was always Hammond in another wig and another coat.' The leading lady was Miss Chester, a voluptuous beauty, but affected and inclined to be vulgar. While dining in an inn, she had embarrassed a fellow actor by taking up the fowl in her fingers, wiping off the sauce on the tablecloth before tearing at it with her teeth. Her acting style was mannered and exaggerated, but this did not daunt Charles Kemble who, seeing her at York, whisked her off to Covent Garden where she often displaced far superior actresses.

Miss Chester's replacement was the more demure Rosina Penley whose 'respectability of private character confers honour upon the profession at large'. No doubt the fact that her brother Montague was the scenic artist at York had facilitated Rosina's engagement. Mansel's circuit now embraced theatres at Hull, Leeds, Wakefield, and Doncaster. The company was obliged to do a lot of shuffling back and forth throughout the year as the York season was from March to May, Leeds from June to September, Hull at the end of the year. But the company also visited Wakefield and Doncaster for their respective seasons over the races, and returned twice to York for the July assizes and August races.

Rosina, still described as from the Theatre Royal, Bath – this being her highest accolade to date – made her first appearance at York as Juliet to Calvert's Romeo. It would be tedious to recite a list of all the roles she played, but it is easy to see that she was much more suitably cast than she had been at Bath four years earlier – in *Brutus* she was his daughter not his wife. In *She Stoops to Conquer* she played Kate Hardcastle, in *The Rivals* she was Lydia Languish, in *The School for Scandal* Lady Teazle; all these were light comedy roles in which Rosina could display her pertness and vivacity. But Rosina was also given leading tragedy parts – Cordelia to Calvert's Lear, Belvidera in *Venice Preserved*, a classic that first appeared in 1682, and Jane Shore – the role that had entranced the Parisian aficionados.

Of course, as the repertoire mainly comprised the typical pot boilers, melodramas and farces, she had her fair share of dross to wade through too; even Calvert was obliged to turn his hand to lighter fare than the Bard. Rosina appeared in the popular play *Wild Oats*, chosen by Mr Doré the principal dancer for his benefit, during which he danced a hornpipe in wooden shoes and real fetters while playing the violin, a feat he claimed was unique to him. Did anybody else even *want* to do it?

York circuit manager Mansel was an educated man, the author of *Free Thoughts upon Methodists, Actors and the Influence of the Stage* and *A Short Struggle for Stage or No Stage* a counter to the sermons of Rev Thomas Best a minister in Sheffield who habitually thundered against the evils of the stage. Mansel took the opportunity to combat these accusations of immorality by printing counter-arguments on his playbills.

Unlike many actor-managers, Mansel had high standards and tried to improve the standing of the theatre in society. He maintained a number of classics in the repertory of his theatres, and on several occasions engaged the eminent actor William Charles Macready.

MR MACREADY

Mr Mansel is happy in having it in his Power to announce to the Public that he has engaged the above Gentleman for FIVE NIGHTS. As Mr Macready is universally acknowledged to be One of the very best Tragedians of the Age, he is, of course, in great request; the Difficulty of procuring his Aid, and the Remuneration which he justly requires, both compel the Manager to declare that there can be no half price on his nights.

This statement, somewhat quaint by modern PR standards, meant that the regular custom of allowing people to enter mid-way through the evening at half the usual admission price would not be allowed on these nights. Macready's repertoire comprised a selection of his 'biggest hits'. Star actors like Macready and Kean spent their lives touring the country repeating the parts which brought them to fame, supported by the resident company in whichever provincial theatre was prepared to pay their fee. Providing the money was commensurate with his own estimation of his status, Macready was prepared to work anywhere, Thackeray nicknaming him 'McGreedy'.

So that Macready is not unjustly maligned, your author must put on record another aspect of the great tragedian. In August 1826 Macready was departing for a tour of America and had agreed to play one night's farewell at Birmingham. The house was packed and highly successful, but in the night thieves broke in and stole the takings of £200 leaving Brunton the manager with a total loss. Macready not only waived his share of the takings, but agreed to play another night in a different play without remuneration. As another good house resulted, the manager was fully reimbursed. In this case 'McGenerous' – Thackeray should be told!

High-minded though he be, Mansel could not afford to present Shakespeare and worthy material exclusively; his programmes were just as cluttered up with melodramas, pantomimes, farces and ephemeral garbage as other managers. This is a sample of the sort of thing that the early 19th century theatregoer enjoyed:

> From the rapturous applause bestowed on Mr Yarnold's
> *Four Tom Cats*, on Tuesday evening, July 29th,
> he will *(for this night only)* introduce his
> FOUR REAL DUCKS
> which he will (Harness on the Stage) put to a Grotesque
> Carriage– mount the Box and
> DRIVE THEM FOUR IN HAND
> several times round and across the stage, a thing never
> before attempted by any Person other than himself.

Robert Mansel was clearly a decent man and a just employer. When one of his actors suddenly died in Leeds, he immediately leapt into the breach:

> For the Benefit of Master Henry Williams
>
> The Public are respectfully informed, that in consequence of the embarrassed Affairs of the late Mr Williams, Mr Mansel has appointed the above Night for the Benefit of his Son, and makes no doubt it will meet with that support, which a generous Public ever bestow on the Children of the unfortunate.

Mansel and Rosina must have been happy with each other as he re-booked her for the following year, again with Calvert and Hammond, and it was much a repeat of same theatres, same repertoire and, probably, same audiences. The main novelty was that the York theatre had been fitted out with gas at a cost of £200. Wakefield theatre had also been transformed by gas. This new form of lighting had been introduced to London theatres in 1817 and was now spreading through the provinces, though the Haymarket, the last London theatre to give up its candles, did not succumb until 1843. With Mansel's policy of improving his venues only held back by costs, he sought to persuade the theatre freeholders to pay, or assist, to improve their holdings.

The Hull theatre where Mansel's company played several weeks was not the same one as when Tate Wilkinson had gained its patent. The current theatre had been built by Wilkinson's son in 1810 when the town's population had grown to 35,000. It was large, containing three tiers of boxes, two galleries, and a pit, with accommodation for 1,700. The stage was 54 feet deep and they would have needed all of that when Mr Cooke's troupe of Equestrians performed *The Cataract of the Ganges*. This was a copy of the latest hit spectacle from Drury Lane where Rosina's brother Sam Jr was currently playing Iran a young Hindu warrior.

Because there were no copyright agreements in those days – the Dramatic Copyright Act not being introduced until 1833 – plays that were London hits found their way on to the provincial stages very rapidly; though how six horses, roaring torrents of water and a daring escape by horseback through blazing fires could be recreated effectively on the majority of far smaller provincial stages gives one pause.

Mansel also booked Mr Cooke's troupe for the older and rather smaller Leeds theatre. With the playbill for *Timour the Tartar* promising a tournament and grand combat on horseback in Act 1, and an attack on Timour's castle with infantry and cavalry and the destruction of the fortress in Act 2, it must have been quite terrifying to sit on the front row!

Benefit performances came at the end of each stand in the circuit and, as the Hull segment neared its close, Rosina chose for her benefit *Wives as They Were and Maids as They Are* a play dating from the year she was born. Written by Elizabeth Inchbald, who was reputed to have received £800 for it, thus reflecting her status as a top playwright, it had held the stage ever since and, as with many other companies, had been a regular in the J & P repertoire. Mrs Inchbald's most remembered play today is *Lovers' Vows* as it appears in Jane Austen's *Mansfield Park*.

Unfortunately, Rosina's benefit on the Thirteenth Fashionable Night brought a major public rift between actress and manager.

The conduct of the audience in those times appears appalling to us today as they assumed the right of censure, expecting the actors, and even the manager, to kowtow to them. Nowadays, if we are displeased with some aspect of a play or performance we either do not go, or, having gone, walk out in the interval. In Georgian times the audience stayed, not only to boo, but to argue with the players on stage, demand the manager be sent for, hold up proceedings until they received what they considered was their due apology and so on.

The most extreme example in theatre history was the Old Price Riots of 1809. When the new Covent Garden theatre re-opened after being destroyed by fire, the management raised the box prices from 6/- to 7/-, and the pit from 3/6 to 4/-. There was strong objection raised to this but, rather than today when the public will simply stay away, instead of refusing to attend they came nightly at half-price and spent the evening in riotous clamour shouting down the actors. This uproar carried on for 67 nights until the management capitulated and restored the former prices.

Robert Mansel did not have anything like that to cope with, but he was expected to grovel to his audience. It appears that a 'gentleman friend' of Rosina Penley had, without her knowledge, posted large bills advertising her benefit. This had affronted the manager who discharged her, dating from the end of the Hull stand. As a result of these playbills, the theatre was filled with people who had come to see Miss Penley rather than the entertainments offered. The officers of the 17th Regiment attended in a body and the house was well-filled. Miss Penley was greeted with wild enthusiasm, and all went swimmingly until half way through the play when Mr Mansel entered in the role of Bronzeley. The audience hissed, groaned, and shouted 'Off! Off!' causing such a racket the actor could not carry on. Eventually, managing to gain quiet, he asked in what way he had offended, thereby starting the audience off again. One local character stood on his seat haranguing the manager, causing officers present in the pit to attempt arresting him, but other members of the audience prevented them. After a long argument between manager and audience the play was suffered to carry on, Mansel being greeted with cold sullen indifference, whereas the audience went over the top when any of the other performers entered. Miss Penley was cheered and overwhelmed with plaudits. Although several constables were present, no arrests were made.

The house was well filled when Mansel's own benefit came a few days later. He requested that the play may be allowed to proceed, and at the conclusion he would make a statement regarding the position of Miss Penley. After some grumbling and disputation this was agreed to, and after the end of the last act he addressed the house. He stated he had taken offence at his managerial properties being invaded and he would continue to defend that position. He had been accused of being a tyrannical manager who could dismiss any player he disliked, not a stance that any manager need take up, as all theatrical contracts had an eight-weeks-notice clause that would more effectively serve the purpose. While these were his managerial rights, he realised he had made an error of judgment and that, in this instance, one night's severe discipline was sufficient. Leading on Miss Penley by the hand he publicly apologised and re-instated her.

It may seem odd that a manager should be so exercised about extra advertising that fills his theatre, but even today it cannot be permitted for an actor, of his own volition, to self-publicise himself at the expense of his colleagues.

Not long after, the futility of such things hit home in a striking manner. At the end of the season in October, Mansel took a coach to London in order to see the latest opera *Der Freischutz* with a view to bringing out the piece in his theatres. Unable to obtain an inside seat from Doncaster, he travelled on the outside to Stamford where an inside vacancy would occur. Taken ill, he was forced to abandon the coach at Wansford where he sought a bed at the Haycock Inn. He died the following day of an apoplectic fit.

As an actor Mansel excelled in light genteel comedy, and as a manager he ensured his theatres were worthy of patronage. In his *Memoirs* Macready called Mansel 'one of the few in this profession entitled to the distinction of a thorough gentleman.'

The company was kept going by two of the actors – Downe and Faulkner – taking over in partnership, thus ensuring that the planned season carried on to the end. In January a local poet gave a summary of each actor in verse:

> A handkerchief to hide your grief,
> Take care you do not leave behind;
> For PENLEY'S power, of tears a shower
> Will draw down each fair cheek, you'll find.
> Charming, slim Miss Penley, O,
> Clever, modest Penley, O,
> Your hands so soft
> Will clap her oft –
> She's worth a host – is Penley, O!

Rosina had her benefit on 28 January 1825 but when the season ended in March her two fellow actors, acquiring the lease for the following season, dispensed with Rosina's services. The partnership lasted only a short time as Faulkner and Downe did not get on, but for some reason Rosina was back at Hull in June and at her benefit gave a final farewell address.

She was well out of it as the partners' acrimony grew until after a performance of the pantomime *Aladdin* where the scenery collapsed, the curtain closed on a scene of chaos and disarray, the audience hearing the partners shouting in anger while Faulkner's leg was broken in the fight.

When the company moved to York, Faulkner having had long-standing financial problems that sent him crazy, attempted to hang himself. Guarded by friends, he eluded them in the night and drowned himself in the river Ouse, leaving five small motherless children – Faulkner being a widower – now fatherless too.

It was a fortunate actor who could now rely on an entire year's work with one company. The circuit system was cracking up, with many managers controlling fewer theatres, and having financial difficulty in holding on to them for more than a year at a time. Managements were renting theatres for a few weeks only, thus the Penley sisters, in common with their fellow actors, were obliged to take engagements for limited short seasons, dashing hither and thither all over the place.

From her two years with Mansel's company on the York circuit, Rosina had laid the foundations of her future career as a leading lady. Under her belt she now had the tragedy repertory of Lady Macbeth, Juliet, Desdemona, Cordelia, Gertrude, Lady Constance and Queen Elizabeth in Shakespeare; with Jane Shore, Belvidere, Elvira, and Millwood etc in other tragedies, plus the leading roles in light comedy – Kate Hardcastle, Lydia Languish, Lady Teazle etc. She could call on a whole host of parts in comedies, dramas and afterpieces, and she delighted in playing exotic roles, many of them characters whose names began with a Z such as:

Zorayda in *The Mountaineers*   Zamine in *Cataract of the Ganges*
Zorilda in *Timour the Tartar*   Zelie in *The Slave*
Zephyrina in *The Lady and the Devil*

As Rosina was trailing round the York circuit for Mansel in 1824, sisters Phoebe and Emma who were also now free-ranging individuals, were enjoying a more settled existence in the refined ambiance of Cheltenham Spa. The town owed its popularity to the medicinal spring discovered early in the 18th century which wooed health-seeking visitors to take the waters. Parks, avenues and promenades, along with elegant assembly rooms, pump rooms and other amenities were created, making Cheltenham second only to Bath as an upper-class holiday resort. The famous racecourse has occupied its current position since 1831.

The first theatre was built in 1782 encouraging the play-loving George III to linger several weeks when he visited in 1788, further boosting the fashionable attraction of the town. By 1801 the population was still only 3000 but rapidly expanding (over the next 50 years it reached 35,000) and a new larger theatre was built in 1805.

Yates was the current manager and he had recruited a strong company including his new wife the former Miss Brunton and Mr & Mrs Woulds from Bath. Although Cheltenham liked to think of itself as a place of refinement, Yates was not above booking Mr Simpson and his dogs Carlo and Lion in an 'Indian Melo Drama' *The Indian Chief; or the Sailor and his Dogs* in which 'the interesting Tricks and Sagacity of these Wonderful Dogs stand unequalled in any other Theatre in the United Kingdom'.

At the end of the season a benefit was held for the widow and children of Mr Thompson a member of the company who had died. Two actors left after their show at Covent Garden to travel through the night in order to take part in this charitable play, which was Mrs Centlivre's 1714 hit *The Wonder*. The leading roles were taken by Colonel Berkeley – a local amateur – as Don Felix, and Phoebe Penley as Violante, the role made famous by Dora Jordan. The local *Journal* stated the role was 'most effectively and judiciously performed by Miss Penley. Indeed, we have often witnessed the exertions of this young and promising actress in various parts of the kingdom, and we have been surprised that such talents have so long been suffered to slumber upon the boards of a Provincial Theatre.' The night raised £112 which is probably twice as much as Thompson's benefit would have brought had he still been alive.

SCENE FIVE

1826 - 1828

GLASGOW, CHELTENHAM, NEWCASTLE, COVENTRY, WINDSOR, MANCHESTER, SHEFFIELD; RETIREMENT AND COMEBACK

FROM MARCH TO MAY of 1826 Rosina was in Glasgow. Macready, visiting for the first time in two years, played for five nights, opening with Macbeth – Rosina giving her Lady Macbeth – and closed with Virginius, Rosina as Virginia his daughter. With Hammond also engaged as leading comedy man in the Glasgow company, it must have seemed a bit like being back on the Mansel circuit.

Another familiar name to visit was the diminutive Miss Clara Fisher who had appeared as a seven-year-old for Sampson Penley at Windsor. Doing the rounds ever since, now eight years on, Clara was still only fifteen. She appeared as Tell's son in *William Tell*, with Rosina playing her mother. In the afterpiece 'The magnificent Melo-Dramatic Spectacle of *Aladdin; or The Wonderful Lamp*' Rosina played the thigh-slapping breeches role of Aladdin. So from worried mother to boyish hero in one night!

Phoebe and Emma were once again booked at Cheltenham where the manager was now Mr Cooke. The season opened on 29 June and in September they were joined by Rosina who was prominently billed with a clutch of 'eminent amateurs'.

While many theatres of the time often had amateurs occasionally venturing leading roles on the local stage, Cheltenham's public seems to have been forever inflicted by several eminent resident amateurs. These were led by Colonel Berkeley, his younger brother Captain Augustus Berkeley and Mr Banks. The Colonel, a notorious reprobate who had an affair with the wife of Sir Henry Vane Tempest, was described by Mrs Arbuthnot the diarist and social observer as 'a vulgar, narrow-minded man, for his great pleasure seems to be to act the sort of King of Cheltenham, where all the vulgar misses make a great piece of work with him'. He was dismissed by Greville the diarist as 'an arrant blackguard' and 'notorious for general worthlessness'. As Berkeley was the heir to an earldom, the largest landowner in the area and an MP, Cooke may be excused for the loan of his stage, and readily forgiven his permanent unctuous fawning.

Rosina made her debut in *Romeo and Juliet* giving her Juliet to Captain Berkeley's Romeo and, needless-to-say, the house was packed for the occasion – it was Mrs Cooke's benefit – the amateurs meeting with 'loud and repeated acclamations.' It was rumoured that Charles Kemble of Covent Garden was to attend with a view to engaging Rosina for the London stage, 'providing report has not over-rated her histrionic talents.' Actually, the distinguished veteran Kemble was guesting for a few days, drawing crowded and appreciative audiences, something of a rarity at Cheltenham. Rosina played Lady Teazle to Kemble's Charles Surface, but she was not whisked off to Covent Garden, as the voluptuous Miss Chester had been, so must not have cut the mustard.

On a later second showing of *Romeo and Juliet*, the *Herald* newspaper – much less unctuous than the *Journal* – severely changed tack and panned the whole lot of them. Captain Berkeley's Romeo was a caricature more fitted for *Bombastes Furioso* the burlesque send-up of tragic opera, and the general standard of the amateurs was so bad that no wonder the attendance was markedly down on the previous effort. The editor hoped that their previous complaints had brought this about, as they were indignant at the way the Berkeleys' rank, fortune and talents were misapplied. More forcefully, the query was whether the immensely rich Berkeleys should be poncing about the stage lavishing money and time upon this idle amusement instead of alleviating the unfortunate starving inhabitants of the district. Uncomfortably, the newspaper also had second thoughts about Rosina:

> Our previous impressions of Miss R Penley have, indeed, been considerably weakened, and we are not disposed to regard her personation of the young, lovely, and sensitive *Juliet* with even the moderate degree of favour it first excited. The appearance of this lady by no means ranks among the requisites which her character demanded, and whenever she proved partially successful in realising her conceptions of its energy, or its tenderness, we were irresistibly struck with a sense of the great natural difficulties it was necessary to overcome.

It is interesting that a similar description of Rosina's appearance persuaded the French that she was an excellent tragic actress by succeeding in spite of not having the accustomed personal attributes, whereas in Cheltenham the lack of those qualities damned her acting prowess.

After Sampson Penley had given up the Coventry theatre to clear his debts and gone to give his all in Paris, the lease was taken up by Elliston of

Theatre Royal, Cheltenham.

The Public are respectfully informed that

Mr. C. Kemble

Of the Theatre Royal, Covent Garden,

Is engaged for Two Nights Only,

And will make his first appearance

On THURSDAY, Sept. 14, 1826,

When will be Performed the favorite Comedy of the

School for Scandal.

Charles Surface, Mr. C. KEMBLE,

Sir Peter Teazle, ... Mr. F. MATHEWS——Sir Oliver Surface, ... Mr. ATKINS
Joseph Surface, ... Mr. MATHEWS——Careless, ... Mr. COOKE
Crabtree, ... Mr. STRICKLAND——Moses, ... Mr. FISHER
Trip, ... Mr. MELVILLE — Snake, ... Mr. GRANBY
Rowley, ... Mr. WALTON— Servant, ... Mr. BLACKER

Lady Teazle, Miss R. PENLEY

For that Night Only.

Lady Sneerwell, ... Mrs. COOKE
Mrs. Candour, ... Miss PENLEY——Maria, ... Miss E. PENLEY

After which, the favorite Farce of

The Promissory Note

Mr. Markham, ... Mr. BARRY
Scamper, ... Mr. MATHEWS——Nicks, ... Mr. F. MATHEWS
Fubbs, ... Mr. BLACKER——Stubbs, ... Mr. SMITH

Cicely, ... Mrs. COOKE
Mrs. Markham, ... Miss PENLEY——Caroline, ... Miss E. PENLEY

Tickets and Places to be had of Mr. Adamson at the Box Office, at the Theatre.

Doors to be opened at a quarter before 7--To begin at quarter past Seven.

Boxes 5s--Pit 2s 6d--Gallery 1s 6d--Second Price at 9--Boxes 3s--Pit 1s 6d--Gallery 1s

T. SHENTON, Printer, Rose and Crown Passage, Cheltenham.

This night was Rosina's big chance to make a London debut. Charles Kemble the manager of Covent Garden was engaged for two nights at Cheltenham, and Rosina was especially placed to play Lady Teazle by way of an audition. Both her sisters were in the supporting cast. Alas she did not impress Kemble and was doomed to remain a provincial actress for many more years.

Drury Lane until he, in turn, relinquished it in face of imminent bankruptcy. The theatre now passed under the control of a Mr Watson who engaged Phoebe Penley for a season there commencing in December 1826. Miss Penley 'formerly so great a favourite in this city' was announced as Meg Merrilies in *Guy Mannering* by desire of the Mayor and Corporation. The manager, expecting Miss Penley to be a draw, featured her name in large bold type on the playbill. She was similarly featured when playing Lady Macbeth. Four nights later Watson was advertising Miss Rosina Penley 'engaged expressly for this evening' in that old war-horse *Wives as They Were and Maids as They Are.*

Coventry must have been a very brief stop for both the sisters as, at the start of the New Year, Rosina joined the Manchester company under the management of Hammond & Raymond making her debut in an afterpiece as Lady Elizabeth Freelove in *The Day After the Wedding*, a farce dating from 1808 written by Mrs Charles Kemble who created the role. The Manchester theatre tended to book stars and 'name' performers for short terms to head the resident company. For the first three weeks of 1827 Ducrow and his horses were the star attraction, and Rosina found herself playing roles such as Eudocia in *The Siege of Missolonghi*, Rhudina in *Napoleon's Retreat from Russia*, and a Wife in *The Battle of Waterloo*. All these piffling characters in what were basically equestrian displays.

When Ducrow left, Rosina played two of her regular roles – Meg Merrilies and Helen McGregor – before again having her chances blighted by the next guest stars – Miss Foote, who played all the leads, and Mr Sinclair, a singer, which ensured most items presented were musical ones. Rosina was not a singer, a singular handicap for an actress of those times, so was overlooked during his stay. It was, however, a bonus for another member of the company Miss Mary Field who, chiefly engaged for her singing prowess, was in her second year at Manchester.

All improved for Rosina with the next guest star – her ex-colleague Mr Salter from the old J & P company – as he specialised in the same plays as Rosina. She was his leading lady during his stay, playing Lady Macbeth, Emma in *William Tell* and so on, but again, as Miss Kelly a star from Covent Garden was also booked for two weeks, it meant that Rosina had to forego Jane Shore, Elvira, and others of her repertoire and play lesser roles supporting the star. She played her usual Queen when Kean made a flying visit to give his Richard III, as Miss Kelly took Lady Anne, a role that Rosina very rarely played.

Throughout March and April, Rosina played leading roles from her customary repertoire, the season closing on 30 April. Rather oddly there was then an 'after season' of extra weeks in May which brought Miss Kelly back to play, amongst other things, Volumnia in *Coriolanus* relegating Rosina to Virgilia, the hero's wife rather than her usual role of mother. So a patchy season prestige-wise for Rosina at Manchester, but a solid five months work at a No 1 provincial venue.

Rosina's elder sister Phoebe was also doing well as, during the same months, she was in the resident company at the Theatre Royal, Newcastle under the management of Samuel Wall Nicholson. The leading man was S W Butler the son of the Samuel Butler who built the theatre at Richmond, Yorkshire, now the only surviving complete Georgian theatre in the country. Butler Jr succeeded to his father's circuit which embraced Harrogate, Ripon, Kendal, Whitby, Northallerton and Beverley. By 1830 the circuit, like so many others, had collapsed and Butler Jr was earning his crust as a tragedian. An imposing figure standing 6ft 4in, he had a commanding presence and loud voice that overwhelmed in some of the smaller country theatres.

Phoebe was engaged mainly for the leading tragedy roles such as Elvira in *Pizarro*, while Miss Jervis and Miss Cleaver took the far more frequent comedy and musical leads.

A potentially serious accident which could have proved fatal occurred to Miss Jervis while perched up on a piece of scenic rock in *The Flying Dutchman*. In the storm scene which is such a feature of this play, her flimsy dress caught fire from a side-light. The actress immediately jumped down to the stage where willing hands extinguished the flames.

A costume catching fire was a regular hazard in the days of candles, oil lights and even gas lighting. Surprisingly, 35 years later conditions were no safer. You can still see a plaque relating to such a case among the ceramic tablets at Postman's Park in London:

> SARAH SMITH, PANTOMIME ARTISTE. AT PRINCE'S THEATRE DIED OF TERRIBLE INJURIES RECEIVED WHEN ATTEMPTING IN HER INFLAMMABLE DRESS TO EXTINGUISH THE FLAMES WHICH HAD ENVELOPED HER COMPANION. JANUARY 24TH 1863.

The most common reason to build a new theatre was that the previous one had been destroyed by fire.

Miss Jervis, fortunate in getting away with a scorching and a fright, was indisposed for several days, Phoebe taking over her roles. Miss Cleaver was not having a happy time either, as she received a series of anonymous letters addressing her with 'unmanly insolence'. The writer urged her to appear at her benefit night in 'a certain indecent male attire', otherwise he would communicate with many of the best families in the area advising them not to visit the theatre that night as 'some shocking disaster will take place'. Attempting to ignore these threats, Miss Cleaver issued the playbill for her performance, upon which the stalker sent an even coarser and more insulting letter in which he said he would notify the Barracks, the Mansion House and very respectable families warning them of an explosion of gas. All these details are set out on a playbill which concludes 'Is a Female, because she is an Actress, to be thus grossly insulted? Is she to be deserted because she will not comply with the insolent Request of a base, anonymous Letter Writer?' These rhetorical questions were not answered, but the offensive letters were put on public display in the hope that somebody would recognise the writing of the sender.

When Phoebe's benefit came in May it took place on the 'Twentieth Fashionable Evening', a plum night to have for one's benefit. Phoebe had recruited Hammond, formerly of Newcastle but now at Liverpool and Manchester, and her sister Emma for the event.

During the Newcastle season, the African Roscius, who was constantly touring the provinces on special guest appearances at this time, performed three parts from his specialised repertoire which took advantage of the novelty value of his colour – his principal roles being Othello, Gambia in *The Slave,* and Oroonoko in Thomas Southerne's 1695 adaptation of an Aphra Behn novel. In these plays Phoebe played Emilia, Mrs Lindeberg and Imoinda.

The African Roscius was Mr Keene an American 'man of colour'. He made his debut as a teenager in London's Royalty theatre in 1825 and, not causing much attention, then went on an ever-lasting tour of the provinces playing guest appearances for a few days at various venues. Keene's real name was Ira Aldridge and he adopted the name of Keene either in tribute to the great Edmund Kean or in an early crude 'passing off' attempt to attract the public. However, actually a very good actor, he surprised those members of the public who may have been colour-prejudiced. The African Roscius was to play a larger role in the lives of all the Penley sisters very soon.

Phoebe and Rosina returned to Cheltenham from June to October, and when Liston visited to play his famous eponymous role in *Paul Pry,* we read a rare review of Phoebe:

> The Mrs Subtle of Miss Penley was an admirable piece of acting. The deep treachery, and the artificial designs of this hateful specimen of duplicity, were sustained by this lady in a manner calculated to uphold the reputation for just conception of character, which she has long maintained on our stage.

Once again the girls were called upon to support the amateurs. The convention of the time – that amateurs were not named in advertisements and playbills – was rather odd as everybody knew the Berkeleys were at it again. The amateurs even muscled in on the professionals' benefit nights, so when Terry announced his night the cast list read: *Knights of the Cross* 'Richard Coeur de Lion, Sir Kenneth, Sir Thomas of Gilsland by the Distinguished Amateurs; Berengaria: Miss Penley, Edith Plantagenet: Miss R Penley' Then in the afterpiece *Simpson & Son* 'Mr Simpson: Mr Terry, Mr Bromley by the Amateur who plays Richard.' Very quaint!

It is a matter of regret that there are so few reviews of our sisterly trio, so it is rather rubbing in the salt to find that when the theatre presented *A New Way to Pay Old Debts* an entire column was devoted to Colonel Berkeley's interpretation of the leading role as though he were Edmund Kean himself. Phoebe is fobbed off with 'Miss Penley supported the character she has obtained for correctness in her acting.' And in the afterpiece: 'Miss Penley has been, in our opinion, seldom more effective than as the virtuous and unfortunate Marguerite.'

Five years after the Paris debacle of their father and the breaking up of the J & P company, all three girls were now established as individual principal actresses, Phoebe and Rosina having gained some renown in their profession, albeit Emma still regarded as 'promising'. Phoebe was now thirty-three, Rosina thirty-two, and Emma twenty-three. The old small country circuits that had sustained the J & P company of old were rapidly breaking up, with many theatres closing. Newer managers had replaced the ones of Sampson Penley's generation and they were operating on far tighter budgets attracting diminishing audiences. The Penley sisters had stepped up into a higher league of the much larger theatres in industrial towns in the midlands and north of England.

Surprisingly, none of the sisters had been engaged by their brother Sam since he had taken over the lease of the Windsor theatre, presumably because they could do better elsewhere. In 1827, Emma was the first of the three, and while Phoebe and Rosina were at Cheltenham, she was the leading lady at Windsor for the six week season. Sam, keeping his expenses down, did not engage any star names, or indeed any London performers, instead relying on a permanent company, leading lady Emma appearing in practically everything every night. The repertory was not taxing and she was seldom required to venture into her sisters' tragedy repertory, though with Younge as her leading man she played the Queen in *Richard III* and Lady Macbeth to crowded houses.

From 5 November until the end of January, Phoebe and Emma — both described as from the Theatre Royal Cheltenham — were engaged by Butler, formerly the leading man at Newcastle, when he newly took the lease of the Sheffield theatre. Butler advertised a rather large roster of names, listing 20 actors and 12 actresses plus a 14 piece band. Amongst the actresses was Miss Cleaver — also from Newcastle — and Miss Field, who had met Rosina at the beginning of the year at Manchester, and was now introduced to her sisters. We have already seen how Miss Field became a regular in Sam Jr's company.

At the end of season the Penley girls chose *King Lear* for their benefit with Butler as Lear. Miss Field contributed the 'celebrated Bavarian Air of *Buy a Broom* in character'.

At the start of 1828, Keene the African Roscius joined the resident company at the Coventry theatre (now managed by a Mr Melmoth) alternating between Birmingham and Coventry. The company was poor, but Keene was singled out for praise in many roles, and when the season ended Keene himself leased the theatre, opening on 3 March 1828. He was only twenty years old and had no previous managerial experience, relying on players he had worked with for his company. The first review of the company in the press stated that old favourites Mr Aylmer, Mr Richards and 'those very estimable ladies, and excellent actresses, the sisters Penley, are engaged, and perform with more than their accustomed ability.' A week later the paper remarked 'these Ladies still retain their accustomed power among their Coventry Friends, and are general favourites.' The two sisters engaged were Phoebe and Emma.

Mr Aylmer turned out to be not only an old favourite but an extremely poorly one too, and very soon a benefit was organised for the poor old chap publicised in the most heart-rending terms:

> Coventry Theatre — We understand that Mr Aylmer has announced his benefit for to-night, and it is under severe illness that Mr. Aylmer appeals to the generosity of the

public. It is to be hoped that the evils incident to his profession will not be severely felt by him, and that, through the act of a generous public, his sorrows will be soothed, and the extremity of his affliction, in some measure, relieved. Bowed down by disease, it is not to be supposed that his own exertions will be characterised by extraordinary excellence, but the performances will have the most powerful attraction for the benevolent, as they are for the benefit of an individual whom we believe to be deserving, and whom we know to be distressed.

Alas, the benefit did him little good as he died the following day.

Unfortunately, Keene had also erred in choosing both his low comedian – whose humour was lower than necessary – and two actors whose well-wishers, 'if they were true friends', would be wise to instantly dissuade them from a stage career. Like many provincial theatres, Coventry staggered on from manager to manager, each one attempting to succeed where his predecessor had failed. Keene's company, while superior to Melmoth's, was not of sufficient attraction to overcome the customary apathy to the venue.

Phoebe and Emma put in sterling work during the season, while their manager Mr Keene appeared rarely in person, performing only on four occasions. On 24 March, Emma took her benefit, and not only was Phoebe in the company as she had been all season, they were joined from Glasgow by sister Rosina too. She stayed on to play again a couple of days later, all three together once more.

Keene, realising he was on a loser and neglecting his own career was unwise, closed his company down on 27 April and resumed his career as a leading man. Dropping the pseudonym, he went into Europe under his own name, becoming a star attraction in several countries.

The season staggered on a few more days with Rosina staying on at Coventry to take part with Emma in Phoebe's benefit night on 12 May, whereupon she and Emma announced their performance in *The Serjeant's Wife* as being their last appearance on any stage. Amazement all round! Usually, actresses retiring from the stage at a young age did so because they 'married out'. But in this case, most surprisingly, on leaving the company the two sisters set up a dress-making business in Coventry. Emma, who had really yet to take off as an actress, one could understand, but Rosina appeared to be doing well, constantly working as a leading lady at venues all over the place. Perhaps it was the lack of a settled existence that was getting to her, or perhaps the work was getting harder to find. It could be that from the time of being there with their father, Coventry had been particularly pleasant, and fruitful friendships made. Perhaps their Aunt Frances (Mrs William Penley), who had done a similar thing a dozen years previously, was the inspiration? Whatever the reason, and there is nothing but surmise to account for this astonishing development, the two women took advertisements in the Coventry papers advertising their dressmaking abilities.

MISSES R. & E. PENLEY,
HAVING retired from the Theatrical Profession, return their
most grateful acknowledgments to the inhabitants of
Coventry, for the flattering partiality and very liberal
patronage with which they have been honoured, and beg to
inform them that, encouraged by numerous friends, they
intend commencing an establishment in HERTFORD-STREET,
where every description of
MILLINERY AND LADIES' DRESSES
will be made with the strictest punctuality and in the newest
Parisian fashions, for which purpose the MISSES PENLEY
(independent of having Agents in France, where they were
initiated to the business), have procured an Assistant from
one of the first houses in London; and in respectfully
soliciting the favours of those friends, whose patronage in the
profession they have withdrawn from, it will ever be their
pride to remember, the Misses Penley venture to hope they
will not be less fortunate in securing approbation and
success.
The MISSES PENLEYS' Show Room will open on
MONDAY, MAY 12.

The Penley dress-making business presumably turned out a bit of a mistake as in September Rosina joined brother Sam Jr's company at Windsor for the last five nights of the season – the playbills trumpeting her name in large type. It is likely that the Windsor audiences were not aware she had retired anyway, it not being billed as a 'comeback'. In fact, the local press opined, after seeing her play Imogene in the tragedy *Bertram*, that she must surely be destined for the London boards before very long.

Then in November, Rosina and Emma were reported to be successfully playing first-rate characters at the theatre on the Isle of Jersey. It may be thought that in 1828 a theatre on Jersey might be a primitive barn-like affair, but not so. In May of that year a splendid new stone building with a frontage of classical columns and a Greek pediment was opened in the Royal Crescent in St Helier. Their manager was Henry Hughes, but the theatre itself was used on short lets by both English and French visiting companies.

SCENE SIX

1829 - 1830

EXETER, CAMBRIDGE, LIVERPOOL, CHELTENHAM & THE YORK CIRCUIT

IN FEBRUARY 1829, Mr H Hughes announced he had taken the Exeter theatre. This was not the same theatre that Mr & Mrs William Penley had joined in 1798 and laboured until 1801 – that had burned down in 1820, this new building arising the following year. Neither was it the same Mr Hughes – he had died in 1814, renowned as the manager of Sadler's Wells. The manager now was Henry Hughes, presumably a son or other kinsman. As in many other areas, the glory days of Exeter were in the past, the theatre having fallen into torpor and bad management with a series of fly-by-night managers.

After some weeks of refurbishment and redecoration, the season advertised to commence on Monday 23 February, was delayed by a day as the company, returning by sea from its Jersey and Guernsey foray, faced several days of contrary winds. The opening night's production was Sheridan's *Pizarro*, and the press and public were indulgent under the circumstances of a company still reeling from a boisterous sea journey melding with new colleagues. Unfortunately, one disagreeable patron sitting prominently in the middle of the front row kept up a loudly-spoken barrage of sneers until Gaskell the leading man stopped the play to appeal to the house. He was widely supported and the malcontent was hissed and booed until driven from the auditorium.

Poor behaviour would seem to have been endemic at the theatre as one report concluded:

> There is a practice prevailing in our theatre which, whilst it must be most annoying to those on the stage, it is not less offensively felt by that part of the audience who occupy the pit, – it is that of throwing orange-peel, etc from the Gallery. To the Proprietors of the Theatre it is most injurious, whilst it reflects disgrace on the city itself; – that it is the act of wanton and thoughtless youngsters, male and female, is known – but why is it not repressed? Let an active peace-officer, who shall be remunerated for his services, be stationed for a few nights in the Gallery, and the first offenders, after due caution, promptly proceeded against, and we err greatly if an Exeter audience be not soon found as similar assemblages in other places.

So it seems that even in those days authority was reluctant to discipline the bad social behaviour of young people.

Whether the misbehaviour of the gallery helped to keep customers away or not, business was slow, only getting going when guest stars were employed. Miss Foote appeared for four days before going on to the Plymouth theatre. Advertisements proclaimed that during the last four years she had travelled over 18,000 miles and fulfilled in excess of three hundred different engagements throughout the British Isles. Now contemplating retirement, this being in the nature of a farewell tour, it would be the last chance of seeing this popular star. Maria Foote was a pretty, personable, singing and dancing actress with a career at both Covent Garden and Drury Lane, who held the public in thrall, Theodore Hook writing:

> If all the world I were to lose.
> I'd heed it not a farden,
> If only there was left to me
> One *Foote* of Covent Garden.

Hook was not alone in his admiration. On the first night of her season at Covent Garden in 1825, she set a house record by attracting the sum of £900.16.0 to the box office. But basically she owed her star status to a very public breach-of-promise case. On retiring in 1831 she married the Earl of Harrington.

Dowton guested for a few nights, and the previously deficient orchestra was beefed up to the satisfaction of all. However, on the night *The Poor Gentleman* was given, the prompter was so audible to the audience he might as well have plonked his chair in the middle of the stage and let the actors perform in dumb show. Emma Penley did not find favour:

> Miss E Penley was by no means so happy as Emily Worthington – there was a whine of tone and an affectation of manner that did not harmonize with the character; this actress, together with her sister, are young ladies of good sense, and this is a fault they will easily correct – let them attend to nature more than the school, and they will win their way to public favour.

It seems odd to lump both sisters together for the same fault while criticising one. Emma was young and not greatly tested, but Rosina, now thirty-three, had a wealth of experience playing larger roles than those she was allotted at Exeter.

> *The Youthful Queen,* a new piece, was brought out, and elicited, we are sorry to add from the almost empty benches,

well merited applause; indeed we wonder that such energy is displayed, when such a chilling prospect appears before them.

In this play, Rosina 'assumed the air of Majesty with dignity and effect.' In the tragedy of *Bertram*

> Miss Penley poured all her energy into the part of Imogene, and developed talent of no ordinary kind whilst portraying a character abounding with vigorous passages, and still more vigorous conceptions of incident and situation, as well as requiring considerable dramatic action.

Rosina became involved in another on-stage accident in the middle of her performance as Imogene – the very role the Windsor press deemed an ideal entrée to the London stage – when a stage hand allowed a heavy backcloth to descend, almost striking the actors on the head. Such accidents were not commonplace, but by no means rare. Four months later at the Plymouth theatre, Charles Mathews was in mid-flow amusing his many fans when the stage curtain above him gave way, crashing down on to his head and neck 'the violence of the blow rendering him perfectly insensible' for two hours. Two actresses at Bath were hoisted in the air when the apparatus by which they were suspended gave way causing both to fall to the stage, one breaking a leg, the other, whilst not suffering a fracture, being severely injured. Fire was not the only hazard to be encountered in the theatres of the time, though still all too common – the Theatre Royal, Glasgow where Rosina had recently performed had just burned down.

Another of Rosina's standard roles was Meg Merrilies in *Guy Mannering* and she gave a 'very correct personification of that strange character', though one critic said 'the character is among the strongest drawn of the northern bard, and few have succeeded in the personation of it, and on this night even Miss Penley fell short of a preceding perform-ance.' That 'even' would seem to indicate that Rosina was generally regarded as normally pretty top-notch.

A role new to Rosina was Celestina the wife of Count Malacini in *The Dumb Savoyard*. This was an example of a genre of drama very popular in Georgian times, that of works based on the man-monkey character. There were a number of these plays wherein an actor, dressed in a skin, personated an ape (usually dubbed a chimpanzee). The attraction of these plays was that the actor scrambled about the auditorium performing monkey-like antics such as taking people's hats and placing them on other folks' heads, snatching chocolates and so on, provoking general mirth and mayhem. Some actors specialising in the man-monkey role, appeared in no other work, and were expert acrobats, more often the role was given to a young actor, not always successfully as in this report of a performance at Drury Lane the previous year:

> Master Wieland, who plays the monkey in the afterpiece, had to climb up the side scene at the commencement of the piece. By some accident he lost his hold, and fell from a height of 12 or 14 feet upon the stage, and came on his side and head, and was carried off by the performers who were taking part in the scene. . . . The panoramic scenery was then exhibited, and the curtain fell. Mr Browne then once more came forward, and stated that Master Wieland had been removed to his house under the care of a surgeon, and that his hurt was dangerous.

It was a new play and young Wieland had been playing the role for little more than a week. He suffered severe lacerations to head and shoulders and two fractured ribs. A month later he was back performing the part once more. While playing the role in Edinburgh in July, he fell again but managed two more nights before he had to cancel. However, after a night off he finished the contract with two further performances. The artistes who specialised in the pantomime side of the business were very susceptible to injury. Joseph Grimaldi – the greatest clown of them all – was obliged to retire when his legs would no longer support him.

At Exeter the role of the man-monkey was taken by an adult actor – Mr H Hughes Jr, a regular member of the company. His portrayal so delighted the audience that they demanded a repeat showing, and he chose the same play for his benefit.

Being a younger woman, Emma played ingénue roles such as daughters, and in *Charles XII of Sweden* she played Ulrica for several performances which caused the comment that Emma was 'an improving actress'. For her benefit in May Emma chose *Much Ado About Nothing*, but we do not know which role she played, probably Hero.

Mr Simpson, a lesser member of the company must have had Rosina and Emma's approval – or affection? – as he was also engaged by Sam Jr, when all three left Exeter to return to Windsor for the summer season. In *Othello* Rosina, giving up her usual role of Desdemona to her younger sister, played Emilia on that occasion. Mr Simpson was given Sam's usual role of Cassio while Sam exerted himself as Iago.

One attraction of note during this season was a musical play called *The Invincibles; or, Ladies Turned to Soldiers*. The tenuous excuse for a plot is that a group of soldiers is confined to barracks for some misdemeanour, and their mistresses contrive to visit them by dressing in the uniforms of the French Invincibles. The actresses masquerade under ridiculous names, Rosina being Corporal Ajax Moustache and Emma as Hannibal del Epée. The troupe is then challenged to perform soldiers' drill, manual exercise, marching etc. 'From these circumstances a variety of odd and ludicrous incidents occur, altogether forming one of the most laughable, and at the same time, one of the most pleasing dramas that have ever yet secured the APPROBATION OF THE PUBLIC'. The play was repeated four times during the season, and in some future programmes the drilling scene was extracted to stand alone as a comedy sketch.

In *A Cure for the Heartache* Emma was praised for playing well:

> From the few opportunities we have had of judging of this young lady's performances, we should say she is on the high road to the highest honours of her profession. Her style is the true one; and her greatest fault is, that it is not enough ambitious. Her acting appears the result of feeling, directed by no common intelligence; let her have confidence and proceed.

Following Windsor, Rosina went to Cambridge, a venue new to her, where she was engaged for the first line in comedy replacing Mrs Hannam who was obliged to retire through ill-health. Miss Poole was the tragedienne of the company. It is a tribute to Rosina's ability that she could encompass both the standard tragedy repertoire and the high comedy one, thus playing in *The Rivals*, (her Lydia Languish receiving local praise) Juliana in *The Honeymoon* – a role she must have seen her Aunt Frances play many times with the J & P company – and similar parts. She was only in her early thirties, but the long experience of treading the boards since a child, permanently closeted in theatres surrounded by players of every stamp and quality, must have ensured that she absorbed the widest range of fundamentals in her bones.

However, one opportunity to wear her tragedy hat arose when James Reynolds took to the stage. This man was an amateur appearing on a theatrical stage for the first time. He was very well known in Cambridge as the driver of the stagecoach, an occupation that enabled the local newspapers to have fun with some rather laboured puns. Surprisingly, this amateur elected to perform Iago in *Othello*, the fourth longest and one of the hardest parts in Shakespeare, calling for subtle acting and delicate shifts of character. A great challenge for an amateur, and Mr Reynolds obviously had no idea what he was taking on. In the event he looks to have done remarkably well in the scenes with Rodrigo and Desdemona and in his soliloquies, but he was uncomfortable in the scenes with Othello. This is not surprising as his Othello was Wallack, the Anglo-American actor, a minor star of great experience. So Reynolds was let down lightly by the press who concluded 'we were quite captivated by the Desdemona of Miss Penley.' Whether Miss Poole thought it beneath her to act with an amateur we do not know, but Rosina was used to tackling anything and, as Desdemona was one of her customary roles, she was in a position to helpfully nurse the amateur along.

Because of time-honoured virulent opposition by the University authorities, the Theatre Royal at Cambridge was actually situated outside the city boundary at Barnwell. It still survives in the form of a Buddhist temple, but is very important in theatre history as, apart from being a survivor from 1814, in 1926 it was transformed into Terence Gray's Festival theatre, which explored the staging theories of the theatrical guru Edward Gordon Craig. The stage incorporating several of the Gray innovations still survives.

The 1829 season lasted no more than three or four weeks after which a few of the actors, including Rosina, went on to Bury St Edmunds ('I didn't know he was dead!' *Trad.*), Rosina once more playing the comedy repertoire including Mrs Jordan's famous role Violante in *The Wonder, a Woman Keeps a Secret*. Miss Poole was again entrusted with the tragic repertoire, but her Portia left a lot to be desired as her depiction of a lawyer spoke – so – slowly – that – the – audience – could – take – a – nap between words. Rosina could have shown them!

However, the Bury critic was somewhat stricter than the Cambridge one and said 'we certainly cannot speak in praise of the Lady Teazle of Miss Penley. In the Farce, however, this young lady was inimitable.' In *Spring and Autumn* Miss Penley was 'the exact picture of a "Bride at Fifty"'. It seems as though the Bury St Edmunds audience preferred a more robust kind of humour rather than high comedy.

Again, the season was under a month, after which the company dispersed. Short seasons of this nature were getting more customary with a manager, often an actor-manager, taking a theatre for two or three weeks and recruiting actors for that limited period. Players needed to travel more extensively to find a shrinking amount of work. The old circuit system where a long-serving troupe travelled together round a regular series of towns was becoming almost extinct.

In August 1829, *Freeman's Journal* proclaimed that no stars were making any money except at Liverpool, Edinburgh and Dublin. No doubt an exaggeration, but an indication how there was a general slump throughout the country. Even so, optimistic managers carried on in adverse conditions.

While Rosina was dodging hither and thither, Phoebe had returned to her old haunt at Cheltenham where Cooke had once more taken over the lease. He held an exceptionally long season opening on 29 June when the attraction was Harriet Smithson, the actress who had been the toast of Paris two years before. The afterpiece was *Gil Blas* with 'our favourite actress Miss Penley' in the breeches part of the Boy of Santillane 'eliciting repeated applause'. The following evening, Phoebe was obliged to play second fiddle as Alicia to Miss Smithson's Jane Shore – 'we have seldom seen these difficult characters supported with greater effect in a provincial theatre.'

In July, Wieland the accident prone man-monkey appeared in *The Dumb Savoyard & His Monkey*. Now a Mr rather than a Master, he was still playing the same role though branching out into the pantomime world as he also played Clown as partner to the older Mr Howell, an 'experienced Harlequin', in *The Doubtful Son* with Miss Cooke, the boss's daughter as Columbine. On the same bill Phoebe was in the main attraction:

> We cannot pass over the dramatic amusements of the week, without expressing our sincere admiration of the very effective manner in which Miss Penley personated the character of Tullia in the tragedy of *Brutus*. The dignity of the Roman lady, and the haughty bearing of the imperious Queen, were well preserved throughout the piece, while the mad scenes were delineated with a wild energy and intensity of feeling that reached the hearts of the audience

Although his season would eventually stretch until closing on 26 November, Cooke was not really faring much better than elsewhere and on 3 August he announced:

Reduced Prices of Admission

Mr Cooke begs leave to inform the Nobility, Gentry and Public at large, that it having been suggested to him a Reduction in the Price of Admission to the Boxes would be favourably received by the Patrons of the Theatre, and deeply impressed with gratitude for past favours and anxious to meet the wishes of his friends.

He has made the following Reduction

which he hopes will prove satisfactory and secure to him
the patronage of the Public: viz, Boxes 4s 0d (Second
Price 2s 6d) Pit 2s 6d (Second Price 1s 6d)
Gallery 1s 0d – No Second Price to the Gallery

This was a ploy that was becoming commonplace, even in the London theatres, where regular prices that had been constant for decades were desperately slashed.

A playbill dated 4 November 1829 advertises Miss Penley's benefit. This is an excerpt from the Memoirs of actor Robert Dyer:

> I had an opportunity to be of service to my friend Miss Penley, by going over to Cheltenham, and playing *Wallace* and *Tekeli* for her benefit, with a company whose proper sphere was a barn; for a more wretched set, with the exception of Cooke and Wilton, never violated the drama's sacred laws. Yet these actors were tolerated by the audience of a fashionable watering place, though, certainly, the fashionables, who go, not to see, but to be seen, deserve none better.

This matches the playbill but, according to a newspaper item, the advertised benefit was postponed because of the extremely wet weather and re-scheduled for 20 November. So the assumption must be that Dyer arrived and the show took place but was not considered as a benefit. The newly advertised benefit had different attractions: *She Stoops to Conquer* with Phoebe giving her Kate Hardcastle, as Portia in the Trial Scene from *The Merchant of Venice*, and Edmond in *The Blind Boy*. Phoebe was a popular performer in Cheltenham from her several seasons there and the local newspaper was certainly a fan:

> Having had frequent opportunities of criticising the performances of Miss Penley, we can with justice pronounce her equal to any provincial actress upon the English stage in the genteel comedy, tragedy and melo-drama, and we congratulate our readers on the opportunity they will have of appreciating her talents in each of these walks of the drama.

Presumably the same critic/fan wrote the review in the following week's newspaper:

> On Friday last, the theatre was respectably patronised by an audience who were capable of appreciating the talented performance of Miss Penley, in Goldsmith's celebrated comedy of *She Stoops to Conquer*. We have never seen the abilities of this young lady displayed to greater advantage than in the scene where she first meets with Young Marlow; and afterwards in her spirited and chaste personation of the

barmaid — indeed, throughout the whole play her acting embodied all that could be required in genteel comedy. The trial scene from the *Merchant of Venice*, in which she sustained the part of Portia, was a fine specimen of her tragic powers, and elicited frequent bursts of applause; while, as Edmond, in the *Blind Boy* she afforded the most unqualified pleasure to the lovers of melo drame. As an old favourite on our boards, we regret that Miss Penley's benefit was not more numerously attended, which may have been partly owing to the extreme coldness of the weather; but we have every reason to congratulate that young lady on the éclat and general approbation which distinguished the amusements of the evening.

Alas, the weather once again conspired to reduce Phoebe's possible audience. In those days it was not simply a matter of a tiresome chore to work to a thin audience, at a benefit all the profits of the performance accrued to the beneficiary, so every shilling really mattered. It is all very well being lauded as the equal to any actress on the provincial stage – what about the money?

A manager called Palmer opened a winter season at Lewes on 19 December 1829 with the doyen of man-monkeys M Gouffe as opening attraction. This most notable man-monkey had a very long career at the Surrey Theatre by actually being two different men – John Hornshaw in the 1820s and Sam Todd in the late 1830s. The earlier M Gouffe had recently been to court to make grievous complaints about his errant wife who nightly 'took other men home to his bed'. She was permanently drunk and had contracted 'a loathsome disease'. He had lost a contract worth £20 a week at Drury Lane because of her drunken behaviour on being refused admission to see him. Threatening to turn her out of his home where she was breaking the furniture, she replied by saying she would hawk penny flowers round bars, making sure people knew she was the wife of Gouffe the famous performer. He was advised to either divorce her or get a legal separation and pay her an allowance. Even reasonably affluent successful stage stars can have their problems.

After several days of Gouffe's monkey tricks, the following production was the *Forest of Bondy* with Mr Coney's celebrated performing dog. But Palmer also gave his customers sterner fare as this was succeeded by *Jane Shore* with Miss Penley in the title role. Unfortunately, the performance was but thinly attended. We have no way of knowing which Miss Penley was engaged in this season as no record of a Miss Penley has surfaced elsewhere during December 1829 and January 1830.

What is of great interest is that for Miss Penley's benefit which comprised *Speed the Plough* and *The Maid and the Magpie* 'our old manager, Mr Penley, performed.' This is by far the latest mention of old Sampson Penley whom we last saw in action exporting potted shrimps from Calais four years previously. Was he still working somewhere, perhaps still trouping round the continent, or was he dragged out of retirement to boost his daughter's takings which would auger to be disappointing in view of the generally poor business? Did he do any more performances before his death two years later? Probably we shall never know.

We do know that Palmer, closing the season in early February, lost over £100 on the season, an excuse for the poor business being the excessive number of parties given in Lewes. Though promising to have another attempt in summer, in the event Palmer was replaced by an optimistic Mr Roberds.

Rosina, having bobbed about East Anglia, possibly thinking *she* also was the equal to any actress on the provincial stage, next appeared at Liverpool where W J Hammond, in partnership with Richard Raymond, had taken the lease of the Pantheon theatre and renamed it the Liver after the fabulous bird from which Liverpool takes its name. The Liver Theatre was not the chief theatre in Liverpool, that distinction belonging to the Theatre Royal, where the salaries ranged from £1 to £5 as opposed to the £1 to £2.10.0 of the Liver.

Rosina soon made herself popular with the Liverpool audiences, and when Hammond put on a benefit for the funds to create a permanent asylum for the casual poor, an Address, written expressly for the occasion by a Lady of Liverpool was

> spoken by that clever and most popular actress, Miss Penley, a lady whose merits the Liverpool audience have so fully allowed, and who now (her benefit taking place tomorrow evening) so justly looks to them for those substantial marks of their favour, to which an amiable and assiduous public character give her such sterling claims.

Unfortunately, coming among the actors' benefits at the end of season rather than earlier in winter, the asylum benefit was not as well attended as anticipated so that the receipts were small. Hammond and Raymond charged the organisers £30 for the use of the theatre but, in view of the feeble returns, knocked £10 off the hire charge. Mrs Caddick's address was feelingly delivered to great applause by Miss Penley and an encore demanded but, circumstances seeming inappropriate, it was declined.

For her benefit Rosina played in *The Lost Son*, her regular benefit stand-by *The Actress of All Work* in which she sustained six different characters, *Hob in the Well*, ending with a popular melodrama in which Mr Parsloe the celebrated man-monkey would appear.

Parsloe, yet another of the intriguing actors specialising in the man-monkey genre, had been engaged to appear in *Perouse; or the Desolate Island*. This play by John Fawcett, based on a former one by Kotzebue, first appeared in London in 1801 and was, probably, the most popular of all the monkey dramas. La Pérouse is the only survivor of a shipwreck, and ends up in the company of a native woman on an island located somewhere 'north of Japan'. A ship with Madame de la Pérouse and her son on board arrives to rescue La Pérouse. Umba, the native woman – played by Rosina Penley – with whom La Pérouse has been living, is jealous and violent. She betrays him to her hostile countrymen, who swoop in and capture La Pérouse, his wife and their son. They are all about to be killed, but are saved through the intervention of a loyal and intelligent chimpanzee. The play was a fictional concept of what might have happened to the survivors of a real life French shipwreck in 1785.

E J Parsloe had been playing 'skin' roles ever since a boy at Covent Garden in 1816. Parsloe also played clown in pantomime and, two years after this appearance with Rosina, took a pantomime company to the Bowery theatre in New York. On the voyage out he injured himself severely by falling down the companionway. Despite this he did his best to rouse the customary mirth; but the audiences were small and on the fourth night the unfortunate clown, broken down by illness and mental anxiety, actually burst into tears onstage and was obliged to retire. He died the next day lamenting that he had ever left his wife and family in England.

Another guest artiste at Liverpool was T P Cooke who played his famous role of William in *Black-Eyed Susan* with Rosina in the title role. The play, which held the stage for many years, was written by Douglas Jerrold – the brother of Mrs Hammond, the boss's wife. The Jerrold parents, members of the J & P troupe back in 1799, had gone on to run their own company in Kent. The child Rosina may well have been play-mates with the equally young Jerrolds.

In the Georgian and Regency theatre there were many family and business connections that linked managers, players and venues together. The stage was like a village. Actors undoubtedly relied on the 'grapevine' to hear about seasons coming up, who was managing where, and so on. Players made friends of other actors and actresses, ensuring rumours and gossip passed around the profession to personal advantage. If an actor obtained a position as, say, low comedy man, he would be quite likely to ask if the other lines had been cast, then either suggest a friend to the manager or send a message to a colleague. It is significant how often the same players' names crop up in distant parts of the country for various different managements. Well-established actors would have many contacts in their address book, and no doubt a manager seeking to engage Rosina Penley and she was unavailable, would be referred to Phoebe or Emma.

At the end of the Liverpool season it was announced that Hammond's benefit raised £108 and Rosina's 'in excess of £70'. Not a bad haul for one night's work considering that a working man, or indeed the general run of actors, would have to work all year for that sum. It was the benefit system that enabled managers to keep wages low, and stars to make prodigious amounts of money. Actors of repute such as Grimaldi, Kean or Macready, and even lesser names like Oxberry, Dowton, and Elliston were regularly engaged with a provincial company for four or five nights at a decent flat fee plus a benefit. Thus they could, and did, go the rounds having a benefit nearly every week.

Hammond had also acquired the lease of the York/Hull circuit which included Leeds. The theatre there was a Tate Wilkinson relic that had seen better days, a typical old Georgian theatre measuring 86ft by 40ft divided equally into stage and auditorium. Seating around 600, it was a cold, draughty and cheerless place situated south of the river away from the town centre and, as by this time the area was becoming increasingly industrialised, hardly an enticing place to visit. Wakefield and Doncaster were other towns in the circuit but visited far more rarely. Although Raymond was not Hammond's partner in this venture he was employed as an actor with Mrs Raymond, and Rosina was returning to the circuit after six years. Rather oddly, in Leeds the local summary of the company said of Rosina the interval 'seems to have produced its effect for she wants natural ease, though tall and graceful in figure. In other respects she is entitled to commendation.' Whatever that was supposed to mean!

Frederick Calvert had spent ten years on the York circuit, starting out as a beginner and ending up as leading man. Back in 1823, as Rosina's colleague, he had played, among other parts, Romeo to her Juliet, and they had been the Macbeths. He had retired to be an academic at the end of the

1829 season, but Hammond lured him back to do a week of guest star appearances in Leeds at the beginning of his tenancy, cashing in on the popularity of a local favourite now no longer to be seen. Calvert played for six nights with mainly Shakespeare plays – *Othello* in which Rosina played Desdemona, *Hamlet* when she played Gertrude, *Julius Caesar* (Portia), *Macbeth* (Lady M), and also *Venice Preserved* when she was Elvira. This gives another example of the workload that actors were expected to undertake.

Any doubts about Rosina's acting prowess were swept aside by the tail-end of the season when we read:

> Miss Penley. – We perceive our old favourite, Miss Penley, takes her Benefit on Monday next, and we hope she will have a bumper, for she certainly is highly deserving of the best support of the lovers of the drama. Her talents are of the first order, her general correctness, the elegance of her wardrobe, and the appropriateness of her costume, are demonstrations of her industry and discernment, and what is above all these, the respectability of her private character, confers honour upon the profession at large.

One patron, much taken with the company, wrote a very long letter of praise including the following critique of Miss R Penley:

> But have I not a word for the gentle, the tender, and affectionate Desdemona? Oh! yes, I could dilate at considerable length in praise of Miss Penley's personification of this amiable character, but must of necessity check my inclination. I have seen the part represented by the principal metropolitan actresses, and can truly say, that never was I more gratified, nor my feelings more powerfully led captive. Miss P's voice is peculiarly adapted to characters of a passive nature; it is sweet, clear, and possesses a quality of tone which, like the minor key in music, shoots unerringly to the heart. I will conclude this article by selecting one or two instances wherein I thought her particularly effective, – the scene where she importunes so strongly for Cassio's restoration to his lost office – the tender sympathy which she evinces for Othello's indisposition, as yet ignorant of the cause of it – the transient irradiation of her features when Iago flatters her that all will yet be well – the whole of the death bed scene, and especially that part of it where she implores for mercy. Will she be offended if I in one instance point out what I consider a fault? The mono-syllable *not* is seldom used but significantly; to give full effect to it, therefore, it should be *well* and *fully* pronounced. Miss P pronounces it as though it were *nut*, the sound of which, though it may be more pleasing, is less dignified and not

proper. The costume (with one exception, and that is the fair heroine,) was appropriate. Why does not Miss P impart to her robe maker, a knowledge of the Venetian costume? Does she not think there is much inconsistency in the wife of Othello being dressed *a la Anglaise!*

Lowly actresses, not having robe makers, were obliged to costume themselves as best they may and, with a different play every night, their resources must have been stretched to the limit; no wonder they were sometimes clad out of period or place. This critique is quoted at length as it tells us more about Rosina than the usual odd lines about 'correct reading' or 'performed admirably' she merits from the professional critics. It also shows that there was critical discernment by playgoers, and the productions were not simply thrown on in any old rickety manner.

There appears to have been a dichotomy in the typical audience of the period. On the one hand we read of appalling noisy behaviour with missiles being thrown at the stage, tearing up benches and smashing chandeliers, on the other the erudite professional criticism of Coleridge, Leigh Hunt, Hazlitt and others still valued to this day. As above, we also see examples of the ordinary playgoer expressing his opinions at length, often about trivial matters. A typical example is a newspaper discussion about whether Young – playing Hamlet – should have his men swear upon the hilt of his sword or the blade. And few actors of any era have had the amount of critical minutiae devoted to them as Edmund Kean.

While Rosina was charming her public in Leeds, both her sisters were now working for brother Sam Jr at Windsor in the customary summer season. Emma was taking many leading roles, rarely having a night off, extending her repertory into the same territory as her elder sisters. All the familiar plays came round again and Emma played Black-Eyed Susan, Angela in *The Castle Spectre*, and similar roles that she must have often seen her sisters perform. Back again came *The Invincibles* with Emma repeating her Hannibal Del Epée. For her benefit she chose to play Emma, Tell's wife, in *William Tell*, a mother role that both Rosina and Phoebe often played. During the season Phoebe appeared occasionally in the more tragic parts such as Lady Macbeth, but Miss Dunbar carried the main weight of that repertoire.

The Hammond troupe visited Doncaster for three weeks in September with Rosina billed as 'her first appearance here these five years'. In October, the next stop for the Hammond company was a season at

Hull. The theatre, newly and elegantly painted, and the stage reconstructed on the latest principles, resulted in a delayed opening. Presumably Hammond was aware that the previous manager Mr Cummins had lost £2,300 on his ill-fated season at Hull. Hammond was well-known on the circuit as an actor in previous companies, but this was his first attempt at management there. As at Leeds, Calvert allowed himself to be wooed back by his old confrère to do a special week at the beginning of the venture.

For his benefit Calvert, presenting a selection of scenes from various plays of Shakespeare, was taken to task by the local paper that said it degraded both Shakespeare and the performer. However, it conceded that Calvert drew a full and fashionable house for the first time that season, pleasing his many supporters.

An actor new to the company, Mr Keppell, essayed the title role in *Hamlet* and proved 'graceful in his action and clear in his enunciation' but 'he introduced many new readings in the part, more ingenious than rational, and tinctured with no small share of affectation.' It was decided he was a useful actor in the line that the company sadly lacked, but Hamlet was 'too high a flight for him.' This brings home to us how conventional the readings of leading parts were expected to be, actors trying out interpretations different from the norm were accused of being 'incorrect' or 'false'. This slavish adherence to convention was one factor in the ability of actors to roll up and play with an unfamiliar company completely without rehearsal. Old actors used to speak of their 'points', meaning certain effects that they always utilised in their portrayals. The points of famous actors were so extensively copied that they became sacrosanct to the interpretation of the character. Acting in the 19th century was very different from the present day when every actor essaying Hamlet will spend weeks exploring the character in extensive rehearsals, seeking some new revelations that shed light on the enigmatic character. Few modern actors would consciously copy effects from a previous interpretation of the role, in fact he would deliberately go out of his way not to resemble a forerunner.

Perhaps poor Mr Keppell was actually a very good actor simply ahead of his time? Or it may be a case of the critic suffering a bilious attack, as he went on to say 'the music, throughout, was only one degree removed from execrable.'

SCENE SEVEN
1831 - 1832
NEWCASTLE, THE YORK CIRCUIT, LIVERPOOL, AND NORTHAMPTON

A S THE YEAR turned into 1831, Phoebe went with her brother Sam Jr for his first season at Newcastle. We have already seen what diarist Waldie thought about it when looking at Sam Jr's career as a manager. This was also the season when Miss Field was first employed by the Penleys.

While Phoebe was at Newcastle, with Ternan as her leading man, sister Emma was playing secondary roles at Edinburgh where Miss Jarman was leading lady. Miss Jarman had made good progress since her years at Bath, when Rosina had worked with her some 12 years previously in her first disastrous foray away from the J & P company. Miss Jarman had appeared in London with both Charles Kemble and Edmund Kean and had now established herself in Scotland as Edinburgh's drama queen.

Although Emma was resigned to lesser parts, her more important supporting roles included Celia in *As You Like It*, Olivia in *Twelfth Night*, Maria in *The School For Scandal* and Hero in *Much Ado About Nothing* when the local press stated 'We like Miss Penley's performance as Hero, although with reference to her person there was something ludicrous in Benedict styling her "Leonato's short daughter"'. The Penley girls must have been above average height, as elsewhere Rosina was described as 'tall and stately'.

Rosina, meanwhile, remained with Hammond for a second year roaming around his varied circuit. In January, Hammond engaged the famous and notorious Edmund Kean, now on his rapidly-failing last legs, to play at several venues and Rosina was there to offer her support. At York, Kean played three nights, his first being thinly attended, but business improving on the two succeeding nights. By now, with his unreliability notorious, the citizens of York were, perhaps, waiting to make sure the actor actually turned up.

Continuing on to Leeds for five nights Kean performed some of his most famous roles including Shylock in *The Merchant of Venice* with Rosina as Portia, and Mr Keppell, the unsatisfactory Hamlet, making his Leeds debut as Bassanio. Kean's other plays were *Othello* (Rosina as Desdemona, Keppell as Iago), *Richard III* (Rosina as the Queen, Keppell as Richmond),

The Iron Chest and *A New Way to Pay Old Debts*. The playbills announced 'Notwithstanding the heavy expense attending this engagement, NO ALTERATION will be made in the PRICES. The Theatre is well Aired, and good Fires are constantly kept.' Nowadays we usually do not have to consider whether we are likely to be cold at the theatre in January.

The troupe proceeded to Wakefield where, for one night only, Kean appeared as Shylock before departing elsewhere on his never-ending peregrinations, while the Hammond company returned to its base at Hull until ending the season on 18 March.

Back at York for the season proper, it was a very different attraction that captivated the audience – the best pantomime ever staged up to that time. Hammond had engaged the Ridgway Brothers, a trio of dancers and pantomimists, which effectively brought a different aspect to the normal programming. The production of *Harlequin Pedlar* was staged every night for an entire week of consecutive performances, a rare event in the provinces at that time. The scenery was very effective, the *Fairy Grotto* and the *View of the Liverpool and Manchester Railway* especially commended. This latter, which seems rather odd and underwhelming to modern eyes, was a moving diorama painted on 3000 yards of canvas which rolled across the stage depicting all the sights to be seen on a journey between the towns. The scene painters had copied pictures taken by artists on the spot, and in the days before photography a huge coloured painting was a rarity, so one stretching on and on a distinct novelty. The Ridgway Brothers in the leading roles were a great hit though taken to task

> in two instances, in the gambling-scene where the clown divests himself of a certain portion of his habiliments; and the incident of the Lady's bustle, – we think oversteps the bounds of decency, and would recommend their omission.

Apparently, losing one's trousers is not only considered unamusing, but mentioning the name of the garment is itself indecent!

Heading the tragedy strength of the company were Rosina Penley and Samuel Butler with whom she had recently played at Exeter. Butler had actually taken on the management of the York theatre for a year – suffering major financial loss – prior to Hammond acquiring the lease, so was a local favourite. Rosina had a particularly busy night when, for Butler's benefit, she was Gertrude in the third act of Hamlet, Cordelia in the third act of *King Lear*, Lady Macbeth in the fifth act of *Macbeth* and Volumnia in the fifth act of *Coriolanus*. And on top of all that, in the afterpiece she was Mary Parker in a nautical drama called *Richard Parker*.

What a prodigious memory the actor of yesteryear possessed – and some of us today cannot even remember where we put our spectacles!

Yet another onstage accident befell Rosina when the discharge from a gun injured her thumb and lacerated her left hand, causing a shock to her entire arm. But there was no cause for alarm as the game gal carried on regardless. Rosina does seem to have been somewhat accident prone.

As Rosina moved on to Leeds with the Hammond company, brother Sam Jr and sister Phoebe closed the Newcastle season and returned to Windsor for the June Race Week. It was a notably weak company apart from the Penleys, even Ternan not arousing much enthusiasm. Performances were every night, as usual during Race Week, but several plays were given twice – either a sign of popularity or, as here, a money-saving gesture.

There were only a couple of days between the close of the Newcastle season and the re-opening for Race Week in that town and, as the regular company had disbanded and departed, a scratch team moved in, with Emma Penley as leading lady. Now at the height of their powers, all three sisters were playing separately all over the place. Emma's next contract was at Northampton opening on 11 July when Mr Hamilton took a new company for a season opening with *The Merchant of Venice*.

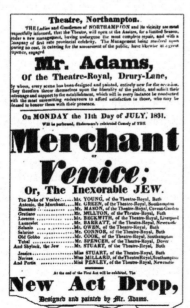

Emma Penley, now emulating her elder sisters, was playing leading tragedy roles. Manager Hamilton had gathered players from many of the Theatres Royal throughout the country for a summer season at Northampton.

Many of the actors, including leading man Mr Stuart, were from the Theatre Royal, Bath. Stuart's daughter essayed Jessica, and Mr Mason, playing Bassanio was reputed to be a nephew of John Philip Kemble. A featured attraction of the season was the expensive engagement of Mr Adams of Drury Lane who painted entirely new scenery throughout. Like many theatres at this time, companies were formed on an *ad hoc* basis and rarely survived more than one or two seasons. As business slumped over the weeks extra attractions were drafted in – the famous Gouffe, doyen of man-monkey actors, and the African Roscius among them. The season closed on 23 September indicating a reasonably successful season, and Emma was engaged for the following year.

While Emma was giving forth in Northampton, sister Phoebe was having another summer season with brother Sam Jr at Windsor. Miss Cleaver and Miss Field from Newcastle were also in the company. The always supportive local newspaper summed up the season:

> With regard to Miss Penley we cannot speak in too high terms of this lady's performances, her Donna Violante was sustained with the utmost dignity and purity, and in all the fascinating simplicity this character is so well calculated to display; who would for a moment hesitate in trusting their secrets with the fair sex, after once seeing Miss Penley in this character?

At the conclusion of the Windsor season Phoebe went with Sam Jr, Miss Field and most of the Windsor company to Leicester. Dodd was the low comedian, proving himself just as popular at Leicester as he was at Windsor; Waldron was tragedian. In *Wallace*, which was praised for the authentic Scottish dress of the ensemble, Phoebe as wife to Wallace 'approached to perfection, not a tone nor a cadence of her voice, but reached the heart; not a motion nor an attitude was without its impressive grace.'

Still in Hammond's company summering at Leeds, Rosina and the very tall Mr Butler repeated their joint repertoire including the title roles in *Romeo and Juliet*, *Coriolanus* with Rosina playing Volumnia, and *The Tempest* with Butler as Prospero and Rosina as Miranda. One had to be versatile to play the hero's fourteen-year-old lover in one play, his mother in another and his daughter in a third! Rosina coped with anything thrown at her as, apart from the tragic repertoire, she still played roles such as Lady Teazle in *The School for Scandal*.

William Macready came as guest star for six nights towards the end of the season, with Rosina providing stalwart support. In retirement, looking back on her career Rosina could claim that she had many times acted with the two greatest actors of the day – Kean and Macready.

Hammond journeyed to London to see the coronation of William IV on 9 September 1831. Brother to the late George IV, William was reluctant to have a coronation at all, but it was necessary by law, so he determined to have it done as economically as possible. Hammond's purpose was to obtain particulars of the pageantry so he could reproduce it on his stages.

While the boss was in London, the Brothers Ridgway had their benefit doing most of the night themselves, picking the plums from their extensive repertoire of pantomimes, sketches and dances. One item that Mr J Ridgway presented was *Grecian Statues*. These poses purported to be living copies of famous classical statuary – the discus thrower, the dying gladiator, Ajax defying the lightning, and so on. One assumes Mr J Ridgway had a particularly well-developed body. *Poses plastiques* or *tableaux vivants* – originally living copies of famous pictures with people dressed in period clothes and theatrically lit – later became infamous as nearly nude bodies creating an erotic entertainment with scenes such as *Nymphs Bathing* and *Diana the Huntress*. These sleazy entertainments flourished in Victorian London at venues like the Hall of Rome, the Coal Hole, and the Cyder Cellar. The famous Windmill Theatre, which operated from 1932 to 1964 featuring nude *tableaux vivants* on stage, was the last of a dishonourable line. Such shows are now unnecessary when unlimited pornography of the most debased kind is readily obtainable on one's home computer.

On Hammond's return from London he mounted his new spectacle:

The Royal Coronation of
King William IV and Queen Adelaide
With entirely New Scenery painted by Mr.
DONALDSON, from Sketches taken on the spot by Mr.
W. J. HAMMOND, who having been an eye witness of the
whole ceremony, is enabled to produce it in a style of
Magnificence not to be surpassed by any provincial
Theatre in the Kingdom.
The characteristic Dresses, Royal Robes, &c. &c. by Miss
Smith and Assistants from London. The Machinery by
Mr. Breckell and Assistants. The Properties by Mr.
Dearlove.
THE KING AND QUEEN'S REGALIA
BY LONDON ARTISTS,
ACTUALLY MODELLED FROM THE ORIGINALS.

251

When the only opportunity the provinces had of gleaning anything of the coronation was via written descriptions and drawings, such a display was expected to be a huge attraction. Coronations in the 20th century have been visible to all on the cinema screen, and that of Elizabeth II available to all who had access to a television could see it as it took place. No doubt the next will be immediately visible on our mobile phones.

Hammond's circuit ended at Hull where his troupe, including the Ridgway Brothers, went through the same gamut of attractions, though the leading man here was Mr Mude. Of course, the principal feature was the representation of the late Coronation:

> The pageant is very cleverly got up. The scene of the interior of the Abbey it very splendid, and the whole gives a very vivid idea of the ceremony of the coronation, the investing the King and Queen with the crown, sceptre, and other regalia. It was received with great applause; but we regret to say the attendance was not adequate to the exertions of the manager in producing so magnificent a spectacle.

This must have been disappointing to Hammond after such an effort. Perhaps the stolid burghers of Hull preferred more solid fare because audiences improved, including a crowded house for *Macbeth* when both Mr Mude's and Miss Penley's characterisations were of 'sterling excellence.' However, benefits were announced as the season's closing approached, and the newspaper again referred to the disappointing business in a forthright manner:

> We beg to remind our readers, that another opportunity is afforded, of lightening the failure of the season to the lessee, in the benefit of Mrs W J Hammond, which takes place on Tuesday evening next. On her own account, also, Mrs H has considerable claims to the patronage of the public, which we are sure will not be forgotten on this occasion. The bill of fare is unusually attractive, and as the closing night of the season, we shall not err in anticipating a bumper.

The season may have been disappointing, but life goes on and, for Rosina, this meant sticking with Hammond when Raymond became his partner once more for the Liverpool season.

Hammond and Raymond's money situation cannot have been too dire as the partners instigated a 'complete and beautiful renovation' at the Liver Theatre. The fronts of the boxes were newly painted with various subjects from ancient history and highly burnished with gold mouldings. A new elegant light blue curtain, in the fashion of the French theatres, replaced the old one. The backs of the boxes were adorned with a handsome paper in the Continental mode, and new fashionable private boxes added.

More surprisingly was the extraordinary large roster of players they advertised – 19 actors and 14 actresses being mentioned by name. From time to time these resident members were also augmented by star visitors from the London theatres. Actresses from the York circuit were Mrs Raymond, Miss Penley, Mrs Jerrold and Mrs W J Hammond, billed as 'their first appearance these two years.' As the Liver Theatre was not the main theatre in Liverpool it probably had to try and punch above its weight to compete.

In a new farce called *Love and Mystery*, Miss Penley played Celeste the heroine, 'a character in which that young lady displayed much of the grace and versatility of talent which have enabled her to rank high in her profession.'

Rosina was Black-Eyed Susan when the famous T P Cooke came again for a few days to present his popular roles. Cooke was the creator of the monster in the first dramatisation of Mary Shelley's *Frankenstein* and this, together with his jack-tar William and Long Tom Coffin, accounted for the vast majority of his performances throughout his career.

Four years after the J & P company was howled off the stage in Paris, at the very same Théâtre Porte-Saint-Martin, T P Cooke had appeared in this version of the Frankenstein story called *Le Monstre*. It caused such a furore that the colour he painted himself became the fashion of the day in Paris, giving a new colour to gloves, *Vert de Monstre* (monster green). Cooke achieved 80 performances of the play in Paris alone, causing all the Parisian ladies to fall in love with him, with several 'desiring to take him home.' He had first achieved fame in 1822 playing Long Tom Coffin in *The Pilot*, a role he played 562 times. He followed this success with *Le Monstre* which he played 365 times, but his biggest hit, and why he is still remembered, is his honest upright British tar William in Jerrold's *Black-Eyed Susan* in which he eventually achieved 783 performances.

For his benefit night, Cooke not only gave his famous William again, but also appeared in the play *Nelson*, and posed as a series of living statuary from antiquity. Rosina's night featured her as *The Bride of Eighty*. Benefit nights were always an opportunity to produce something novel and original, but one of the oddest must have been the unusual attraction included on Mr Ferrers the Prompter's night when he undertook to make a pair of shoes in five minutes!

Both Phoebe and Rosina were engaged at the Windsor theatre for the summer season of 1832 starting at the very end of July with three nights starring Kean. The star opened with his Shylock and Rosina gave her Portia, Sam Jr was Gratiano. The leading man for the season was Ternan from Newcastle and Edinburgh. He played Iago to Kean's Othello, with Rosina as Desdemona and Sam Jr in his old role of Cassio which he had played many times with Kean at Drury Lane. The final night of the three had been firstly advertised as *Richard III* – undoubtedly Kean's finest role. Whether his strength was failing him because he was, after all, doing alternate nights at his own theatre at Richmond, in the event his final offering was *The Stranger*, with Rosina giving her Mrs Haller. The three houses were 'tolerably good' but the season overall was disappointing.

Rosina's appearances were many and varied during the season, sister Phoebe's scarce and intermittent. For her benefit Rosina intended playing that long-time favourite of the J & P company *The Honeymoon* but 'was induced by receiving numerous applications from Her Friends' to change it to the new drama of *The Rent Day* which had been given earlier in the season. The evening ended with *Tekeli* – another old J & P war horse – with Phoebe playing the heroine her Aunt Frances used to do, and Sam Jr, who in younger days used to play the title role, now settling for Bras-de-Fer, the cowardly soldier that Uncle William often played.

Emma Penley returned to Northampton for the summer season, again conducted by Hamilton, but this time in conjunction with Parry of Covent Garden. The season opened on 16 July and Emma was the only cast member retained from the previous season along with – 'at a considerable expense' – the scenic artist Mr Adams of Drury Lane. The only evidence for Emma's roles in the season comprise a press cutting for 11 August 1832 showing she played Rachel Heywood in *The Rent Day*, and another stating that for her benefit Emma chose *The Jealous Wife* and *The Maid and the Magpie*. Emma had the advantage that her benefit was under the patronage of not only the Northampton and Sulby Cricket Clubs but also George Payne Esquire of Sulby Hall. A local character, this gentleman had inherited not only the Hall but a rent-roll of £17,000 a year and £300,000 in ready cash. However, he was not only a profligate but also a betting mug prone to backing nearly all the horses in a race and still not finding the winner. In one race alone he lost £33,000 on one horse. This wastrel eventually had to sell Sulby Hall, a mansion of some distinction built by Sir John Soane. The season ended on 24 September.

SCENE EIGHT
1833 - 1836
LEICESTER, EDINBURGH, SHEFFIELD AND BIRMINGHAM

A S USUAL, AFTER the Eton boys had quit school for their holiday, on 30 July Sam Jr opened his Windsor theatre, employing both Rosina and Phoebe. Anderson was brought down from Newcastle as leading man, making his debut by portraying *Grecian Statues* posing on a raised pedestal. This gimmick, first launched by the equestrian Ducrow and widely copied, purported to be an educational presentation of authentic ancient sculpture appealing to students of the fine arts. As we have seen, many actors, including the great T P Cooke, seized on the idea as a method of titillating their female fans.

For their shared benefit night on 5 September, Rosina was Clari in 'the admired opera' *Clari; or the Broken-hearted Father.* Usually sub-titled *The Maid of Milan*, this piece by the American John Howard Payne with music by Sir Henry Bishop introduced what has been called the most famous song in the world – *Home Sweet Home.*

Rosina and Anderson left before the end of the season to open Belville Penley and Anderson's first season as managers at Leicester with *The Belle's Stratagem* and *Katherine & Petruchio*, David Garrick's version of *The Taming of the Shrew* which replaced Shakespeare's original for 200 years. First impressions of the new company stated 'Mr Anderson is an actor of great ability, and Miss Rosina Penley is a very effective performer, but Miss Stohwasser bids fair to be the favourite from the charming naivety of her manner.'

Having helped brother Belville launch his foray into management, Rosina left Leicester before the end of the season to take up a place at Edinburgh, which being a principal provincial theatre paid enhanced salaries ranging from a guinea to £5. When that theatre opened for the winter season in October 1833, regular favourite Miss Jarman, Rosina's old colleague from Bath, was due to return supported by tragedian Mr Stuart, another ex-Bath player who had partnered Emma Penley at Northampton. Miss Jarman, now in a higher league having established herself both in London and Edinburgh, could not take up her position immediately as she was contracted at the Victoria Theatre in London. Until she arrived 'Miss Penley, a lady who has long held a distinguished rank in her profession, and whose sister acted here three years ago' was holding the fort.

> Miss Penley, from Newcastle, made her first appearance here in the part of Meg Merrilies, and also made a good hit. Her voice is not perhaps so powerful, although clearer, than that of our old friend Mrs Stanley; but her style and manner reminded us very much of the latter; she was warmly applauded throughout.

Unfortunately, Rosina does not seem to have hit the spot, as a review of *Macbeth* somewhat grudgingly said:

> Our new tragedian, Mr Stuart, appeared . . . in the arduous character of Macbeth; the most we can venture honestly to say of his presentation is, that it was tolerably respectable and this is also all that can in verity be said of Miss Penley's Lady Macbeth.

However, according to the report it did not much matter about the tragedians, as Shakespeare's tragedies had been finely acted in the past only to be received by empty benches. The report concluded menacingly:

> Indeed if our theatre amusements are not better patronised than they have been for some years back, we shall soon lose them altogether, for the manager must in self-defence, shut the doors before he is utterly ruined. We still, however, augur better things.

Another ominous sign of a drastic falling off of theatre business – if a capital city such as Edinburgh was not attracting custom it is not surprising that lesser towns were feeling the pinch, and country theatres falling like ninepins. In order to keep the business flowing, the Edinburgh manager lowered his admission prices, and the owners agreed a lower rental from the 2000 guineas previously demanded.

Theatre rents had plummeted over the last four or five years – the rent for the Dublin theatre was now £900 whereas it had formerly been £3000; Bath theatre, in the doldrums for some time, could only attract a manager by cutting its rent to a similar £900, and the patent houses in London were now let several thousand pounds cheaper than only five years before.

Miss Jarman having arrived, Rosina was free to join her former manager W J Hammond who had taken the lease of the Sheffield theatre. His winter season ran from 4 November to 20 December. After which she returned to Newcastle for the 1833/34 season for brother Sam Jr, teaming up again with Younge, Anderson and the engaging Miss Stohwasser 'and a very pretty face she has too. In addition to her being a very interesting woman, she is a very fair actress . . . we have no doubt of her becoming a favourite with the Newcastle audience.' As we have been told more than once that Rosina was not conventionally pretty, it is possible that she was rather peeved with all these eulogies showered on the attractive Miss Stohwasser. At Rosina's benefit in April, Mrs Penley, who can only have been Sam Jr's wife, once again appeared. Perhaps she saved herself just to appear on family benefit nights, always playing the same part?

In May 1834 Rosina was back with W J Hammond's company at Sheffield to open the spring season with *Macbeth*, Rosina as Lady M and Anderson (his first appearance) as Macduff – no doubt Rosina helped him get the gig.

Hammond advertised he had, under public pressure, reduced the box price from 4/- to 3/, (pit and gallery remaining at 2/- and 1/-). He was by no means the only manager reducing his prices in the nationwide slump. Hammond's 1834 Sheffield season lasted until 21 June during which time Charles Kean, son of the late Edmund, guested playing all his father's principal roles, supported by both Rosina and Anderson.

Charles Kean as Hamlet

Sheffield, it may be remembered, was the town where the Revd Thomas Best had been thundering his anti-theatre sermons for the past 20 years, so it is pleasant to learn that the theatre was still functioning in spite of his worst efforts as this crackpot went on trying to deprive the citizens of Sheffield their harmless pleasures until his death in 1865. At least Best did not go to the extremity of the Rev Phin of Wick who refused to baptise, marry or bury any parishioner who had attended a theatre!

One of Hammond's actors Thomas Boddie, took Hull's Adelphi Theatre for a short season opening on 7 July, advertising that Hammond, Rosina Penley and Anderson would be appearing in turn for 5 days each. Hammond was the first, appearing in *The Battle of Austerlitz* and the afterpiece *Peccadilloes* for two nights, followed by two further plays. Hammond, Boddie and stage manager Ferrers were taken to court by the proprietors of the Theatre Royal on the grounds that these actors were acting in an unlicensed theatre, the standard penalty being £50 for each part played. Thus Hammond would be obliged to fork out a total of £200,

Boddie and Ferrers £50 each.

Two magistrates had to agree to the guilt or innocence whereas the pair trying this case unusually disagreed. The defendants could neither be convicted nor acquitted. The only way out of the impasse was to withdraw the charges. The prosecutors agreed, providing the actors did not appear ever again at the Adelphi which they were determined to crush as it transgressed their patent.

Needless-to-say Rosina and Anderson did not make their advertised appearances. Though not all heeded the warning, as another actor called Ingleton then took the Adelphi and he too was summoned to appear before the magistrates but fled the town. He was pursued by the town constable who found him acting at Knottingley, arresting him while still in make-up and costume. As Ingleton could not afford to pay the penalties imposed he was sent to the treadmill for three months. An appeal was granted by the prime minister and his sentence fortunately remitted.

Hammond should have known better – he had had the lease of the Theatre Royal himself. He later dropped all his provincial interests, taking instead, with brother-in-law Douglas Jerrold, the lease of the Strand Theatre in London from May 1836 which he made into a home for light comedy and farce. This he relinquished to take on the management of Drury Lane from October 1839, lasting only until March 1840 when he was imprisoned owing debts of £8000. Released after a year, Hammond dabbled with other ventures before going to America in 1848, promptly dying there of dysentery.

At the end of July 1834 Rosina was back at Windsor for brother Sam's annual season. Also there were Younge, Anderson, the delightful Miss Stohwasser and the inevitable Mr Dodd who sang either 'A Comic Song', 'A New Comic Song' or 'A Favourite Comic Song' on every programme.

On 8 September, Rosina's benefit play was *The Merchant of Venice* in which she played Portia, Younge was Shylock and the beguiling Miss Stohwasser was Nerissa. Phoebe appeared at the benefit, being billed as 'her first and only appearance during the season'. Anderson was not in the play as he opened that night at Leicester with his own company and had already left Windsor. Younge also left for Leicester after Rosina's benefit.

Rosina was not in the Leicester season, she returned with Hammond to Doncaster in October where, instead of her usual role of Virginia the daughter in *Virginius*, she was now merely Servia the nurse. Rosina was now thirty-eight and beginning to show her age. The Doncaster stay being only a matter of two weeks or so, the company then moved on to Sheffield for the winter season, but it was a mere stop off on the way to Newcastle for Rosina as on 22 December she opened there with Anderson in *Romeo and Juliet*. The company was headed by Sam Jr in person, with Dodd, Windsor's favourite low comedy man, and the charming Miss Stohwasser.

Actors were now undertaking far more travelling, chasing diminishing work in shorter bursts. It was only the major towns that were still running regular seasons, and actors were not staying for the entirety, but coming and going on piecemeal contracts.

At the conclusion of the Newcastle season both Rosina and Dodd were back at Windsor for the annual Race Week heading a 'respectable company' which 'produced a number of new and popular pieces, but we are sorry to say the house was poorly attended.' So the audiences did not find the pieces as popular as the manager thought they would.

The Miss Penley in brother Belville's Cheltenham company when that season opened on 29 June was Phoebe, who as a well-established favourite in the town from seasons over the previous ten years, was billed as 'of the Theatre Royal, Newcastle and formerly of this theatre.' The season at Cheltenham closed on 28 August and the entire company, including Phoebe, moved to Leicester for several weeks before returning to Cheltenham for a winter season.

Rosina was at Windsor again for the 1835 summer season. This seemed to be the one fixed point in her year and – although there is very little evidence – no doubt she filled in with short bursts at other venues. However, as the theatre seasons, circuits and venues were all contracting she would probably be having more periods 'resting' than she would have liked.

One year must have seemed very much like another at Windsor with annual bespeaks from Princess Augusta, Queen Adelaide, the local MPs, other district dignitaries and organisations in turn. Similarly, many of the same players and plays were dredged up year after year, repeatedly featuring the familiar titles *Black-Eyed Susan*, *The Mountaineers*, *Jane Shore*, *Pizarro* and so on over and over.

Othello was still regularly performed, probably Shakespeare's most popular play of the period. Now Kean was in his grave, his role at Windsor was played by Mr Willis 'from the London Stage', the ever reliable Younge was Iago, Sam Jr gave his Cassio and Rosina was Desdemona. 'We think we never saw *Othello* performed better in the country.'

By necessity, new plays were introduced, some very successfully – *The Man o' War's Man; or Tom Cringle's Log* for one. There was a full house when Queen Adelaide commanded a new comedy: J B Buckstone's *Married Life* in which Rosina had some 'serious acting' to do as the jealous Mrs Lynx which she did, as always, 'extremely well.' Buckstone had started out as a teenage actor with the J & P company at Peckham in 1818, going on to have a career both as a major playwright and a star comic actor. His ghost is said to haunt the Haymarket theatre.

The local newspaper regarded *Pizarro* as Sheridan's best play and deservedly popular: 'Miss Penley's personation of the unhappy Elvira was an admirable performance, and fully justifies our former opinion of her powers.' Of course, it is never done today, Sheridan's fame resting on repeated productions of his two fine comedies *The Rivals* and *The School for Scandal.* Rosina 'took a benefit on which occasion we were glad to see a most respectable attendance, as it showed in what estimation this lady and her performances are held. . . The acting was generally speaking very good, particularly that of Mr and Miss Penley.'

As the season closed, there was confidence that, despite the poor start to the season, Mr Penley would not have lost money as it ended strongly with good houses. Of Rosina Penley:

> This lady possesses talents of not ordinary kind. If we would name any one or two characters in which she is seen to advantage we would mention her *Lady Townley* and *Esmeralda*, in both of which she displays very considerable talent, which she takes every opportunity of cultivating.

Rosina went northwards again to Newcastle where she was once again leading lady, this time working for her brother Montague who had taken over the manager's reins from Sam Jr.

Montague had assembled mainly a roster of actors new to Newcastle, Mr Cowle was leading man with Rosina who was welcomed with:

> Miss Penley's style of acting is so well known, that any description of her performance is unnecessary. She generally gives evidence of a good conception of her parts, but with a little less effort, whether of gesticulation, action, or voice, as circumstances may require, she would often be more truly effective.

This critic no doubt sat in a prime place in the pit or boxes. Rosina had to play in a theatre where the gallery alone held 750 people, no wonder she tended to be broad. However, in an early production of that old war-horse *Pizarro* 'nothing could be more discreditable than the way it was misrepresented.' Beyond Miss Penley, Mrs Cowle, Wood and Maddocks scarcely an individual knew what to say or do. Cowle as Rolla was 'shamefully imperfect' and could not have been worse if he had been in the position of the originator of the part on the first night. This referred to the infamous occasion at Drury Lane when J P Kemble had Sheridan locked in a room still writing the last scenes of the play, passing them out page by page while the actors were enacting what had gone before. It is remarkable that this play, first performed in 1799, running for 31 consecutive nights, is now forgotten. *Pizarro* promptly went into print engendering 20 editions and sales of 30,000 copies in one year alone. The play became one of the most popular throughout the entire 19th century, but is now considered of little merit.

Poor Mr Cowle came in for some stick again when, under the patronage of Lady Ravensworth, he played Macbeth. He showed powers of high order in the famous dagger scene but, after the second act, he went completely to pot either forgetting the words or, more likely, never having known them. He resorted to what actors call 'winging it' – making it up as he went along. To make up common words in place of Shakespeare's lines was as 'reprehensible as it was foolish.' Rosina as Lady M acted well throughout, which must have been a work of art playing opposite a husband who did not know what he was saying. One wonders if Lady Ravensworth asked for her money back.

The likely reason for this farrago of nonsense is that Cowle had never played the role (one that was in every tragedian's repertory) and when Montague Penley accepted the commission from the local aristocrat he was not aware of the fact and had to set Cowle to learning it. Montague had probably hired an actor who was economical, but not actually an established tragedian.

Fortunately, a major success came along in the form of *The Jewess*. The splendour of the manner in which the piece was mounted and the chaste and effective acting of the principal performers (including Mr Cowle!) was considered more responsible for its success than the intrinsic merits of the drama.

This popular work, chosen as the last night's attraction, was also for the benefit of Rosina

> who has been so many years before a Newcastle audience, as
> to render encomium a work of supererogation. It must suffice
> to say that the friends of the drama – ever ready to patronise
> sterling professional talent, when accompanied, as in the case
> of Miss Penley, with spotless private character and conduct –
> gave her a real 'bumper'.

During the evening Rosina delivered an epilogue full of smart illusions to the railroads in progress, the public improvements to the town, and the drama generally. More importantly to the theatre and its audiences she made references to the fact that this was the last night of the old building as it stood in the way of a new road scheme. A brand new theatre was promised when the drama would spring up revitalised anew. This was officially the last night of the old theatre, though it would open again for one last time during Newcastle Race Week, the true last performance taking place on 25 June 1836. The reference to railways may have seemed clever at the time, but little did the actors know that this progress in transport would destroy their way of life.

As usual, Windsor beckoned for Rosina to spend the 1836 summer season with brother Sam's company where *inter alia* she gave her esteemed portrayal in *The Jewess*. Thence to Birmingham where, under the management of Mr Armistead, she opened the winter season on 26 September as Letitia Hardy in *The Belle's Stratagem*. Although a legitimate Theatre Royal, Armistead, also being a circus manager elsewhere, gave his public a hefty dose of lighter fare including Four Chinese Brothers 'whose performances are a puzzle for the Faculty', Madam Frost on the tightrope and Monsieur Stonet the Flying Phenomenon on the Corde Volante. Another exotic attraction was the 'Troope Elastique of Real Bedouin Arabs' which was most likely a group of Moroccan tumblers, still a staple diet of travelling circuses today.

In amongst all this, Rosina played her standard repertoire but also, for the only time so far discovered, she played Rosalind in *As You Like It* – a part that would seem to have been ideal for all the tall Penley sisters. One of the main afterpiece attractions that ran for several nights was *Othello Travestie* a silly send-up of the play with cross-dressing players. Rosina was not asked to take part in this or other farces and fatuous fare. Now regarded more and more as a tragedy queen, she did not totally eschew comedy and still acted Julia in *The Rivals* and other classic pieces. However, tragedy, strong drama and Shakespeare were her strengths, and during the run at Birmingham she paired with the leading man Waldron in *Macbeth*, *The Merchant of Venice*, *Henry VIII*, *Hamlet*, and *Richard III*.

On one occasion Mr C Pemberton, a local lecturer and authority on Shakespeare, offered his services for a special performance in aid of the Building Fund for the Mechanics' Institute. For this night Waldron, who was also offering his valuable talents, stepped down to the role of Macduff. It is astonishing how readily actors of the time could switch parts at the drop of a hat. One has the feeling that they carried entire plays permanently in their heads and could drag out whichever role the manager requested. Rosina, of course, played Lady Macbeth with many tragedians – Ternan, Younge, Salter, Butler, Stuart, Calvert, Mude, Hamilton, Cowle, Charles Kean, and the greatest of them all William Macready. Although she worked many times with the famous Edmund Kean, there is no record of them playing the Macbeths together.

Now she was supporting not an actor but an academic, though as she had nursed many an amateur through a variety of roles she is hardly likely to have been daunted by the prospect. A section of the Birmingham Choral Society was roped in to assist in the proceedings, as the play always included singing witches and the music of Matthew Locke.

The final headliner of the season was Mr Ord's Stud of Nineteen Horses which was engaged for several nights; Mr Ord not only showing conventional 'equestrian manoeuvres' but inserting his horses into the plays *Richard Turpin*, *Ivanhoe*, and *El Hyder* in which Rosina gave one of her collection of Z-named lovelies, in this case Princess Zaida. Rosina's final night was 13 December, enabling her to go straight to Newcastle in time for the opening of the new theatre.

The opening night playbill for the new Theatre Royal at Newcastle under the management of Montague Penley

SCENE NINE

1837 - 1840
THE NEW THEATRE AT NEWCASTLE; WINDSOR AND COVENT GARDEN

A S MIGHT HAVE been expected, in spite of the rapid progress in building the new theatre in Newcastle, there was a delay in opening. It was 20 February 1837 before Montague Penley's first night in a theatre that, apart from the three major theatres in London, was trumpeted as the finest in the country. With Younge and Rosina leading the troupe, the assembled company was not, on paper, a particularly outstanding one. After the first-night excitements and complaints of the new theatre, once the company had settled in, Mrs Haller in *The Stranger*, another of Rosina's fail-safe roles, provided throughout

> the most perfect specimen we have yet seen of her mode of delivery – which, beautiful as it generally is, and remarkable for the good taste by which it is directed, was on this occasion peculiarly manifest.

Later came *Rosina*, an old war-horse from the J & P repertory, a very popular light opera composed by William Shield with a libretto by Frances Moore Brooke, an author well-known in London literary and theatrical circles. Mrs Brooke, married to a clergyman, spent some years in Canada and wrote the first novel ever published in that country. She is now a feminist icon. *Rosina*, written on her return to England, was first performed at Covent Garden in 1782. The work was a forerunner of English comic opera and modern musical comedy. Like *The Beggar's Opera* of 50 years previously, it used folk and popular melodies, including the air that was also used by Burns for *Auld Lang Syne*. It also may have been the inspiration for Sampson Penley to name his children, as out of the seven characters there are Phoebe, Rosina, Capt Belville and William.

On Whit Monday, *The Jewess*, the play that had been such a success at the old theatre, was revived by public demand for two nights with Rosina in her original role. For her benefit on the Fifteenth Fashionable Night, Rosina chose *Married Life* the play by Buckstone in which the tangled but innocent relationships between five married couples looked forward to the 'teacup and saucer' plays of T W Robertson. Another attraction was Rosina reciting Collins' *Ode on the Passions* accompanied by *tableaux vivants*.

This poem, set to music, was a favourite for benefits, with several verses covering fear, anger, despair etc. Having each passion depicted in living pictures could only have added interest to something that today would be considered rather tedious.

Once again Rosina returned to Windsor for the summer season in 1837. She was now forty-one and her work appears to have become restricted to her brothers' companies – Montague in the north and Sam Jr in the south. At Windsor that year the company was a mix of new and unfamiliar names and, as had become the norm of late, the season got off to a slow start despite Sam delaying the opening until 7 August. Business gradually picked up towards the season's end, and there was a packed house when the new queen Victoria (who had come to the throne on 20 June) commanded and attended a performance.

The season closed on 16 September.

Rosina on her regular rota returned to Newcastle where the theatre opened on 30 October for the 1837/38 season, and Montague engaged Sheridan Knowles and his protégé Miss Elphinstone to give a fillip to the start of the proceedings.

Mrs Mayoress (as the wife of the Mayor was quaintly styled in Newcastle) gave her patronage to a performance of *The Honeymoon*. Of all the plays performed over the years, this particular one has the most resonance for the Penley family. It entered the J & P repertoire soon after it was written in 1804 and all the Penley children grew up with it as it was regularly performed on their father's circuit. As seen in Act Two, the part of the Mock Duke in the play was William Penley's calling card at Drury Lane, a position he maintained for over ten years.

At Newcastle, Corrie, a regular in Montague's company, played Jaques the Mock Duke, and Rosina's Julianna was 'performed with much judgment; and when the lady becomes conscious of the impropriety of her former conduct, every thing done and said by Miss P was really affecting.'

> The gradual fading away of disappointed vanity, and the gradual growth of real esteem and affection for her manly husband, were as truly given by Miss Penley.

Of course Rosina was good in the role; she had been playing it for years, her name being against the part on a bill with her father's company at Hastings 20 years previously.

In February, came a new drama translated from the French called *Walshi; or the Queen of Bohemia* with beautiful scenery and superb dresses. 'The expense in bringing out this piece must have been great, and the Manager is justly entitled to the support of the public for his exertions.'

The title role 'was played by Miss Penley and we certainly never saw her acquit herself with more talent.' It sounds to be the usual kind of hokum, with Walshi coveting the throne of Bohemia, assisted to it by Graffe an adventurer, who, imprisoned by the perfidious queen, escapes and hurls the queen from the battlements to her death, being filled with remorse when he discovers she was his mother. There appears to be no written trace of this work and it may have been Montague's own version of the story, as he made a few unsuccessful attempts at writing plays.

Montague and Rosina were devastated at the news that their brother Sampson Penley Jr had died in Paris on 27 May 1838. Sam had actively been making arrangements to return, with his family, to resume control of the Windsor theatre. His death created a sudden and immediate void as the June Race Week was imminent. Montague immediately stepped into his late brother's shoes putting in a company for Race Week and, as at Newcastle, permanently taking Sam Jr's place at Windsor.

Whatever the personal affect on Rosina, professionally she carried on as she had been accustomed over the latter years, working the summer season at Windsor. The change of manager would have made little difference to her; the installation of gas, new for the summer, with redecoration of the auditorium would have been a bigger change. Gas and new decor notwithstanding, the season got off to its usual sluggish start with thin houses. Montague was praised for putting in the best company seen for many years, and engaging Mrs Nisbett as a guest artiste. The leading tragedian was Samuel Phelps who would go on to be the actor-manager at Sadlers' Wells and usher in modern practices in performing Shakespeare, historically taking his place between Macready and Irving as the major classical actor of the day.

Rosina took part in *The Provok'd Husband* selected for the benefit arranged for Sam Jr's widow. When her own benefit came round the play was, yet again, *The Honeymoon*, but as Mrs Nisbett had been retained, the part of Julianna, for which Rosina had been much praised in Newcastle, was played by the star. This must have been peeving for Rosina but was common practice. The local actor always had to stand down, the guest star having priority. Every night of the year in a theatre somewhere in the provinces there would be the local tragedian glowering at the man from London who, having come to usurp him for two or three nights, would then gaily disappear with as much money as the local favourite could earn in a year.

By the end of the season the early thin houses had been forgotten and the local press lavished praise on the talented company, the sparkling society in the boxes, and the full houses. It was generally agreed that the 1838 season had been one of the best ever witnessed in Windsor. This is not surprising as Montague had brought leading actors of superior quality, and Rosina was still described as 'our favourite.'

Rosina was not engaged for the winter season at Newcastle. Montague had engaged Mr and Mrs Ternan to lead the company for the opening weeks. Mrs Ternan was the former Miss Jarman, the leading lady for whom Rosina had deputised five years previously at Edinburgh. Miss Jarman had married Thomas Ternan in 1834 and the couple had immediately sailed to America where they toured for three years with great success. On their return, the Ternans had found they were as popular as ever in both Edinburgh and Newcastle.

Neither was Rosina involved in Montague's disastrous foray into the London big time, next working for her brother for the customary Windsor summer season in 1839 when the opening guest artistes were Mr & Mrs Keeley, followed by Mrs Nisbett and her sister Jane Mordaunt. Montague had great faith in Mrs Nisbett and the two Misses Mordaunt, having booked them for Race Weeks in Newcastle in 1838 and 1839.

In that old war-horse by Colman the Younger *Heir at Law*, Rosina gave her Cicely Homespun 'with her accustomed excellence, and was much and deservedly applauded.' At the age of forty-three Rosina was obviously still able to play rustic maidens. She played Helen McGregor in the opera *Rob Roy*, a role she had often played before, sometimes with Macready. For her benefit Rosina chose *The Heart of Midlothian* and *Black-Eyed Susan*, deservedly appreciated by the public who crowded the house. It was the best house of the season and proof that Rosina's admirers were still plentiful.

The desperate Montague in December 1839 elected to venture the first winter season at Windsor for many years. Once again he turned to sister Rosina and brother Belville for assistance, with a company led by Maddocks and Cooke, and old favourite low comedian Dodd back after a four-year absence.

Rosina gave her *Jane Shore* yet again – 'an excellent piece of performance, and that lady fully sustained the reputation which her former exertions have earned for her.' When Mr and Mrs Maddocks took their benefit they were 'not patronised to the extent to which their talents entitle them'. In *William Tell*, Maddocks as William Tell ably supported his character, as did Rosina playing Tell's wife Emma, yet another role Rosina had played many times, often with Macready.

For Belville's benefit the play was Bulwer Lytton's *The Lady of Lyons* which had been first performed at Covent Garden as recently as 15 February 1838 with Macready playing the lead. Bulwer Lytton wrote only three plays, all highly successful, and was considered to be in the vanguard of modern drama.

Rosina, although having performed in many of the leading theatres of the land as well as a large number of undistinguished ones in small obscure towns, had never had the opportunity of playing in a London theatre. When, back in 1826, Charles Kemble visited Cheltenham to witness the performance of Miss R Penley from the Glasgow Theatre prior to engaging her for the London Boards, she acted Lady Teazle to his Charles Surface in *The School for Scandal*. He must not have been impressed, because no offer was forthcoming. At last in January 1840, Rosina had her chance to tread the boards of Covent Garden when she was engaged to play Gertrude in *Hamlet*.

Covent Garden's glory days were well over. The theatre had been through a series of short-stay managers and was currently leased to Charles Mathews and his wife Madame Vestris who were doing excellent business with opera, pantomimes and musical works in general, the drama aspect taking second place. The afterpiece on the *Hamlet* night was the 16th performance of the pantomime *Harlequin and the Merry Devil of Edmonton; or the Great Bed of Ware*. The *Windsor and Eton Express* was pleased to write:

> MISS R PENLEY – This well known and much respected actress who has successfully performed the principal female characters at our Theatre Royal, as well as most of the principal provincial theatres in the kingdom, for some years, made her first appearance before a London audience on Monday night, at the Theatre Royal Covent Garden. The part assigned to her was the Queen, in Shakespeare's tragedy of *Hamlet*, a character, which although not a heavy one, requires on the part of the performer much discernment, discretion, and experience, combined with no little talent. The many friends and admirers of this lady's public and private character in this neighbourhood will be glad to learn that her first appearance on the metropolitan boards was as successful as they could have possibly wished it. The house was well filled, and the performances of the evening went off remarkably well.

Rosina was next cast as Britannia in a Grand Masque entitled *The Fortunate Isles* – more pageantry than drama, mounted to celebrate Queen Victoria's marriage to Prince Albert – that played as an afterpiece for some 17 evenings between 21 February and 13 March. Full of historical allegory, Madame Vestris as Liberty, together with Time, Fame, Honour and Victory discover Britannia the genius of the isle whom they combine to bless. Then left alone, Britannia is assailed in turn by the Genii of Saxony, Denmark, and Normandy; a fierce conflict between each, the scene ends with Britannia bound in chains. But all is well as Liberty re-enters and Britannia's chains fall free. This entire allegory was but a preliminary to a spectacular romp through the high spots of British history.

On 16 March Rosina played Lady Capulet in *Romeo and Juliet*, the pantomime *Harlequin and the Merry Devil of Edmonton; or the Great Bed of Ware* clocking up its 46th performance the same night. Romeo was Anderson, Belville's old partner, still playing the ardent youth, but Rosina, once his Juliet, now playing his mother-in-law.

Anderson, often criticised for his barn-storming type performances, lost all decorum in his grief, throwing himself on the ground, roaring and blubbering like 'a great lubberly boy who had received a horse-whipping'. Neither did it help when leaving Juliet after the balcony scene, he posed, taking up what he deemed a picturesque attitude, but stumbled into Juliet, the kerfuffle causing hearty laughter at his maladroitness.

Mercutio was Vandenhoff, a popular principal tragedian in the provinces, but a second-rater in London, and, making her London debut as Juliet, Miss Jane Mordaunt the sister of Mrs Nisbett, who had been appearing regularly at Windsor over the previous two years. The *Theatrical Observer* made this rather prejudicial comment prior to the event: 'this young lady must throw a little more animation into her acting than she is wont to do, to stand any chance of success.'

After two performances the paper told its readers that Miss Mordaunt was no higher than the general respectable Juliets and 'if her friends lead her to think she will one day become a star, it is nothing more or less than downright cruelty.' The *London Standard* agreed with a host of damning comment, saying she did nothing that might not be done by any clever young lady after a few elocution lessons and instructions when to raise her arm, clasp her hands etc. Her friends called for her at the end, thus reviving the press strictures that this foolish custom should be abolished, as it was cruel to fill a young mind with hopes that even the most ignorant could see would never be realised.

The rather harsh verdicts went on to say that she was to be replaced by another actress who had been favourably received in the role at Drury Lane. 'But what could have induced Miss Mordaunt's friends (?) to imagine she could play, even second-rate tragic characters, is beyond conception.'

When the play was done for the third time, Miss Emmeline Montague was the Juliet and played it admirably, 'we may fearlessly avouch that one of these days she will be a star.' She did not exactly become a star, but an established actress, who, on one occasion, was called upon by Dickens to replace one of his amateurs when the theatre was too large for her to cope. Miss Montague retired from the stage in 1848 after marrying the actor Henry Compton who had played the Apothecary at her debut, later becoming the best Shakespearean clown of the day. The actress Fay Compton and author Compton Mackenzie were their grandchildren.

The theatre of Rosina's day could be pitiless and cruel to young women, and during her career Rosina herself had suffered many setbacks. Balancing open hostility, the public could be excessively indulgent to their old favourites, as was shown when Charles Kemble made a come-back to the Covent Garden stage where he had once been manager. He had retired through ill-health on 2 January 1837, making a tear-stained farewell speech, his collapsing frame supported by fellow actors. Now sixty-five, he was returning after four years absence to play some of his old successes. His first re-appearance – as Charles Surface in *The School for Scandal* – was by command of the queen, and the theatre was packed as soon as the doors opened, the takings exceeding £600. Kemble's appearance was greeted by roars of applause, and at the end the queen desired to see Mr Kemble who, waiting on her after the play, received her approbation for his performance and her command that the following evening he should play Mercutio in *Romeo and Juliet.*

The play was given with the usual cast, Miss Montague, Anderson, Miss R Penley etc, Vandenhoff standing down for Kemble to give his Mercutio, a part he had taken up later in life when his daughter started playing Juliet and he could no longer conceivably be Romeo. Again the house was crowded, with the queen and Prince Albert present. It was an unofficial visit by royalty and they lurked in the shadows of their box. At the end of the play, after Kemble had acceded to the demand of the audience by re-appearing to bow and finally exit, a great clamour arose from the pit which at first appeared to be a desire for the queen and Prince Albert to show themselves. On the contrary, the fuss was because a lady in the adjacent box was leaning out trying to peer round next door! The pit denizens had a proper attitude, it was not a state occasion but a private visit, and knew when the royals must not be disturbed. The yelling and hooting continued until the miscreant lady and her party quitted their box in embarrassment.

Kemble went on to play other items in his repertoire that had no place for Rosina. Finally, for his farewell performance on 10 April 1840 he chose to play Hamlet, his most famous tragic role – the versatile Charles Kemble was actually considered better in the high comedy department. Again Victoria and Albert were present to see this memorable theatrical occasion, rumours spreading that he was to be knighted by the queen at the end of it. It remained nothing but a rumour, the first actor to be knighted did not

Charles Kemble
Pictured at the time of his farewell to the stage in April 1840

happen for another 55 years when the accolade fell on Henry Irving.

Again the house was crowded, for this really was to be the actor's final farewell. Of all the Kembles, Charles was the most loved by the public and, throughout our story of the Penleys, he has been a major recurring figure. Rosina must have felt that an era was ending when she played Gertrude, mother to the now pensionable Hamlet who had played the same role for her father in Brussels 26 years previously. Kemble's delivery was now so measured, giving equal weight to the small scenes as the great speeches, that his unusually deliberate manner, together with long intervals between the acts, led to the final curtain falling an hour past the scheduled time. No doubt he was both conserving his failing strength and reluctant to finally leave the stage. He maintained his vigour to the end, fenced with his usual skill and almost recaptured the elasticity of his youth.

He was, of course, unanimously called for at the end, his speedy re-appearance bringing the pit to its feet, leaping on to the benches shouting bravos and waving hats and handkerchiefs. Kemble, bowing repeatedly with his usual inimitable grace, retired without making a speech.

> We observed none of the Parisian nonsense of wreaths, chaplets and bouquets, and we were glad of it, for the truly English testimonials C Kemble received were much more gratifying.

Ironically, though today Gertrude is considered a leading role normally played by mature actresses that, if not stars, are well-known, in the lengthy review in *Theatrical Observer* the actress does not warrant a mention, though the actors of the Ghost and the Gravedigger are praised. Poor Rosina was presumably included in the statement 'the others did their best.'

Kemble's final performance also concluded Rosina's short run at Covent Garden; Mathews and Vestris putting on little drama, but running pantomimes and burlettas etc for long runs until 1842 when they gave up the theatre. An indication of the parlous state of theatricals in the capital was that Covent Garden, one of the two major patent theatres in the land, then stood virtually unused for three years apart from brief lettings, orchestral concerts and, in place of the annual pantomime, an exhibition of curious shrubs and plants from around the world.

After playing to full houses in a theatre seating over 3000 people, it was something of a come-down for Rosina to return to Windsor for the usual poorly attended summer season for brother Montague. But she had been in the theatre game long enough to know that it was a world of ups and downs and, as a player aged, the downs came along more often than the ups. The first week did good business as Montague had engaged William Farren from Covent Garden for four nights, successfully countering the usual blight of thin houses at the start of the season. Unfortunately, with Montague no longer able to afford star names, business dwindled and, even with a strong company of provincial artistes and some good new plays, business was poor. Rosina, now forty-four, took something of a back seat, giving up some of her roles to younger actresses, retaining others such as Mrs Haller. Rosina's benefit was *Macbeth* in which she played Lady M to Edmund Glover's Macbeth, yet another thane to add to her collection.

The season ran from 27 July to 5 September 1840.

SCENE TEN
1841 AND AFTER
ROSINA MANAGES WINDSOR AND RETURNS TO BATH

ON 6 JUNE 1841, the first national census took place. Phoebe and Emma Penley, untraceable for the last five years, can now be found living together at 39 Parrock Street, Milton, Gravesend. The likely explanation for the sisters' absence in the theatre is that Phoebe was ill and that Emma was caring for her. The census gives Phoebe's age as thirty-five and Emma's as twenty-five. Even accounting for the fact that at this census adult ages were rounded down to the multiple of five below the true age, this is wildly inaccurate as both Phoebe and Emma were at least ten years older. The most exhaustive search has not revealed the where-abouts of Rosina in this census.

Sampson Penley and his brother-in-law John Jonas had first taken the old Windsor theatre back in 1812, and occupied the new one from its inception in 1815. Penley's sons Sampson Jr, and now Montague had both managed the venue. The provincial theatre scene in 1841 was not propitious, business was in the doldrums. Very few theatres were actually thriving, most in some state between staggering on and closure. Liverpool, formerly one of the most lucrative houses, was closed because of the manager's huge losses. The York circuit where Rosina had been a regular favourite was cut down to York, Leeds and Hull and barely covered expenses. Even the fashionable towns were suffering: Cheltenham theatre, which rather oddly for a popular thriving spa town had always been a loser, had burnt down. Gloucester had been closed for two years though the rent was nominal. Brighton, another town expected to be a money maker, only did business when a particular top star appeared. Norwich was closed half the year and did nothing much when it was open. The whole of the Kent circuit was described as 'miserable'.

The new theatre that had been built at Leicester after Belville Penley & Anderson's time was already a white elephant. The only theatre that any of the Penleys had leased that was doing decent business was Newcastle, under Ternan. Unfortunately, that too would soon come to an end when Ternan had a mental breakdown and was confined in Bethnal Green asylum, dying there two years later.

Montague announced the opening of his Windsor 1841 summer season with the engagement of Mrs Honey for three nights. The company members were new to Windsor, gathered from all the provincial theatres royal, desperate actors at the ready for the picking up. The acting manager was Lacy from Brighton and Sheffield, and leading lady was Miss Cooper from Covent Garden. Only Dodd and Rosina were from previous companies. Belville, having supported his brother on his recent ventures but subsequently moving to Bath with his wife, was no longer employed.

In the event, the season opened on 3 August with the long established pantomimists Howell and T Matthews guest stars in the ancient *Three Fingered Jack*, the equally venerable *Valentine & Orson*, and various pantomime dance routines. It is reported that 'those two gentlemen well and ably sustained the reputation which they had deservedly attained; and, indeed, during the week, their reception has been a series of nightly triumphs such as are seldom seen in our theatre.' It sounds very much like 'give them the old hokum' working its magic again.

Then something very strange happened. Suddenly Montague is no longer the manager, he and his wife going to live in France. Whether this was urgently fleeing to avoid financial problems – as in the case of his father and brother who resorted to the expedient – cannot be determined. The situation remaining somewhat odd, and unexplained by the local newspaper, it does suggest that he was yet another Penley eluding potential bankruptcy or imprisonment.

Whatever the truth of the circumstances, the Penley banner was still flying high as, to the rescue, galloping up on her white charger, came Rosina herself to mastermind the summer season of 1841. Whether the handover to Rosina was planned and orderly, or a face-saving scramble, she nevertheless came in for praise from the local press as being an improvement on Montague in that she had selected a company of actors superior to the ones he provided:

> Her high talent in the histrionic art is a fair guarantee of her powers to please in her new capacity. The first grand proof of her abilities has already been made apparent in the selection of her company, for take them 'all in all' we have no hesitation in saying that a more powerful cast never graced the boards of a Windsor theatre.—Miss Penley has, no doubt, (and very correctly) observed that a second rate company are not suitable to the taste of the people of Windsor, possessing as they do the facilities of visiting the metropolitan houses. We now hope to see that Windsor spirit and Windsor

gallantry will manifest themselves in the highest degree in rewarding and encouraging this lady in her new undertaking.

In this short piece the critic is surely guilty of exaggeration in stating a more powerful cast had never been seen in Windsor. He is also flattering his readers and finally appealing to their better nature to support the venture.

Other local newspapers agreed that Rosina's company, far out-stripping her brother's, was thus better entitled to the public's patronage, with more chance of success than previous attempts by 'some of her family'. It is always safer throwing stones at a person after they have gone. On one night the play was commanded by Queen Victoria – this was in the days when she was amused – and Prince Albert commanded the plays on another night. Coupling royalty with the attractions always resulted in a boost in takings. Queen Victoria was a keen theatre-goer between the ages of thirteen and forty-two, visiting all kinds of attractions, often two or three times a week; after Albert died she never entered a theatre again.

Rosina relied greatly on T H Lacy as stage manager, and apart from Dodd there was a clean sweep of acting personnel. Rather strangely, considering Rosina was always regarded as a local favourite and something of a draw, she did not appear very much in person. Surely she did not have delusions of grandeur after her four months at Covent Garden? Perhaps she was too pre-occupied with all the chores of management and must surely have regretted the absence of Belville.

The main success of the season was *The Ladies Club* by Mark Lemon in which a group of wives get their own back on errant husbands, absent at their clubs, by forming one of their own. Much humour was engendered by ladies behaving in their own club just like their menfolk do.

As the season was drawing rapidly to its close the public was urged to visit the theatre, if only to see Miss Cooper, the company's most attractive feature and a favourite of the metropolitan stage, and 'though the company is generally good, it is no difficult task to discover the vast superiority of this lady.'

Dodd's benefit was a bumper, and Lacy's respectable. Howell and Matthews were re-booked for the last three nights to perk up the takings. For Rosina's benefit the 'new comedy of *London Assurance*' and the old Eastern Romance *The Evil Eye* were presented. The last night of the season was the benefit for Montague with *The Lady of the Lake* as the attraction, with the popular *The Ladies Club* being resurrected. Considering that Montague had taken some stick in recent press reviews praising his sister, one wonders what the audience was like on his benefit night, whether he had already departed for France at that point, or was still in the country. Beneficiaries did not have to be present for their special nights; often an absentee shareholder was entitled to one, or the descendents of the author.

Thus the season ended, but it had not been a success. The final verdict can be left to the *Buckinghamshire Herald* newspaper:

> Miss Penley has been indefatigable in her exertions to cater for the public taste. Some of the most popular plays in our language have been produced, and sustained by respectable performances, yet the house has seldom been filled, and like the shop of Romeo's apothecary, there has been almost nightly 'a beggarly account of empty boxes.' To us it appears that the appetite of the Windsor public for such amusements is rather dull; for in no other way can we account for the want of patronage bestowed on the establishment, as there cannot exist the slightest doubt that the entertainments and the performers are infinitely superior to those which the previous manager of the theatre ever produced on our boards. It is therefore to be regretted that Miss Penley has not met with that general encouragement to which she is entitled, from the labour and expense she has incurred.

It is also to be hoped that Rosina did not have to dig too deeply into her hard-won savings at this juncture in her life. She was now back to being a jobbing actress at the age of forty-five, a time when actresses realise that the leading parts are always for younger women, and they have to reconcile themselves to playing mothers and dowager duchesses. Even in the early Victorian period it was unfeasible to have middle-aged Juliets and Desdemonas. On the family front, Rosina had long ago lost brother William who died in France, four years previously brother Sampson died in Paris, and now Montague had exiled himself to Paris. Together with her bitter memories of how her father's company had been treated in that gay city she must have hated both country and capital. We do not know how often she saw her sisters, now in spinster-like retirement in Gravesend, but with Phoebe an invalid it was hardly likely to have been a jolly household.

Brother Belville and his wife now lived in Bath and, whether they had any influence or not, Bath was also the town where Rosina continued her career. Once second only to the London patents, Bath had been through several periods of financial crisis with a frequent change of managers.

On 4 December 1841 Mr Hay of the Exeter and Plymouth theatres commenced a season at the Theatre Royal, Bath. This may well have been the same Hay who proved an ineffective low comedy man when employed by Sam Jr at Newcastle back in 1830. New to the town, his first advertisements were very lengthy, the language respectful, but with the grovelling tenor of earlier years giving way to a mild form of lecturing, as he appealed in particular to the tradesmen of the city to support the theatre and regretted that

> many estimable and conscientious persons are, from mistaken prejudice, opposed to that art which has, more than any other, tended to the civilisation of mankind – fancying evils in a theatre which (whatever may have been in the olden time) fortunately, now exist only in their imaginations.

Hay's company included Mr and Mrs Woulds who were long-serving players at the theatre, Woulds having first arrived at Bath in 1811. He had taken the lease himself from 1834 to 1838, but relinquished it because of his losses, mainly caused by an influenza epidemic that confined two-thirds of the population indoors for weeks. Woulds, who also managed the Cardiff and Swansea theatres, was made bankrupt in 1840, hence was back in the ranks of 'merely players'. As Mrs Woulds had recently been at Windsor, perhaps she was the link that enabled Miss R Penley to be included in the company.

The leading lady was Miss Vining, with Miss Connor and Miss Wood as principal female support, Rosina coming pretty low down in the pecking order. She made her first appearance as Mrs Cerulen Fizgig (a Blue Stocking) in an afterpiece. Her next appearance was as Servia, Nurse to Virginia, in *Virginius*. Ten years previously she had still been playing the daughter, now she was the nurse. Although most of her roles were now neighbours, mothers and widows, Rosina still maintained some of her old parts – Lady Randolph in *Douglas*, Gertrude in *Hamlet*, the Queen in *Richard III*, (actually all mothers – she had been playing above her age for years), Elvira in *Pizarro* and Emilia in *Othello*. Most surprisingly, she was cast in *A Midsummer Night's Dream* as Hermia, one of the young lovers, so she must have been wearing reasonably well.

Alas, the same could not be said of the theatre as houses were depressingly thin. The committee of tradesmen – formed to raise a Subscription Ticket Fund as a result of Hay's badgering – appealed to drama lovers to support a subscribers' night.

One of the recent regular successful visitors was Charles Kean, son of the late famous Edmund, now a star to compete with Macready. The young Kean always did well at Bath playing to full houses, but as his salary demands were half of the gross receipts he was hardly a money spinner. Not everybody thought he was worth his money, *Punch* magazine punning 'Mr Kean may justly appeal against the income tax on the ground of being over-rated.'

Charles Kean was engaged for four nights. He had recently married actress Ellen Tree who had been a favourite at Bath, but she did not accompany her husband on this occasion, the bride of two days playing at near-by Bristol. On 2 February, Rosina played Gertrude to Kean's Hamlet, and on 4 February played the Queen in *Richard III*, a decade after similar pairings with his father. Rosina was also in the other two nights of Kean's visit when he performed in *The Lady of Lyons* and *The Stranger*, but in the latter play she had to concede her old role of Mrs Haller to Miss Vining, the company's leading lady.

Kean returned for one night only on 19 February to give his Shylock in *The Merchant of Venice* with *The Lady of Lyons* as an afterpiece. Rosina was not in the main play – Miss Vining taking Portia – but was in the afterpiece. Although Bath had been a prestigious theatre in past days, it had now lost much of its shine, as had Rosina herself. Simply because of age she was no longer cast in the leading roles she had sustained for most of her life. Just as the city's theatre was a faded echo of its former days, so Rosina's parts no longer lived up to her past reputation.

Rosina's last performance with the company was on 25 April playing Madam Ankastran in *Gustavus III*, and when *Richard III* was given on 2, 12 and 14 May she was no longer there to play the Queen. On 23 May, manager Hay had his benefit, then promptly did a moonlight flit leaving his company in the lurch. It transpired that wages, only forthcoming in dribbles of shillings until 7 May, had ceased altogether. Hay had decamped owing a total of £350 (£28,000 in today's money) in theatre wages.

It would seem that Rosina had ceased to trust the shady Mr Hay earlier than most. It often happens in these cases (which still occur occasionally in the theatre at the present time) that the actors go along with the manager's excuses, giving him the benefit of the doubt until the older and wiser ones decide to cut their losses and leave. The younger, more naive and unemployable, stick it out, fobbed off with paltry hand-outs, until the final collapse leaves everybody, including the manager, destitute.

In an effort to assist the unfortunate players, Woulds headed a committee which arranged with the theatre trustees to hold two benefit concerts on 6 and 11 June hoping to raise sufficient money to distribute to the company in lieu of their wages, enabling them to travel on to other engagements or back to their homes. An appeal to Charles Kean to come and play for two nights elicited a reply stating his commitments would not permit, but he sent £20 towards the fund, which one supposes is the least he could do after screwing so much from the exchequer on many previous visits. The local gas company agreed to light the theatre free of charge. Alas, the local inhabitants were not so generous, and a total of only £97.15.0 was raised from the two performances. Therefore, as a last desperate attempt, a third and final performance was given on 23 June with all seats at half-price from the beginning of the evening.

Rosina's vast experience and knowledge of her father's often hand-to-mouth working methods will have given her sufficient warning, and no doubt she made her exit without too much of a loss a month before the debacle. It was an ignominious end to the season at Bath, and an utter disgrace to occur in a theatre that had once been recognised as second in the entire country only to Drury Lane and Covent Garden.

On 17 June 1842 Phoebe Penley died at 39 Parrock Street, Gravesend, aged forty-six years. The death certificate indicated she had been ill for some years, which no doubt explains her fewer and more irregular appearances then her final absence.

In March 1848, Emma married Henry Juteffe Paull, an accountant from Devon; a widower whose first wife had died in 1844 leaving him with two daughters. In the 1851 census, Emma, now Mrs Paull, is correctly listed as aged forty-five and her husband forty-three living at 3 Hauley Road, Islington. Her stepchildren Ellen and Ada are sixteen and ten. A visitor at this address in Islington is Rosina Penley aged fifty-four. The Paull family, at some juncture, must have then returned to Devon as Henry Juteffe Paull died at St Thomas in Devon in June 1865. In the 1871 census, Emma Paull is living with one step-daughter Ellen at 4 Cliff Terrace, Budleigh Salterton, and in the 1881 census at Victoria Place, Budleigh Salterton, again with Ellen. Presumably, Ellen never married and the younger step-daughter did. Emma died in March 1891 at St Thomas aged eighty-five.

And what of Rosina? So far nothing has turned up to indicate that she went on acting after that horrendous season at Bath. But she may well have been beavering away in some obscure company like a latter day Mrs

Beynon who ploughed on year after year, unremarked, in Jonas & Penley's company. The search for further information goes on, only one other sighting having emerged:

LITERARY INSTITUTION, BLACKHEATH.
MISS PENLEY, teacher of Elocution, and formerly of the
Theatre Royal Covent Garden and Edinburgh, respectfully
announces her intention of giving a
DRAMATIC AND MUSICAL SOIREE,
at the above Institution, on Thursday Eve, Feb. 13th, 1851
in which she will be assisted by
MISS C WARMAN
the young Lady whose first appearance was so pre-eminently
successful at the New Institution, at Deptford, and pupil of
Miss Elder, of Bexley House, Greenwich, who will preside at
the Pianoforte on this occasion.
Admission 1/-; Reserved seats 2/-.
A limited number of tickets to be had at the Institution; of
Mr. Millard, printer, High-road, Lee; and at Bexley House,
Greenwich.
Mr. Wheatley's omnibuses will leave the Centurion,
Deptford, and the White Hart, Greenwich, at 7 o'clock.
Charge 6d.

As will be noted, this event was some nine years after her Bath season. What had she been doing? Where did she live? Had she retired from the stage? Did she make her living as a teacher of elocution? Was this soirée a 'one-off' or a regular event? So many questions and so few answers! What can be revealed is that on the night of the above concert the 'highly respectable audience had to console themselves for the absence of Miss Penley, caused by illness'. Miss C Warman, who brilliantly performed on her own, gave universal satisfaction, everything going off very well.

Nowadays, when we are accustomed to the sight of semi-naked teenage pop stars cheerfully cavorting on our home screens performing lewd gestures, and actresses exposing their breasts at the drop of a bra with full frontal nudity of both sexes commonplace in Shakespeare and the classics, it is difficult to imagine that in former times, actresses were socially in an awkward position.

Young actresses were often regarded as little better than prostitutes, and most actresses in the 18th and 19th century came from acting families. The double standards of the time meant that men could admire, worship, and attempt to seduce an actress, yet would never dream of introducing her into their social or domestic circle. William Macready, the respectable head of the profession, himself, claimed it was impossible for a young woman working in the theatre to remain virtuous.

As a result, most actresses either married actors or 'married out' leaving the theatre, their previous life becoming a dark secret never to be spoken of again, as did Sampson Penley's sister Esther after marrying her pork butcher and settling down in Folkestone.

The upper classes, many themselves louche by nature, were not as censorious as the newly burgeoning middle class, and some of the more glittering actresses of the period were fortunate to marry into the aristocracy, such as Anastasia Robinson who became the Countess of Peterborough. Other actresses with their post-marriage titles include:

Miss Mellon	Duchess of St. Albans
Miss Fenton	Duchess of Bolton
Miss Farren	Countess of Derby
Miss Brunton	Countess of Craven
Miss O'Neill	Lady Beecher
Miss Stephens	Countess of Essex
Miss Foote	Countess of Harrington
Miss Paton	Lady Lenox
Mrs Nisbett	Lady Boothby

But it was very different for the unmarried woman who pursued a career. At a time when a young woman was expected to be obedient to her father until marriage, then subservient to a husband thereafter, a lone woman in control of her own destiny was regarded with suspicion. Prior to the Married Women's Property Act of 1870, on marriage a wife's property and income became her husband's, hence the aim of improvident young men seeking marriage with rich widows! Married women had few legal rights and were by law not recognized as a separate legal being.

Women who earned their own living, disporting themselves on the public stage pretending to be ladies, speaking and dressing in a superior fashion when they were actually working women, could not, by that very fact, be respectable because ladies did not work. To show off one's talents, skills and beauty to the public gaze was immodest – and respectable women were females of decorum and modesty. While a certain type of actress had no qualms about flaunting her body in scanty garments, many actresses themselves were unhappy about displaying their bodies, especially when required to wear tights or revealing garments, feeling themselves despised by respectable people.

For an actress like Rosina Penley to spend all her life on the stage as a single woman, finding her own work, negotiating her own contracts, travelling on coaches the length of this country and abroad, passing from ingénue roles, through drama queens, to end playing mothers and dowager duchesses, is quite an achievement. We do not know if she had lovers, ever fell prey to the casting couch or relied on the protection of a rich gentleman, but as far as her public image proclaimed she was regularly complimented not only for her acting ability but for her innate respectability.

It is highly significant how often newspapers in the 19th century would praise an actress for her figure, looks, personal charms, talent, voice, diction, elegance, simplicity, tenderness, etc, etc, but above all for a 'private character strictly unblemished'.

In the spirit of the times it is creditable that throughout her career Rosina was commended for her natural morality [author's emphasis]:

o Her talents are of the first order, her general correctness, the elegance of her wardrobe, and the appropriateness of her costume, are demonstrations of her industry and discernment, and **what is above all these, the respectability of her private character,** confers honour upon the profession at large. LEEDS

o The Misses Penley – **Their excellent private character,** conjoined with their professional skill, rendered them a valuable acquisition to the stage. COVENTRY

o Miss Penley, a lady whose merits the Liverpool audience have so fully allowed, and who now (her benefit taking place tomorrow evening) so justly looks to them for those substantial marks of their favour, to which an **amiable private and assiduous public character** give her such sterling claim. LIVERPOOL

o Miss Penley a lady **who has long held a distinguished rank** in her profession. EDINBURGH

o ever ready to patronise sterling professional talent, when accompanied, as in the case of Miss Penley, **with spotless private character and conduct** – gave her a real 'bumper'. NEWCASTLE

Rosina never married. As mentioned above, in the 1851 census she is reported as living with her sister Emma, giving governess as her occupation. In the 1861 census, Rosina is listed as a visitor in the house of William Cooper at Crouch End, Hornsey, London. Her age is given as sixty, but she was actually sixty-four. Her occupation is unclear, so is the connection with Cooper, unless it be via the Miss Cooper Rosina hired as leading lady at Windsor, or the Cooper, long-time leading actor and stage manager at Covent Garden. By the 1871 census she is listed, correctly aged seventy-four, as living at Moore Lane, Budleigh Salterton with Mr & Mrs Henry Edwards to whom she was linked via Sampson Jr's wife.

Bath Stage History in a footnote states: 'Miss Penley, who was connected with the stage for many years, died at Budleigh Salterton, Devon in 1879, in her 83rd year. She was a sister of Mr Belville Penley, of Bath.' Most curiously, throughout the book, the author, who is Belville Sampson Penley, the only son of Belville Penley by his second wife, does not allude to the fact that Rosina was his aunt.

More informally and kindly, a memoir in *The Era* of 2 March 1889 written by Claude Ashley Anson Penley, the only son of Rosina's famous painter cousin Aaron to reach maturity, a lawyer and a noted amateur actor himself, says:

> She was a wonderful woman to the last, of commanding figure, and with a lovely voice. She was a magnificent reciter and a great Shakespearean scholar. I was on the most affectionate and intimate terms with her until her death, and have listened with the greatest interest to the old theatrical stories she loved to tell and told so well. I always understood her Lady Macbeth was a grand performance and Talma, the great actor, after witnessing it, paid her the compliment to say that he considered her to be one of the then greatest living actresses. Tate Wilkinson [presumably the grandson of the famous Tate Wilkinson] presented her with the copy of *Cymbeline* used by Mrs Siddons when studying Imogen, with her notes and business written in her own handwriting in it, stating he thought in her hands it would be in its most worthy holding. The book is now in my possession.

No record of Rosina playing Imogen has been found, though she died most appropriately on 23 April – Shakespeare's birthday.

Rosina Penley's character may have been in the title but the star of the show was Madame Vestris, the actress-manager of Covent Garden. In partnership with her husband Charles Mathews, together they made the theatre the home of light entertainment, relegating drama to less importance.

ACT FIVE

MONTAGUE PENLEY

'the liberal and deserving manager'

SCENE ONE
1816 - 1818
ACTOR AND SCENIC-ARTIST

MONTAGUE PENLEY was Sampson and Lucy Penley's fourth child and second son, born at Folkestone on 5 May 1799. He was seven years younger than his brother Sampson Jr. Unlike his sisters, Montague, rarely appearing on the stage as a child, was most likely at school for some years, probably at the grammar school at Alton in Hampshire run by his aunt's brother Mr Saulez. This is surmise, but William and Frances Penley sent their sons William and Aaron there and they, in turn, had some of their own children attend the school. Both William and Aaron became professional artists as also did Montague, so it would seem that was a particular strength of the tuition.

At the age of seventeen, Montague's name first appears in a theatre advertisement, not as an actor but as a scenic artist. In August 1816, at his father's recently acquired Windsor theatre, *The Miller and his Men* was announced. This was a new production 'with New Scenery, Dresses and Decorations. The whole got up under the direction of Mr S Penley. The Scenery painted by Mr M Penley.'

In the theatre of the time, a complete new production was a major undertaking as generally nearly all plays used stock scenery – a few all-purpose backcloths proving suitable for most plays. Although advertisements often trumpeted new scenery, usually this would really mean one or two new scenes amongst a lot of old tat. Windsor, being a newly built theatre, required the management to build up a stock of scenery. A scene with an exploding mill effect would have to be specially devised, and prove its worth via many repetitions. Montague's scenery was still going strong at Windsor in the 1830s.

The play opens with a sunset view of the mill at work, situated on a rocky eminence surrounded by a lake. Other scenes show the miller's men passing in boats; bandits carousing in a cavern; the powder magazine with its secret entrance; a near view of the mill and finally a grand view of the destruction of the mill. Montague must have been a very busy young man creating all these.

Montague was also stepping out as an actor, his range being that of Second Light Comedian. In a new farce called *My Landlady's Gown* he was cast as Monsieur Genlis, a comic Frenchman with an ear-trumpet.

As Montague, playing small roles, was low down the pecking order of the company, he seldom managed to get his name on the press advertisements unless it was a major production such as *Othello*, where he played Montano. In a small country company such as J & P, the Second Light Comedian had to double-up as Second Tragedian; if he proved to be a talented scenic artist too, he should never be out of work. Montague's new scenery at Windsor was highly praised.

By 1818 J & P was at its major family strength. There is a playbill extant for Penley's Windsor company playing the Hastings theatre with family members Mr Penley (Sampson) with his offspring Mr M Penley (Montague), Mr W Penley (William), Miss Penley (Phoebe), Miss R Penley (Rosina), Miss E Penley (Emma), and brother-in-law Mr Jonas. Sampson's eldest son, having left the family company, and now a Drury Lane actor, younger brothers Montague and William, nineteen and seventeen respectively, were promoted to playing major roles. All Sampson's daughters were working, and the only offspring remaining not yet employed regularly was the ten-year-old Belville, although he was occasionally dragged in for pages etc. While Sam Jr was no longer in the family fold, he is represented on this particular Hastings playbill, the afterpiece being his popular farce *The Sleeping Draught*.

When the J & P company revived the neglected Lewes theatre in November 1819, the necessary new painting and decorating tasks fell to Montague, and he also had to refurbish the scenery stock and paint a new front drop. The scenery and dresses in *The Miller and his Men*, presumably brought over from Windsor, 'were beautiful', and a similar comment served to praise the new production of *Pizarro* which Montague had also painted.

The following year Montague was beavering away again on the circuit both as actor and scenic artist. In *Macbeth* he was cast as Lennox which would not have taxed him much and, for his sisters benefit night, painted the scenery for a new production of *The Vampire* in which he also took a principal role.

SCENE TWO
1821 - 1835
THE SEMI-INVISIBLE MAN

FOR THE SUMMER of 1821, Montague broke away from the family's season at Windsor as brother Sam Jr recruited him for the previously described tour of Elliston's Midlands circuit. This was probably the first time that Montague had worked out of the family fold. It must have been beneficial for his immediate boss to be his big brother. The company was based at Leamington Spa with visits to Weedon, Warwick, Birmingham, Northampton &c. During the season at Leamington Spa, the company acted every Wednesday night at Coventry, when Sam provided vehicles known as pleasure cars, six players generally crammed into each. Returning after the play to Leamington, they would pass through the village of Kenilworth about one o'clock in the morning where the actors enjoyed singing *God Save the King*, in full chorus, in honour of the revels of the Earl of Leicester held for Queen Elizabeth back in 1575. It was probably a jolly and carefree existence for a young actor, but no doubt the honest villagers came to dread going to bed on Wednesdays! It was on this tour that Montague played Prince Leopold in Elliston's famous facsimile Coronation Procession, and Sam had his spat with the magistrates of Coventry.

Breaking completely free from family ties the following year, Montague obtained the position of scenic artist at York. Theatre manager Robert Mansel instigated some major alterations at the theatre that changed the auditorium layout from the traditional rectangular form to a semi-circular plan. This was the latest fad, with the boxes gradually receding to become the 'horseshoe' plan of the circle. Mansel also included new retiring rooms and refreshment bars, all these facilities being funded by the shareholders of the theatre.

The proscenium and wings were painted by Montague, also several of the new scenes for productions including *Twelfth Night*, Faucet's melodrama *The Miller's Maid* and Dibdin's *Ninth Statue* providing 'the favourite temple with revolving pillars illuminated with gerino fire.' Whatever gerino fire may be! On 15 April, for his benefit, he designed and painted a variety of new scenery for the play *The Pirate; or The Wild Woman of Zetland*. Montague is credited with supplying several scenes at various theatres on Mansel's circuit.

During the next few years Montague Penley becomes elusive, with no definite trace between 1822 and 1825. There are very rare occasional glimpses of a Mr Penley during that period which may well be Montague, but could just as easily be his father eking out a living after the collapse of his own company, or a brother. So it is with diffidence the following entries have been placed under Montague's name.

The season at the Olympic Circus in Liverpool ended at the end of March 1824, and during the last week a joint benefit was held for Mr Penley, Mr Newton and the Misses Usher. In the early days of the 19th century there was not the clear-cut division between theatre entertainment and circus that we have today. Circuses presented a similar repertoire to the melodramas of the minor theatres, and even Drury Lane would have spectacles with horses, plays with performing dogs and rope-walkers. Circuses were usually presented in permanent or semi-permanent buildings rather than the canvas 'big tops' of later days, and had stages as well as rings. At the Olympic Circus in one advertisement alone are mentioned *Timour the Tartar*, *The Miller's Daughter*, *Little Red Riding Hood*, *The Forest of Bondy* and *Cataract of the Ganges*, all of which could regularly be seen in conventional theatres.

The clown was Mr Usher, second only in fame to Joseph Grimaldi, who gaining his early start in Liverpool, returned there on a regular basis. His daughters were sharing in the benefit with Mr Newton who appears to be a singer of comic songs. But what was the position of Mr Penley? Obviously not as scenic artist, as their names appear on the advertisements and do not include Penley.

In February of the following year there were two further advertisements in the Liverpool newspaper with the name of Mr Penley. In February, the Theatre Royal announced a benefit for Mr Ryley and among the players was Mr Penley taking part in both the main play and the afterpiece. Mr Newton was also billed singing a comic song. On 1 March the Olympic Circus announced *Valentine and Orson* for Mr Penley's benefit. Whichever Mr Penley was present at Liverpool, he must have played at least two winter seasons at the Olympic Circus.

Montague Penley rests on firmer ground in 1824 as he was back at Windsor, assisting his brother Sam Jr in various ways. Firstly he completely renovated the house prior to the summer opening, painting the walls in various pinks, and antique pictures on the box fronts. 'The effect when lighted up is truly beautiful. Mr Montague Penley, whose abilities as an artist in this line are very great, has been unremittingly employed during the last month in the execution of these embellishments.' He went on to act as Box Office manager, supporting actor and resident scene painter.

For a new production of *The Revolt of the Greeks*, Montague painted six entirely new scenes culminating in a grand battle scene: 'Exterior of the Palace and Fort, with Minarets and Cupolas rising above, the whole projecting into the sea – The Turks are attacked by sea and land – The Greek Fleet is seen advancing – Bomb-shells are discharged into the Castle – The Castle discovered on fire – Flames reflected by the water – The Turks fly in disorder, and the Greeks are ultimately triumphant.'

Cooke, the circus owner of the Liverpool Olympic, had a circus building erected in Sheffield during March 1825 – also named Olympic – and ran a season there until mid-June, after which the building was swiftly torn down. This would have little concern for us except that the mysterious Mr Penley of the Liverpool venue also pops up at Sheffield, again in company with the singing Mr Newton. However, on this occasion the clown was Mr Boulter not Usher. Presumably this Mr Penley (who may not be Montague, but could well be his father) stayed the full season at Sheffield but the only mention he gets is 'Mr Penley's representation of an English boatswain is excellent.'

Montague certainly returned to Windsor for the 1825 summer season when the big production was the opera *Der Freischutz*.

> The dresses appear to be the most characteristic we have yet seen. The exhibition of the scenery called forth the warmest expressions of approbation, especially the picturesque German village, mills, and monuments, and the waterfall landscape, which are painted with a knowledge of his art most creditable to the talents of Mr Montague Penley, the artist. We did not conceive the incantation could have been made so horribly effective.

The success of this piece was out of all proportion to the normal fare and Montague's scenery was a great deal to do with it. The opera was repeated for the next two nights, then on with something more conventional. This was not to the local newspaper's liking:

> We cannot conceive the reason why so sudden a stop should have been given to the representation of *Der Freischutz*, unless the manager was apprehensive that his store of horrors would prove too powerful for the nerves of his auditory, as, indeed, we hear that several person fainted, and were obliged to be removed from the Theatre, during its performance.

> Certainly in point of scenic effect, dresses, and other appropriate dramatic accompaniments, this piece may fairly take precedence of any drama ever brought forward on our boards, and we make no question but that its speedy reproduction would be very successfully attempted.

On the principle of giving the customers what they want, Sam Jr immediately billed its repetition under the patronage of Countess Harcourt. Perhaps she fancied a dollop of the shivering fits, and fainting in lumps! The ever faithful Princess Augusta, who was always bespeaking plays, followed the next night with a royal command for the conventional comedy *The Road to Ruin*.

No doubt Montague was expected to come up with an effective monster for *The Anaconda; or The Serpent of Ceylon* which rapidly followed. A six-week season soon passes, especially when the theatre is closed on some nights, so all too soon came Montague's benefit night when he chose the comedy *The Way to Get Married* and the melodrama *The Black Forest*, the playbill having his name in the largest of enormous type, which may be an indication of his local popularity.

He returned in 1826 being staunch support to brother Sam throughout the season; amongst his many roles Montague played Sir Benjamin Backbite in *The School for Scandal*, Bob Handy in *Speed the Plough*, and Master Slender in *The Merry Wives of Windsor*.

The repertoire did not vary much from year to year: 'The melodrama of *The Miller and his Men* has been submitted to the public in a most creditable manner, and appeared to afford general satisfaction.' However, new plays were introduced from time to time, and a big success at the very end of the season was *The Pilot; or A Tale of the Sea*. This burletta by Edward Fitzball, based on the novel by James Fenimore Cooper, had very recently run at the Adelphi for 200 nights making a star of T P Cooke. In the Windsor production, 'Long Tom Coffin stood forth the favourite of the night, and was very cleverly acted by Mr M Penley.' There are some parts that are actor-proof and it would seem that Long Tom Coffin was such an example, because whoever plays the role – in whatever production, in every theatre – seems to be showered with praise. Certainly the Windsor critic was enamoured of the piece. He remarks that the manager was lacking in thought not to have produced the play earlier in the season, when he would have got more mileage out of it, rather than at the season's end when few people will have chance to see it. When the season closed it had been one of the most successful the local newspaper could remember. Montague had been busy throughout, appearing as an actor nearly every night, albeit in supporting roles.

Montague had been carrying on four distinct professions as actor, scene painter, artist and a teacher of art. He now advertised himself in the Windsor newspaper as a drawing master under the patronage of HRH Princess Augusta, who was the fifty-eight-year-old unmarried second daughter of George III. He states he specialises in crayon drawing, claiming to have studied the art under Monsieur Cheni, professor of the Academie Royale in Paris. This would account for some of the gaps in his scanty biography. In the flowery obsequious manner of the time he writes: 'Montague Penley cannot enter on the present avocation without returning his sincere acknowledgements of gratitude to the inhabitants of Windsor and its vicinity, for the kind favours he has so many years experienced, and at the same time ventures to hope for a continuance of that support which will ever be his study to deserve.'

Now he had turned his back on the theatre to concentrate on his art, advertising himself as a Professor of Drawing and Perspective at an 'Academy of Drawing'. Promising 'those young gentlemen who may wish to be instructed in this elegant and useful accomplishment, the satisfaction of rapidly obtaining a correct eye and easy style,' his terms were one guinea a quarter. Private families and seminaries were also punctually attended.

In 1829, Montague John Jackson Penley married Laetitia Sarah Didsbury at Bloomsbury in London. They do not appear to have been blessed with children. In 1833, an announcement appeared in the local press informing friends that the Mesdames Didsbury and Penley had moved their school from Upton to Crescent House at Clarence Crescent, Windsor. It was hoped that the superiority of the air would prove advantageous to the pupils. They also assured parents that their system of tuition, having been pursued with great success for many years, would be continued, combined with the comforts of a private family. From this we must assume that Montague married a schoolteacher and, now moving to new premises, his wife's and sister-in-law's school provided shared facilities with Montague's Drawing Academy which operated twice a week from the same building – presumably their combined home.

Montague seems to have severed all connection with the Windsor theatre though still living in the area. It was announced in September 1835 that a set of drawings by Mr M Penley, depicting the monkeys in the Pavilion on Monkey Island in the Thames near Bray, had been drawn on to zinc plates. The Duke of Marlborough had built the pavilion on an island he had purchased, decorating the interior with captivating and unique scenes of monkeys doing rather humanlike activities – shooting, fishing, smoking and so on. Done by French artist Andieu de Clermont prior to 1738, they were quite ravaged by the time Montague made his sketches. Montague also had a set of six local churches etched on to zinc plates by a Mr Fairland. Both sets were expected to be popular and gain extensive local sales.

The Pavilion on Monkey Island

SCENE THREE
1835 – 1838
NEWCASTLE AND WINDSOR

AFTER A PERIOD of total darkness, Montague, apparently having eschewed the theatre for years, emerges into the spotlight to reveal he has adopted yet another occupation – that of theatre manager. In December 1835 he took over the lease of the Newcastle Theatre from his brother Sam. It had been clear from the beginning that Sam was not enamoured of his north-east venue and had suffered financial problems there, so it is no wonder that he quit, especially if he suffered from ill health. But it is surprising that Montague, who must have been aware of all his brother's troubles, should think it a good idea to choose to go into theatre management at a time when theatres throughout the land were struggling.

To ensure there was no doubt a new regime was starting, he placed the following advertisement:

THEATRE ROYAL, NEWCASTLE

MR MONTAGUE PENLEY, in announcing the Performances for the OPENING of the Theatre, begs most respectfully to observe, that he has spared neither Trouble or Expense in procuring an efficient Company of approved Talent. The Orchestra will be continued on the same Scale of Excellence, forming one of the finest Theatrical Bands out of London. Particular Attention will also be paid to the Scenic Department, and Novelties (already in Preparation) will be produced with greater Effect and Splendour than possibly ever witnessed at this Theatre; neither Exertion of Attention will be wanting to render the Entertainments throughout the Season worthy the Support of the liberal Patrons of the Drama. On MONDAY, December 14th 1835, the Performances will commence with the New Nautical Drama, now acting in London with unprecedented Success, entitled MY POLL AND MY PARTNER JOE, with new scenery, Machinery, and Dresses. The Overture by a full Orchestra, under the Direction of Mr C Miller.
NB: Great Attention has been paid to the Airing of the Theatre.

The fact that Montague was trumpeting the scenery as being more splendid than previously, indicates that he had not been responsible for it under his brother's regime. One aspect that Montague retained was the orchestra which was a feature of this theatre. When Sam had taken the theatre, the Musical Director Charles Miller came with it, and on Sam's publicity for the 1833 season the band numbered 26 players, and in 1834 23 musicians were listed by name. Most provincial theatre orchestras of the time would probably comprise half that number at best. Miller was a respected name in Newcastle and he will feature prominently in future dealings with Montague.

A correspondent raised the point that often a good orchestra betokened an indifferent company. Montague's main actors were Cowle, Wood, Moulton and Hudspeth, with Williams a powerful singer; the female leads were Rosina Penley and Mrs Cowle. The correspondent was correct, it was a weak company; the kindest that could be said being no actor was of such brilliance he overwhelmed the others.

The orchestra was to the fore in the pantomime *Father Red Cap*, as was the scenery, including a panorama of Virginia Water surrounded by pictures of 'interesting objects' in the area. This work was by Montague and, considering that Virginia Water is a lake in Windsor Great Park, one assumes it was painted for the Windsor audience's delectation rather than the Geordies. However, local folk were more delighted by a dioramic view of the New Green Market painted by Mr Gompetz. The optical illusion of the cathedral great hall with its massive pillars made the spectator feel he was actually present. Unfortunately, the same critic could not give unqualified praise to the acting. Miss Parsloe – surely some kin of the famous man-monkey – as Columbine was certainly lively and vivacious, but wanted delicacy in climbing on to Harlequin's back. Similarly, her action of whirling around on one leg with the other stretched out to its full extent while clad in an exceptionally scanty dress might be judiciously dispensed with. We are in pre-Tiller Girl territory here – never mind Hot Gossip, and the raunchy semi-nude pop stars *de nos jours*.

One successful production, when both scenery and acting prowess were deemed excellent, was the play *The Jewess* which attracted crowded houses each time it was performed.

The Easter Monday attraction was a topical 'military spectacle', almost documentary in nature, *Fieschi, the Assassin of Paris*. Giuseppe Marco Fieschi was the chief conspirator with two accomplices in an attempt on the life of King Louis-Philippe of France in July 1835. He contrived an 'infernal machine' of 20 gun barrels, to be fired simultaneously. As Louis-Philippe was passing along the Boulevard du Temple, accompanied by his three sons and a numerous staff, the device was fired from an upper storey. A ball grazed the king's forehead, the king and the princes escaping essentially unharmed, but 18 people were killed and many wounded. Fieschi, himself severely wounded by the discharge of his machine, vainly attempted to escape. He was condemned to death, and was guillotined. New scenery depicted various Parisian scenes created from on-the-spot sketches of the event.

Montague continued the practice of dubbing Fridays as 'Fashionable Night' and naturally that night was the one usually chosen for bespeaks. The Thirteenth Fashionable Night was by desire and under the Patronage of the High Sheriff of Northumberland when Auber's popular opera of *Masaniello* was performed. The Fourteenth Fashionable Night was Montague's benefit, for which he promised a new self-penned comic drama in three acts. It looks as though Montague intended copying his big brother as a playwright as well as a manager. On the last night of the season, for Rosina's benefit *The Jewess*, in which she played the lead, was brought back.

Though it was the season end, Montague opened it for one more time for the annual Race Week, making, as was customary, a speech on the last night. This was a particularly emotional occasion for the audience. It was the last night of the building that had been standing since 1789. It was to be demolished for the creation of a new main road. Quoting appropriate lines from *The Tempest*, Montague asked rhetorically if the drama would perish with the roof, answering himself by stating that, Phoenix-like, it will rise with redoubled ardour in the new theatre that will be superior to any in the kingdom.

Montague had already succeeded in his tender for painting the scenery at the new theatre, and now learned that his tender for the three-year management lease was also accepted.

The new theatre at Newcastle-upon-Tyne.

Montague Penley was the first manager with a three-year lease.

Much grander than its predecessor, the building remains today, though the interior has had two complete alterations.

The new theatre opened – several weeks later than scheduled – on 20 February 1837. The interior was splendid, with opulent gilt ornaments and painted panels each containing a beautiful group of dancing boys painted by Montague and Mr John Reed. The ceiling, from which hung a central cut-glass chandelier, was decorated with painted panels full of nymphs and musical instruments. The proscenium arch was lavishly ornamented with the royal arms, the boxes lined with a rich crimson paper, and the whole of the seating covered in crimson moreen. After reading of this magnificence, it is quite alarming to learn that 'the gallery floor is lined with lead to prevent nuisances'.

The newly painted scenes by Montague and others were praised, but the lighting, considering the number of lights, was not as brilliant as expected, and adverse comments were paramount. Not only was the auditorium gloomy, but the rotunda and stairs were dangerously under-lit. It was announced Argand burners were to be introduced. It is surprising that gas was not installed in a new theatre in a major city such as Newcastle; at this period gas lighting in theatres had become commonplace. An innovation at the London theatres from 1815 onwards, gas provided not only a brighter, cleaner light, but cheaper running costs. Candles were a major expense and even in small theatres, when consumed by the thousands, the cost of even the very cheapest tallow candles mounted up. Simple oil lamps had been improved by the patent Argand lamp which had a circular wick and chimney glass. Most theatres utilised a combination of oil and candles and, even after it was introduced, gas ran in tandem with older forms for some decades.

Some idea of the cost of lighting can be discerned from figures for Covent Garden in 1810 when nightly 270 wax candles were burned in the auditorium glass chandeliers, 300 Argand lamps lit the stage and scenery, with a similar number in the corridors and staircases. By the time the Newcastle theatre opened it was calculated that the same amount of light cost 1/- in candles, whale oil in Argand lamps 6½d, coal gas 2¾d. Many much smaller theatres had gone over to gas years before as the smoke and smell of the older methods were an inconvenience, if not actually injurious to the health of members of the audience. Montague's brother Belville and his partner Anderson had at this time already gone over to gas in their small circuit of old country theatres.

It may well be that the lack of gas was a deliberate policy as the old Newcastle theatre had installed gas during major alterations in 1817 which was responsible for a fire breaking out. Seven lives were lost and several more people severely injured caused by the press of the gallery crowd who, having got through the top exit, were unable to get through the closed lower exit. As a result gas was banished and wax and oil only illuminated the auditorium for the rest of the old theatre's existence.

Montague's new theatre was swimming very much against the tide, as other theatres were actively changing over to gas because wax and oil had been the usual cause of the many theatre fires throughout the years. Though it has to be said that as late as 1828 gas came vividly into disrepute when an explosion of a gasometer inside Covent Garden Theatre led to all apparatus for making gas being removed from the building. While gas illumination was retained on the stage, it would be supplied directly from the mains of the Chartered Gas Company. The rest of the building: auditorium, corridors and front of the house reverting to oil lighting. Presumably if the gas supply proved dangerous it would only be the actors and stage crew that would suffer. The Adelphi and the English Opera House both announced they would do the same as a safety measure, and The King's Theatre announced they would rely on wax candles only.

So there was also more recent precedent for being wary of gas, but perhaps it was simply that the installation of gas piping would have further delayed the opening of the new theatre. The speed of erection was commented on: 'Considering the rapidity with which the building has been erected, the interior, particularly the boxes and pit, are remarkably dry.'

Montague's new Newcastle company was headed by Mr R Younge of Drury Lane who had often been seen at Windsor, and the leading lady was again the faithful Rosina Penley. The pair played Shylock and Portia for the delayed opening play *The Merchant of Venice* which had some short-comings in performance, although Younge as Shylock was 'scarcely in any part to be found fault with' and Rosina played Portia with 'considerable discrimination' but 'the other performers seemed hardly to have a due conception of their respective parts.' One local newspaper explained:

> It would be improper as well as unfair to criticise the performances on the first night. The company had been brought from nearly every part of the kingdom; they were, consequently, strangers to each other, and unaccustomed to act in concert. Besides, several of them had only that day arrived, having been allowed only a few hours' leisure to study their parts, with the additional disadvantage of labouring under the effects of long and fatiguing journeys.

Fortunately, as all the attention was on the new building – to use a modern actors' expression – they 'got away with it'.

The local newspapers seemed to be at loggerheads over the new theatre, one supporting Montague to the hilt, and another constantly sniping at the company. Montague appears to have consistently lacked first-class actors in his companies, probably from an unwillingness to pay more than he found necessary, a fault that he inherited from his father. Sam Jr, from his experience of Drury Lane – the top theatre in the country – had learned discrimination, recognising the quality of actors, accepting one had to pay over the minimum to engage them. Montague preferred to spend his money on spectacle and music, for Mr Charles Miller was back too, leading the excessively large orchestra.

The orchestra was greatly admired for its rendition of the *Tancredi* overture of Rossini on the occasion of the visit of the Mayor and Mrs Mayoress to the new theatre. On entering their box, the party was greeted with universal cheering by a full house. As an indication of how audience numbers swelled on nights of notable patronage, £10 more than ever before was taken in the boxes and a further £10 returned to people who had paid for box seats but could not gain admittance. The new theatre's capacity, at the same price structure as before, took some £20 more than the former one.

Montague mounted a new production of *Chevy Chase* concocted by him from old border ballads telling the story of a famous battle between Scottish raiders and the Percys of Northumberland. The essence of the thing was pageantry rather than drama.

The opening season in the new theatre had been marred not only by the murky lighting, but a public spat in the press. Successive harvest failures in the previous two years had meant that the people of the Highlands and Islands of Scotland began 1837 with an almost total lack of food. Half of the population of 167,000 was totally destitute. Mr Watson a professor of music, conveyed to the Mayor the charitable idea of mounting a concert at the theatre to raise funds for 'the distressed Highlanders'. This worthy then took it upon himself to pass the proposal on to Montague, who promptly called upon Watson. Montague said that he would require £20 rental for the theatre. As this sum would leave a remote chance of yielding much profit, Watson and the Mayor were compelled to drop the idea. When Montague was challenged about this £20 charge, he denied the statement, causing Watson to get on his high horse requesting an apology for being charged with a falsehood. Not having received any reply to his private letters, Watson had one published in all the local newspapers demanding Montague 'to justify your Conduct, or by your Silence allow yourself to be stigmatized with that Odium which you have wished to cast upon me.'

Montague, compelled to defend himself, said that £20 was the minimum cost of running the theatre for a night, he had contributed many times to worthy causes, and he thought the concert would not attract customers. He agreed he had demanded £20, but added that he had offered the valuable gratuitous use of the Assembly Rooms or Music Hall instead, which Mr Watson had declined. There he assumed the matter had ended until receiving a letter 'written in such terms as I thought it my duty to avoid noticing.' After one or two sly digs, he concluded:

> I trust the public will consider my anxiety to vindicate myself from an insidious attack, a sufficient excuse for intruding upon their notice matters which can be of so little interest to them. Deeply sensible of their liberal patronage, I take the opportunity of assuring my kind friends I shall be ever ready to promote their wishes in forwarding any benevolent purpose; and with this explanation I take leave of the subject, and of Mr Watson.

Watson came back with a lengthy seven-point letter setting out again the facts as he saw them, together with copies of the two private letters he had sent Montague. He too signed off with a leave-taking flourish, and there the matter ended. The spat was trivial, but theatre managers of the time were very much beholden to their local audience, and adverse factions could make a very nasty dent in the normal business. Fortunately, with the season coming to its end, no doubt any unpleasantness would have been forgotten by the time the theatre next re-opened.

Local man Charles Miller, who had provided the orchestra for many years, placed a rather mysterious advertisement stating 'in consequence of unexpected Impediments having been thrown in the Way of his taking a Benefit at the Theatre this Season, as usual, he most respectfully solicits their Patronage and Interest at a Benefit Concert . . . at the Music Hall, Blackett Street.' This would seem to indicate another kind of dispute with Montague, who increasingly appears to lack what today we would call 'people skills', although he did give £1 towards the debtors in the local prison. Any kind of basic comfort in prison (including food!) had to be paid for and, as many prisoners were literally destitute, it was customary for individuals as well as charities to make occasional small donations.

Montague's second season at Newcastle opened in November 1837 with Mr Lee as leading man. If this is the same Mr Lee who was Kean's secretary and understudy, he did not please the gallery in one of Kean's most famous roles – that of Sir Edward Mortimer in *The Iron Chest* – as they laughed uproariously at his death scene and were vehement in their disapprobation. But *interdum vulgus rectum videt* ['the rabble is sometimes right'] agreed one newspaper review, as the play, which the critic regarded as deficient in any dramatic regard, was, amongst other faults, soporific. It was further suggested that Mr Lee might have to yield the first characters to someone better skilled in the art of the sixth commandment ['thou shalt not commit murder']. 'Mr Penley should be careful in his selection for the public entertainment, and choose pieces adapted to the talents of his company, and not those which, to be at all endurable require the perfection of histrionic talent.'

Montague's company was again found wanting. Montague, obviously fully aware of this, engaged the noted actor and playwright Sheridan Knowles to appear in his own most famous play *The Hunchback*, supported by his protégé Miss Elphinstone. The local critic, ecstatic about Miss Elphinstone, devoted the bulk of his review to expressing how wonderful she was. Of Knowles he was more circumspect, admitting that his role was a quiet but languid one, giving little opportunities for an actor to display his talents. Miss Penley 'performed very cleverly' but 'it was a pity to find such beautiful language as is put into the mouth of Lydia, rendered utterly unintelligible by Miss Le Batt's hurried and pointless mode of delivery.'

In February came *Walshi; or the Queen of Bohemia*, with its beautiful scenery and superb dresses. The play was well acted by all, but very thinly attended though Montague put it on for at least three nights.

When brother Sam Jr beat a hasty retreat to France, Montague had no idea he was to end up in control of the Windsor theatre, but his brother's sudden and inopportune death in Paris thrust him into that position. Thus he was placed as Sam Jr had been previously – running two theatres 300 miles apart. Montague's first Windsor chore was to book the company and open the theatre for the annual Race Week in June 1838. He followed the practice of staging an early performance for the boys of Eton college prior to the normal one that attracted the race-goers.

As usual, the young toffs got up to their high jinks, scrambling all over the auditorium, calling out to the players, firing missiles at the band, and similar japes. The Hon Thomas Milles – the son of Lord Sondes – a young gentleman of fifteen or sixteen years of age, and a pack of chums gained admission to the gallery then let themselves down into the boxes and pit. In this instance one boy held Milles's hands in the gallery, while another stood in the boxes underneath to guide his feet to the pillar. The gallery boy let go too early and Milles crashed into the pit. He was carried into the greenroom (the back-stage room where actors gather) and surgeons speedily arrived in the shape of Sir J Chapman and Mr Soley who discovered the boy had a severe fracture to the head and other injuries of a serious nature. The injured lad was taken home in a carriage and was 'believed to be out of danger but still lies in a very bad state.' This was a disastrous start to Montague's regime at the Windsor theatre.

However, when the season proper opened on 31 July Montague had not only refurbished the place, but gone to the expense of installing gas lighting. The *Windsor & Eton Express* reported:

> Our theatre has never been opened with so much spirit and elegance as it has been this season, by the new manager Mr Montague Penley. He has already produced a rapid succession of the most popular pieces, got up with great taste and splendour, and his *corps dramatique* is the most efficient we ever remember seeing at this or any other provincial theatre. That universal favourite, Mrs Nisbett has been gratifying us this week with her inimitable performances in several of her most popular characters. We are pleased to find that the public have testified their sense of the manager's liberality and good taste by affording him bumpers every evening.

It was a first-class company indeed. The leading man was Samuel Phelps who had recently made his London debut and was recognised by Macready as a potential rival. Mrs Nisbett was a star recognised as the Mrs Jordan of her day. The company included her two sisters, the Misses Mordaunt, Mr Corrie down from Newcastle, and Rosina.

On the 11 August, there was a benefit for Sam's widow who remained in France, and a special one for supporting actor Mr Howe who had sustained a serious accident at rehearsal when a gun went off in his face. For several days one eye was in danger, but finally it was announced there was no probability of his losing his sight. However, his face was likely to be permanently disfigured – not a jolly prospect for anybody, much less an actor. The new young queen sent him £10.

Mrs Nisbett proved to be a popular attraction and she prolonged her stay, working every evening, sometimes in both main play and afterpiece. However, when the benefits came round Mrs Nisbett took second place, the biggest audience being for Rosina Penley.

The season closed with Montague's benefit:

> We heartily congratulate him on his having experienced one
> of the most brilliant seasons ever remembered at Windsor;
> there has scarcely been a night since the opening of the
> theatre but the house has been crowded . . . this proves that a
> talented company is sure to meet with liberal encouragement
> here. Our favourite Miss Penley has been playing with her
> usual success, and the public have testified their approbation
> of her talent by giving her a splendid benefit.

It looks as though Montague not only affected a seamless changeover
from his deceased brother, but mightily improved things too. It was not to
last very long.

After Windsor's success receded into history, Montague headed north
again for the 1838/39 season at Newcastle. Having realised the difference
star names and popular favourites made to his business, he engaged Mr &
Mrs Ternan, who were big in Newcastle, for a month prior to their
appearances at Drury Lane, Mr Corrie was back, as was Charles Miller
leading the orchestra as usual.

However, the big news in Newcastle in December 1838 was the
brutal murder of a bank clerk at the Newcastle Savings Bank, the building
then being set on fire in an attempt to conceal the crime. The unfortunate
employee was Joseph Millie, a fifty-four-year-old widower, father of
several children, the eldest being fourteen.

> On Monday evening, Mr Penley the respected manager of
> our Theatre Royal, gave the receipts of the house, free of all
> deductions, for the benefit of the orphan children of the late
> Mr Millie. The receipts of the boxes were £18.4s, the pit £11,
> the gallery £21.5s – total £50.9s'

A capacity house held about £150 so it looks as though only a third of a
house turned out to aid the unfortunate orphans. The 'liberal and
deserving manager' also held a benefit in aid of the Eye Infirmary and
(after deducting expenses) the sum of £23.14.0 was raised. Still, Montague
had done his bit for charity and, hopefully, redeemed himself in the eyes of
Mr Watson's supporters.

SCENE FOUR
1839
LONDON

HAVING PREVIOUSLY run his Newcastle seasons into June, it is surprising that in 1839 Montague closed in March, taking his benefit which raised over £94. The reason for the early closure is quite startling – he had taken a three-year lease of the English Opera House in London and restored the old name of the Lyceum.

The Lyceum was the third theatre on the site, having been built in 1834 by Samuel Beazley to replace the previous one he had designed in 1809, which had been temporarily occupied by the Drury Lane company for three years when its own theatre had burned to the ground. That Lyceum itself was destroyed by fire in February 1830 giving Beazley an opportunity to create a brand new theatre incorporating fresh and novel ideas. He laid great stress on the foyers, saloons and circulating areas, bringing in French ideas such as a shallow projecting balcony with a canopy over, placed in front of the conventional dress circle. The number of private boxes available to rent by the season, week or day, was far larger. As it was intended as an opera house, the décor featured musical insignia, medallions of composers, and floral ornamentation. The proscenium opening was 34ft and the total stage width 67ft. Externally, the façade was dominated by six mighty columns which are, of course, still there to this day, although the building behind was replaced many years ago. This was the theatre, only six years old, of which Montague had taken the lease.

His father Sampson had attempted a London season at the tiny Tottenham Street theatre back in 1810 and failed; now 30 years on, he himself was risking a similar venture. The situation was, however, even more financially perilous than in his father's day. The patents still applied so, by the existing regulations, Montague would only be able to present light musical pieces and melodramas. There were now many more theatres in the rapidly expanding populace of London, but still only three had patents for legitimate drama. Times were changing and the ploys to get round the increasingly lax restrictions becoming so feeble as to be almost non-existent. The minor theatres were putting on plays in virtually the same manner as the patent houses, simply having a chord struck on the pit piano at intervals so that it conformed to the regulations. Regular attempts by the minors were made to scrap the patents: 'we hope ere long to find all restrictions removed, and every theatre at liberty to play the regular drama, without impediment or molestation' but that was not to be for several more years.

More importantly, theatre business was in the doldrums. Macready having managed Covent Garden for two years, had just announced he was giving it up. Bunn at Drury Lane had abandoned drama in favour of musical concerts, and there was competition from several large minor theatres with regular audiences.

For his company, Montague relied on provincial players known to him personally, including Corrie from Newcastle, and Miss Mordaunt from Windsor. He attempted to engage Mrs Nisbett who had been such a hit at Windsor, but she was now contracted by Madame Vestris who refused to release her, 'choosing rather to pay her a very handsome salary, to lie on the shelf at the Olympic.' His sole London players were Vale, a comedian whom he brought out of retirement, and Mrs Stirling who had also recently retired. Having made a name for herself in the London minor theatres, she retired at the early age of twenty-six; realising her error she was now returning to the stage as Montague's leading lady.

Penley planned his admission prices to be 'moderate and judicious' compared to the main theatres. In spite of its newness, the theatre had been newly re-decorated, ornamented with vases and statues front of house, presenting a light, chaste and agreeable appearance on the opening night, the success of which all the newspapers, professing he deserved, cordially wished him.

The opening night was 1 April 1839, not a very auspicious date. Three new pieces were presented, all of them successful; they were *Dark Deeds*, *The Silver Crescent* and *Lady Mary Wortley Montague* which, from the pen of a lady belonging to the upper circles of society, was a musical drama concerning 'the peculiar adventures which befell her ladyship on the occasion of her stolen marriage.' The subject was a popular scandal of 100 years earlier when, rather than marry her approved suitor with the unlikely name of Clotworthy Skeffington, she eloped with the man who became the Ambassador to Turkey.

The newspapers did Montague's venture proud, as he gathered many column inches of comment and review. Inevitably, they harped on the fact that, apart from young Mrs Stirling, and the reclaimed veteran Vale, the players were totally unknown in London – a strong indication of how the provinces were still regarded as inferior to the capital. One or two newspapers expressed stronger doubts about the venture:

> . . . a set of performers that, with a single exception, are altogether new to London. It was a hazardous experiment, and, without some decided and even brilliant success on the part of individual actors in so novel a company, almost certain of failure. . . .

> . . . a company, save with a few exceptions, of provincial artists. . . . Among the performers who acquitted themselves in a meritorious way, we must point out Messrs Neville and Saville and Mrs Stirling . . . in the third piece the scenery and dresses are of a most magnificent description.

> . . . an almost entire company new to the London boards, and no failures, is indeed a novelty in our theatrical annals – and such we congratulate Mr Penley on the success of the experiment, and assure our readers, that though strangers, there are few companies in London with whom they need fear a comparison . . . we feel assured that this will prove one of the most favoured theatres.

> . . . To introduce almost an entire company from the provinces is a bold attempt. It was never made but once, and then it failed. . . . What we did see of Mr Penley's new importations, several of them are far superior to some established favourites, and few of them would have suffered by any comparison that could be drawn. . . . Mr Penley has done theatricals a real lasting benefit by his spirited project.

Others decided not to rush in until they had seen further productions. The *Champion* thought the new company from the provinces bid fair to make a noble stand on grounds stronger than mere novelty, reserving judgment until the company had been tested with better material than the ephemeral Easter offerings. Alas, there were few further offerings at all. Even at Montague's judicious prices the public was not tempted.

As had been customary at all theatres for over a century, half-price admission was offered at a certain point in the evening. By way of an attraction for the half-price visitors, a concert *à la Musard*, was given, the stage 'being thrown open to the audience at the end of the second piece.' Musard, a French musician, had introduced open air concerts in Paris in the English style. His programmes comprised overtures, waltzes, popular instrumental solos and quadrilles. In January, the orchestra of the English Opera House had started a series of promenade concerts dubbed *à la Musard* and these were very popular, some dozen taking place up to the time of Montague's management. This is thought to be the first use of the expression 'promenade concert'. Other theatres took up the idea, Drury

Lane running a series of *concerts d'été* with an orchestra of 100 players and singers, charging only 1/- in the promenade and 2/- in the boxes. One recent concert was claimed to have had no fewer than 4700 people attending. Very much of the moment, these concerts were inordinately popular, ousting drama. Of course, the promenade 'free and easy' was a new fad, and throughout London all kinds of venues were launching them.

Penley's interval concert was an attempt to jump on the bandwagon. The Lyceum orchestra, on a more modest scale than Drury Lane, was conducted by the ubiquitous Charles Miller. It made little difference and the already bargain admission prices were reduced further to 2/-, 1/- and 6d. This was desperation as theatre prices throughout the country had been stable for decades, even the little Tenterden country theatre in his father's day had functioned on the standard 3/-, 2/- and 1/- formula. The London patent theatres normally had a top price of 7/-, so to reduce prices to such a drastically low level signalled an obvious cry of despair.

Reduced prices and free musical concerts in the interval proving fruitless, Penley's Lyceum theatre closed. It did not re-open; his project had failed within 11 days.

> The want of public patronage has compelled him to close his theatre. A kind of bastard Musard enabled him to prolong the performance a few evenings, but the opening of Drury Lane as a concert room destroyed the attempt.

Sections of the press castigated the public at large for not supporting the company, not giving it a fair trial, flocking to promenade concerts rather than the theatre, attending performances by performing animals rather than human artists, and so forth. It is always easy to be wise after the event, but the project was severely under-capitalised, crashing within a fortnight of opening night and leaving Montague ruined. A new, obviously hazardous, venture needed ample backing to nurse it through the early months until the appeal of the shows was recognised as being worthwhile. Montague clearly had an advance budget of no more than one week, relying on immediate takings to fund the following week.

After Penley's precipitate departure the theatre was used for concerts by the Band of the Coldstream Guards, these playing to very full houses. Then it was taken by the composer Michael Balfe, best remembered for his opera *The Bohemian Girl* and songs such as *I Dreamt I Dwelt in Marble Halls*, *Come into the Garden Maude* and *Excelsior*. He too only lasted a short time. The following year, M Musard himself, coming from Paris, gave a highly successful series of promenade concerts at the venue.

SCENE FIVE
1839 AND AFTER
FAREWELL

MONTAGUE PENLEY HAD flopped in London but he still had his leases of Newcastle and Windsor. On the heels of his failure, he opened the customary Race Week at Windsor. Unfortunately, a further obstacle was put in the way:

> The Windsor Theatre Royal opened on Monday night, for the race week, Mrs Stirling being the principal 'star' engaged by Mr Penley. Although the prices have been reduced nearly one half, yet at the end of the first piece there were only thirteen persons in the boxes, nineteen in the pit, and eight in the gallery. The Provost of Eton has not only issued strict injunctions that the Eton boys shall not enter the Theatre, but he has forbidden the manager to draw up the curtain until a quarter past eight o'clock, this being the hour at which the boys are compelled to be within their domiciles. The provost has been induced to come to this determination in consequence of one of the scholars, during the last race week, in attempting to climb from the boxes to the gallery, falling into the pit, and severely injuring himself.

The annual roistering in the theatre had eventually gone too far. Mrs Stirling, the star of the thwarted season at the Lyceum, must have trusted Montague, even after that aborted venture. No doubt, as still happens today, being owed money by the promoter, she was persuaded by him that her loss, and more, would be recouped by a new venture and, as actors are perennially foolishly optimistic, went along with the scheme. However, all her biographer has to say about the affair was:

> Penley, a provincial manager of experience and good repute, had induced a number of actors and actresses to throw up lucrative engagements at Glasgow, Newcastle, Bath, and other provincial towns, and accompany him to the Lyceum. They would naturally suppose that he had brought with him the wherewithal to tide his company over any initial failure. In fact, he was merely gambling on the chance of success. After eleven nights' performance, five nights' salary only were paid, and much distress resulted to the players, who, with the one exception of the leading lady, were unknown in London, and whose provincial posts were already filled.

Also in June, tenders were invited for the future lease of the Newcastle theatre, Penley's three-year deal ending in November. Montague made an effort for the Race Week there by booking Mrs Nisbett and her sister Miss J Mordaunt and business was good.

The *Newcastle Journal*, always kind to Montague, told its readers that the lease was coming up for renewal and that the theatre had been under control of the Penley family for about nine years, 'during the whole of which period it has been conducted in a manner satisfactory to the public, profitable to the shareholders, and creditable to the lessees.' The paper recommended Mr Montague Penley, the present lessee, as 'we know no one who has greater claims on the consideration of the shareholders, or one whose efficiency, and above all, whose cultivated taste, extensive experience, and sound discrimination, afford a better guarantee for the general excellence of the performances, and the proper conduct of the establishment in all its departments.'

These rather blatant untruths sound so much like a tender application one suspects that Montague may have been greasing a few palms. The managers offering tenders were Monro of Birmingham, Beverley of Sunderland, Ternan of Rochester, Penley of Windsor, W Watson of Newcastle, and Hooper of London.

The decision went with Ternan who received 35 votes, whereas Penley got 15, Watson and Beverley one apiece and the others none. Ternan was to have a three-year lease at £410 per annum. Ternan, a local favourite, had appeared, with his wife, as a visiting artist during both Sam Jr's and Montague's managements. Montague no doubt now regretted that he had ever engaged the popular tragedian. Of course, the proprietors would have been influenced by Montague's failure – if he could not pay his debts in London, how would be pay his rent in Newcastle? Also, it has to be said that reviews of the plays during the latter end of his tenure indicate that his companies were on the weak side.

In the theatre success can be overnight. Unfortunately, as Montague was to find, failure clings and is hard to shake off. He still had a few months in Newcastle until his lease expired and, if he could put on some money-spinning shows, had a chance of recouping something from the wreckage. Mr Miller the erstwhile bandmaster did not help with his public letter to the press:

> I beg to address a few Lines to you, in Consequence of having learnt that a Report has been industriously circulated in Newcastle, to the Effect, that I was the immediate Cause of

the Failure of Mr Penley's Speculation at the English Opera House, London, in having, as is stated, persuaded the Band not to play etc. I shall simply state, that the Allegation is as distant from Truth, as the Conduct of the Manager towards those who placed Faith in his Engagement has been at Variance with that of Propriety and Honour. *The only true Cause of the Band and Performers refusing to play was the Non-payment of their Salaries.*

Having, in full Reliance upon Mr Penley's Fidelity in the Completion of a Compact deliberately entered into, broken up my own Establishment in Newcastle, and sacrificed many lucrative Engagements, it is to suppose me devoid of all Reason, and utterly destitute of the commonest Degree of common Sense, to give Credence, for a Moment, to the Assertion, that, in the very Commencement of the Season, I should recklessly attempt to injure an Establishment on which *I was dependent* for the Remuneration of my own Exertions for the very Means of Support and Maintenance, and on the Success of which my own Prospects in London in a great Measure depended. I was guilty of no such insanity. My only Object in this Letter is to vindicate my Character from the unjust Aspersions of Parties, who seem to spurn *Truth* to the same Degree that they scorn the Force of the stringent Obligations of Justice and of Honour.

I am, Gentlemen,

Your very obedient Servant,

Charles Miller

This letter to the editors suggests that Montague Penley was making all kinds of preposterous excuses for his failure at the Lyceum, presumably in an attempt to conceal his lack of financial probity whilst the tendering process was in progress.

Like all the Penleys, Montague was a fighter and was prepared to have a last throw of the dice. In July, he engaged some juvenile dancers: Master and Miss Marshall, and Miss Taylor who seem popular and/or cheap enough to have had their engagement extended. Then, just prior to closing, there was a benefit night for the Ladies and Gentlemen of the Theatre. One wonders if that was in lieu of salary? Then a further night for the benefit of Mr M Penley himself, when the main attraction was a revised version of *The Beaux Stratagem* and the old 1803 farce *Raising the Wind*, in which Mr M Penley himself played Jeremy Diddler 'being his First and Only Appearance here.' No doubt band leader Miller considered it appropriate casting, as the character is a needy artful swindler who gave his name to the word 'diddle' as a synonym for cheat.

Montague was now reduced to his Windsor venue only which he opened on 5 August 1839, returning to the customary prices. On 17 August, the *Odd Fellow* reported 'The houses have been wretchedly bad, in spite of the engagement of those very clever people, Mr and Mrs Keeley.' However, the *Champion* reported that the manager had experienced thus far a most prosperous season. The company generally, 'of a much higher order than normally met with in provincial towns', included Mrs Nisbett, Miss J Mordaunt and Miss R Penley, while the stage manager – Mr Baker of Drury Lane – had been 'vital in the running and prosperity of the theatre and deserved a bumper benefit'. These widely disparate opinions make ascertaining the truth quite impossible.

The fighting Montague had a final throw at the Newcastle dice. Nothing loath, though he was surrendering his lease in November, Montague opened Newcastle at the end of September attempting to make some money back while still having the use of a theatre. He booked Sheridan Knowles and the personable Miss Elphinstone 'of whom eulogy is supererogatory'. Knowles was not much better at handling his own finances than Montague; also, after several hit plays, he had fallen out with his champion Macready who disliked his flaunting of Miss Elphinstone, a young lady who had returned with the married Knowles from a USA tour in 1834. Knowles continued the flaunting until his wife died, then made Miss Elphinstone a respectable married woman. In 1844 he suddenly dropped the theatre and became a Baptist preacher, receiving a £200 annual pension from Sir Robert Peel in 1848.

Montague's final attraction before the closure of his lease was Mr and Mrs Woods, with a reputation for quality singing in the north-east, who finally and firmly closed Montague's venture for good on 8 November with *La Somnambula* being a benefit for Mrs Woods. It was a crowded house and thus ended eight years of Penley management.

Montague, surely by now getting heartily sick of the theatre business, was back at Windsor to produce the first winter season for many years. 'Every care has been taken to render the Theatre comfortable, by the introduction of Stoves, and Fires being constantly kept.' His chances of retrieving some of his losses were now centred on the Windsor theatre alone, and he must take every opportunity to milk it. A winter season was a risky venture, especially as provincial theatre business was universally depressed. The company was led by Maddocks and the Cooke family from Cheltenham, with Miss R Penley and local favourite Dodd providing support. Rosina had not been involved in Montague's Lyceum venture, nor in the last Newcastle season, but brother Belville was roped in again as Acting Manager. Once more the season had a slow start, with scarcely 50 people in the theatre on opening night, but audiences built after the second week.

The play of *Jack Sheppard* had been recently staged at the Adelphi with tremendous success, and the Windsor audience likewise approved of Penley's version. Sheppard was played by a female at the Adelphi, so at Windsor Miss Cooke essayed the role with much acclaim. The remarkable jail-breaking deeds and criminal exploits of the eponymous villain dated back 100 years to a time when the public's glee was aroused by the futile efforts of Jonathan Wild the self-styled 'Thief Taker General' to capture the man. Wild was actually another gang leader, responsible for getting some sixty enemies hanged for a cash reward, and had a vast network of operatives in collusion with the authorities. Interest had been recently revived by Harrison Ainsworth's serialised novel *Jack Sheppard* which was outselling *Oliver Twist*. The actual skeleton of Wild, who was executed in 1725, was a curiosity belonging to Mr Fowler, Surgeon of Sheet Street, Windsor. History does not tell us if Mr Fowler cashed-in on Montague's production of *Jack Sheppard* by displaying the macabre relic. The skeleton now reposes at the Royal College of Surgeons Hunterian Museum in Lincoln's Inn Fields.

Contemporary interest was aroused when the best house of the season gathered to witness the performance of a 'distinguished Amateur' in the character of Pierre, in Otway's tragedy of *Venice Preserved*. Three gentlemen of fashion had a wager wherein one would masquerade as a musician, one as a coachman and one as an actor, the one raising the most money by his foolery being the winner. The unnamed person – actually a Mr FitzRoberts – who was to be the actor, undertook to play two comedy roles and two tragic roles at four different theatres, Windsor being the first. This poor chap was starting at a disadvantage, having agreed with Penley to pay £20 for the expenses of the house, then split the proceeds equally. '£20 in the present state of theatricals is far from being a joke.'

> The performance of the piece went off with great *éclat*, and the 'Amateur' was ably supported, particularly by Miss Rosina Penley, as Belvidera, and Mr Maddocks, as Jaffier. At the termination of the tragedy the 'Amateur' was called for by the audience, and in the modern London style he obeyed the mandate, made his obeisance in return for the compliment paid him, and retired amidst considerable applause.

On Dodd's benefit, a drama called *The Climbing Boy* was enacted with Miss Cooke's younger sister – only twelve years old – in the title part. One wonders if Rosina, looking from her forty-three years at the youthful Cooke sisters, recalled with nostalgia when she and her sisters played such juvenile roles with the J & P company.

Sheridan Knowles, that favourite guest artiste of Montague, appeared in some of his own plays, apparently *sans* Miss Elphinstone, but his appearance led to the local paper expressing surprise and grief that the audiences were so poor:

> We were sorry to observe so thin a house, as we had anticipated the novelty of one of the first authors of the day playing the principal character in one of his own pieces, would have at least induced the inhabitants of *this* town to have attended in greater numbers.

Many people in Windsor had said that if the manager were to introduce stars, more people would attend the theatre. However, when the manager engaged star names the audience was not boosted enough to warrant the extra expense of star salaries.

The final week brought the customary bespeaks and patronage nights, and the *Reading Mercury* 'calculated that Mr Penley would reap a well merited reward for his perseverance and exertions. The houses during the week have been unexpectedly well attended.' Whereas *The Theatrical Observer* observed 'The Windsor Theatre was compelled to close on Friday last. Every attraction put forth by the management has been attended with ill success . . . the wonderful abilities of Mr Maddocks! and Miss Penley! . . . totally unappreciated by the good folks of Windsor.' Again, from our standpoint 170 years later, whom can we believe?

In June, Montague decided that the usual tiresome task of assembling a company of actors and putting on a different play every night for Race Week was not worthwhile. The likelihood of diminished audiences was imminent and he could not afford to risk further losses. The theatre was let out for exhibitions by The Royal Wizard of the South. This magician, George Barnardo Eagle, also performed under the names Barnardo and Na Barno. The most famous conjuror of the day was John Henry Anderson who, hailing from Scotland, was dubbed The Great Wizard of the North. George Eagle shamelessly plagiarised Anderson's show and methodology, offering a complete evening's entertainment which was more economical to stage than a troupe of actors with a repertoire of plays. 'The house was moderately well attended on every evening, and the performances of the Royal Wizard were very cleverly gone through, being loudly and frequently applauded.'

Whether Montague had lost money or not on the winter season, he was back at Windsor in summer. As the opening attraction, he booked William Farren for four nights to play his most famous roles. Farren's first London appearance was in 1818 at Covent Garden as Sir Peter Teazle in Sheridan's *The School for Scandal*, a part with which his name will always be associated; an instant popular and critical success, he remained so for many years. Lord Ogelby in *The Clandestine Marriage* was another of his personal plums. After a long career at both the patent houses, Farren was currently part of Madame Vestris's company at the Olympic, with a ten-year shelf life still ahead of him. He played crusty old bachelors, jealous old husbands, stormy fathers, worrying uncles, or ancient fops with ghastly pretensions to amiability and was among the most highly regarded actors of his time. He was popular with the Windsor audience, and business was gratifying.

Most of Montague's company were new names from various theatres royal throughout the provinces including Mrs Woulds from Bath playing 'ladies of a certain age'; only Rosina, Dodd and stage manager and second lead Baker being from previous years. In a contrast to the old favourite plays of Farren, Bulwer Lytton's latest work *The Lady of Lyons* was produced. Alas, once Farren had gone, business was pretty doleful and even the kindly local newspaper could not hide the fact:

> The whole of the performances this week have gone off with great éclat, but we regret to say that the audiences have not been so great as the exertions of the manager and the talent of the company merit. The company is much stronger, in point of talent, than it has been for some years, and the manager deserves the highest public patronage for his exertions in catering for their amusement.

Although a full and varied season of shows, the public was not flocking. Business improved as it always did for the last week of the bespeaks and benefits, but compared to previous years even they lacked custom. Baker and Dodd pulled in reasonable audiences for their benefits, but the Le Batt sisters were 'below mediocrity in numbers'. The *Theatrical Observer* pointedly reporting: 'Windsor Theatre: On Thursday last the performances here were for a benefit! On the rising of the curtain there were four in the pit, four in the gallery and boxes entirely empty. At half-price the curtain fell to less than forty shillings.' Edmund Glover, the leading man, not only roped in his mother – Mrs Glover being a popular grande dame of the current stage – but his dog. At the dénouement, this animal, supposed to attack the villain of the piece, rather delayed things by standing staring at the audience, barking vociferously. The dog was obviously a pet and not a trained performer.

Considering reviews in various newspapers along the way, the final local report on the summer must have been flavoured with more than a pinch of salt:

> The season, we are glad to say, has been a prosperous one. Indeed the theatre has deserved and has obtained this season a very large share of distinguished patronage, including no less personages than the Sovereign, her illustrious Consort, and her Royal Highness the Duchess of Kent, all of whom have liberally contributed to the treasury of the manager, and also to the purses of two or three of the principal performers. The prospect is therefore, we trust, highly favourable to the manager, and will induce him the next season not to relax his efforts in securing, as he has done this season, a respectable and talented company and good and popular pieces,

For the winter holiday period some amateurs mounted a few shows with the professional assistance of the Misses Mordaunt, sisters of Mrs Nisbett, as Montague did not attempt another winter season, thereby confirming the last one had not made money. Neither did he attempt a Race Week in 1841 on the grounds that the Provost of Eton College would not let the performances commence until 8.15pm.

Montague announced the opening of his Windsor 1841 summer season with the engagement of Mrs Honey for three nights. Again, the company members were new to Windsor, gathered from all the provincial theatres royal. But, as we have already seen, Montague did not stay to mastermind the season but fled to France, leaving his sister Rosina to cope with Windsor. As far as can be ascertained, Montague never entered a theatre ever again.

In Paris, Montague occupied himself painting and copying pictures in the Louvre. A travel book of the time *How to Enjoy Paris in 1842* gave this useful tip on page 409: 'As many purchasers of pictures often want them cleaned and restored, I would recommend them to a countryman for that purpose, M Penley 11 Rue Romford, whose efforts I have seen effect a complete resuscitation upon a dingy and almost incomprehensible subject.' Montague also exhibited, and the *Explication des ouvrages sculpture, architecture, gravure et lithographie des artistes vivants exposés au Musée Royal* lists Montague

Penley, now at 18 rue de la Ferme-des-Mathurius, showing a work entitled *Bonheur et Malheur* in an exhibition in March 1846.

In Paris, Mr and Mrs Penley were able to visit Montague's sister-in-law, the widow of Sampson Penley Jr, who remained in that city with her children, living off the pension provided by the Drury Lane Fund, and by teaching.

On returning to England in 1847, Mr & Mrs Montague Penley settled in Brighton at 1 Wykeham Terrace, Montague describing himself as a painter. By the 1871 census, his address was 3 Montpelier Crescent and he was a widower, Letitia having died in June 1866. His occupation is given as an artist and teacher of painting. Mary A Emery was named as an unmarried visitor aged fifty. This lady was still visiting (oh yes?!) at the time of the 1881 census when Montague was listed as a retired artist. He died in December 1881 at Brighton aged eighty-two.

Montague's prowess as a painter is impossible to assess as there seem to be no works readily available to view. However, there is an extant print which ties together his theatrical roots and his artistic talent, although its provenance is clouded in mystery. The picture exists as an engraving described as *Exterior of Sandwich Theatre Previous to a Rehearsal*, the publisher and printer given as J Didsbury of 22 Southampton Street, The Strand, who must surely have been a relative of Montague's wife, née Didsbury. A copy is now in the Parker Collection in Margate library with a suggested date of 1840. Some years ago Kent libraries issued a greetings card with the picture captioned *Exterior of Sandwich Theatre c1780*. It depicts a somewhat broken-down barn-type theatre with a shield bearing the date 1762, indicating when the theatre was built or converted. The date circa 1780 put on it by the card printer is, presumably, an educated guess based on the clothing of the figures in the picture.

Compared to brother Sam's biography, the lack of available evidence has resulted in a rather halting version of Montague's theatrical career which ran on a parallel time scale. Belville, the third brother, was also a manager but never an adult actor, and his short career – often linked with his brothers – is considered in the following chapters.

Exterior of Sandwich Theatre Previous to a Rehearsal
The theatre depicted is probably the one at the New Inn which
was visited by Mrs Sarah Baker's Company at various times between
1772 and 1790

ACT SIX

MR BELVILLE PENLEY

'a spirited and deverving manager'

and

MRS BELVILLE PENLEY

'who sang delightfully and was encored.'

SCENE ONE
1831 - 1833
BELVILLE PENLEY MEETS MARY FIELD

BELVILLE PENLEY WAS Sampson and Lucy's youngest child, born in Folkestone, he was baptised on 29 June 1808 at Rye. He was the second child to be thus named, a predecessor being born on 30 June 1804 in Folkestone, and buried at Eastbourne on 10 September of the same year.

Belville was not destined to become an actor although as a child he briefly surfaced in his father's company. Indeed, he claimed to have been playing a child's part in Brussels on the night before the battle of Waterloo. He recalled being clad in a regimental suit given to him by English officers, and remembered the triumphant return of the army and a subsequent visit to the battlefield.

Apart from a few appearances as a page and similar roles in 1820, the highlight being his appearance as Tom Thumb, Belville did not appear as an actor growing up into adult roles as did all his brothers and sisters. There appears to be no cogent reason why this should be so. Surrounded by players, he must have lived and breathed in theatres, even if spending time away at school.

It is as an adult of twenty-two that Belville comes to our notice functioning as Box Book Keeper at Newcastle for big brother Sam's 1830/31 inaugural season. In the company was Mary Field, a singer who hailed from Bath and had been on the stage for several years. She was in the Birmingham company in 1825 being billed as 'her first appearance in England since her return from the Continent', and at Manchester in 1826. Engaged as a singer rather than actress, Miss Field was cast in roles such as Rowena in *Ivanhoe* and Clymante in *Native Land*, plays which were classed as musical dramas or operas. When not employed in the main play of the evening she might be in a musical afterpiece such as *Love Laughs at Locksmiths*, or simply singing solos or duets interpolated within or between plays. Retained at Manchester for the 1827 season in the same line of business, she met Rosina Penley, presumably for the first time, who was also engaged at Manchester for the season. Mary Field had further seasons at Manchester. In 1828 she was cast as Ophelia, and in 1829 her parts included Ariel in *The Tempest*, and Ophelia again which she gave with the Hamlet of no less an actor than Charles Kemble.

At Newcastle, her charms enraptured John Waldie, he of the copious journals. Whilst carping at the actors, he seems rather smitten with Miss Field who sings delightfully:

> 7 January 1831 – Penley's Windsor Company: A Miss Field, tho' plain, is neat and has a lovely voice and sings tolerably.
>
> 12 January 1831 – Miss Field was ill and did not sing which spoiled all as the others were poor.
>
> 21 Jan 1831 – Miss Field sang delightfully and was encored in the second song.
>
> 18 February 1831 – Miss Field in Harriet sang *Should He Upbraid* very well – tho songs in a higher key suit her more – but she has a charming facility and clearness of intonation.

Waldie was not the only man to be wooed by Miss Field's charms, a fact which led to a scandal in the public prints as shall soon be seen.

The Newcastle season closed at the end of May with a well attended benefit for Mr Belville Penley. Miss Field joined Sam Jr's Windsor company for the summer season, going on to Leicester with many of the other players. Her singing was quite a hit with the Leicester audiences and she was singled out for the songs *Young Cavalier* and *Lo! Hear the Gentle Lark* 'although Miss Field's eyes seemed to wander with disapprobation to the clumsy flute accompanier, who certainly annoyed some parts of the company.' Though on another occasion: 'Miss Field had not a fair scope for her talent; the music was seriously curtailed; but the songs allotted to her were given with taste and effect.' Miss Field also had difficulties with the acoustic of the auditorium which prevented her from being heard at her best.

Although Windsor and Leicester were not top venues, Miss Field, having been around some years, had also gained much experience in more important theatres like Bath and Manchester, this standing her in good stead at the end of the Leicester season when she became a member of the singing company at Drury Lane itself:

> In the entertainment of *Rosina* there were also two debuts, a Mr Templeton, from Edinburgh, and a Miss Field, from Bath, as Rosina; the young lady cannot boast of much personal charms, and her voice, though tolerably sweet, seems not sufficiently powerful for the vast arena of this Theatre; she met with but a moderate share of applause – even the air of *Whilst with Village Maids I Stray* did not produce an encore.

The huge 3000-seat auditoriums of Covent Garden and Drury Lane were double the size of other theatres and often a considerable problem of audibility faced newcomers from the provinces.

Other parts she played included Lucinda in *Love in a Village* after which the *Theatrical Observer* said 'Miss Field improves upon acquaintance; she sang and acted, as Lucinda, very pleasingly.' As Jeannette in *The Love Charm; or The Village Coquette* '. . . it could not be sung better than by Miss Field.' But on 25 November, Miss Field's singing in *Lionel and Clarissa* was 'anything but harmonious'.

Both *Love in a Village* (with music by Thomas Arne, now considered as the first English comic opera) and *Lionel and Clarissa* were by Isaac Bickerstaffe dating from the 1760s. Bickerstaffe was a sodomite who in 1772 was publicly exposed in a scurrilous lampoon which associated him (totally falsely) with Garrick. As a result he fled to France where he spent the rest of his life in penury, writing fruitlessly for money to Garrick who, not wishing to be further tainted by an unwarranted slur, refused to even open the letters. Bickerstaffe is thought to have died around 1812, forsaken and abandoned, whilst his works remained as popular as ever.

On 29 November, Miss Field was cast as Ninette in the drama *Clari; or the Maid of Milan*. Then, the day after a performance of *Rob Roy Macgregor*, the *Theatrical Observer* observed:

> We would recommend a certain lady, who was unquestionably the most *prominent* personage in the drama, though not the *greatest* actress, to change the word Miss, which now precedes her name, into Mistress; if she cannot get anyone to make her an *honest woman*, she may assume a *nom de theatre,* for in her present *situation* propriety demands that she be called Mistress. As this is not her first *misfortune,* nor, if the scandalous world is to be believed, likely to be her last, a matronly appellation is the more necessary for her. – 'Assume a virtue if you have it not.'

It would appear from this not too subtle observation that Miss Field was great with child, and not for the first time. It seems a bit much to accuse her in advance by saying it was not likely to be her last, even if she had been putting herself about a bit. The father of the child was revealed on 4 February 1832 when she performed Elvira for the first time in the Grand Opera of *Masaniello* being billed as 'Mrs Belville Penley (late Miss Field)' the *Theatrical Observer* observing '*Masaniello* was the afterpiece, in which Miss Field (who has taken our advice and assumed the appellation of Mrs B Penley) played *Elvira.*'

Masaniello proved popular, being repeated five times in February alone. In fact the subject – the uprising of fishermen in Naples in 1647 – was quite widespread at the time, with several different dramatic versions current, including an equestrian one at the Surrey Theatre. The one at Drury Lane was based on *La Muette de Portici* by Auber.

Belville was at Newcastle in his managerial capacity for his brother once more. The company included the twenty-one-year-old James R Anderson, son of a Scottish actor, who had stage experience from an early age. Prior to Newcastle he had worked in Nottingham. The two young men got on very well together, making plans to go into management.

Meanwhile, Belville's paramour, getting embarrassingly large, was one of the singing witches in Macready's *Macbeth*; one of the ladies of the court in *The Daemon; or the Mystic Branch*, from Meyerbeer's *Robert le Diable*; one of the gypsies in *Der Alchymist*, from a novel by Washington Irving, music by Louis Spohr; and amongst the priests, virgins, matrons etc in *Pizarro*. All were roles where she could conveniently be tucked away at the back of the chorus.

Surprisingly, on 31 March 1832, she played the role of Katty in *Rob Roy Macgregor* again, and in early May repeated her Lucinda in *Love in a Village*, one critic remarking 'Mrs B Penley should rather call on *Lucina* than be called *Lucinda*; her appearance must have justified the worst suspicions of her censorious aunt.' The smart-aleck critic assumed his readers would know Lucina was the Roman goddess of pregnant women.

Belville may have returned from Newcastle in time for the birth of his son Walter Belville Penley. As far as records tell, this was Mary's first child; whether the cutting remark about it not being so was merely malicious rumour, or whether a previous unknown or unacknowledged bastard existed, cannot be ascertained. Mary would have been about twenty-six and Belville two years younger.

Mrs B Penley, as Mary Field was now professionally known, returned to Drury Lane for the 1832/33 season. She does not appear to have taken part in the summer season at Windsor, but Anderson was there, as were Rosina and Phoebe.

SCENE TWO
1833 - 1838
THE PENLEY & ANDERSON COMPANY

ON 9 SEPTEMBER 1833, Belville Penley and J R Anderson went into management, launching a season at Leicester. Yes, the very same theatre that brother Sam had occupied two years previously. A major improvement was the installation of gas lighting replacing oil which 'from its smell and smoke, has for so many years been a cause of great complaint, and prevented many persons from visiting this place of amusement' and was now 'entirely removed from the interior of the theatre.'

Entirely new and superbly executed scenery was promised, including an act drop by Mr Nicholls of Newcastle. No doubt some of the other scenery had been gleaned from Newcastle, and probably Windsor too. The company was led by Anderson, with Rosina as leading lady. Miss Stohwasser was likely to become a favourite of the town because of her naive manner. Anderson looked on her with favour too. There were other actors from Windsor, some of whom had also been in Sam's company at Leicester.

Mrs B Penley was unavailable to accompany her 'husband' as she had been re-engaged at Drury Lane, although her star had fallen and she was cast mainly in chorus roles. The management of the theatre had passed to Alfred Bunn, as Capt Polhill the previous lease-holder had lost £80,000 during his tenancy. Bunn negotiated a lower rental, paying £6000 for the year where his predecessor had been charged £8000. It was an alarming drop from the heyday of Elliston who forked out £10,000 each year, and the clearest evidence of how even in the capital theatre business was struggling.

Bunn also controlled Covent Garden and was using his players indiscriminately at either theatre. Having one company spread over both theatres was an economy measure as business was in decline, the previous season losing £10,000. Bunn was actually asking some of his performers to appear at both Covent Garden and Drury Lane theatres on the same evening, forcing them to run from one stage-door to the other in full costume and makeup to avoid missing an entrance.

While the major London theatres were struggling, Belville and Anderson in their more modest house were not doing much better. In spite of encouraging notices in the local press, when the season came to an end it was reported:

> Messrs Penley and Anderson whose labours have just ended have met with so unfortunate and inadequate a requital. It is evident to all that they have redeemed the Theatre from the discredit into which it had fallen for a series of successive years, and we hope again to meet the same company with as few alterations as necessity may dictate.

Belville and James, not giving up easily, agreed to take the theatre again for the following season. They then returned to Newcastle for Sam Jr, taking Miss Stohwasser with them.

Mary Field had another child by Belville Penley, a daughter called Louisa who was baptised on 20 April 1834. In spite of the *nom de théâtre* of Mrs B Penley, adopted to squash malicious rumours, Mary was still an unmarried woman, a situation finally rectified on 1 July 1834 when the pair married at Tottenham, London.

In September 1834, Penley & Anderson returned to the Leicester theatre to be greeted with boosting publicity in the local paper. However, this was somewhat undermined by concluding 'the great pecuniary loss sustained by Messrs Penley and Anderson last season, will it is to be hoped be repaid them by a liberal patronage they are catering with perseverance, and deserve the support of a discerning public.' It helps nobody to be reminded of previous failure!

Whereas gas had been trumpeted as the feature of their first season, the attraction this time was an augmented orchestra. Anderson was again leading man, and prominently featured was Mrs B Penley, heralded with this twee announcement:

> Miss Field, a favourite during her former brief stay, will revisit us with a change of name, but, we hope, unchanged in her title to approbation: indeed we have little to fear with respect to our fair vocalist, as it is seldom that ladies lose their 'sweet voices' by entering into wedlock. The company comprises other old favourites.

Younge, like Anderson coming directly from Windsor, was second lead, Watson was the male singer and Boddie the low comedy man; a new addition was the dancer Miss Parsloe, she of the scanty attire and extending legs. Unfortunately, the season commenced with a very thin house, and the advertised attraction of *The Poor Gentleman* had to be replaced with another play as Mr and Mrs Gardiner, contracted as principal performers in the piece, did not turn up.

An actor not arriving was an everyday hazard in the days when travel was by road. Though the coaching system was incredibly well-developed, with a 1000 vehicles leaving London daily and a network of inns, stables, ostlers, and blacksmiths supporting travel throughout the land, hazards remained. There were constant dangers on the road – accidents, impassable roads, and highwaymen on isolated stretches of countryside. Apart from these normal travelling hazards, the costs for an out-of-work actor may have been prohibitive of his taking up a job offer. All well and good if he had time to hitch-hike, or the manager sent him an advance, otherwise he had to pay the cost of a coach at 2d to 3d a mile, half-price if travelling outside. It was also necessary to have plenty of ready money as overnight stops and refreshment halts had to be paid for, plus a multitude of extra expenses such as tipping the coachman and guard 1/- per stage of about 30 miles. Apart from the legitimate bill at an inn, there were tips for the chambermaid (6d a night) the 'boots'(2d), and the head waiter (1/-). Even the porter taking your portmanteau upstairs removed his hat with a 'pray remember the porter, Sir.'

Coach services were just as subject to delay as railways and aeroplanes are today. Actors travelling long distances may well miss connections as coaches could be halted by bad weather, mechanical accident or lame horses. On one occasion, Miss Foote travelled from Grantham to London (120 miles). 'On descending the hill at Barnet, at ten o'clock at night, one of the horses fell down and severely hurt the rider, while the other began to show much intemperance. In this dilemma, one of the York coaches passed, and the passengers assisted this Lady from her situation.' At another time, Mr De Camp's Company of Comedians on its way to Sheffield had the entire coach overturned because it was top-heavy, resulting in 19 passengers all 'more or less injured'.

Towards the end of his ramshackle touring life, Edmund Kean was prone to not arriving as planned, usually because he was prone somewhere else. With arrangements depending entirely on correspondence, sometimes there was a genuine misunderstanding as to what had been agreed. A letter from Kean to his secretary reads: 'Dear Lee, What day do I open at Cheltenham. The stupid son of a bitch has not dated his letter, write me Birmingham . . .' Nothing was planned very far ahead, hence the daily issue of playbills. On one day, at the foot of the bill, the public may be informed the next attraction would be such-and-such, only for it to be changed entirely when the next day's playbill was posted. Because newspapers of the time were generally weekly, up-to-date information was carried on the daily playbills rather than in advertisements.

Actors could also arrive earlier than expected and have to wait around until required. One actor arriving at a country theatre the day before his contract started put up at the local inn. After dining and enquiring the whereabouts of the theatre, the pot-boy was deputed to conduct him to the place which was down an obscure dark alley. Finding his new employer backstage while the show was in progress, the actor introduced himself, and the next he knew he was onstage performing in the afterpiece!

At Leicester, Mr & Mrs Gardiner never did arrive so Mrs B Penley sang *Lo Hear the Gentle Lark* 'with much taste, this Lady's voice is clear and melodious; her high notes possess not only power but a pleasing distinctness.' Alas, as the season progressed Mrs B Penley struggled to get across to the audience.

The local press was very supportive with many complimentary reviews and urges to the public to support the deserving and spirited managers. Adverse comments were rare:

> The piece was performed passably well: higher praise we cannot accord, the company being unsuited for tragedy. In farce, indeed, the company is qualified to shine.
>
> Miss Parsloe whose dancing is of the first order. We do not like to find fault with a Lady if we cannot praise, but we must say without any over-strained notions of decency, that the dress would look better if not quite so short. The Italian Opera House and the Leicester Theatre are different spheres.

Presumably Miss Parsloe, who keeps offending the critics with her antics, persists because her public rather likes them. Penley & Anderson were not going to be dismissed as mere farceurs so the following week the resident company gave a 'wretched performance' of *Richard III*. Then the duo mounted a grand opera *Gustavus the Third* by Auber. The scenery and costumes were lavish, music superb and Mrs B Penley gave her songs 'with that taste and feeling which invariably distinguishes this lady's singing, there was no unnecessary display of exertion, no torturing the gamut into fits to elicit a hand or two from the gods.' Which is one way of looking at it, but a correspondent who wrote to praise and recommend the production to his fellow citizens commented 'Mrs Penley was tolerably good; her singing is calculated to please, but in acting she certainly does not excel.'

However, in spite of gas, augmented orchestra and a first-rate company, there were complaints about the acoustic of the auditorium with which Mrs B Penley struggled. The great William Macready visited for a night playing Hamlet to a crowded house but, labouring under an indisposition, was something of a disappointment. Another star performer imported for a night was John Braham, a singer with a high reputation, whose vocal power remained undiminished even at sixty years of age. These visits now showed up a flaw in the theatre; the sound was lost through some error in its construction. It was because of this that Mrs B Penley's voice was never heard to advantage.

As the season ended, the usual benefits took place, Belville's announced with the leaden raillery of the local press:

> Mr B Penley, the senior Manager, will take his benefit . . .
> This gentleman, though he treads not the boards in presence
> of the audience, is not idle *behind* the curtain as a caterer for
> the public amusement. This consideration, we hope, will
> induce a numerous attendance *before* the curtain, as the
> reward of his unseen but efficient services.

Alas, the attendance was not as good as expected. Supporting actor Mr Skerrett fared even worse as his turnout barely covered expenses, proof indeed that an actor could lose rather than gain from his benefit. When the season closed, the local press hoped it had been a successful one for the spirited managers, as their exertions had been indefatigable, though judging from the response to the benefits that looks unlikely.

To the Penley siblings it must have seemed that their lives were much the same from one year to the next, the same plays coming round with monotonous regularity, and with only the occasional new work really making an impression, everything much the same as in their father's day. But events in the wider world were changing society all the time – 1835 saw Fox Talbot expose the first negative photograph; the last canal to be constructed; the introduction of the hansom cab, and, unknown to the world, Charles Darwin was taking a voyage on the *Beagle*. The theatre world itself was changing too – the clamour of the minor theatres for the overthrow of the patent system was becoming deafening, and the Excise Act of 1835 enabled theatres to have bars within the building.

Mrs B Penley, returning to her home town, joined the Bath Theatre for the 1835 season that opened at the end of December. The manager was the long-serving Bath actor Woulds, and leading man was another Bath favourite Mr Stuart. Macready appeared frequently, and it is thought he had concealed financial backing in the theatre.

Mrs BP who had been taken to task for being a wooden actress at

Leicester was regarded very differently by the Bath press:

> Her efforts have been extremely well received and deservedly
> so. This lady possesses a merit which is unfortunately
> somewhat rare among theatrical vocalists. She always proves
> herself aware that, to give full effect to an opera, there is
> required such a thing as *acting*, as well as singing. Her best
> attention is, therefore, always devoted to the business of the
> stage, and, in her hands, the proprieties of the scene never
> suffer.

Mrs BP took her benefit in May when her brother Mr Henry Field, a long-time Bath resident, played Fra Diavolo in the opera of that name. The last night of season came on 14 May which was Woulds's benefit. He was praised for all his efforts – putting into the season double what the most sanguine expectations can have been, far exceeding his promises, bringing the latest novelties, presenting plays of a high standard, assembling a dramatic company of unparalleled quality in any provincial theatre. But what was his reward for all this effort and zeal? At the close of his labours he faced a frightening loss. Surprisingly, Woulds managed the place for another four years before finally going bust, returning to being merely on the acting strength for the next manager when, as we have seen, Rosina Penley joined the ill-fated theatre.

The two young entrepreneurs Penley & Anderson, extending their horizons just as Belville's father old Sampson Penley had done, took the leases of both Cheltenham and Gloucester theatres. These theatres had been part of a circuit, run for over 40 years by three generations of the Boles Watson family. P & A trumpeted the Gloucester theatre would now be lit by gas.

The Cheltenham Theatre opened for a summer season on 29 June with Phoebe Penley who had often appeared at the theatre over the previous ten years for other managers. Formerly this venue had a long season that ran from the end of June until the end of November, but P & A changed that system by closing on 28 August so the entire company could move to Leicester for the regular autumn visit opening on 9 September.

The Leicester company, announced for 'an unusually short season', comprised Anderson, Phoebe Penley, Mrs Belville Penley, and Osborne, Hall and Hudspeth all from Cheltenham. The season was not helped by competition from a fair with Wombwell's menagerie, and a visit from Batty's circus which promised the spectacle of The Battle of Waterloo. No doubt Belville would recall that 20 years previously, as a tot, he had visited the actual battlefield. Mrs B Penley seemed to have found the measure of the acoustic as there were no adverse comments made during this season. The major production was the musical drama *Masaniello* when the company was augmented with Monsieur Silvain and Mlle Pauline from the Royal Academy Paris and Italian Opera London. M Silvain, starting life as Jack Sullivan a waterman's boy, had been plucked by chance off the streets by Winston of Drury Lane to act as a 'double' for a girl in a pantomime. Later, the same boy was a last-minute substitute in Hullin's clown troupe and, from there, assisted by his Frenchified name, rose to be a principal dancer and a highly respected artiste of considerable merit.

Leicester closed on 29 October, enabling Belville to open the Cheltenham theatre again for 'an experimental winter season' commencing on 2 November with *Othello*, Phoebe playing Emilia. Hitherto, the theatre season had been strictly a summer affair, and this new departure was something of a shot in the dark, P & A reducing the prices in an attempt to attract customers. In spite of bringing in Mrs Coleman Pope, a leading lady from Covent Garden, business was generally disappointing. Mrs Coleman Pope was destined to be Lady Macbeth to Macready's thane during the Astor Place Riot of 1849, remaining in America as one of their leading actresses until dying in New York in 1880.

Phoebe Penley took her benefit on 2 February, and as Anderson's benefit loomed imminently the local *Chronicle* newspaper – always supportive of P & A – sent hearty wishes for a bumper turn-out on several grounds. As a manager he had spared no expense to gratify his public, in spite of scanty encouragement he had not relaxed his efforts to present pleasing shows. His acting merits, universally admired by all, were of a very high order. All these virtues combined in one man deserved an over-flowing house. Belville's benefit, in which his wife and brother-in-law Henry Field were the principals, closed the season on 27 February. The experimental winter season had not been a success. Perhaps Belville should have taken notice of brother Sam at Windsor who had dropped the winter season there years ago.

P & A then opened for two days on 26 and 27 March for the Spring Race Meeting, presenting Auber's grand opera *Gustavus III*, the lavish production from Leicester, but the local *Looker On* reported the house was by no means crowded and, if future houses were to be no better, then Messrs Penley and Anderson would have 'little cause of congratulating themselves', which reads remarkably mean spirited. The *Looker On* appears to have delighted in showing the theatre in a poor light, whereas the *Chronicle* devoted several inches to reviewing the productions each week.

As early as April, Penley & Anderson announced their plans for a June opening, trumpeting the engagement of Mr & Mrs Yates, popular players in the town, Yates having been a previous manager. They also admitted to the folly of their winter season:

> Having learnt by experience that cheap admission and a limited company will never meet with support from a Cheltenham audience, they have determined once more to make a bold venture, with a powerful company, and first rate novelties, to meet the expenditure of which, they are under the necessity of RAISING THE PRICES TO THE ORIGINAL SCALE and they feel confident that the arrangements they have made will leave the public no cause of complaint.

In the same issue as this advertisement, an editorial laboured the same point saying that several recent managements had not reflected the elevated tone of society in Cheltenham, and should ever remember they are catering for an audience whose powers of judgment are at least the equal to those of any in the empire. Nothing like blowing your own trumpet! Cheltenham folk did not want low-class melodrama degrading the drama with displays of coarse passion and violent crime. After 50 lines of rubbing in these assertions, the writer then cheers up saying that Penley & Anderson, agreeing with this theory, will be elevating the drama with a first-class company presenting refined entertainments. Miss Eliza Crisp was to be foremost among the company, and *The Jewess* and *The Siege of Rochelle* would be mounted early in the season under the direction of Mr Yates, with Mrs Yates and Miss Betts from Drury Lane making guest appearances. Yates was advertised as touring with a magnificent wardrobe of costumes.

Prior to the season opening, on 30 May 1836 at Kensington church Mr J R Anderson manager of the Cheltenham, Gloucester and Leicester theatres was married to Miss Georgina Stohwasser of Ivy House, Richmond, Surrey. Thereafter, the personable Miss Stohwasser worked under the more mundane cognomen Mrs Anderson.

On 6 June, Belville and Anderson opened the summer season at Cheltenham without – according to the *Looker On* – the new scenery, machinery, dresses or decoration that had been promised on the playbills. The new company was not very new either and provided little to praise. In the opening play *The Poor Gentleman*, Mr Osborne was considered 'worth fifty times the wretched fellow who successfully murdered the Old

Corporal, one of the best characters in the piece'. Miss Crisp, a good actress and a local favourite, was taken to task for not dressing her characters properly, her version of the daughter of a half-pay officer being dolled up in white satin like a young countess on her wedding day. The opening night was but thinly attended according to the *Looker On*, numerous and fashionable according to the *Chronicle*. How can one believe what one reads from two centuries ago?

While awaiting the Yates and their splendours, a tenor called Fraser was engaged, and with support from Mrs B Penley – the only family member in the company – and bass Edwards, 'several excellent operatic pieces' were brought forward.

Mrs B Penley, not only to the fore in the company, also gave private lessons in English, French and Italian singing. Mrs B Penley was becoming more known for her vocal prowess than any attempt at acting, and her husband encouraged this by arranging concerts of music with other vocalists and musicians. These concerts were usually headed by Belville's brother-in-law Henry Field, an eminent pianist, as both Mary and her brother were constantly in demand in the region.

With genuine armour from Paris, dresses and banners from Drury Lane, and entirely new scenery, on 18 June *The Jewess* was – at last – produced. The audience was promised a grand parade of armoured knights, Grand Marshall, electors and ambassadors all mounted on fully caparisoned steeds. All this was under the control of Yates who was stage manager at Drury Lane. The play ran for four performances winning a rave review for Mrs Yates in the leading role, and eulogies for the magnificent spectacles of a gorgeous character that alone were worth twice the admission price. The only quibble was that whilst the horses 'armed cap-a-pie in complete steel' behaved remarkably well, the biped supers needed a little extra drilling.

Penley & Anderson 'impressed with a due sense of gratitude for the very liberal patronage they have hitherto received and anxious to retain the support and good opinion of the Public', for race week, which was actually two days, went on to present Monsieur Silvain the 'unrivalled dancer' – fortunately minus the louche Miss Parsloe – and Mr Dobbs the 'celebrated Comic Writer and Singer of the Theatre Royal, Drury Lane.' On top of these attractions the enterprising managers also booked Monsieur Hengler, artist in fireworks to royalty, to give a brilliant display of 'pyrotechnical wonders'.

In spite of the protestations of elevated taste, the opera of *Lestocq* was thinly attended on the two nights of its presentation, while Dobbs brought in the public with his original comic songs into which he cleverly inserted local topics. The next guest star was Goldsmid, a comic actor who had previously appeared during the winter season, but the houses were not very well attended. Then came Charles Mathews who had much greater success. Having spent some years as an architect apprenticed to Pugin, Mathews had only recently followed his famous father on to the stage. He soon made an impression; becoming the finest light comedian of the age, marrying Madame Vestris, and managing several theatres.

In September, Macready gave his Virginius to a good house and Hamlet to a poorer one, the so-called discriminating Cheltenham audience preferring Sheridan Knowles to Shakespeare. During his visit Macready was robbed of his watch, purse and other valuables by 'a scoundrel he had employed to dress him'. Macready was followed by Knowles himself with his talented and beautiful protégé Miss Elphinstone. Unfortunately, just as brother Montague was to find at Windsor a couple of years later, Knowles was not a draw. The *Chronicle* went to town using much of its lengthy review to castigate the public for not supporting this worthy actor and playwright.

When that regular favourite *George Barnwell* was presented, the *Chronicle*, condemning the play at great length, deplored its perennial popularity. The public seemingly never tired of the tale of the innocent young apprentice seduced by a prostitute using her whiles to extort money from the youth who gradually succumbs to theft and murder. Ostensibly written, on the lines of the *Rake's Progress*, as a warning to youth, the scenes of degradation as Barnwell sinks lower offended the newspaper's high-tone notions of propriety, and it declared the play should be banned from the stage altogether.

In October, the Penley & Anderson company split its resources to carry out a week in Gloucester, leaving Miss Crisp as the only player of worth in Cheltenham. This was for the Gloucester races, the regular season in that town being in winter.

Coming to its end on 25 November, the Cheltenham season had proved an up-and-down affair as regards business, or as the local paper quaintly described it, 'very much like "the uncertain glory of an April day" exhibiting more of cloud than sun'. The young managers' main problem was a universal one: providing special highlights in the way of guest stars and spectacular events left the remainder of the season in mundane normality which was not then supported. Also, as at Leicester, unlooked for competition came from Wombwell's menagerie and Batty's Circus who separately visited the town during the season.

When the benefits were held, Miss Crisp offered the currently popular *Othello Travestie* which was much deplored by the newspaper who thought this kind of low-class entertainment making mock of the Bard should not be allowed on the hallowed Cheltenham stage. The fact that Anderson played Emilia in drag cannot have helped much!

One of the rare gleams of sun blessed the benefit of Mrs B Penley which was a bumper, but the 'returns on the season had not been commensurate with the managers' efforts.' This sentence was recurring more and more in newspaper reports throughout the land and, though every manager was still described as 'spirited', it must have been getting much harder to remain so.

There was no Penley & Anderson autumn season at Leicester to follow, as the proprietors of the theatre had elected to pull the building down and rebuild. It must have been recognised that the twenty-five-year-old theatre had severe shortcomings but, as the venue had proved unprofitable for a varied number of managers, it seems brave to go to the expense of a brand-new theatre. Building had commenced in April, and the new premises would be ready for opening as usual in September, but with a new manager Mr Munro. As Penley had had trouble filling the seats in the previous building, it is oddly remarkable that the new theatre had accommodation for 1200. An innovation being that every alternate row of benches in the pit had a backrest.

Having lost Leicester, Penley & Anderson concentrated on a winter season at Gloucester which opened in December and ran until April 1837. The company relied heavily on Anderson, along with regulars Osborne, Hudspeth and Mr & Mrs Hunt. Mrs B Penley was not engaged. Having given birth to another son during the year, she seems thereafter to have eschewed the stage in favour of concert appearances.

The problem at Gloucester was the dearth of support from the local gentry:

> A lack of encouragement has by no means induced our managers to relax their exertions, and their efforts, backed by those of the company, have been really so meritorious that we have been quite grieved to observe the paucity of persons in the boxes during the past week. Even the productions of Shakespeare seem to have lost their wonted influence in this portion of the house. Henry IV was very creditably

performed, and Mr Anderson in Hotspur, and Osborne in Sir John Falstaff, received, as they deserved, great applause from a pit and gallery well-filled.

Anderson also gave his Shylock and Richard III during the season.

In an effort to attract the toffs, P & A engaged several guest artistes including popular veteran Mrs Nisbett, and provincial star tragedian Vandenhoff giving his Virginius and Lear. To tempt non-drama lovers they offered Four Celebrated Hungarian Singers in national costume, and Mr H C Cooper the virtuoso violinist pupil of Signor Spagnoletti.

All was to little avail as, on the last night – it also being his benefit – Anderson closed the season with this speech:

> This evening closes one of the most unfortunate and unprofitable seasons we have known since we commenced management . . . and I think you will be generous enough to allow that we have done all that Managers could do to prove we were most desirous to retain the good opinion of those liberal friends who so kindly supported us during our first campaign. The Theatre, which was unworthy to receive the patrons of the Drama, has been at a very great expense converted and improved, so as to place it on a scale superior to provincial establishments; all the novelties which could be procured, were in succession produced; all the stars that could be spared from their splendid stations in the London hemisphere, have appeared before you; . . . yet, with all our efforts, the season has been a most lamentable failure, owing, I must acknowledge, more, much more, to unfortunate circumstances, the unhealthy season, and the depression of trade, than to the want of your kind exertions in our behalf. Notwithstanding all our losses, . . . it is with unfeigned pleasure I inform you that we have renewed our lease of the Cheltenham and Gloucester theatres, and at the commencement of the regular season, next winter, we shall have the honour of again appearing before you. Ladies and Gentlemen, on behalf of my partner Mr Penley, the company, and myself, I beg to offer my best thanks, and respectfully bid you farewell.

It would be inconceivable that the partners should return to Gloucester, and they did not do so. Prior to the Cheltenham 1837 season P & A came up with the wheeze of a subscription system with 100 transferable tickets priced at three guineas each for the dress-circle, and two-and-a-half guineas for the upper-circle boxes. This would secure the lessees against certain loss and guarantee patrons a first-rate company. Performances would be on Tuesday and Saturday each week, curtain-up was now 8pm instead of 7pm – a sign that the upper classes were now dining later – and once again the hope was expressed that the spirited and persevering managers would succeed. Newspapers applied these two adjectives to theatrical managers *ad nauseam*.

The season commenced on 3 July with *The School for Scandal* but, after only a few nights' performances, in common with all theatres, had to be suspended for the funeral of William IV. The season closed on 18 October, the scheme, a ploy that other managers including old Sampson Penley had tried before, not proving successful. As the *Looker On* pointed out, Cheltenham had invested so much money, time and trouble on its outdoor attractions to please summer visitors that not many people considered going indoors to the Drama. Perhaps if the season were to be held at a different time of year it would have a right to expect better business. Throughout history to the present day, the time has never 'been right' for the theatre manager. An old anecdote tells of the manager looking out at his sparse audience at a third-rate East-End music hall and sighing 'It's the polo at Hurlingham.'

Anderson and Penley could not go on leasing theatres that they were unable to fill, and debts were mounting. On 4 September 1838 in the Court of Relief of Insolvent Debtors James Robertson Anderson and Belville Penley were jointly sued as managers of the Leicester, Cheltenham and Gloucester theatres with debts of £570 (£45,000 in today's money). On 28 September Anderson applied to have his insolvency discharged by claiming the 'benefit of the act'. While Anderson was in jail, a £23.15.2 debt due to him had been paid into the court for the use of his creditors. Anderson applied to retain some theatrical properties he possessed and, when asked the value, replied that he did not know. The lawyer for the chief creditor asked 'Are they worth £5, £10 or 10/-?' to which the insolvent replied 'More likely 10/-' which raised a laugh from the bench. The lawyer, presuming the properties were 'fine regal dresses', the court allowed Anderson to keep them as being of more use to him than anyone else, and the insolvent was discharged.

The Cheltenham theatre that had caused so much grief to the partners burned down on 3 May the following year, giving even more grief to the succeeding manager.

SCENE THREE
1838 AND AFTER
FAREWELL

ALTHOUGH SENIOR MANAGER, there was, strangely, no further mention of Belville in the insolvency proceedings and he headed off to Newcastle to his position as Box Office Manager, opening the 1838/39 season on 5 November for the currently more successful Montague.

Belville's erstwhile partner James R Anderson gained employment in Macready's Covent Garden company, firstly playing Florizel in *The Winter's Tale*, then going on to essay Edmund to the great man's Lear – though condemned for being 'showy and vulgar', 'superficial and melodramatic' and had 'an appearance of self-satisfaction that was particularly offensive.' Anderson graduated to leading roles including, amongst others, Othello and Iago, and was a popular leading man opposite Helena Faucit. Eventually becoming manager of Drury Lane in 1849 he relinquished it in 1851, citing the loss of thousands of pounds

James R Anderson

because of the Great Exhibition. Acting in both America and Australia, he was recognised as an actor of some distinction, with a fine speaking voice which deteriorated in his later years. In 1895 he was attacked and garrotted in a London street, dying a few days later at the age of eighty-four.

Belville did not bounce back so readily or so successfully as his former partner when he turned to assisting his brother Montague in his next venture – the ill-fated Lyceum season in which Mrs Belville Penley was a leading performer. This was a case of from frying pan to fire, Montague's season, as we have seen, turning into a miserable ten-day failure with meagre audiences and unpaid performers. Sticking with Montague, he and Mrs BP were engaged at Windsor for the summer season, where Rosina was also employed.

As Belville's experience as a theatre manager seems to have been entirely one of 'a beggarly account of empty boxes,' in 1841 Mr & Mrs

Belville Penley retreated to Mary's home town of Bath. Both Mary and her brother, having served in the Bath theatre company in the past, had a reputation amongst the musical cognoscenti of the area.

Mrs Belville Penley, no longer professing to be an actress, gained additional local renown as a principal soloist at concerts of sacred music, and was engaged regularly for such events. It is interesting to note that a typical one-night concert at the Bristol Assembly Rooms interrupts a week when all the other nights were taken up with Promenade Concerts *à la Musard*. The Bristol Choral Society admission prices were 2/6d and 1/6d with books of words at 3d each, whereas the fashionable and popular promenade concerts were only 1/-.

Belville's wife, the once fetching Miss Field, now looks permanently transmuted into the grand dame of religious oratorio. Although still only in her mid-thirties, the name Mrs Belville Penley conjures up – probably most unfairly – an image of a stout large-bosomed diva in a black gown and ropes of pearls. Her brother, Henry Field, a musician of distinction, had been pianist to the Emperor of Russia, and the two siblings held an annual matinee concert throughout the 1840s. These came to an abrupt halt in 1848 when, after 40 minutes of brilliant pianistics, Henry starting to falter noticeably, collapsed after playing the final note of Prudent's *Des Huguenots*. Coming to his senses under medical supervision, it was at first thought he had fainted through the heat in the crowded room, but some days later his symptoms worsened and he died.

Belville Penley, giving up all theatrical pretensions, became Superintendent of Baths. The census for 1841 lists him living at Hot Bath House, Bath Street, with wife Mary listed as a Professor of Singing. They now had four children: Walter Belville, Louisa, Florence and Henry. In 1842 Walter Belville gained one of three free scholarships out of seventeen applicants to Bath Grammar School. In 1843 the five-year-old Henry William Penley died, and a new baby Henry Montague Penley was born.

By the 1851 census the family was living at 18 Great Stanhope Street. Belville was still Superintendant of Baths, Mary still a Professor of Singing, Walter, now eighteen, a draper's assistant, and two further children – Frederick and Mary had been born. Mrs Belville Penley, née Mary Field, died in December 1855 in Southampton.

In 1857, Belville announced he had leased the Roman Bath and Hot Medicinal Springs in York Street, so was once again in management, though the famous Roman Bath was very different from the declining theatres he had previously managed. In September 1861, at the age of fifty-three, Belville remarried, his new wife being Emma Louisa Dutton, a lady of Bath some twenty-eight years younger than himself. They had one son Belville Sampson Penley who was born on 17 October 1861. Again Belville had managed to impregnate a lady well before wedlock. Two further children were born, and died, in 1863. Belville Jr became the editor of the *Bath Herald* from 1886 to 1925 and author of *The Bath Stage: a history of dramatic representations in Bath* published in 1892. W B Penley, credited with research for the book, was Belville's first born son Walter. Old Belville Penley was still alive at the time of the book's writing, so he was probably the fount of any research, but perhaps he was too enfeebled to take much interest as he died on 20 March 1893 at Bath, his second wife dying on 12 June 1904, also at Bath.

> The death of Mr Belville Penley, which has just occurred at Bath, removes an actor who had faced the footlights prior to the battle of Waterloo. On the night before the great engagement his father's company was actually performing in Brussels, Mr Penley himself playing a child's part, attired in a regimental suit given him by English officers. He remembered witnessing the entry of the victorious army into the city, and also a subsequent visit to the scene of the battle. Mr Penley belonged to a theatrical family. His sister, Miss Rosina Penley, was considered by Talma to be the greatest actress of her day. On many occasions she played the leading role with Macready in *Macbeth*.

EPILOGUE

I N SPITE OF THE most detailed research John Jonas remains an enigmatic figure. All we can truly say is that he lived and died, married Sampson Penley's sister, and became an actor-manager with his brother-in-law. His parents were possibly circus or fairground performers, he probably started his show business career as an acrobat and clown. In his youth he ran a puppet show at London fairs. Jonas remains a shadowy figure confounding the most diligent research. In some respects two or three of his offspring fare better, leaving a more definite place, albeit modest, in theatre history. All that is currently known about the Jonases is encompassed within the foregoing pages and in the additional chapter named 'Curtain Call' that concludes this book.

Sampson Penley is not as obscure, but his life and family have not until now been prised out of the gloom of history, and his chief claims to fame, long forgotten, once more remembered. His was the first English theatre company to tour the continent after the rout of Napoleon, and the first English theatre company to visit Paris since Elizabethan times. He successfully managed many theatres for nigh on 30 years before succumbing to financial ruin. He was a practical man of the theatre in all its aspects. A manager in Georgian times did not have a huge staff of secretaries, advertising men, photographers, poster-designing graphic artists and entire PR departments; much less producers, directors, casting directors, costume and lighting designers, movement and voice coaches, dramaturgs and all the rest of the modern theatre panoply.

Like all managers of the day, Sampson Penley had to lease theatres, apply for licences, arrange transport, engage artistes, contrive scenery, plan a different programme each day, cast the plays, arrange newspaper advertising, draw up playbills, get them printed, have them posted up, conduct rehearsals, be the accountant, and probably play a leading role in a multitude of plays. Often he had to do all this for several venues, simultaneously, in the days when communications were by horse-drawn coaches.

No doubt Penley's dreams were more grandiose than his capabilities, but the workload revealed is prodigious and, considering how much still remains concealed in the mists of time, we can only boggle at the versatility and sheer hard graft of the man.

The wonder is that he was by no means unique. The Jonas & Penley set-up was typical of the age, there were other families who toured their own particular circuits, procreating and training large numbers of children. Their theatres were much the same, the repertoires identical and business practices closely similar. Except to a handful of dedicated theatre historians all these are long forgotten. The light now shed on Jonas & Penley also illumines their colleagues and rivals.

Although strolling players had been plying their often unwelcome craft for hundreds of years, progressing only from 'rogues and vagabonds' to 'gipsies, tramps and thieves', it was not until the 1788 act brought, if not respectability, at least acceptability. Licensing by local magistrates brought official approval and decency to the provincial theatre. When circuits were established, enabling the various troupes of players to visit the same towns year by year, the managers and many of the personnel became familiar faces to the residents. Friendships were formed, and the growth and development of children noted each time a troupe paid its regular visit.

Although there was traffic of actors between the provinces and London theatres, as we have seen with William Penley and Sampson Penley Jr, they were poles apart; just as there was the huge gulf in the 1940s/1950s between the West End and the 'local rep'. In both periods the provincial theatre emulated the metropolis by copying London productions, inevitably losing much of the originals' appeal through lack of money, facilities and talented actors.

Yet for all its faults the late Georgian provincial theatre thrived. It was an industry. One estimate claimed there were some 8000 competent professional actors plying their trade throughout the country, with as many again scraping a living, though their abilities passed only a self-assessment.

Though within five years of the 1788 act the country was at war with France, continuing to be so until 1815, the period was a boom time for the theatre. Encampments of militia men drafted in from all over the country were assembled to guard the south coast against invasion, thus enhancing the permanent population of many towns. All these men sought diversion in between their drilling and military duties. The regular populations were thriving through increased wages which had risen by two-thirds and, in spite of war, social life carried on as normal with plenty of money around from increased harvests.

In the immediate post-war period, agriculture passed suddenly from prosperity to extreme depression. Taxes had increased during the time of war: the poor-rate had quadrupled, the county-rate had risen sevenfold, a property tax had been imposed on owners and occupiers of land, an extra tax on agricultural horses, plus war duties on hops and malting barley. These were bearable in times of record harvests and inflated corn prices, but suddenly corn prices plummeted. Thousands of acres of land went untenanted or uncultivated. Farms were abandoned by poverty-stricken occupiers, money was suddenly scarce. Going to the theatre became an unnecessary expense.

As business at many country theatres had been artificially increased by the presence of army and navy personnel stationed in their area, with the end of the Napoleonic wars, this element of the audience also promptly disappeared.

Agricultural distress continued for many years, with select committees trying to find ways to combat the deplorable farming conditions. As late as 1833, in spite of rent reductions, which in Sussex amounted to 63%, there was scarcely a solvent tenant in the Wealds of Sussex and Kent, and many farmers, having lost all they had, were working on the roads. Neither did towns escape this new poverty. Agricultural workers fled from the fields to the factories, flooding the market with excess labour at a time when owners were installing machinery that was making their workers redundant. By 1830, machine-breaking Luddites roamed the towns, and Captain Swing Riots set the country ablaze.

But through all, the actor still plied his trade. In the country theatres an unchanging diet of second-rate drama, relying on a great number of old war-horses, provided an entertainment becoming increasingly stale. Year after year, the same plays were churned out – *The Wonder* (1784), *Lovers' Vows* (1780), *The Stranger* (1798) were examples of plays all still in the repertory in 1855. The reader cannot but have noticed the repetition of play titles at all periods throughout the preceding chapters.

The circuit system collapsed and players no longer travelled as a troupe, isolated short seasons with actors specially recruited becoming the norm. Small theatres could no longer afford the exorbitant salaries demanded by visiting top stars, and the new generation of good actors was unwilling to work for the low salaries of their predecessors, resulting in a general lowering of standards in the market towns.

Mrs Holbrook, that purveyor of theatrical gloom and doom, claimed the falling standards were caused by the lack of the cultured intelligent managers of her youth. These had been replaced by despotic ignoramuses who crushed any initiative shown by their underlings. As in many fields, when a person gives up because his income has fallen, he is replaced by someone who is prepared to do the job more cheaply. Rarely is an underpaid newcomer equal in skill to a seasoned practitioner. Managers who attempted to fill the place of companies like J & P could only combat diminishing audiences by employing fewer and cheaper actors.

Audiences were no longer prepared to accept low standards in their own provincial towns, expecting their shows to equal the quality of the London theatres; though these too were also in decline. Whereas in 1765 Drury Lane and Covent Garden each had a nightly expense of no more than £70, by 1823 with the much larger theatres this had increased to £200, one reason being the exorbitant salaries now demanded by stars. A comparison offered in 1840 shows 50 years previously top names like Munden, Quick and Fawcett received £14 a week in London, J P Kemble the top star and manager of Covent Garden having the highest rate at £36. Now Kemble's successor Macready was on £25 per night. Liston the comic actor, who first appeared in London in 1805 at £17 a week, in 1823 received £50 a week, retiring twelve years later by which time his salary was £20 a night.

It was not only that the theatre had become moribund, society itself was changing. With the accession of Queen Victoria came a rising middle class respecting family values and strict morality. Backs were turned on the licentiousness of the Georgian era. Non-conformist chapels sprang up everywhere, many theatre buildings being taken over and converted for the new purpose. Where theatres survived, clergymen thundered against the sins of the stage, and being seen at a theatre could destroy a person's reputation for piety in a closed community.

Unlike their childhood days when the Jonas and Penley children spent their years going round a circuit of country towns of modest population, their adult selves were to be found working seasons in manufacturing towns such as Manchester, Newcastle, Glasgow, Nottingham and Liverpool, all places booming as generators of the Industrial Revolution with rapidly expanding populations. Only in these larger towns were theatres able to function, hardly thriving, but generally lurching from crisis to crisis, with local newspapers regularly bemoaning poor attendances. It was in these circumstances that Sampson Penley's children sought their living. Though practical conditions in lighting and transport improved, the vitality of the theatre waned with the same stale repertoire of hoary old plays dragged out annually.

To the old itinerant actor brought up in a world of stage coaches, the coming of the railways would have seemed a boon. But, with the network expanding rapidly throughout the land, it had the opposite effect. In the year Victoria ascended the throne, London and Birmingham were first joined by rail. In 1841, one Thomas Cook organised an excursion for 500 Leicester men to go to a temperance meeting at Loughborough. In 1844, the first day excursion ran from London to Brighton. In 1846, a new line was built to that sweet little village by the sea – Blackpool. The common man could now travel throughout the land at an economic price.

When Victoria came to the throne in 1837 it was not just another new monarch, it heralded a complete change to a way of life; upper class people even changing their eating habits so they dined later, and more lengthily, than previous generations. They were still at dinner when the theatre curtain rose.

The story of the Jonas and Penley families starts with the Theatrical Representations Act of 1788, and ends with the Theatre Regulation act of 1843. All through this period the London theatre world had been bound by the irksome oligopoly of the three patent theatres Drury Lane, Covent Garden and the Haymarket. With the huge expansion of the metropolitan population many other theatres had sprung up, but were unable to function on the same level plane as the three with their jealously guarded patents. By 1843 the minor theatres had virtually smashed through the regulations, putting on plays exactly as in the patent theatres, except for playing a chord on the piano each act, to claim they were presenting a musical piece. Equally, the patent theatres, in their desperation to fill seats, were resorting to the same melodramas and spectacles as the minor houses.

The abolishment of the patents at last officially ended the farcical situation. All theatres were licensed on the same basis, and all could present the same entertainments. However, new rules were also imposed, and one that would prove detrimental to the legitimate theatre was the banning of food and drink in the auditorium. As the straight theatre had declined, the song-and-supper room providing musical entertainment had arisen. As a result of the 1843 act, theatres divided into two distinct streams: either a theatre presenting plays, or a music hall providing light entertainment with food and drink. The majority of the populace favouring music halls, eventually great and grand buildings arose to cater for the masses. By 1850 there were 58 theatres in London, but 100 music halls; by 1854 there were 300.

But sadly there was no longer a place for the actors of the Jonas and Penley troupe.

AFTERWORD

THOUGH STRAIGHT THEATRE took a deep dip after 1843, it was not permanent, and the railways did eventually prove a boon to the provincial theatre, as complete tours of London productions replaced resident stock companies. A West End success could regularly be sent out on No 1 tours to the principal towns, followed by No 2 tours to lesser venues, and even No 3 tours to the 'sticks'. There were favourite stars who eschewed London, but pulled in the punters in the provinces. There were managements who specialised in buying the touring rights of the latest successes. The productions were mainly comedies, melodramas, period romances and frothy musicals, with only a sprinkling of Shakespeare and classics.

With the conversion of Belville to master of thermal baths, brother Montague into professional artist, and the retirement or death of the Penley sisters, the acting Penleys had long ago disappeared. However, there was a brief thespian flowering in a succeeding generation of the family into this later form of showbusiness.

William Sydney Penley was, by far, the most famous of all the Penley actors. Known as W S Penley he was descended from the son of William Penley of Drury Lane who married on Christmas Day without telling his family. William Jr had eight children the eldest son being William George Robinson Penley (1823-1902). This chap was adventurous enough to emigrate to Australia, but came back a year later because 'sheep were being sold at 1/- each'. Becoming a school master in Margate, he married in 1850 and W S Penley was born on 19 November 1852 at St. Peters, Margate, Kent. Four years later W G R Penley was yet another Penley dragged before the Court of Insolvency.

However, he must have survived all that as W S Penley was educated in London, where his father had a school, and studied singing at the Chapel Royal Choir. He was a chorister at the Chapel Royal and at Westminster Abbey.

W S Penley made his stage debut at the age of nineteen at the Court Theatre, and in 1875 was in the original production of Gilbert and Sullivan's *Trial by Jury* at the Royalty Theatre in London and on tour. In November of that year, after the opera had returned to the Royalty, he was promoted from the chorus to the role of the Foreman of the Jury. He continued in that role when *Trial by Jury* toured again and transferred to the Opera Comique late in 1876. Apart from this role, he played many others in light opera, including Sir Joseph Porter in *HMS Pinafore*.

In 1884, he achieved his first major triumph when he took over the role of Revd Robert Spalding in *The Private Secretary* from Sir Herbert Beerbohm Tree, and was famous for his portrayal for many years.

However, W S Penley's greatest success, and the play that ensures him a firm place in theatrical history, is Brandon Thomas's farce *Charley's Aunt*, claimed to be based on a true incident and specially written for Penley. On 29 February 1892, Penley produced the comedy at the Theatre Royal, Bury St. Edmunds, appearing in the role of Lord Fancourt Babberley, an undergraduate at Oxford, who impersonates Donna Lucia, his friend Charley's aunt from Brazil – 'Where the nuts come from.' The play was a success, and Penley then produced it in London at the Royalty Theatre in December 1892, after which it transferred to the Globe Theatre in 1893. *Charley's Aunt* became an unprecedented hit, running for 1,466 performances in London, a historic record that lasted for decades. The original run finally ended in December 1896, but the play was revived several times afterwards. Penley is said to have earned £200,000 from *Charley's Aunt* alone.

In 1900, Penley rebuilt the Novelty Theatre renaming it the Great Queen Street Theatre. There he did yet more revivals of *The Private Secretary* and *Charley's Aunt*, retiring from acting in 1901, but managing his theatre until 1907.

W S Penley died at the age of sixty at his home in St Leonards-on-Sea, Sussex after a two-month illness. His grave is in Hastings Borough Cemetery.

Author Brandon Thomas also made a fortune out of *Charley's Aunt*, it being constantly revived, and still performed to this day.

The Theatre Royal, Bury St Edmunds is of much greater importance than simply the theatre where *Charley's Aunt* had its debut and where Rosina Penley appeared in 1829 playing, among other roles, Lady Teazle and Violante. Built in 1819, it is Britain's only fully operational surviving Regency theatre. In 2007 it was restored, as closely as modern-day regulations allow, to its original state. The horseshoe-shaped auditorium, originally seating almost 800 people (now 350), is a prime example of the later development of the Georgian theatre such as the Penleys' Windsor building. It is a step up from the more primitive rectangular country theatre example provided by the 1788 Richmond Georgian Theatre. The third member of the extant trio of Georgian theatres is the Theatre Royal Bristol built in 1766. In constant use over the years to the present time, it has had considerable alterations to keep the premises up to date, whereas the former two both had long periods of closure when they were used as brewery storage cellars, thus retaining their ancient features.

MR. W. S. PENLEY.—"Charley's Aunt."

William Penley of Drury Lane 1773 – 1838
↓
William Henry Saulez Penley 1793 – 1866
↓
William George Robinson Penley 1823 – 1902
↓
William Sydney Penley of *Charley's Aunt* fame 1852 – 1912

CURTAIN CALL

THE CHILDREN OF JONAS

IT IS A MATTER FOR regret that the Jonas family is bewildering – to say the least. Compared to accessible material regarding the Penley family, similar record of the Jonases is practically non-existent. The name of John Jonas, brother-in-law and business partner of Sampson Penley, appears regularly on playbills of Jonas & Penley productions, but there is barely a newspaper review or any other source of information about him. As Sherlock Holmes might have said: 'Other than he acted small roles, played the violin, was a Mason and the father of many children we know nothing.' On baptism records of his children he described his occupation as musician, and his main contribution to the J & P productions may have been as a musician, music being an integral part of the Georgian and Regency theatre. But there is never a mention of musicians on any J & P playbill even when operas and songs are programmed. It was John Jonas who headed the troupe's foray into Europe in 1814 (during which time another Jonas child was born back in England) and, when Sampson Penley was declared insolvent, Jonas did not seem to have been involved financially, yet was in the troupe that attempted to perform in Paris. Although always named first in the partnership, Jonas seems to have had little to do with the management of it, but it is clear he often led the company in the absence of Penley, when more than one unit was functioning at a time. Such as has been discovered about John Jonas is told in the Jonas & Penley section ACT ONE.

Of John's many children there is even less to relate, as few of them took to the stage as adults, and references to them are all too slight to present a coherent narrative. This additional chapter is thus something of a round-up of nebulous mentions and puzzling questions in which your author ceases to be simply a historian, but donning the mantle of the afore-mentioned Sherlock Holmes, diffidently offers alternative solutions to the currently inexplicable.

John & Mary Jonas had ten children, the disparate towns of birth and baptism indicating the itinerant nature of the parents' calling. As children, the Jonases took their place in humorous dance items as the family troupe trailed round and round their venues. As they grew older they also played the inevitable pages, servants etc. However, only two or three of them carried on in showbusiness as adults, and it is these individuals that now occupy the attention. The principal ones are Maria, Joseph and Frederick, who take up the most of this section, but what is known of all the Jonas children is set out in order of birth.

Mary Jonas was born about 1788 which is a backward reckoning from her age stated on her death certificate, as a birth or baptism record has not been discovered. Like her sisters and cousins she took part in childhood dances in her parents' shows, but Jonas's eldest child does not seem to have been very prominent as an adult actress. She only comes into view around 1813 when she would be about twenty-five, but not taking important parts, these going to her younger sister Maria. Both Mary and Maria were included in the 1814 Brussels venture, as was their younger sister Esther. Mary was still acting in 1819 and 1820 as her name appears on some J & P playbills, but she may have retired from theatrical activity thereafter, or simply lapsed into obscurity. In the 1820s, her brother Charles Paul took a teaching job in Wells-next-the-Sea, Norfolk, soon becoming master. In 1841 she appears at his school as housekeeper. About 1842 they moved to a new school in Bungay, Suffolk where Mary died, of serious apoplexy, on 2 February 1847, aged fifty-eight.

John Jonas Jr born on 9 February 1790, baptised 29 August 1790 at Southwark, may have been a 'Master Jonas' as a child. If so, it was a rare occurrence and certainly John Jr never became an adult actor.

This eldest son became a professor of music and married Henrietta Rebecca Butler Cook on 10 February 1820. The couple had six children but only three daughters survived to maturity, the middle one being Elizabeth Gladman Jonas. She was taught the piano by John Field, a composer highly regarded by his contemporaries whose compositions are said to have influenced Brahms, Schumann and Liszt. Field is credited with originating the piano nocturne later popularised by Chopin. He does not seem to be any relation of Mary and Henry Field of Bath.

In 1832 Field gave a concert which included – amongst many celebrated singers and musicians – the debut of seven-year-old Elizabeth Jonas, who was singled out for especial praise. From that beginning Elizabeth achieved some prominence as a prodigy, being commanded to appear twice in one week before the royal family. Her father attended on her, remaining in the royal presence throughout, and Princess Augusta, always such a supporter of the Jonas & Penley seasons at Windsor, stood by the piano 'exhibiting the greatest approbation'. It was through the good offices of Augusta that the recital was arranged. The child was much caressed and nursed by the ladies during the intervals of her performances, and the king and queen received and parted with her in a kind and condescending manner. The king's equerry sent Mr Jonas 'a handsome present for the child' and, shortly after, parent and prodigy went off to Paris.

During the following year, a review of a charity concert at Vauxhall Gardens for the Dispensary for Diseases of the Ear extensively covered the star of the show Signor Paganini, several singers and 'Miss Jonas's performance on the piano' which was 'really astonishing for a child.' She supported Paganini again at Drury Lane when he gave his farewell concert, an event that brought a net profit to the star violinist of £250.

Some three years later, the *Morning Post* was still astonished by the musical prodigy:

> Drury Lane Theatre: Miss Jonas, a young Lady apparently about twelve years of age, performed Czerny's fantasia for the grand pianoforte . . . to say that Miss Jonas was tremendously applauded would convey but a feeble notion of the extraordinary sensation which she created. The members of the orchestra, as well as the hearers in front of the curtain, seemed astonished at the combination of powers which she displayed. The juvenile pianiste gave all due expression to the simple melody, and, in pursuing the ramifications and variations of the composer, she was never at a loss to overcome difficulties, however intricate, and to achieve points of execution however complicated. Her strength is equal in both hands, and whilst the delicacy of touch was particularly observable the precision in the rapid passages was no less remarkable. For one so young in the profession she is in sooth a player of surprising pretensions that would in no small degree put on their mettle many performers of note.

Truly a rave review! In 1836 Elizabeth became a King's Scholar at the Royal Academy of Music, which she left as an Associate in 1841. She taught piano from 1838 to 1850, but ceased public performances as she had become too nervous, and finally poor health caused her to play for her own and friends' amusement only. She died at the age of fifty-three in 1877 leaving £25,000 (over £1million in today's money) through wise investments.

Her father John Jonas Jr had died on 11 December 1868 aged seventy-eight, and is buried at Nunhead cemetery near Peckham.

Joseph Charles Jonas was born on 9 September 1792 at Rotherhithe, baptised exactly a year later at Bermondsey. Not to be confused with a younger brother Charles Paul Jonas, which is easily done as for some reason Joseph often switched his names around becoming Charles Joseph.

The earliest evidence of a stage appearance by Master J Jonas is on a playbill dated 24 June 1803 at Tenterden theatre when, together with Master Jonas (John Jr), Miss Jonas (Mary) and Miss S Jonas (Sophia), he performed A Dance of Negro Children in a plantation scene in the musical entertainment *Paul & Virginia*. The 'Masters and Miss Jonases' performed a comic interlude called *The Soldiers Triumph* at Tenterden in May 1805.

On 5 May 1807 he played Father Cleod in a comic pantomime dance called *The Caledonian Lovers* with two of his sisters and Phoebe and Rosina Penley.

Joseph does not appear again on any extant bills until 1813 when he came into his own during the Tenterden season, and now being twenty-one, billed as Mr J Jonas, appears on many playbills playing small roles, dancing comic dances and singing comic songs.

Joseph, now considered a fully-fledged actor, albeit still confined to minor roles, was also very much a solo dancer and occasional singer. After Tenterden, Joseph went with the rest of the company to Peckham.

Joseph was included in the 1814 foreign J & P tour unit that went to Amsterdam and Flanders. Although the company opened in Brussels on 15 August, curiously Joseph does not feature on any playbills until 10 September, neither is he billed as presenting any comic dances which may have been thought ideal for any non-English speaking spectators. Joseph's connection with the J & P company seemed to be severed after the continental tour.

An isolated press advertisement for 4 October 1816 at the Leicester Theatre announces *The Forest of Bondy* with the principal characters by Messrs Brunton, Elrington, followed by further names, then 'The Dances by Mr Turner, Mrs Turner, Miss Cranfield and Mr Jonas'. This must surely be our Joseph Jonas, although none of the other names have any connection with Jonas or Penley. Brunton is presumably the manager as there are also a Mrs and Miss Brunton listed, and Brunton is known to have been the manager of Brighton and other theatres around that period. A playbill of the Leicester Theatre of 17 October amplifies the presence of Mr Jonas, as he plays Blunt in *King Richard III* and Hans Molkus in *Of Age To-Morrow*, though no dancing is featured.

In 1818 Joseph joined the substantial Surrey Theatre company in

London where his sister Maria was a principal. Situated south of the river, the large Surrey theatre started out as a circus in competition with Astley's located nearby. Under Elliston it had become a theatre licensed for non-dramatic works, being permitted only to show opera, melodrama, pantomime, burletta (a musical play or farce containing rhymed lyrics and resembling comic opera) etc. Surrey shows usually comprised three or four separate works, some of which had large casts, so the actors were very hard working. Unlike the small country theatres such as Joseph was used to with J & P, changing programmes nightly, the Surrey tended to run the same programme in clutches of several nights, resting them, then bringing them back for a further session of several nights.

Joseph's roles were not principal ones, often only 'walk-on' characters such as a guard, cook, soldier etc. Joseph was kept on for 1819/20 and finally the 1820/21 season.

More intriguingly, during the 1823/24 season at the Adelphi in the pantomime *Doctor Faustus and the Black Demon; or, Harlequin and the Seven Fairies of the Grotto* the part of Pantaloon was played by Mr Jonas. This was a major production that had 37 performances between 26 December 1823 and 7 February 1824. It was then brought back on 30 March for a further four performances with a 'double company', meaning there were two Harlequins, two Clowns, two Columbines and two Pantaloons. Mr Jonas was joined by Mr Blanchard as the second Pantaloon 'who will introduce his admired Tea Kettle Duet.' Mr Jonas was then seen no more at the Adelphi.

No doubt this was Joseph Jonas who, as we have seen, was reasonably established at the Surrey in the years up to February 1821. After the disastrous foray with his father and Penley to Paris in 1822, no doubt he returned to pick up his staggering career in the lighter realm of the London minor theatres. Therefore, it is very probable that this was another fleeting glance at the career of the acting/dancing Joseph.

At Easter 1824 Joe was also in the pantomime at Sadler's Wells which went even better than the Adelphi by having a triple company of principals. Joe was one of three Pantaloons, the others being Blanchard again and Henderson. His theatrical career from then on is a mystery.

It is certain that Joseph married at Chelsea in October 1827, and in May 1828 his first daughter Susannah was baptised in Fulham. Joseph's occupation is given as 'fishmonger'. The assumption is that on marriage Joseph gave up the precarious life of an actor/dancer – possibly sustainable as a bachelor, but not a family man – in favour of a more settled conventional mode of life. However, on 24 October 1829 his second daughter Sophia was born; she was baptised on 1 August 1830 at Richmond, her father's occupation now being again 'comedian'. As Sampson Penley Jr had a company at Richmond theatre in the autumn of that year, it rather looks as though Joseph had taken up his profession again, joining his cousin's company. It was a very brief come-back.

In December, two unfortunate events rattled the Joseph Jonas family – the couple's first-born daughter Sophia died and was buried at Fulham, and Joseph was tried for receiving stolen goods.

On 1 December, Charles Joseph Jonas was remanded in Newgate prison indicted for feloniously receiving, on 23 November, 1 piece of silk, containing 30 yards, value 50/-, the goods of John Peters and Thomas Underwood, well knowing it to have been stolen. Apparently his wife had been shoplifting. Although the Christian names are reversed, this is the same Jonas who alternated professions between fishmonger and comic dancer. For unaccountable reasons, on several occasions Joseph preferred to use Charles first. Jonas must have been worried out of his mind, seven years transportation being commonly handed out for what today would be deemed trivial offences. In the event the question of guilt or innocence did not arise, as the case was dismissed because the prosecutor was unable to identify the property.

In August his first son was baptised in Fulham, and Joe's occupation is given as paper hanger, as it is on his second son's baptism in May 1837. In *Pigot's Middlesex Directory* of 1839 Joseph Jonas is listed as a self-employed Paper Hanger and he is one still when daughter Laura was baptised in January 1841. The census of June 1841 shows the family living in Fulham.

The couple had eight children, all baptised in Fulham, listed here by baptismal dates. The letters alongside indicate if Joseph was simply Joseph or Charles Joseph in the parish register, and his given occupation:

Susannah Elizabeth	18/5/1828	J (fishmonger)
Sophia Maria	1/8/1830	J (comedian)
Emma	6/4/1832	J (paper hanger)
Charles John	31/8/1834	CJ (paper hanger)
John Henry	7/5/1837	CJ (paper hanger)
Laura	22/1/1841	J (paper hanger)
George Ernest	22/9/1844	J (paper hanger)
Charlotte Elizabeth	25/1/1848	CJ (paper hanger)

Joseph was still a house decorator when he drowned falling from a boat into the Thames on 21 September 1856 at the age of sixty-four.

Sophia Jonas was born about 1794 at Kingston-upon-Thames, and again no birth records have come to light. In 1813, aged around nineteen, she is seen occasionally on playbills in roles such as Christina in *Ella Rosenberg* and a Singing Witch in *Macbeth*. Although not listed as part of the J & P company in 1814, she may have accompanied it on the continental foray, or been in the company the following year when it is believed it toured again. Although the date and place is not known, she married a merchant named Boudon, and two sons were born in Amsterdam in 1817 and 1819 which seems to indicate that she resided some years on the continent. During their adult lives, these sons spent time in Chile which suggests that Sophia's husband may have had a business there that his sons continued. Sophia did not return to live in England until old age, dying of senile decay and anasarka on 20 May 1883 at Finchley Road aged eighty-nine. She died a widow, leaving £1,600. 12. 1d.

She is very unlikely to have been the Miss S Jonas on the playbills of the Surrey Theatre in 1821 to 1823. That Miss Jonas remains an enigma.

Maria Jonas was born on 30 May 1796. Her baptism was on the same day as that of William Penley's soldier son George Frederick, and Sampson Penley's daughter Rosina – 14 December 1796 at St Nicholas Church, Sevenoaks.

From an early age Maria was recognised for her singing voice, the first indication of her singing a solo song being a playbill for 17 June 1811 when she would be just fifteen years of age. However, she was required to play acting roles too, and was Juba in an afterpiece called *The Prize* (21 June). Although some eight years younger than her sister Mary, and three years younger than her sister Sophia, Maria was the one who performed the most at an early age. The year 1813 was when the seventeen-year-old Maria blossomed forth, and appears on 14 extant playbills for that year at Tenterden.

When the company moved to Peckham she appears on many more playbills. Maria was included in the company which toured Holland, Flanders and France in 1814. In 1816 and 1817 she was one of the 'extremely good looking' actresses 'of full average merit and great personal attractions' at Valenciennes. As described earlier in the section on the Penley sisters, it was Maria's benefit – cancelled to allow Talma the French tragedian to perform – which caused such a flurry of protest and hot-air from Oxberry.

In his memoirs, Thomas Dibdin remarks that in 1817 he wrote a *petit pièce* called *Rather Too Bad* for Miss Jonas, a promising young actress. This was performed at Dibdin's 'own little theatre', the Sans Souci. Maria, obviously moving in London circles, was getting to know the 'right' people, but for the present she spent the summer of 1817 at Windsor, also joining the family company again for the brief winter season at that theatre. Maria Jonas, somewhat like Mary Field, was principally noted for her singing rather than acting abilities, and the Windsor press stated:

> we must speak in terms of high praise; her voice is clear and sweet, her execution scientific, and her taste correct. She promises to become a very pleasing singer, and to acquire a deserved rank amongst the eminent performers of the day.

While eminence may have been promising, more immediate promotion was definite, as Maria was taken into the resident company at the Surrey theatre. The manager Thomas Dibdin clearly had a predilection for Maria Jonas. The Surrey, one of the three large 'transpontine houses' south of the Waterloo Bridge, had a large following from the overspilling London population south of the river. However, as a minor theatre, it was not allowed to perform legitimate drama, but its audience preferred melodrama and musicals anyway.

Maria was engaged to play the part of Sophia Western in a burletta based on Henry Fielding's novel *Tom Jones*. This was a new production and much time, effort and money was expended in mounting it. It opened on 18 January 1818 and ran for the following five evenings:

> the principal feature of the evening, as to novelty, was the introduction of Miss Jonas in the part of Sophia Western. This Lady possesses vocal powers which would do credit to one of our first theatres, and we congratulate the Manager on an acquisition which will not fail to add to the already great respectability of the Surrey, and assist to render it a permanent scene of attraction.

The *Theatrical Inquisitor* added its own encomium calling Maria 'a young lady of rare acquirements in the vocal department, and possessing a voice of most sweet melody.'

Maria must have been pleased to find the London critics chimed in accord with the one at Windsor, and that other doors would open wide for her. The Surrey tended to play the same programme for a full week, but even long-running plays had breaks rather than a continuous run.

Therefore Maria, at that juncture only cast in *Tom Jones* at the Surrey, was free on other nights, popping to Windsor now and then to sing the odd song, and playing a bit part in *Macbeth* when Phoebe played Lady M, or in *Othello* with Phoebe as Emilia and Rosina as Desdemona.

Maria's next role at the Surrey was in another new offering called *The Three Talismans*, an Egyptian spectacle in which she 'sang with great taste and execution. She is a very valuable acquisition.' This had 23 performances by the end of April when her next role was Iris in a comic burletta *The Golden Pippin*. The comic trifle *Rather Too Bad* – which Dibdin claims he wrote for Maria – had 18 performances before she was plunged into her next major part.

How to Write an Opera was a 'Broad Comic, Terrific Extravaganza, in three acts, mixed up with much modern Magnificence'. The third act was a spoof rehearsal of an opera called *Anaconda*, in which Maria played the title role. Amongst the scenic delights promised was 'A Terrific Portrait of the Largest Boa Constrictor in the known World! Which will exhibit awful Proof of his tremendous Capacity to swallow even more than is set down in this advertisement.' This show also ran for 23 performances. In July, Maria's next role was Lydia Melford in *Humphrey Clinker*, a burletta based on Smollett's novel. On 28 August *Tom Jones* was reprised for the last time.

Maria was now a regular principal in the large Surrey company which comprised some 35 actors, 30 actresses and a band of 20, and she succeeded in getting a place in it for her brother Joseph who had been a colleague in the J & P company during 1813 and 1814.

There is something of a mystery in that during November 1821, January 1822 and March 1823 a few existing Surrey playbills list a Miss S Jonas taking inferior roles. The obvious conclusion is that this was Maria's sister Sophia who was three years older, and as a child had acted with the J & P troupe. However, Sophia does not seem to have had any sort of adult acting career, marrying a French merchant named Boudon, probably in Amsterdam, around 1815 when she would be twenty-two. The mysterious Miss S Jonas is completely unaccountable, as there are no other glimpses of such an actress elsewhere at any time.

Dibdin was forced out by financial problems in March 1822, and the theatre was taken by Watkins Burroughs – one of the actors. Maria remained at the Surrey until March 1824 playing a multiplicity of roles though, it has to be said, few were of the stature of her debut at that theatre. She then went abroad once more, playing with the English Theatre in Boulogne where colleagues included a Mr Penley (it is not clear which of the Penleys this was, probably her uncle Sampson on the rebound from his Paris fiasco) and that old J & P stalwart Mrs Beynon. Maria Jonas played the title role in *Rosina* which was in August, and Jessy (with a song) in *The Falls of Clyde* in October, so she must have spent some weeks there.

And there, alas, is all that is known about Maria Jonas. It is quite possible that she married whilst abroad, as did her sisters Sophia and Esther, or married somebody out of the theatre business on returning to England. It is even credible that she married a fellow actor and henceforth went under a married name that has not been identified.

Charlotte Jonas was born on 10 June 1799 probably at Folkestone, baptised 7 April 1800 at Folkestone. She appeared as one of the Ghosts of Murdered Children in *Macbeth* in 1813 with her younger sister Esther and a Penley cousin, and she was a Maid in *Deaf Lover* at Windsor in 1819. A paucity of playbills means we cannot add to these, and all that can be assumed is that she was, at least, still appearing with J & P, albeit in 'walk-on' roles, at the latter date. On 2 August 1824 she married an artist called James Urquhart who changed his name to James Barry, perhaps in admiration for the Irish painter of that name (1741 – 1806). Urquhart died at Croydon in 1852 at the age of forty-eight from Bright's disease of the kidney and anasarka, the informant on the death certificate being Joseph Jonas of Fulham. Charlotte died in 1889 at Finchley Road at the age of eighty-eight, leaving £76. 4. 3d.

Charles Paul Jonas was born on 18 August 1801, baptised 4 September 1801 at Bermondsey. He played two or three boy parts, including Fleance in *Macbeth*, with J & P in 1813, a year when the entire Jonas family seemed to be out in full force, but nothing thereafter. He took a teaching job in Wells-next-the-Sea, Norfolk then became master. In 1842 he moved to a new school in Bungay, Suffolk, then Yoxford where he was buried after dying at Ipswich at the age of seventy-seven in 1878.

Esther Jonas was born in late 1803 or early 1804 and baptised on 15 February 1804 at Henley-on-Thames. She performed as a child from around 1813 in small roles such as Julia in *The Soldier's Daughter*, and Gossamer (attendant to the Fairy) in *Forty Thieves*. She was only a ten-year-old at the time she was included in the Brussels season in 1814 playing several roles, in particular Prince Agib the young prince in *Timour the Tartar*, when a French critic enthused of her remarkable relationship with the audience.

There is no trace of Esther becoming an adult actress, but she may well have stayed on in Brussels as on 9 April 1829 at the British Embassy in Brussels, she married Henry F L Droinet, a pioneer of gas production from Rheims in France. The couple returned to Rheims, Esther dying in 1833.

Henry Jonas was baptised at Folkestone, Kent on 9 April 1806. In 1813, when most of Jonas's children seem to have been roped in during the seasons at Tenterden and Peckham, at the age of seven he played Alonzo's Child in *Pizarro*. It is to be hoped he was small for his age as Sampson Penley Jr playing Rolla would have great difficulty in emulating Kean, Macready and other stars who had been depicted in prints holding the infant aloft in one hand. This seems to be the only time he appeared on stage as a small child, but there is a newspaper advertisement for 1820 at the Windsor theatre for the play *Perouse* in which the Chimpanzee is played by Master Jonas. This can only be Henry aged fourteen, or his younger brother Frederick, more likely the latter.

Nothing further is known of Henry.

Frederick Jonas was born on 30 May 1809 and baptised at Tenterden on 18 August 1809. He was only three years old when his mother died and thirteen when the Jonas & Penley company was defeated in Paris, so he had little opportunity of learning to perform with the family company.

There is no sight of Frederick until he appears as a dancer and bit-part player at Kendal where the season ran from July to September 1830.

21 August Review of the company: 'Messrs May, Jonas, Benson, Hall and Edwards stand, with regard to merit, in the order they are placed. They are generally deficient in their parts – Edwards, most lamentably.'

28 August Review of the company: 'After a dance by Mr Jonas, (which by-the-bye he has *danced* often enough), the very laughable interlude of *Animal Magnetism* was produced.'

4 September Review of the company: 'Mr Jonas exhibits great improvement; he is becoming a clever little fellow, and goes through his line of characters with great judgment.'

A playbill for late in the 1830 season at Kendal features *Perouse* billed as 'first time here these eleven years' in which the Chimpanzee is played by Mr Jonas. The play may have been mounted because for the first time in all those years they have a suitable man in the company to play the chimp, viz Frederick Jonas.

But dancing and pantomime remained Fred's forte and in March 1831 he was with the two Ridgway Brothers, Mr and Miss Usher – all celebrated pantomimists – at the Liver Theatre, Liverpool. For Mr Usher's benefit, Mr Farnes 'will place a real donkey alive on the top of a ladder, which he will balance on his chin, without any deception.'

Fred is likely to be the Mr Jonas in a newspaper report of a theatre company at Bangor in Wales in September 1831. This is evidently a company new to the town that has fitted up the theatre at some expense for a short season. The names of the actors are totally unfamiliar and, although undoubtedly of a lower class of company than J & P, are described as excellent, always perfect in their parts and with 'no shifting to the side-wing, to catch the aid of a prompter.' At the conclusion of the Bangor season the company was moving on to Beaumaris or Holyhead. The newspaper suggested it might also try other towns in North Wales so that inhabitants could see drama at home without having to travel to Liverpool or Chester.

> The Poor Gentleman was most admirably performed. The scenes of dry humour betwixt Sir Robert Bramble and Humphrey Dobbins were extremely well gone through by Messrs Henderson and Jonas.

Humphrey Dobbins is a blunt-speaking valet appearing in two scenes only of the five act play, therefore fitting well with the small roles similarly assigned to Mr Jonas in the Kendal company.

In June 1832 he is reported to be dancing and playing Pantaloon at the Durham theatre where a new company essayed a one month season.

By 1834, Fred was at the Edinburgh theatre playing Pantaloon in the Man in the Moon, a successful pantomime starring the Ridgway Brothers that ran for 23 performances. There had originally been three Ridgways who played Harlequin, Clown and Pantaloon, but George had died at the age of twenty-two from 'rapid consumption' (tubercolosis) hence the need for a replacement. This was followed by another pantomime Aladdin which also had a good run, in which Jonas played the Son of the Vizier. Jonas stayed on after the Ridgway Brothers had left, playing various small roles including the Player King in Hamlet, Fag in The Rivals and Vintner in A New Way to Pay Old Debts, the season eventually ending on 1 June 1834.

September saw Fred with the Ridgway brothers again, this time in Dublin followed by other towns.

Fred and the Ridgways opened in January at Manchester. From 1835 to 1840 Jonas and the Ridgway brothers had regular seasons at Manchester and Liverpool with Mr J Ridgway collecting a bride along the way to complete the quartet by playing Columbine.

Fred Jonas parted company with his colleagues in 1840 when Mr T became Clown at Covent Garden, and Mr & Mrs J went to Norwich. Mr T was Clown at the Garden for four consecutive seasons, getting brother Mr J in on year three and Mrs J as well in year four. Varied actors played Pantaloon.

Further sightings of Frederick are spare indeed. For several months in 1841 he played small roles and danced at Manchester and Liverpool. He then disappeared until a report in the *Era* of a fellow actor's benefit performance at the Manchester Amphitheatre in March 1845, when he was described as 'an actor of considerable utility'.

In December 1847 the *Era* announced that the Dublin pantomime would have Mr Blanchard and Mr Jonas as Pantaloon and Clown. Tom Blanchard was a famous Pantaloon having appeared for years in most of the London theatres including Covent Garden and, as noted above, had in the past performed with Fred's brother Joe. However, this was Mr H Blanchard, presumably a son of old Tom, and in the event he played Clown to Fred's Pantaloon. After the panto ended Fred stayed on for a few weeks playing small roles and dancing.

That is all that can be pieced together from the available evidence of the career of Frederick Jonas – dancer, pantomime performer and small part actor – until we come to his death. This 'clever little fellow' and funny Pantaloon, no longer able to bring joy and laughter to the holiday children, died of tubercolosis on New Year's Eve 1853 in the workhouse at Brownlow Hill, Liverpool. He was forty-four years of age.

Mary Ann Jonas was born on 8 August 1814 at St Paul, Deptford on the day that her father John Jonas was playing in *John Bull* at Antwerp, and baptised on Sunday, 11 September 1814 at Deptford. A mystery surrounds this child because John Jonas's wife had died in 1812. The assumption is that he re-married, although no evidence of this has been found.

And there, alas, the curtain finally falls on all the Jonas cousins of the Penley family.

NOTES

ACT ONE: JONAS & PENLEY

- SCENE ONE

Mrs Penley's Company of Comedians based on *Life of an Actor* by Pierce Egan pages 197/198

Sarah Baker was from a family of fairground acrobats from *Theatre in the provinces in the late 18th and early 19th century with special reference to Sarah Baker in Kent.* Jean Napier Baker

The origins of Mrs Esther Penley are obscure Details of births, marriages and deaths of the Penley family are from *Penley Family of Gloucestershire and Sampson Penley of London* by Frank Hall and b, m & d entries provided by Laurie Jonas

the theatre at Henley-on-Thames information comes from *Under Two Managers* by Paul Ranger and from *The Well-Trod Stage* by Bill Port

Maidstone in Kent performing in a theatre belonging to Mrs Sarah Baker from *Theatre in the provinces in the late 18th and early 19th century with special reference to Sarah Baker in Kent* by Jean Napier Baker, *Taking the Town: a compleat and authentic account of the Thespian Activity in the County of Kent 1737 – 1843* by John Morris and *The Theatric Tourist* by James Winston

a twenty-one year lease of the theatre at Lewes in East Sussex from *The Theatric Tourist* by James Winston

Tenterden theatre information is from *Finding Sampson Penley* by Alan Stockwell

Mrs Baker's Folkestone theatre information regarding the Bayle theatre is taken from the Records in the Bayle Box at Folkestone Library/Museum

playbills from 1803 to 1813 The author has with Laurie Jonas collated a total of 225 playbills for the J & P company, major holdings being with Tenterden and Rye museums, the British Library and a private collector

Mr and Mrs Holbrook All Holbrook material is from *The Dramatist; or Memoirs of the Stage* by Ann Catherine Holbrook

- SCENE TWO

the Carnarvon Militia and the Montgomery Tenterden playbill 11 August 1809

William Henry West Betty from *Mr Dickens & Master Betty* by Alan Stockwell

a new theatre to replace the ramshackle from *The Well-Trod Stage* by Bill Port

The playbill was also used for extra announcements examples from actual extant playbills in Margate library

when the play is a 'bespeak' examples from actual extant playbills

resulting in the drawing of swords from *Hampshire Telegraph & Sussex Chronicle* 12 December 1803

an example of an actual Race Week from *Kentish Gazette* 7 & 14 August 1812

'have given more than usual respectability . . .' *Sussex Advertiser* 26 July 1802

Mr Moritz 'exhibiting several astonishing Deceptions . . .' from *Sussex Advertiser* 9 August 1802

Mr Saxoni the celebrated rope-dancer from *Sussex Advertiser* 23 August 1802

'A Grand Exhibition of Two Transparent Paintings' Playbill 24 June 1800

'a Grand Display of Transparent Fire-Works' Playbill 3 June 1807

There were other managements too Material on Kent managers and theatres from *Theatre in the provinces in the late 18th and early 19th century with special reference to Sarah Baker in Kent* by Jean Napier Baker, *Taking the Town: a compleat and authentic account of the Thespian Activity in the County of Kent 1737 – 1843* by John Morris and *The Theatric Tourist* by James Winston

- SCENE THREE

an example of an actual season is based on playbills of the Tenterden theatre. **A shocking accident occurred** from *Hampshire Telegraph & Sussex Chronicle* 24 Nov 1806

- SCENE FOUR

The history of the Faversham Theatre from *Theatre in the provinces in the late 18th and early 19th century with special reference to Sarah Baker in Kent* by Jean Napier Baker

The company was still there in June from *Kentish Gazette* 20 April 1810, 5 June 1810 and 6 July 1810

- SCENE FIVE

'A considerable expense . . .' from *The Monthly Mirror* Pg 395

The lease was acquired by Sampson Penley . . .this chapter is indebted to *Finding Sampson Penley* by Alan Stockwell and *The History of the Prince of Wales Theatre London, 1771-1903* by Richard L Lorenzen

'Sampson Penley Jr was spirited and interesting' and other press reviews from *Morning Post* 9 October 1810, 29 October 1810, *Morning Chronicle* 18 February 1811 and *The Times* 29 May 1811

- SCENE SIX

J &P attempted a season at Brighton from *Sussex Advertiser* 21 October 1811, 28 October 1811 and 9 December 1811

10th Hussars 'who conducted themselves . . .' from *Sussex Advertiser* 6 January 1812. Other Lewes information from *Sussex Advertiser* 13 January 1812, 27 January 1812 and 3 February 1812

his 'celebrated scene delineating Le Brun's . . .' from *Sussex Advertiser* 16 November 1812

'we heartily wish them better success . . .' *Sussex Advertiser* 2 November 1812

the celebrated performer the SIEUR SANCHEZ from *Sussex Advertiser* 15 February 1813

- SCENE SEVEN

Mrs Jordan is speedily to return . . . from *Caledonian Mercury* 11 January 1800

Owing to the imbecility of the play-folk . . . *Sussex Advertiser* 30 August 1813

- SCENE EIGHT

Many English settle among us . . . from *Carlisle Journal* 21 May 1814

'The British & Foreign Bible Society . . .' from *Stamford Mercury* 6 May 1814

The pioneering actors left on 6 May . . . the material in this chapter is indebted to *Western Popular Theatre (A Dutch Actor's Experiences with English Theatre in Amsterdam May – July 1814)* by Ben Albach, *A Shakespeare Season on the Continent: Brussels 1814 and its Prelude in Amsterdam* by Willem Schrickx in *Neophilologus* Vol 61 No 4 Pgs 619-640, *Booth Memorials* by Asia Booth Clarke and *Histoire du théâtre francais en Belgique depuis son origine jusqu'à nos jours* Olivier, 1878 – 80, 3:5-7 Brussels

'On his part, Sampson Penley sent . . .' from *Sussex Advertiser* 20 June 1814

A young prince has a big part . . . from *A Shakespeare Season on the Continent: Brussels 1814 and its Prelude in Amsterdam* by Willem Schrickx in *Neophilologus* Vol 61 No 4 Pgs 619-640,

'actually performed at Brussels the night before Waterloo . . .' from article by W R Pepper in *Era Almanack 1889*

- SCENE NINE

'The Company are gone to Windsor . . ,' from *Sussex Advertiser* 24 August 1815

Mr S Penley of Drury Lane . . . from *Windsor and Eton Express* 20 August 1815

'Instead of Shylock taking his pound of flesh . . .' the anecdote is from *Hampshire Chronicle* 19 August 1816

- SCENE TEN

The entertainment of *Rosina* . . . *Windsor and Eton Express* 25 August 1817

Booth had spent a period with Thomas Trotter . . . this information is indebted to *Junius Brutus Booth* by Stephen M Archer

'Mr Creswell stated that he had been present . . .' *The Times* 13 January 1818

losses may be made up by 'that future patronage . . .' from *Windsor and Eton Express* 10 January 1819

- SCENE ELEVEN

a new theatre in Coventry . . . this information is indebted to *Coventry's Forgotten Theatre* by Ted Bottle

The Masters of Eton, having discovered . . . from *Bath Chronicle* 1 July 1819

'It appears that clandestine performances . . .' The information in this paragraph comes from a letter to the author from Eleanor Cracknell the archivist at Eton College. There is a book *500 Years of Eton Theatre* by Michael Meredith

In the latter, the veteran Jonas . . . from *Sussex Advertiser* 3 January 1820

- SCENE TWELVE

'The Misses Penley, with the most profound respect . . .' from Rye playbill 24 February 1820

'a Comic, Heroic, Operatic, Tragic, . . .' from Coventry playbill 13 July 1820

The house was crowded . . . from *Windsor and Eton Express* 21 January 1821

- SCENE THIRTEEN

'in some degree compensate . . .' from *Windsor and Eton Express* 1 April 1821

'Messrs Jonas and Penley have wisely abandoned . . .' from *Windsor and Eton Express* 12 July 1821

The success of the season has certainly not . . . from *Windsor and Eton Express* 9 September 1821

- SCENE FOURTEEN

So long as the number of English . . . from *Morning Post* 20 September 1814

Thus in July 1822, when Sampson Penley sought to appear . . . The information in this chapter is indebted to the following sources: *Chroniques pour l'Angleterre* by Stendhal Vol VI Pg 260 et seq; *He Conquered France but Slowly* article in *New York Times* by Joseph L Bergerhoff 18 April 1918; *Memoirs of Henry Beyle aka Stendhal a critical and Biographical Study* by Andrew A Paton; *Le Théâtre Anglais a Paris sous la Restauration* by Joseph Leopold Borgerhoff ; *L'Histoire par le théâtre1789-*

1851: La Restauration by Theodore Muret ; *Du Marasme dramatique en 1819* by J-T Merle; *L'Album* 1821; *Almanach des Spectacles* by A-M Coupart; *France d'antan, Le théâtre romantique* by Paul Ginisty and *Theatrical Anecdotes* by Herman Drederick Johan van Schevichaven, Translated by Jacob Larwood. A more detailed account of the affair using these sources can be found in *Finding Sampson Penley* by Alan Stockwell

Barton was 'a man of peculiar but considerable talent' from *Dramatic Biography & Histrionic Anecdotes* by William Oxberry

We should rejoice that no British Actor . . . from *London Literary Gazette and Journal* 10 August 1822

Our readers will have perused with some surprise . . . from *Glasgow Herald* 12 August 1822

The Vandals have disappeared   *Trewman's Exeter Flying Post* 12 September 1822

- SCENE FIFTEEN

'an old actor, Penley, well-known in France . . .' from *Beaten Paths & Those Who Trod Them* by Thomas Colley Grattan Pgs 201-203

Boulogne English Theatre . . . from *Theatrical Observer* 23 September 1824

'almost the only thing not . . .' from *Library Chronicle of 1825*

ACT TWO: MR & MRS WILLIAM PENLEY

- SCENE ONE

Their Majesties and the Royal Family . . . from *The Times* 25 July 1797

featured 'new dresses and decorations . . .' from *Trewman's Exeter Flying Post* 22 January 1801

Mr Penley presents his duteous Respects . . . from *Trewman's Exeter Flying Post* 5 March 1801

After a long and, we trust, not an unprofitable . . . from *Trewman's Exeter Flying Post* 16 April 1801

Their Majesties honoured the theatre . . . from *The Times* 31 July 1801

'A Mr Penley in the character of a Merry Andrew, . . .' from *The Times* 3 August 1801

- SCENE TWO

'Dr Ollapod, Scrub, Tandem, . . .' from *Monthly Mirror* February 1804

- SCENE THREE

The successor to the lamented Collins . . . from *Hampshire Telegraph & Sussex Chronicle* 22 September 1806

WICKED FORGERIES from *Morning Chronicle* 26 September 1806

'Mr W Penley's Lissardo, in the play . . .' from *Sussex Advertiser* 29 August 1808

'Miss Gayton's admirable dancing . . .' from *Morning Chronicle* 18 October 1808

The late Drury Lane Company performed . . . *Aberdeen Journal* 27 May 1809

'the race ball, on Friday . . .' from *Sussex Advertiser* 31 July 1809

- SCENE FOUR

'The company was numerous . .' *Some Account of the English Stage* by John Genest

The humble petition of George Frederick Penley . . . The application paper for a cadetship by G F Penley is in the Public Record Office

'replete with nonsense and vulgarity, . . .' from *Some Account of the English Stage* by John Genest

Mr Penley as a sailor, Harry Hawser . . . from *Morning Post* 23 July 1813

he sent a further letter imploring to keep his job: . . . This letter was found by Laurie Jonas while searching for J & P playbills at Amsterdam University

Mr Penley (late of the Theatre Royal, Drury Lane) . . . from *Morning Chronicle* 3 October 1816

MRS PENLEY (wife of Wm Penley, . . . from *The Times* 9 September 1816

- SCENE FIVE

'all the popular, new and standard works; . . .' from *Hampshire Telegraph & Portsmouth Gazette* 5 December 1831

ACT THREE: SAMPSON PENLEY JR

- SCENE ONE

A Mr Penley made his *debut* last night . . . *Caledonian Mercury* 4 March 1815

Mr S Penley: This gentleman has been on the Stage . . . from *Biography of the British Stage* by Edward Cape Everard

Mr Penley, as Hotspur, has contrived to do away . . . *Theatrical Inquisitor* Vol 8

We never saw a theatre more crowded . . . from *The Times* 19 September 1815

The coxcombry of Mr S Penley . . . from *The Times* 8 November 1815

We think this actor may improve his performance . . . from *The Times* 7 December 1815

S Penley was the unprincipled servant . . . from *The Times* 2 February 1816

Towards the latter end of December . . . from *Morning Post* 9 April 1818

[The play] is one of the drollest . . . from *Blackwood's Magazine* Volume 3 Pg 83

Without any great abundance . . . from Saunders Newsletter 7 April 1818

The alteration performed on this evening . . . from *Some Account of the English Stage* by John Genest

a long and tedious scene between Lodowick . . . from *Blackwood's Magazine* Volume 3

'With the exception of Stanley as Plume . . .' from *Some Account of the English Stage* by John Genest

- SCENE TWO

At the conclusion Mr Penley appeared . . . *Morning Chronicle* 11 October 1819

Mr Penley offends us at all times . . . from *Theatrical Inquisitor* 1819

'one Hamblin, a wretch . . .' from *The London Theatre 1811-1866 Selections from the Diary of Henry Crabb Robinson*

Mr Penley's Aufidius was endued . . . from *London Literary Gazette and Journal*

Ultimately Mr Kean appeared . . . from Saunders's Newsletter 1 February 1820

The whole comic strength . . . from *New Monthly Magazine* Vol 13 Page 227

a storm of exprobation; . . . *European Magazine and London Review* Vol 77 Pg 60

it met with a decided and deserved condemnation . . . from *London Literary Gazette and Journal* Pg 61

'we cannot think that those . . .' from *New Monthly Magazine* Vol 13 Page 227

'the sound of the trampling of the champion's steed, . . .' from *Criticisms and Dramatic Essays of the English Stage* William Hazlitt 1851 Pgs 83 - 85

- SCENE THREE

'Mr S Penley, of Drury Lane, . . .' from *Theatrical biography: or, The life of an actor and manager* by Francis Courtney Wemyss

***Richard III.* Richard Duke of Gloster** . . *Theatrical Observer* 12 November 1821

'in such a style of throes as no man ever died . . .' from *London Literary Gazette and Journal* 1822 pg 75

'I always take a shag . . .' from *Drury Lane Journal Selections from James Winston's Diaries 1819 – 1827*

there was one very vivid and appalling . . . *New Monthly Magazine* 1822 Pg 107

There was one very vigorous description . . . *Morning Chronicle* 29 January 1822

Penley played the part of Jack Meggot . . . from *The Times* 16 April 1822

Mr Penley's playing Jack Meggott . . . from *The Times* 28 October 1822

'Mr Penley's Jack Meggott . . .' from *Morning Chronicle* 28 October 1822

'Mr Penley always looks like a footman . . .' from *The Times* 17 October 1822

- SCENE FOUR

'far superior to any ever before . . .' from *Windsor & Eton Express* 19 July 1823

'displayed the versatility . . .' from *Windsor & Eton Express* 6 September 1823

Of Thompson and Penley, in *London Literary Gazette and Journal* No 351 Pg 653

when he approached a small cottage *Windsor & Eton Express* 23 August 1823

'Mr Penley was also a very good . . .' from *Theatrical Observer* 20 February 1824

'Penley's Young Contrast was the essence, . . .' from *The Times*. 30 April 1824

The vacation of Eton College . .*Windsor & Eton Express* 4 September 1824

'The gay, the gallant Count Almaviva . . .' from *The Times* 25 October 1824

'Browne, Archer, Penley etc . . .' from *Berkshire Chronicle* 26 February 1825

'rendered it very effectively . . .' from *Theatrical Observer* 12 April 1825

'Mr Penley deserves our favourable mention . .' *Theatrical Observer* 25 May 1825

'Mr Penley played Cassio . . .' from *Theatrical Observer* 27 June 1825

We feel great pleasure in . . . from *Theatrical Observer* 29 June 1825

WHEREAS I, JOHN HEXELL . . . *Windsor and Eton Express* 27 August 1825

'When Booth declined to respond to . . .' from *The Era* 28 February 1885

'Cassio was personated by Mr Penley, . . .' from *The Times* 18 October 1825

- SCENE FIVE

Our Theatre has been opened . . . from *Windsor and Eton Express* 16 June 1827

'On the closing night of Race Week an unfortunate incident occurred . . .'
from *Windsor and Eton Express* 11 July 1829

I found a temporary engagement . . . from *Old Drury Lane: Fifty Years'
Recollections of Author, Actor* Edward Stirling

Our theatre will close tomorrow, . . . from *Berkshire Chronicle* 11 September 1830

We are fearful it has been rather . . . from *Reading Mercury* 13 September 1830

- SCENE SIX

'was not troubled with much . . .' and other excerpts in the paragraph from
Newcastle Journal 25 December 1830

7 January 1831: Penley's Windsor Company . . . from *The Journal of John Waldie
Theatre Commentaries, 1799-1830*: no. 42 [Journal 58]

The classical taste, spirit, and enterprise . . . from *Leicester Chronicle* 24
September 1831

Having introduced to the patronage of the town . . . from *Leicester Chronicle* 8
October 1831

'Penley's William was a faithful . . .' from *Leicester Chronicle* 15 October 1831

'Few weeks exhibit such a variety . . .' from *Leicester Chronicle* 15 October 1831

'On the 15th May, 1833, expired . . .' from *Nine Years of an Actors Life* Robert
Dyer, 1833

our Theatre, too, under the direction of . . . from *Morning Post* 13 August 1834

Two missiles, a stone . . . *Newcastle Journal* 21 February 1835

- SCENE SEVEN

displaying great powers; his . . . *Windsor and Eton Express* 5 September 1835

'Of Mr Penley himself he is the very *beau ideal* . . .' from *Windsor and Eton
Express* 12 September 1835

'their morals and manners . . .' from *Western Times* 29 November 1851

ACT FOUR: ROSINA PENLEY and her sisters PHOEBE & EMMA

- SCENE ONE

in England such a character is entitled . . .' from *Morning Chronicle* 11
September 1817. The whole issue may be followed via *The Times* 11 September
1817, *Morning Post* 12 September 1817, *Morning Chronicle* 16 September 1817,
Morning Post 18 September, *Morning Chronicle* 19 September 1817, *Morning Chronicle*
22 September 1817, *Morning Post* 27 September 1817, *Morning Post* 1 October 1817,
but more readily in *Finding Sampson Penley* by Alan Stockwell

and if applause may be considered approbation . *Theatrical Inquisitor* July 1817

'We have now a company of comedians . . .' *Theatrical Inquisitor* 25 August 1817

It is not often that the receipts of benefit nights . . . these were published at
the end of a lengthy review in *Theatrical Inquisitor* 25 August 1817 and as this
publication was written by Oxberry, one of the actors so blessed, he should know

- SCENE TWO

Miss Penley (daughter of the manager of the Windsor Theatre) . . . from
Bath Chronicle 29 October 1818

Miss Penley has played in *Three Weeks After Marriage* . . . from *Bath Chronicle* 11 November 1818

'Miss Penley represented the young Lady . . .' from *Bath Chronicle* 31 December 1818

- SCENE THREE

'those talents which on former . . .' *Windsor and Eton Express* 21 January 1821

'deserves to be distinguished by a spiritual . . .' from *The Mirror* (French)

Miss R Penley has shown a genuine sensitivity, . . . from *The Mirror* (French)

- SCENE FOUR

'So that Macready is not unjustly maligned . . .' from *Aris's Birmingham Gazette* 28 August 1826

'respectability of private character . . .' from *Leeds Intelligencer* 26 August 1830

'A handkerchief to hide your grief, . . .' from *Hull Packet* 28 January 1825

- SCENE FIVE

'most effectively and judiciously performed . . .' from *Morning Post* 24 November 1824 quoting *Cheltenham Journal*

Our previous impressions of Miss R Penley . . . from *The Times* 22 November 1826 quoting *Cheltenham Herald*

Sarah Smith, pantomime artiste . . . Postman's Park (on St Martin's Le Grand, London, a short distance north of St Paul's cathedral) houses the Memorial to Heroic Self Sacrifice commemorating ordinary people who died while saving the lives of others and who might otherwise be forgotten. It was founded by the Victorian artist George Frederic Watts in the form of individual ceramic tablets.

The Mrs Subtle of Miss Penley . . . from *Cheltenham Chronicle* 31 May 1827

'Phoebe is fobbed off with . . .' from *Cheltenham Chronicle* 20 September 1827

'those very estimable ladies, . . .' from *Coventry Herald* 7 March 1828

'these Ladies still retain their . . .' from *Coventry Herald* 14 March 1828

Coventry Theatre: We understand that Mr Aylmer *Coventry Herald* 9 May 1828

The native inhabitants . . . from The Channel Islands: Jersey, Guernsey, Alderney, etc. by Henry D Inglis

- SCENE SIX

Miss E Penley was by no means so happy . . . from *Trewman's Exeter Flying Post* 12 March 1829

The Youthful Queen, a new piece . . . from *Western Times* 14 March 1829

Miss Penley poured all her energy . . . from *Trewman's Exeter Flying Post* 19 March 1829

'the character is among the strongest . . .' from *Trewman's Exeter Flying Post* 16 April 1829

Master Wieland, who plays the monkey . . . from *Windsor & Eton Express* 19 April 1828

'gold laced unmentionables and . . .' *Exeter & Plymouth Gazette* 9 May 1829

From the few opportunities . . . from *Windsor & Eton Express* 22 August 1829

'we certainly cannot speak in praise . . .' from *Bury & Norwich Post* 11 November 1829

'we have seldom seen these difficult . . .' from *Cheltenham Chronicle* 2 July 1829

We cannot pass over the dramatic amusements . . . from *Cheltenham Chronicle* 6 August 1829

I had an opportunity to . . . *Nine Years of an Actor's Life* by Robert Dyer Pg 124

Having had frequent opportunities . . . *Cheltenham Chronicle* 19 November 1829

On Friday last, the theatre was respectably patronised . . . *Cheltenham Chronicle* 26 November 1829

spoken by that clever and most popular . . . *Liverpool Mercury* 23 April 1830

'E J Parsloe, who must have been some kin . . .' from *Gentleman's Magazine* Vol 268 1890

'seems to have produced its effect for she wants natural ease, . . .' from *Leeds Intelligencer* 3 June 1830

Miss Penley. – We perceive our old favourite, . . . from *Leeds Intelligencer* 26 August 1830

But have I not a word for the gentle . . . from *Leeds Intelligencer* 24 June 1830

'graceful in his action . . .' from *Hull Packet* 23 November 1830 plus other quotations in the paragraph from same source

'the music, throughout, . . .' from *Hull Packet* 23 November 1830

- SCENE SEVEN

'We like Miss Penley's performance . . .' from *Caledonian Mercury* 2 April 1831

in two instances, in the gambling-scene . . . *Yorkshire Gazette* 9 April 1831

With regard to Miss Penley we . . . from *Berkshire Chronicle* 10 September 1831

'approached to perfection . . .' from *Leicester Chronicle* 15 October 1831

The pageant is very cleverly got up. . . . from *Hull Packet* 15 November 1831

We beg to remind our readers . . . from *Hull Packet* 13 December 1831

'a character in which that young lady . . .' from *Liverpool Mercury* 6 January 1832

- SCENE EIGHT

'Mr Anderson is an actor of . . .' from *Leicester Journal* 13 September 1833

Miss Penley, from Newcastle, . . . from *Caledonian Mercury* 10 October 1833

Our new tragedian, Mr Stuart . . . from *Caledonian Mercury* 31 October 1833

Indeed if our theatre amusements . . . from *Caledonian Mercury* 31 October 1833

'and a very pretty face she has . . .' from *Newcastle Journal* 14 December 1833

'respectable company' which 'produced . . .' *Reading Mercury* 22 June 1835

'We think we never saw *Othello* . . .' from *Berkshire Chronicle* 15 August 1835

'Miss Penley's personation of . . .' *Windsor and Eton Express* 5 September 1835

'took a benefit on which occasion . . .' from *Windsor and Eton Express* 5 September 1835

This lady possesses talents of not ordinary kind . . . from *Windsor and Eton Express* 12 September 1835

Miss Penley's style of acting . . . from *Newcastle Journal* 26 December 1835

'nothing could be more discreditable . . .' *Newcastle Journal* 26 December 1835

who has been so many years before . . . from *Newcastle Journal* 14 May 1836

- SCENE NINE

the most perfect specimen we . . . from *Newcastle Journal* 24 February 1837

'performed with much judgment; and . . .' *Newcastle Journal* 19 January 1838

The gradual fading away of disappointed vanity . . . from *Northern Liberator* 20 January 1838

'The expense in bringing out this piece . . .' and rest of paragraph from *Northern Liberator* 10 February 1838

'an excellent piece of performance . . .' from *Windsor and Eton Express* 28 December 1839

MISS R PENLEY.– This well known and much respected . . . from *Windsor and Eton Express*, 25 January 1840

'this young lady must throw . . .' from *Theatrical Observer* 4 March 1840

'if her friends lead her to think . . .' from *Theatrical Observer* 18 March 1840

'But what could have induced . . .' from *Theatrical Observer* 24 March 1840

'we may fearlessly avouch . . .' from *Theatrical Observer* 24 March 1840

We observed none of the Parisian nonsense . . . from *Morning Chronicle* 11 April 1840

- SCENE TEN

'those two gentlemen well and ably ' *Windsor and Eton Express* 7 August 1841

Her high talent in the histrionic art is . . . *Berkshire Chronicle* 7 August 1841

'We were glad to see our old friend Dodd . . .' *Berkshire Chronicle* 7 August 1841

Miss Penley has been indefatigable in . . . from *Bucks Herald* 28 August 1841

many estimable and conscientious persons . . . from *Bath Chronicle* 2 December 1841

Rosina was praised for her natural morality . . . from *Liverpool Mercury* 23 April 1830; *Leeds Intelligencer* 26 August 1830; *Caledonian Mercury* 3 October 1833; *Coventry Herald* 9 May 1828; *Newcastle Journal* 14 May 1836

'highly respectable audience had . . .' *West Kent Guardian* 15 February 1851

'Miss Penley, who was connected . . .' from *The Bath stage: a history of dramatic representations in Bath* by Belville S Penley

ACT FIVE: MONTAGUE PENLEY

- SCENE TWO

'The effect when lighted up . . .' from *Windsor and Eton Express* 24 July 1824

'Exterior of the Palace and Fort . . .' *Windsor and Eton Express* 7 August 1824

The dresses appear to be the . . . from *Windsor and Eton Express* 30 July 1825

We cannot conceive the reason . . . *Windsor and Eton Express* 6 August 1825

'The melodrama of *The Miller and his Men* has been submitted . . .' from *Windsor and Eton Express* 9 September 1826

'*Paul Pry* made his last intrusion . . .' from *Windsor and Eton Express* 9 September 1826

'Long Tom Coffin stood forth the favourite . . .' from *Windsor and Eton Express* 9 September 1826

'We recognise among many names . . .' *Windsor and Eton Express* 2 June 1827

'Montague Penley cannot enter on . . .' *Windsor and Eton Express* 16 Dec 1826

'those young gentlemen who may wish . .' *Windsor and Eton Express* 7 July 1827

- SCENE THREE

THEATRE ROYAL, NEWCASTLE . . . *Newcastle Journal* 5 December 1835

The staircase of the latter is far from . . . from *Public buildings: The Theatre Royal, Historical Account of Newcastle-upon-Tyne: Including the Borough of Gateshead* (1827), pp. 229-231.

'Considering the rapidity . . .' from *Newcastle Journal* 24 February 1837

'Mr Younge's talents as a Tragedian . . .' from *Brighton Patriot* 7 March 1837

It would be improper as well as . . . from *Newcastle Journal* 25 February 1837

'Despite the "damning with faint . . .' from *Newcastle Journal* 25 March 1837

'The celebrated diorama of the town of Majuri . . .' from *Newcastle Journal* 13 May 1837

'to justify your Conduct, . . .' from *Newcastle Courant* 2 June 1837

I trust the public will consider . . . from *Newcastle Courant* 9 June 1837

'in consequence of unexpected Impediments . . .' *Newcastle Journal* 3 June 1837

'Mr Penley should be careful in . . .' from *Northern Liberator* 11 November 1837

'it was a pity to find such . . .' from *Newcastle Journal* 15 December 1837

'The expense in bringing out . . .' from *Northern Liberator* 10 February 1838

Our theatre has never been opened *Windsor and Eton Express* 8 September 1838

We heartily congratulate him on his . . . *Berkshire Chronicle* 15 September 1838

'On Monday evening, Mr Penley . . .' from *The Examiner* 30 December 1838

- SCENE FOUR

'we hope ere long to find . . .' from *The Operative* 16 December 1838

'choosing rather to pay her . . .' from *The Charter* 10 February 1839

'the peculiar adventures which befell . . .' from *Odd Fellow* 30 March 1839

a set of performers that, with . . . from *The Examiner* April 1839

a company, save with a few exceptions . . . from *Odd Fellow* 6 April 1839

an almost entire company new . . . from *The Operative* 7 April 1839

To introduce almost an . . . from *The Era* 7 April 1839

'being thrown open to . . .' from *Theatrical Observer* 9 April 1839

The want of public patronage . . . from *The Era* 21 April 1839

- SCENE FIVE

The Windsor Theatre Royal opened . . . *Windsor and Eton Express* 30 May 1839

Penley, a provincial manager of experience. . . *The Stage Life of Mrs Stirling* by Percy Allen

We cannot, however, allow this opportunity . . . *Newcastle Journal* 29 June 1839

I beg to address a few Lines to you . . . from *Newcastle Courant* 15 November 1839

'Every care has been taken to render . . .' from *Windsor and Eton Express* 14 December 1839

The height of the skeleton . . . from *The History of the Life of Jonathan Wild* Henry Fielding, London 1840

'£20 in the present state of theatricals . . .' *Morning Herald* 31 December 1839

The performance of the piece went . . . from *Windsor and Eton Express* 4 January 1840

'The Windsor Theatre was compelled . . .' *Theatrical Observer* 23 January 1840

We were sorry to observe so thin a house . . . from *Windsor and Eton Express* 18 January 1840

'by far the best house of the present . . .' from *Windsor and Eton Express* 18 January 1840

'calculated that Mr Penley would . . .' from *Reading Mercury* 18 January 1840

'The house was moderately well attended . . .' from *Bucks Herald* 20 June 1840

The whole of the performances this week . . . from *Windsor and Eton Express* 8 August 1840

'Windsor Theatre: On Thursday . . .' from *Theatrical Observer* 26 August 1840

The season, we are glad to say . . . from *Windsor and Eton Express* 5 Sept 1840

ACT SIX: MR & MRS BELVILLE PENLEY

- SCENE ONE

'although Miss Field's eyes seemed . . .' *Leicester Journal* 16 September 1831

'Miss Field had not a fair scope . . .' from *Leicester Chronicle* 24 September 1831

In the entertainment of *Rosina* . . . from *Theatrical Observer* 13 October 1831, other excerpts in this paragraph from *Theatrical Observer* 15 October 1831, *Theatrical Observer* 27 October 1831 and *Theatrical Observer* 4 November 1831

We would recommend a certain lady . . . *Theatrical Observer* 18 January 1832

'Mrs B Penley should rather call on *Lucina* . . .' from *Morning Post* 6 May 1832

- SCENE TWO

'from its smell and smoke, has . . .' from *Leicester Journal* 30 August 1833

Messrs Penley and Anderson whose labours . . . from *Leicester Journal* 6 December 1833

'the great pecuniary loss sustained by . . .' *Leicester Journal* 5 September 1834

Miss Field, a favourite during her former . . . *Leicester Journal* 6 September 1834

'On descending the hill at Barnet . . .' from *Coventry Herald* 25 January 1828

'Dear Lee, What day do I . . .' from *Kean* by Giles Playfair Pg 305

'with much taste, this Lady's . . .' from *Leicester Journal* 12 September 1834

The piece was performed passably well . . . from *Leicester Chronicle* 20 September 1834

Miss Parsloe whose dancing is of the first order . . . from *Leicester Journal* 12 September 1834

'with that taste and feeling which invariably . . .' from *Leicester Journal* 24 October 1834

'Mrs Penley was tolerably good . . .' from *Leicester Chronicle* 24 October 1834

Mr B Penley, the senior Manager, . . . from *Leicester Chronicle* 1 November 1834

Her efforts have been extremely well received . . . from *Bath Chronicle* 12 February 1835

a bumper turn-out on several grounds . . . from *Cheltenham Looker On* 18 February 1836

Having learnt by experience that cheap admission . . . from *Cheltenham Chronicle* 26 May 1836

'worth fifty times the wretched fellow . . .' *Cheltenham Looker On* 11 June 1836

Mrs Belville Penley has announced her . . . *Cheltenham Chronicle* 2 June 1836

'very much like "the uncertain glory . . .' *Cheltenham Chronicle* 27 October 1836

A lack of encouragement has by no means . . . from *Gloucester Journal* 25 February 1837

This evening closes one of . . . from *Gloucester Journal* 29 April 1837

- SCENE THREE

The death of Mr Belville Penley, . . . from *Manchester Courier* 1 April 1893

BOOKS CONSULTED

For dates and casts of Drury Lane, Covent Garden and contemporary comments I have relied mainly on volumes of bound copies of the magazine *Theatrical Observer* and *Some Account of the English Stage* by John Genest. For much of the information about Jonas & Penley's theatres in the south-east I have gone to two unpublished works:

Baker, Jean Napier *Theatre in the provinces in the late 18th and early 19th century with special reference to Sarah Baker in Kent.* A thesis at the University of Kent 2000.

Morris, John *Taking the Town: a compleat and authentic account of the Thespian Activity in the County of Kent 1737 – 1843* A thesis in the V & A theatre collection

From the many published book sources consulted, the following have been the most useful, others are included in the footnotes. STR refers to books published by The Society for Theatre Research.

Allen, Percy *The Stage Life of Mrs Stirling* T F Unwin & Co, London 1922

Archer, Stephen M *Junius Brutus Booth* Southern Illinois University Press 2010

Bottle, Ted *Coventry's Forgotten Theatre* Badger Press, Westbury 2004

Broadbent R J *Annals of the Liverpool Stage* E Howell, Liverpool 1908

Burwick, Fredk, *The Journal of John Waldie Theatre Commentaries, 1799-1830*: University of California 2008

Clarke, Asia Booth *Booth Memorials* Carleton, New York 1866

David Mayer & K Richards (Eds) *Western Popular Theatre* Methuen, London 1975

Denning, Anthony and Ranger, Paul *Theatre in the Cotswolds* STR London 1993

Dibdin, Thomas *The reminiscences of Thomas Dibdin, of the Theatres Royal, Covent Garden, Drury Lane, Haymarket etc,* London 1827

Donaldson, Walter *Recollections of An Actor* J Maxwell & Co, London 1865

Dyer, Robert, *Nine Years of an Actor's Life,* Longman, Rees, Orme, Brown, & Co. London 1833

Egan, Pierce, *Life of an Actor* D Appleton & Co, New York 1904

Era Almanack 1889

Everard, Edward Cape *Biography of the British Stage*

Frost, Thomas, *The Old Showmen & the Old London Fairs* Tinsley Bros, London 1874

Garlick, Görel *To Serve the Purpose of the Drama: The Theatre Designs and Plays of Samuel Beazley 1786-1851* STR London 2003

Genest, John *Some Account of the English Stage* H E Carrington, London 1832

Grattan, Thomas Colley *Beaten Paths & Those Who Trod Them* Chapman & Hall, London 1862

Hall, Frank *Penley Family of Gloucestershire and Sampson Penley of London* 2006

Hazlitt, William *Criticisms and Dramatic Essays of the English Stage* G Routledge & Co, London 1851

Holbrook, Ann Catherine *The Dramatist; or Memoirs of the Stage* Martin & Hunter, Birmingham 1809

Hunt, Leigh *Dramatic Essays* edited by William Archer and R.W.Lowe, W Scott, London 1894

Inglis, Henry D *The Channel Islands: Jersey, Guernsey, Alderney, etc.*

Knight, Charles *Passages of a Working Life during Half a Century* Knight & Co, London 1873

Knight, William G *A Major London Minor: The Surrey Theatre* STR London 1997

Mackenzie, Eneas *Historical Account of Newcastle-upon-Tyne: Including the Borough of Gateshead* 1827

Macready, W C & J C Trewin, *The Journal of W C Macready* Longmans, Green & Co, London 1967

Murray, Christopher *Robert William Elliston, Manager* STR London 1975

Oxberry, William *Dramatic Biography & Histrionic Anecdotes* Vol II & III George Virtue, London

Penley, Belville S *The Bath stage: a history of dramatic representations in Bath* W Lewis, London 1892

Playfair, Giles *Kean* Columbus Books, London 1988

Port, Bill *The Well-Trod Stage* Robinswood 2005

Prince Hermann von Puckler-Muskau *Travels of a German Prince* 1832 R Griffin, Glasgow 1848

Ranger, Paul *Under Two Managers* STR London 2001

Raymond, George *Memoirs of Robert William Elliston* J Mortimer, London 1844

Rede, Leman Thomas *The Road to the Stage* Joseph Smith, London 1827

Robinson, Henry Crabb *The London Theatre 1811-1866 Selections from the Diary of Henry Crabb Robinson* STR London 1966

Rosenfeld, Sybil *The York Theatre* STR London 2001

Stirling, Edward *Old Drury Lane: Fifty Years' Recollections of Author, Actor, and Manager* Chatto & Windus, London 1881

Stockwell, Alan *Finding Sampson Penley* Vesper Hawk 2012

Stockwell, Alan *Mr Dickens & Master Betty* Vesper Hawk 2010

Wemyss, Francis Courtney *Theatrical biography: or, The Life of an Actor and Manager* R Griffin, Glasgow 1848

Winston, James *Drury Lane Journal: Selections from James Winston's Diaries 1819 –1827* STR London 1966

Winston, James *The Theatric Tourist* 1805 STR/British Library Reprint London 2008

NEWSPAPERS AND JOURNALS

Aberdeen Journal   *Bath Chronicle*   *Berkshire Chronicle*

Blackwood's Magazine   *Bucks Herald*   *Bury & Norwich Post*

Caledonian Mercury   *Cheltenham Chronicle*   *Cheltenham Looker On*

Coventry Herald   *European Magazine and London Review*

Exeter & Plymouth Gazette   *Glasgow Herald*

Gloucester Journal   *Hampshire Telegraph & Sussex Chronicle*

Hull Packet   *Kentish Gazette*   *Leeds Intelligencer*

Leicester Chronicle   *Leicester Journal*   *Liverpool Mercury*

London Literary Gazette and Journal   *Manchester Courier*

Morning Chronicle   *Morning Herald*   *Morning Post*

New Monthly Magazine   *Newcastle Courant*   *Newcastle Journal*

Northern Liberator   *Odd Fellow*   *Reading Mercury*

Sussex Advertiser   *The Charter*   *The Era*

The Examiner   *The Mirror* a French newspaper

The Monthly Mirror   *The Operative*   *The Times*

Theatrical Inquisitor   *Theatrical Observer*   *West Kent Guardian*

Trewman's Exeter Flying Post   *Western Times*

Windsor and Eton Express   *Yorkshire Gazette*

ILLUSTRATIONS

Back Cover: A Scene from *A New Way to Pay Old Debts* starring Edmund Kean with Sampson Penley Jr as the young lover Allworth on the left. *Picture by courtesy of* The Garrick Club

Acknowledgments

Primarily, my thanks must go to my e-mail friend and colleague Laurie Jonas the great-grandson x 4 of the John Jonas who was partner and brother-in-law of Sampson Penley. Laurie is a devoted explorer of his family tree and a great advocate of getting photographs, scans and copies of original documents including playbills bearing the Jonas name. From various sources, between us we have now assembled 255 images of playbills of the Jonas & Penley company between 1798 and 1823. Laurie has also tracked down written evidence of the births or baptisms, marriages and deaths of most of the Penleys and Jonases included in this book. I am particularly grateful for his discovery in Amsterdam University Library of the letter from William Penley to the Drury Lane committee pleading to keep his job. Laurie also assiduously pursued Jonas & Penley playbills in the Menken Collection – devoted to Junius Brutus Booth – owned by Mrs Joelle Shefts in the USA. Kate Ramirez, a student researcher from the Hampden-Booth Library, undertook on his behalf to wade through boxes of unsorted material on a quest for J & P playbills, photographs of which have now enhanced our collection.

Several librarians and museum curators have been particularly helpful – Debbie Greaves of Tenterden, Anne Buchanan of Bath, Ann-Rachael Harwood of Cheltenham, Jo Kirkham of Rye, and Mary Hart of Bexhill – but there have been many others that have patiently replied to my e-mail and personal enquiries so thanks to all of you. The British Library collection of playbills on microfilm has been a constant resource entailing several visits, and the V & A theatre collection has also been a fruitful source. The personnel at both these national institutions have, as always, been unflaggingly helpful.

It would be remiss of me not to acknowledge the invaluable assistance of my wife Brenda who acts as my editor, proof reader, grammarian, re-arranger of sentences, placer of commas and general finder of errors. That there are not more solecisms in the text is entirely due to her; any that remain are my responsibility.

APPENDIX I

TABLE OF KNOWN JONAS & PENLEY SEASONS

APPENDIX II

AMSTERDAM SEASON 1814

APPENDIX III

BRUSSELS SEASON 1814

TABLE OF KNOWN JONAS & PENLEY SEASONS

Seasons could be of several months or as short as a week to coincide with local race meetings. The main sources of information are ephemeral playbills and newspaper advertisements so knowledge is scanty and far from complete. The table shows known seasons and venues gleaned mainly from these sources expanded by information from books. These are listed below. The Davey notebooks comprise a collection of 36 volumes compiled by a researcher into many towns in the south of England. As these are written in pencil and are often indecipherable, false assumptions may have been made. Also the accuracy of Davey's entries may in some cases be suspect, but where there are no means of further corroboration they have been assumed to be correct.

Where possible, opening and closing dates of seasons are given. In the case of Race Weeks often an opening date is obtainable but not the closing one. It can be confidently assumed that such 'seasons' are of a few days only. Where a single date is given that is the only knowledge of that season and is usually gleaned from a solitary playbill of an unknown lengthy season. From other sources we know that J & P had long leases of the Folkestone and Hastings theatres from Mrs Sarah Baker, but strangely, and infuriatingly, we have no actual evidence of any activity at either of those venues except for one press advertisement and one playbill.

Birth, baptism places and dates of the Penley and Jonas children are given where known as these *may* provide a clue to the location of the J & P company at the time.

It must be understood that this table represents only a fraction of the total output of J & P over the period; more activity is still to be discovered, and more will remain forever hidden.

M is *Taking the Town: a compleat and authentic account of the Thespian Activity in the County of Kent 1737 – 1843* by John Morris an unpublished manuscript in the V & A Theatre Museum

D is the collection of 'notebooks' by Peter Davey in the V & A Theatre Museum

BA is Archer, Stephen M, *Junius Brutus Booth: Theatrical Prometheus*

BB is Bottle, Ted, *Coventry's Forgotten Theatre*

BG is Grattan, Thomas Colley, *Beaten Paths & Those Who Trod Them*

BH is Highfill et al *Biographical Dictionary of Actors, Actresses, Musicians, Dancers, Managers and Other Stage Personnel in London, 1660 - 1800.*

BN is *Neophilologus* Vol 61 No 4 Pgs 619-640 an article by Willem Schrickx called *A Shakespeare Season on the Continent: Brussels 1814 and its Prelude in Amsterdam.*

BR is Ranger, Paul, *Under Two Managers*

BP is Porter, Henry C, *History of the Theatre in Brighton from 1774 to 1885*

BWPT is *Western Popular Theatre* Editors David Mayer & K Richard

KEY:
pb(s)=playbill(s); ad(s)=press advertisement(s) ; r(s)=press report(s) M =Morris ; D =Davey; BA =Archer; BB =Bottle; BG =Grattan; BH =Highfill; BN =*Neophilologus*; BP=Porter; BR=Ranger; BWPT=*Western Popular Theatre*

DATE	Source	J & P Co. VENUES	Notes and *Family matters*
1788 circa			*Mary born (Mr & Mrs JJ)*
1790			*John Jr born Feb 9, bapt Southwark (Mr & Mrs JJ)*
1792			*Joseph born Sept 9 Rotherhithe (Mr & Mrs JJ) Sampson Jr born Sept 21, bapt Carshalton Oct (Mr & Mrs SP)*
1793			*William Jr born Carshalton Sept (Mr & Mrs WP) Sophia born Kingston (Mr & Mrs JJ)*
1794	**LEWES theatre acquired**		21 year lease
1795	**HENLEY theatre acquired** *Sometime between 1795 & 1800* *Sometime between 1795 & 1800* May 9 October 27 November > December	BR BR M D D	Horsham Dorking Maidstone Eastbourne Lewes	*George born Sevenoaks May 19 (Mr & Mrs WP) Phoebe bapt Minster, Sheppey Jan 18 (Mr & Mrs SP)*
1796	February 23 July > August August 29	BH D D	Hoddesdon Lewes Eastbourne	*Rosina born May 15, bapt Sevenoaks Dec 14 (Mr & Mrs SP) Maria born May 30, bapt Sevenoaks Dec 14 (Mr & Mrs JJ) George bapt Sevenoaks Dec 14 (Mr & Mrs WP)*
1797	January July > August November >	M D D	Maidstone Lewes Lewes	*Frances born Rye (Mr & Mrs WP)*
1798	<January Opens January 16 > April August	D pb, r D	Lewes Henley Lewes	
1799	**TENTERDEN theatre opened** May > July July > Closes on Aug 21	pbs D, ad	Tenterden Lewes	*Montague born Folkestone May 5, bapt Tenterden June 23 (Mr & Mrs SP) Charlotte born Tenterden June 10, bapt Folkestone April 7 1800 (Mr & Mrs JJ)*
1800	June July > August Opens Aug 26 > Sept	pb D,ads D, ad	Lydd Lewes Eastbourne	*Catherine born (Mr & Mrs WP)*
1801	May > July July > August	pb D	Tenterden Lewes	*William born Broadstairs (Mr & Mrs SP)*

	September > October	D	Eastbourne	*Charles born Bermondsey August 18 (Mr & Mrs JJ)*
1802	Opens July 10, Closes on Aug 28 October	D,ads D, r	Lewes Eastbourne	*Robert born and Catherine buried Folkestone March Robert buried Rye December (Mr & Mrs WP)*
1803	January **BATTLE theatre opened - Feb** Opens February 19 > March May > Closes on July 20 July > August September October > December	pb r pb pbs D,r r r	Rye Battle Tenterden Lewes Eastbourne Lewes	
1804	**FOLKESTONE theatre acquired** July > August October > November November > December	 D r D	 Lewes Eastbourne Lewes	*Esther bapt Henley Feb 5 (Mr & Mrs JJ) Belville born Folkestone Jun 30, Bapt Folkestone July 18 ,Buried Eastbourne Sept 10 (Mr & Mrs SP)*
1805	Opens May 6, Closes July 12	pbs	Tenterden	*Emma born Henley Dec 15 (Mr & Mrs SP)*
1806	November November > December	r r	Eastbourne Rye	*Emma bapt Henley Jan 10 (Mr & Mrs SP) Henry bapt Folkestone April 9 (Mr & Mrs JJ) Aaron born Rye May (Mr & Mrs WP)*
1807	Opens May 4, Closes July 8	pbs, ad	Tenterden	
1808	*September?*	?	Lewes	*Belville born Folkestone, bapt Rye June 29 (Mr & Mrs SP)*
1809	June July > August July Opens September 28 October	r pbs r ad pb	Rye Tenterden Lewes Henley Eastbourne	*Frederick bapt Tenterden Sept 30 (Mr & Mrs JJ)*
1810	Opens January 27 January > February Opens April 23, Closes July 7 Opens October 8 >	BP D ads ads	Brighton Folkestone Faversham London	
1811	<June Closes March 11 June > Closes August 10 Opens July 31, Closes August 20 Opens August 12 Opens August 22 Opens August 26 to December Opens October 29, Closes 13Dec Opens December 14>	ads ad pbs ad ad ad pb ads ads	London Lewes Tenterden Lewes Canterbury Eastbourne Peckham Brighton Lewes	 Race Week Race Week Race Week
1812	<Closes January 29 February March	rs r r	Lewes Henley Rye	

	Opens May 13 > July	ads	Faversham	
	Opens July 24, Closes August 3	pbs	Tenterden	
	July 24	pb	Bexhill	
	Opens July 29, Closes Aug 11	r	Lewes	Race Week
	Opens August 13	ad	Eastbourne	
	Opens Aug 11	ad	Canterbury	Race Week
	Opens Aug 3 > September	ads,r	Windsor	
	Opens Aug 24, Closes Oct 15	pbs	Peckham	
	October	D	Folkestone	
	November > December >	D,ads,rs	Lewes	
	Opens December 12 >	BP	Brighton	
1813	< Closes Jan 22	ads, rs	Lewes	Sieur Sanchez appeared at Brighton and Lewes then for 2 days each at Eastbourne, Bexhill, Hastings, & Battle,
	< Closes Feb 16	BP, ads	Brighton	
	February 20	ads, D	Eastbourne	
	February 25, 27	pb	Bexhill	
	May > July	pbs	Tenterden	
	Opens Aug 4, Closes August 17	ads	Lewes	Race Week
	August	r	Canterbury	Race Week
	Opens Aug 30, Closes Nov 13	pbs	Peckham	
1814	April	R	Deptford	*Mary Ann born Deptford August 8 (Mr & Mrs JJ)*
	Opens May 18, Closes July 9	BWPT	Amsterdam	
	July 13, 16	BA	Rotterdam	
	July 22, 27, Aug 3, 4, 8	BA	Antwerp	
	Opens Aug 3, Closes Aug 23	ads	Lewes	Race Week
	Opens August 25	ad	Eastbourne	Race Week
	Opens Aug 15, Closes Nov 22	pbs, BN	Brussels	
	Opens Aug 27, Closes Oct 5	pbs	Peckham	
	November 25, 30	pbs, BA	Ghent	
	Opens Dec 14, Closes Dec 31	BA	Bruges	
1815	Opens January 2, > March	BA, pb	Ostend	
	Opens August 8, Closes Aug 15	ads	Lewes	Race Week
	WINDSOR theatre acquired			
	Opens Aug 21, Closes Sept 16	ads, r	Windsor	
	Opens December 9 >	ads	Windsor	
1816	< Closes January 18	ads, r	Windsor	
	Opens June 10	ads	Windsor	Race Week
	Opens July 30, Closes Sept 14	ads	Windsor	
	September	D	Eastbourne	
	December >	pb, ads	Windsor	
1817	< Closes Jan 18	ads	Windsor	
	Opens May 3, Closes May 31	pbs	Tenterden	
	Opens June 2	ad	Windsor	Race Week
	Aug > Closes Sept 13	ads, r	Windsor	
	Opens Dec 13 >	ads	Windsor	
1818	<Closes January 13	ads	Windsor	
	May 26	pb	Tenterden	
	Opens June 8	ad	Windsor	Race Week
	Opens July 28, Closes Sept 12	ads	Windsor	
	September 17	pb	Hastings	
	October?	D	Peckham	
	Opens Dec 26 >	ads	Windsor	

1819	< Closes Jan 16	ads	Windsor	
	Opens April 12 > Jun	BB	Coventry	
	Opens June 7, Closes June 12	ad	Windsor	Race Week
	Opens Aug 3, Closes Sept 11	ads	Windsor	
	Opens Sept 20 > October	ads	Eastbourne	
	Opens Nov 2 >	ads	Lewes	
1820	< Closes Jan 1	ad	Lewes	
	Opens Jan 4 > March	ad, pbs	Rye	
	Opens May 29, Closes June 3	ad	Windsor	Race Week
	Opens Jun 2, Closes July 28	BB, pbs	Coventry	
	Opens July 31, Closes Sept 16	ads	Windsor	
	Opens Aug 9, Closes August 22	ads	Lewes	
	Opens Aug 24, Closes Sept 5	ads	Eastbourne	
	Penley acquires DOVER Theatre			Sometime in 1820 Dover
	November	ad	Dover	added to J & P theatres
	Opens Dec 26 >	ads	Windsor	
1821	< Closes Jan 13	ads	Windsor	
	Opens Feb 23, Closes March 23	BB	Coventry	
	April (Easter)	r	Windsor	
	June	r	Windsor	Race Week
	Opens Aug 2, Closes Sept 15	ads, r	Windsor	Re-opened for a further week for Egham Races
1822	Opens July 31, Closes August 1	r	Paris	Stopped by riots
	Opens August 20, Closes Oct 19	r	Paris	Rue Chantereine Theatre
	November 8, November 20	pbs	Calais	
	November 23, December 26	D, ads	Dover	'returned from Paris'
1823	November 17	pb	Dunkirk	
1824	'Early summer'	BG	Boulogne	Last recorded performance of J & P company

The author would welcome any information that could be added to this table.
Please contact www.vesperhawk.com

List of productions presented by Jonas & Penley at the German Theatre in Amsterdam in 1814		
May 18	The Honeymoon	The Weather-Cock
May 21	John Bull; or an Englishman's Fireside	The Bee Hive
May 23	Hamlet	The Benevolent Tar
May 25	Speed the Plough	Raising the Wind
May 28	The Jew	The Benevolent Tar
May 31	The Soldier's Daughter	Fortune's Frolic
June 2	The Wonder: a Woman Keeps a Secret	Ways and Means
June 4	Lovers' Vows	The Miller and His Men
June 6	Barbarossa	The Miller and His Men
June 8	The Mountaineers	The Jew and the Doctor
June 13	Romeo & Juliet	The Sleepwalker
June 15	The Peasant Boy	High Life Below Stairs
June 18	The Stranger	Of Age Tomorrow
June 20	The Voice of Nature	The Forty Thieves
June 22	George Barnwell	The Forty Thieves
June 25	The Stranger	Of Age Tomorrow
June 27	The Battle of Hexham	Don Juan
July 1	Alexander	Don Juan
July 2	She Stoops to Conquer	Inkle and Yariko
July 4	The Busy Body	Highland Reel
July 6	Follies of a Day	Inkle and Yariko
July 9	Laugh When You Can	The Mogul Tale

From a note to Ben Albach's article in *Western Popular Theatre* which gives more details of the plays. His list omitted June 13 and July 4, these have been included from other sources. Other stray performances may not have been gathered through lack of any identification.

List of productions presented by Jonas & Penley at the Theatre du Parc in Brussels in 1814. (First three dates at Theatre de Monnaie)			
Mon	August 15	John Bull	Of Age Tomorrow
Wed	August 17	The Honeymoon	Raising the Wind
Fri	August 19	The Soldier's Daughter	Lovers' Quarrels
Mon	August 22	Ways & Means	Travellers Benighted
Tues	August 23	A Cure for the Heartache	Travellers Benighted
Fri	August 26	The Stranger	The Beehive
Mon	August 29	The Wonder	The Weathercock
Tues	August 30	She Stoops to Conquer	The Sleepwalker
Thurs	Sept 1	The Stranger	Raising the Wind
Tues	Sept 6	The Wonder	Fortune's Frolics
Thurs	Sept 8	The Soldier's Daughter	The Beehive
Sat	Sept 10	The School for Scandal	Of Age Tomorrow
Tues	Sept 13	The Busy Body	The Purse
Tues	Sept 20	The Iron Chest	The Village Lawyer
Thurs	Sept 22	The Wonder	Ways & Means
Sat	Sept 24	The Honeymoon	The Purse
Mon	Sept 26	Hamlet	Personation
Sat	Oct 1	Richard III	Personation
Mon	Oct 3	The Mountaineers	The Prize
Wed	Oct 5	Romeo & Juliet	The Wedding Day
Sat	Oct 8	Hamlet	The Devil to Pay
Mon	Oct 10	The Provoked Husband	My Grandmother
Wed	Oct 12	Macbeth	The Wedding Day
Sat	Oct 15	The Rivals	High Life Below Stairs
Tues	Oct 18	The Road to Ruin	Don Juan
Thurs	Oct 20	Incle & Yarico	Don Juan
Sat	Oct 22	Love in a Village	The Review
Fri	Oct 28	A Tale of Mystery	The Poor Soldier
Sat	Oct 29	The Beehive	Timour the Tartar
Tues	Nov 1	Sieur Franke (Equilibrist)	Timour the Tartar
Fri	Nov 4	John Bull	Timour the Tartar
Sat	Nov 5	Sieur Franke (Equilibrist)	Travellers Benighted
Tues	Nov 8	The Castle Spectre	Travellers Benighted
Sat	Nov 12	Earl of Warwick	The Romp
Wed	Nov 14	The Weathercock	Blue Devils
Tues	Nov 22	Othello	Tom Thumb
Other stray performances may have been missed through a lack of identification.			

INDEX
and
TIME LINE

Plays are listed separately at the end of the index.

Penley, Sampson, [*see also*] & P] **13** to
110 *passim*, **113, 122, 130, 131, 135,
140, 144, 161, 168, 201, 202, 204,
205, 206, 209, 211, 222, 223, 228,
241, 264, 273, 276, 281, 287, 288,
305, 321, 330, 337, 343, 346, 357,
362, 363, 366, 367**
Penley, Sampson Jr, **4, 17, 23, 34, 41,
42, 43, 44, 47, 49, 57, 59, 60, 62,
68, 69, 71, 72, 73, 75, 80, 87, 93,
106, 107, 127, 135, 136, 137, 145** to
197 *passim*, **202, 203, 204, 205, 206,
209, 217, 229, 231, 235, 245, 247,
249, 250, 254, 255, 256, 257, 259,
260, 265, 266, 273, 277, 283, 287,
288, 289, 290, 292, 300, 302, 310,
317, 322, 326, 340, 344, 362, 367**
Penley, William (son of Sampson) **17,
47, 49, 54, 72, 83, 86, 93, 102, 110,
202, 209, 210, 276, 288,**
Penley, William (brother of Sampson)
**13, 14, 17, 33, 39, 44, 108, 109,
110, 113** to 144 *passim*, **148, 150,
151, 201, 232, 254, 265, 287, 344,
351, 363**
Penley, William Henry Saulez, **113, 138,
139, 140, 141, 142**
Penley, W S (actor-manager), **351, 352**
playbill, **18, 25, 26, 33, 44, 60, 61, 77,
85, 103, 105, 106, 113, 127, 180,
181, 217, 225, 227, 239, 288, 292,
328, 357, 360, 363, 367**
Poole, Miss (actress), **236, 237**
Prince Albert, **143, 269, 270, 275**
Prince of Wales, Prince Regent, [*see also*
George IV] **1, 43, 45, 74, 83, 88,
131, 178**
Princess Augusta, **86, 87, 179, 186,
194, 259, 292, 293, 358**

Q

Queen Adelaide, **194, 251, 259, 260**
Queen Charlotte, **41, 68, 119, 120, 124,
127, 133, 134, 140, 169**
Queen Victoria, **143, 195, 265,269,
271, 275, 346, 347**
Quick, Mr (actor), **119, 121, 126, 130,
346**

R

Rackham, Mr (actor), **19, 25, 33, 36, 49,
124**
Raymond, Mr (actor), **139, 225, 241,
243, 252, 253**
Richmond, Surrey, **183, 188, 190, 196,
254, 332**
Richmond, Yorkshire, **32, 226, 352**
Ridgway Brothers (pantomimists), **248,
251, 252, 368, 369**
Rochester, **12, 30, 310**
Rotterdam, **56, 59**
Rue Chantereine, **99, 100, 101**
Rye, **16, 31, 36, 37, 46, 48, 49, 82, 83,
84, 87, 122, 125, 133, 210, 321**

S

Salter, Mr (actor), **61, 78, 80, 82, 84,
85, 97, 206, 209, 263**
Sanches, Sieur (entertainer), **51**
Sandford, Mr (actor), **115, 116**
Saxoni, Mr (entertainer) **28**
Serle, Mr (actor), **106, 107**
Shakespeare, **2, 5, 34, 37, 62, 63, 68,
82, 94, 95, 96, 97, 101, 106, 116,
117, 148, 149, 153, 158, 163, 165,
167, 171, 179, 180, 201, 212, 213,
214, 216, 220, 236, 244, 246, 255,
256, 259, 261, 262, 263, 266, 268,
280, 283, 334, 335, 351**
Sheffield, **5, 140, 141, 215, 229, 256,
257, 259, 274, 291, 327**
Sherborne School, **120, 124, 133**
Sheridan, R B (playwright & manager),
**23, 82, 101, 124, 125, 127, 128,
131, 147, 169, 193, 207, 232, 260,
261, 314, 315**
Shiffner, Capt (MP), **46, 50**
Siddons, Sarah (actress) **11, 20, 23, 82,
121, 125, 132, 147, 148, 207, 208,
210, 213, 283**
Silvain, M (dancer), **331, 333**
Smithson, Harriet (actress), **102, 106,
107, 238**
Stackwood, Mr (actor), **19, 49, 57**
Stirling, Mrs (actress), **306, 307, 309**
Stohwasser, Miss (actress), **191, 192,
255, 256, 257, 258, 259, 325, 326,
332**

PLAYS

TIME LINE

1798, 13, 17, 113, 115, 232, 345

1799, 17, 18, 114, 115, 242, 261, 287, 366

1800, 35, 53, 93, 115, 366

1801, 17, 113, 115, 117, 119, 140, 221, 232, 242, 366

1802, 41, 121

1803, 11, 18, 19, 33, 122, 125, 214, 311, 360, 366

1804, 19, 20, 22, 23, 25, 35, 37, 123, 124, 126, 265, 321, 366

1805, 23, 25, 29, 31, 33, 35, 80, 114, 115, 121, 201, 202, 221, 346, 360

1806, 22, 29, 35, 67, 125, 127, 137, 152, 207, 366, 367

1807, 29, 31, 32, 34, 35, 45, 59, 127, 202, 360

1808, 37, 127, 128, 225, 321

1809, 37, 128, 129, 218, 305, 367

1810, 37, 38, 39, 40, 41, 42, 67, 114, 217, 298, 305

1811, 40, 43, 44, 45, 53, 125, 130, 131, 133, 202, 277, 363

1812, 27, 38, 44, 46, 47, 48, 49, 51, 64, 67, 109, 131, 132, 133, 147, 167, 202, 214, 273, 323, 369

1813, 19, 43, 50, 52, 55, 91, 92, 134, 358, 360, 363, 365, 366, 367

1814, 29, 38, 52, 55, 56, 57, 62, 63, 64, 78, 83, 88, 93, 94, 134, 135, 139, 144, 147, 148, 150, 176, 190, 202, 232, 237, 357, 358, 363, 365, 366, 369

1815, 65, 66, 68, 76, 81, 136, 147, 148, 150, 168, 273, 298, 344, 365

1816, 60, 66, 69, 71, 80, 87, 93, 105, 106, 131, 136, 137, 138, 143, 151, 170, 202, 242, 287, 360, 363

1817, 42, 74, 75, 76, 77, 78, 139, 151, 154, 201, 202, 203, 217, 298, 363, 364

1818, 74, 78, 81, 139, 140, 142, 151, 156, 206, 214, 257, 260, 287, 288, 315, 360, 364

1819, 80, 88, 95, 140, 147, 157, 209, 288, 352, 358, 361, 363, 366

1820, 82, 83, 88, 106, 157, 158, 160, 206, 210, 211, 232, 321, 358, 361, 367

1821, 88, 95, 162, 163, 212, 214, 289, 361, 363, 365

1822, 71, 88, 92, 94, 95, 102, 103, 110, 140, 162, 167, 168, 211, 212, 253, 257, 290, 361, 365

1823, 105, 142, 168, 169, 171, 214, 243, 346, 351, 361, 363, 365

1824, 105, 106, 172, 221, 290, 361, 365, 366

1825, 107, 132, 175, 214, 220, 227, 233, 290, 291, 321

1826, 93, 168, 169, 177, 216, 222, 225, 268, 292, 321

1827, 178, 179, 225, 228, 361

1828, 95, 179, 222, 229, 231, 299, 321, 361, 362

1829, 30, 178, 180, 183, 232, 237, 238, 239, 240, 241, 244, 293, 321, 352, 362, 367

1830, 140, 181, 183, 184, 226, 232, 241, 277, 305, 321, 345, 362, 367

1831, 140, 178, 183, 185, 186, 187, 221, 233, 247, 251, 321, 322, 368

1832, 108, 109, 110, 141, 188, 247, 254, 257, 323, 324, 358, 362, 368

1833, 183, 190, 191, 217, 255, 256, 258, 293, 296, 321, 325, 345, 367

1834, 191, 257, 258, 267, 277, 296, 305, 312, 326, 362, 368, 379, 384, 385

The time line is a reference to the pages that cover a particular year. For example, picking a year at random, we can see what several of our various family members are doing – more than likely totally unknown to each other – in **1824**.

Pages 105 and 106: *Sampson Penley is destitute in France and begs Edmund Kean to appear for him at Boulogne*

Page 172: *Sam Penley Jr opens his Windsor season and returns to Drury Lane where the press castigates the national theatre for putting on spectacles for children instead of drama*

Page 221: *Rosina Penley is touring the York circuit which embraces Hull and Leeds. Sisters Phoebe and Emma are working at Cheltenham*

Page 290: *Montague Penley is repainting the interior of the Windsor theatre in assorted pinks*

Page 361: *Joe Jonas is playing Pantaloon at Sadler's Wells*

Page 365: *Maria Jonas is at the Surrey Theatre before going to the English theatre at Boulogne*

Page 366: *Charlotte Jonas marries an artist called James Urquhart*

CPSIA information can be obtained
at www.ICGtesting.com
Printed in the USA
LVOW13*0112030717

540137LV00023B/686/P